Abraham, Ancestry, and Ethnicity in Luke's Gospel

Abraham, Ancestry, and Ethnicity in Luke's Gospel

From These Stones

Andrew Benko

LEXINGTON BOOKS/FORTRESS ACADEMIC
Lanham • Boulder • New York • London

Published by Lexington Books/Fortress Academic
Lexington Books is an imprint of The Rowman & Littlefield Publishing Group, Inc.
4501 Forbes Boulevard, Suite 200, Lanham, Maryland 20706
www.rowman.com

86-90 Paul Street, London EC2A 4NE, United Kingdom

Copyright © 2025 by The Rowman & Littlefield Publishing Group, Inc.

All rights reserved. No part of this book may be reproduced in any form or by any electronic or mechanical means, including information storage and retrieval systems, without written permission from the publisher, except by a reviewer who may quote passages in a review.

British Library Cataloguing in Publication Information Available

Library of Congress Cataloging-in-Publication Data Available

ISBN 978-1-9787-1446-5 (cloth : alk. paper)
ISBN 978-1-9787-1447-2 (electronic)

Contents

Introduction: From These Stones		vii
1	*Ethnos* and Racial Fluidity in Antiquity	1
2	"The Rock from Which You Were Hewn": Abraham in Judean Racial Reasoning	59
3	"Our Ancestor Abraham": Abraham in the Infancy Narratives	97
4	"We Have a Father—Abraham": Abraham as Ancestor and Ethnic Founder in Luke	117
5	*Whose* Ancestors? Genealogical Reconfiguration in Luke–Acts	167
Conclusion: Carving a New People from an Old Block		227
Bibliography		235
Index Subjects		247
About the Author		253

Introduction

From These Stones

Don't begin to tell yourselves, "We have Abraham as our ancestor," for I tell you—God can raise up children for Abraham from these stones.— Luke 3:8[1]

In a long, cool, air-conditioned room in Caria, Turkey, a remarkable series of marble reliefs stands along two facing walls. These fragmentary stones are what remains of the art from a *sebasteion*, or Temple of the Emperors, erected in first-century Aphrodisias. Inscriptions indicate that the construction of this complex began during the reign of Tiberius Caesar, but damage caused by an earthquake during the time of Claudius necessitated a second fundraising campaign so that the complex was not fully completed until sometime during Nero's reign.[2]

With this ambitious project, local elites expressed their loyalty to and participation within Rome's empire. Its artistic schema asserted the honorable place of the Carian people among the races of the empire in two distinct ways. First, a series of mythological and historical scenes lining its south portico depicted Rome's founding and rise to power. These panels included depictions of both Aphrodite and Aeneas, reminding the visitor that the city's patron goddess and namesake was none other than the mother of Rome's primal founder. Stressing this link affirmed that the Carians and the latter-day Romans were, as it were, related peoples, both descended from Aphrodite.[3] Second, a series of personified *ethnē* (races) lined the temple's south portico. Each relief depicted an idealized female figure standing atop a base; each base bore the name of a race above a garlanded male face.[4] While only fifteen intact figures and bases have been recovered, the size of the complex indicates that as many as fifty of these panels might once have decorated the temple. One of the recovered bases reads: ΕΘΝΟΥΣ ΙΥΔΑΙΩΝ, "the race of

Figure 0.1 "Ethnous Ioudaiōn (the race of the Judeans)" Pedestal, from the Sebasteion in Aphrodisias, First Century. *Source*: Andrew Benko.

the Judeans" (see figure 0.1).[5] We see, then, that in first-century Aphrodisias, the city's elites affirmed their ethnic connection to Rome, and claimed an honorable standing for their own race partially *by way of contrast with other peoples*. On these walls, Judeans were just one of the several races these local elites used to "think with."

Just a few decades[6] after the completion of Aphrodisias' *sebasteion*, another major work was underway—one that would also attempt to carve out a proud identity for its own audience, whom it would situate honorably within the wider Roman οικουμενη ("civilized world," "empire"). Like the *sebasteion*, it was an ambitious project, for this work, Luke–Acts,[7] aimed to provide an "orderly account" of the beginnings of Christianity (or "The Way," as the author also calls it).[8] Like the *sebasteion*, it would require funding from wealthy benefactors who would need to be thanked—in two dedicatory prologues, rather than chiseled inscriptions (Luke 1:1–4; Acts 1:1–2). Like the *sebasteion*, it would be completed in stages, for it straddled two volumes,

Introduction ix

in two distinct genres: a Hellenistic-style *bios* ("life") and a "history" of the movement's early days.[9] Both the *sebasteion* and Luke–Acts strongly emphasize myth, history, and ancestry, as they set out to portray various peoples (*ethnē*) in particular ways. Both are, in other words, instances of what we might call "racial reasoning."[10] And, much like the *sebasteion*, Luke–Acts would use Judeans to "think with"—although in a very different way.[11]

TOPIC, THESIS, AND APPROACH

This book will read Luke's gospel with an eye toward ethnicity, asking how Luke (re)constructs the ethnic identity of those who follow "The Way." To consider how Luke's racializing rhetoric would have worked in its original context, we will attend to then-current notions of race, rather than impose modern definitions upon the text.[12] I call this an "*ethnos*-conscious approach," foregrounding the ancient term for race to differentiate it from "ethnocritical" readings, which more typically privilege models drawn from contemporary anthropology or sociology, and which often lean more heavily on *modern* definitions of race or ethnicity.[13]

Over the past three decades, scholarly understandings of ethnicity in antiquity have shifted enormously. A generation of classicists, eager to challenge the implicit racism of earlier classical scholarship, has brought new rigor to our reading of ancient texts about ethnicity. Armed with the emerging consensus from the social sciences that "race" (or "ethnicity") is a social construct rather than an objective reality, and that it is a construct whose definition can shift over time and across cultures, classicists and New Testament scholars alike have suggested that we ought to attend to *ancient rhetoric itself* to learn what "race" meant.[14] Classicists such as Jonathan Hall, Benjamin Isaac, Denise McCoskey, and Mary Boatwright have all re-examined classical literature dealing with ethnicity.[15] In their scholarship, such factors as ancestry, kinship, homeland, and distinctive culture emerge as significant aspects of how the ancients tended to conceptualize "ethnicity."

Over the past two decades, and largely taking up the challenge laid out in Denise Buell's landmark study *Why This New Race?*, New Testament scholars have turned their attention to ethnicity and racial reasoning in early Christian literature.[16] An enormous amount of work has been devoted to ethnicity in the New Testament, examining Paul's letters, Acts, and the gospels—including not only Matthew and John, but even Q.[17] Despite the growing energy around this subject, book-length treatments of the race in *Luke's* gospel are sadly lacking. This volume aims to address this gap in the field.

If we wish to consider Luke's treatment of ethnicity, Abraham is a promising place to start. Ancestry was a crucial element of how race was constructed

x   *Introduction*

in the ancient world—and for Judeans, Abraham was the ancestor *par excellence*. Abraham is mentioned more often in Luke than in the other two synoptic gospels combined.[18] From the very beginning of his gospel, Luke affirms that Jesus descends from Abraham, and the story of Zechariah and Elizabeth mirrors the story of Abraham and Sarah.[19] In Luke's account of John's ministry, the Baptist warns the "brood (*gennēmata*) of vipers" in the crowd not to tell themselves, "We have Abraham as our father," for God can raise up children for Abraham even from "these stones" (3:8). As Jonathan Hall reminds us, ancient ethnicity could often be boiled down to the question "Can you, or can you not, claim descent from *x*?"[20] Therefore, Luke's repeated invocation of Abraham, often as someone's "father/ancestor," is racial rhetoric and invites the reader to consider the role of Abraham in Luke's racial reasoning. Clearly, the patriarch occupies a significant place in the evangelist's thought.

I will read such invocations of Abraham in light of his function in Second Temple literature, as the ancestor of the Judeans (e.g., *L.A.B.* 23:5, *Pss.Sol.* 9:9) and "founder of the race" (Philo *Abr.* 276), while also occasionally being considered a point of surprising contact between Judeans and the *ethnē* (e.g., Ps. Eup. *Pr.Ev.*9.17.2–9; Artapanus in *Pr.Ev.* 9.18.1) or even the ancestor of non-Jewish *ethnē* (e.g., Jos. *Ant.* 1:239ff; *Ant.* 12.225ff; 1 Macc. 12:21). As many scholars of ethnicity in antiquity have demonstrated, although ancestry presents itself as a "fixed" fact, it could be surprisingly "fluid" in practice. Genealogies were contested, revised, or invented to draw new connections, or boundaries, between races.[21] Luke selectively aligns himself with certain Second Temple Abraham trajectories, especially those which present Abraham as a "model convert," and against other trajectories which use Abraham to emphasize the distance between Judeans and others.[22] I will argue that Luke partially deconstructs Judean self-understanding as the *sperma Abraam* ("seed" or "descendants of Abraham") by implying that Abraham (and other Israelite "founding fathers") will not acknowledge the paternity of simply *anyone* who calls him "father" (Luke 16:24–31); rather, Abraham is properly the ancestor of those who follow his ways (best exemplified in "the Way," the nascent Christian movement), even if they are from the nations (3:8b; 13:28–29).

To contextualize Luke's racial reasoning, we will consider ancient discussions of conversion and apostasy. Modern readers of the gospel tend to view "religion" as a fairly distinct category of human identity, separable from "race," and therefore do not understand conversion as a racial issue. But Luke's original audience would be informed by then-contemporary ideas, rather than modern ones. Many ancient writers treat conversion as the abandonment of one people's ancestral traditions and religious practices, and the adopting of another's.[23] Such abandonment/adoption had serious ramifications for one's social, cultural, and familial identities. Abraham was

Introduction xi

regarded as a model convert precisely for his willingness to leave behind his homeland, his kindred, and his way of life, in order to pursue God's will.[24] Because ancient discussions of peoples often focused upon their distinctive way of life (itself inherited from their ancestors), these changes also had *ethnic* implications.[25] Religion was not a separate facet of identity which could be abstracted from race; rather, it was deeply implicated in the construction of ethnic identity. Therefore, a shift in one might enact a shift in the other.[26] Ancient sources frequently spoke as if converts had joined a new *people*, not merely a new "religion."

For Luke, Abraham's "children" are those who share his willingness to leave relatives, home, and customs, if that is what it takes to escape idolatry and serve God. Conversely, those who are *unwilling* to pursue God's purposes are no true children of his, even if they are his genealogical descendants—even, indeed, if their very unwillingness to abandon their customs is based on a sense of loyalty to Abraham![27] Thus, the ethnic identity of both non-Christian Judeans *and* Christian gentiles is destabilized by Luke's use of the patriarch: Judeans *qua* Judeans can no longer presume upon the perceived benefits of being Abraham's heirs, unless they conform to his faith (as Luke understands it), and conversely, God can raise "children of Abraham" even from "these stones" (Luke 3:8), redefining even gentile believers as descendants of Abraham. Both Judeans and gentiles are reconfigured by Luke's reasoning: (most) Judeans' connection to Abraham is attenuated, and Christian gentiles' connection to their *own* ancestors is also attenuated, as they abandon their ways and take on Abraham's.[28]

This book will argue that Luke offers a new layer of ethnic identity Luke to gentile believers, as adjunct members of Abraham's family tree. This implicitly reconstructs the racial categories which were so frequently defined by ancestry: Judeans who fail to model Abraham's faith will derive no benefits from him, and conversely, deserving non-Judeans could be reckoned among his children. Indeed, Luke's use of Abraham is only one facet of his reconfiguration of Judean ancestors more generally. Luke partially deconstructs the notion of ancestry itself; he implies that ethnic benefits are not inherited from ascribed descent (assigned at birth) but are rather derived from one's "subscriptive" descent (subscribing to the model of the ancestors).[29] Throughout the gospel, Luke attempts to demonstrate that various ancestors and "founding fathers" of Israel, including Noah, Abraham, Moses, David, and the prophets, as well as "archetypal" Judeans such as Simeon and Anna, all eagerly anticipated what is now fulfilled in Jesus.[30] Jesus is the requital of their hopes, the culmination of their prophecies, and the fulfillment of God's promises to them.[31] Therefore, those who recognize Jesus as their salvation follow in these figures' footsteps, and can (correctly) claim them as their ancestors. Conversely, those who reject Jesus have alternate ancestors

xii   *Introduction*

assigned to them; their claims upon Israel's righteous ancestors are questionable, and they are described as the *actual* descendants of those who killed the prophets (11:47–51; 6:22–23, 26; Acts 7:51–53). There are, it seems, two competing "lineages" within the Jewish race—one normative and praiseworthy, and one shameful—which can be assigned to individuals (seemingly regardless of their genealogical descent!) based on how they respond to Jesus.

CHAPTER STRUCTURE AND PROSPECT

This introduction has broached the subject of ethnicity in Luke's gospel and laid out the thesis that Luke values, but reconfigures, ancestral connections to such figures as Abraham. Luke's rhetoric redefines the relationship of individuals to pre-existing racial categories, themselves (largely) built upon the notion of descent from these founders. I have also briefly introduced my "*ethnos*-conscious approach," anticipating the next chapter.

Chapter 1, "*Ethnos* and Racial Fluidity in Antiquity," will lay out the methodology for the following chapters. Of foremost concern for this project is the question: "What did people mean, *in Luke's day*, by race?"[32] An *ethnos*-conscious approach privileges ancient conceptions of race over modern ones, allowing ancient sources to tell us what "race" actually meant *to them*, rather than imposing modern race theory onto antiquity. After surveying examples of ancient racial discourse, we will propose a tentative model of what race/ethnicity typically comprised in Mediterranean antiquity. I will argue that, in the ancient world, ethnicity most frequently consisted of the notions of (1) shared descent, (2) shared homeland, and (3) shared distinctive way of life.[33]

This chapter will also survey some of the functions of racial reasoning in antiquity. Racial rhetoric could connect races, contrast races, and include or exclude individuals within ethnic groups. While race *presented* itself as an essential "given,"it was actually a fluid and contestable category. Ethnic fluidity was most obvious when it came to such factors as religious adherence, changes in way of life, and the creative editing of genealogies—whether the genealogies of individuals (e.g., Herod's "blue-blooded" Jewish genealogy drawn up by his court scribe Nicolas),[34] or entire peoples (the creation of "ethnic genealogies," which explained how entire peoples could be related through the "discovery" of a shared ancestor).[35] Racial thinking was also deeply implicated in the production of imperial ideology, and in various provincial peoples' responses to the empire. Later, we shall see these strategies at work in Luke's own racial reasoning.

Chapter 2, "The Rock From Which You Were Hewn," will survey some of the ways the figure of Abraham was used in Jewish literature. Most importantly, we will consider how the ancestor was deployed in the construction

Introduction xiii

of ethnicity. For example, Abraham could be invoked to strengthen Judeans' sense of ethnic solidarity, exhort them to hold fast to their customs, or discourage them from marrying gentiles.[36] Abraham could, then, serve a "particularizing" function, emphasizing the distance between Judeans and others. However, some discussion of Abraham could have the opposite effect: he could be a source of (often surprising) connections between Judeans and other races. Particular attention will be given to Hellenistic reworkings of Abraham stories which linked him with other peoples, whether culturally or genealogically, as well as to traditions regarding him as a "model" convert.

Chapter 3, "Our Ancestor Abraham," will examine the racial implications of the Infancy Narratives and genealogy of Luke 1–2. We will consider the allusions to ancestral promises and covenants in prophetic songs (Luke 1:54–55, 72–72, etc.) and how Zechariah and Elizabeth (1:6–7, 18) echo the story of Abraham and Sarah. Luke 1–2 strongly emphasizes the prototypical Judaism of Jesus and his family, and its hymns express strong in-group hopes for the salvation of Israel.[37] At the same time, they also foreshadow the eventual inclusion of the "nations" in these hopes. Chapter 4, "We Have a Father—Abraham," will consider how the rest of Luke's gospel characterizes the patriarch as ancestor, ethnic founder,[38] and benefactor, and will consider what this means for the ethnic identity of those who call him "father." Some of this will be found in Luke's unique material, just as telling is how the evangelist reframes material from Q or Mark into his own Lukan framework. For example, the parable of Lazarus (16:19–31) amplifies and clarifies the Baptist's warnings not to assume ethnic Judeans will automatically benefit from their descent from Abraham (3:8).

We will, by this time, begin to recognize Luke's use of Abraham as part of a wider theme: his surprising claim that Israelites cannot assume they will automatically derive benefits or blessings from their status as the descendants of the patriarchs. In chapter 5, "*Whose* Ancestors?," we will consider how the entire notion of ancestral descent is "troubled" throughout the Third Gospel. Those who reject Jesus are the descendants, not of Abraham (3:8), but of those who killed the prophets (11:47, cf. Acts 7:52; Luke 13:34), whatever their "factual" descent. Similarly, those who adhere to the faith and model of the patriarchs *are* their descendants, whatever the genealogical facts may be. Luke's use of Abraham plays a part in this, but the trope encompasses a host of ancestral figures, both from Israel's past and from various gentile races. Because ethnicity was so fundamentally tied to ancestry in the ancient world, this slipperiness in the attribution of *ancestry* implies a corresponding fluidity to *racial identity,* as well.

I will propose that one's ethnic ancestry, to Luke, is not (only) a matter of ascriptive descent (i.e., that which is attributed to one at birth), but more importantly a matter of subscriptive descent; that is, you are someone's

xiv *Introduction*

descendant if you who subscribe to their ways (*ethē*). To support this notion, we will consider examples of similar thinking in antiquity, including "father/child" language applied to those who have "descended" from certain "lineages" of teaching, from teacher ("father") to student ("son") over the course of generations. Also pertinent in this regard is the so-called "fictive kinship" language used within many Greco-Roman associations. We will also consider examples of how religious conversion could be seen as a (partial) realignment of one's *ethnic* identity. Luke's use of Abraham (and other ancestors) creates space for gentile followers of "The Way" to imagine themselves to be aligned with, and indeed children of, Abraham, and to think of themselves as possessing a now-hybridized ethnic identity: they are now "Israelites" by adherence to Abraham's faith, while remaining "gentiles" to some degree. While this possibility is implied in Luke, it remains largely an "uncashed check" at the end of the Third Gospel. But Luke has amply laid the groundwork for such reasoning, which will be paid off in full during the course of his second volume, Acts.

Finally, the conclusion will consider the ethical implications of Luke's racial reasoning. For latter-day Christians, some of these possibilities are to be celebrated, but others are more problematic. Rather positive (or at least neutral) is Luke's conviction that members of all races may be fully incorporated in the people who know God in Jesus and understand themselves to be meaningfully related as a result. But Luke also reconfigures the racial identity of both those who accept *and those who reject*, Jesus. Gentile followers of "the Way" can only be rightfully understood by reference to *Israel's* myths, history, and ancestry, giving an unmistakably *ethnic* quality to Christian identity. Recognizing this dynamic within Luke challenges traditional interpretations of Christianity as a "universal" (racially unmarked) movement—a characterization almost always constructed in opposition to the supposedly "exclusive" Jews.[39] Recognizing the (claimed) Abrahamic identity of gentiles-in-Christ forces us to rethink the pervasive scholarly contrast between a "non-racial" Christianity and "racial" Judaism—if anything, Luke wishes to suggest the *Jewishness* of his gentiles![40] On the other hand, the way Luke undermines the ethnic identity of *non*-Christian Judeans is extremely problematic. In questioning whether non-Christian Judeans have a meaningful connection to Abraham or to other renowned Israelites—and in telling them "*your* ancestors" killed the prophets—Luke's rhetoric has contributed directly to later supersessionist constructions of Christianity as the "true Israel," as somehow "better Jews" than the (majority of) Jews themselves.

One subject which falls outside the scope of this study should be noted at the outset. This book will *not* discuss Luke's assessment of Samaritan ethnicity in significant depth. Although Samaritans *are* of significant interest

Introduction xv

to Luke (Luke 10:25–37; 17:11–19),[41] he does not significantly explore or reconfigure their *ancestry*—this book's angle of approach.[42]

FINDING ONE'S PEDESTAL: CHRISTIANS AMONG THE *ETHNĒ*

Like the Aphrodisian *Sebasteion*, Luke–Acts employs racial reasoning to construct an honorable identity for its intended audience. The imperial temple complex did this by invoking shared ancestry between Carians and Romans, rehearsing mythical/historical traditions, and contrasting their own race with other races subjugated by the empire. Luke does this by implying shared ancestry between Judean and gentile Christ-believers,[43] by rehearsing Judaism's mythical/historical traditions (reinterpreted as the common inheritance of all who confess Christ), and by contrasting Christ-believers with non-Christian Judeans.

The racial reasoning in the *sebasteion's* artistic schema was largely based on the implicit contrast between the Carians and the various *ethnē* who stood along the south portico, in various poses which imply their defeat, subjugation, or pacified status.[44] The reasoning in Luke's literary schema is also largely based upon contrast: non-Christian Judeans are depicted in a particular way in order to make claims about Christians (both Israelite and gentile) by contrast.[45] We might imagine that actual, living, flesh-and-blood members of the various *ethnē* depicted in Aphrodisias would object to the way their races were constructed in those reliefs. Similarly, many flesh-and-blood Judeans of Luke's day would likely object to the way that Luke–Acts characterizes them.[46]

Race is a socially conditioned category, rather than an objective reality. The meaning of "race" is perpetually being articulated and performed—and its various meanings are continually challenged or accepted, revised or modified. This means that competing definitions of the category can circulate at the very same time. For example, although some strands within Second Temple Judaism emphasized strict genealogical descent in their construction of Jewishness (e.g., *Jub.* 30:7–15; Tob. 4:12–13; 4QMMT 75–82), others were quite open to gentiles joining the race, as long as they adopted their cultural and religious practices (e.g., Jos. *C. Ap.* 2.210; Philo *Virt.* 195; *Spec.* 1.317).[47] Luke capitalizes on the pre-existing idea that "Judean" was a semipermeable identity, to affirm an Israelite identity for gentile Christians. His construction of this new identity downplays *literal* descent, but creatively invokes the *idea* of ancestry by adherence to the hope and faith of the ancestors. Similarly, Luke downplays or reinterprets the legal regulations within the Torah, while

xvi   *Introduction*

creatively reinterpreting loyalty to Torah as one's recognition of Jesus as the culmination of promises found therein.

Because "race" is a thing made of discourse, the characterization of *particular races* can be contested. Totally different assessments of any given race jostle and compete at the same moment in time. For example, although some gentiles had a fairly positive view of Judean traditions and were drawn to their teachings (*Virt.* 102; *Ant.* 20.34–42; Luke 7:4–5),[48] others caricatured them as subversive, antisocial atheists (Tacitus, *Hist.* 5.3.1; Philostratus *Vita. Apoll.* 5.33), who supposedly posed an almost existential threat to traditional ways of life (Jos. *Ant.* 13.245; Diodorus, *Bib.Hist.* 34–35.1.1). In the face of such criticism, Judeans creatively affirmed the honor of their people by emphasizing its extreme antiquity, recalling high-profile gentiles who have favored them, or even asserting that various arts or sciences had actually originated with them.[49] Faced with ethnic critics, these Judeans asserted that they were both a civilized and civili*zing*, people.

Nevertheless, in the period after the Jewish Revolt, Christ-believers may have felt defensive about their identification with a race now widely associated with unrest and rebellion. Luke eases his audience's potential discomfort by associating "the Way" with those aspects of Judaism most acceptable to outsiders, while characterizing its enemies with many of the same negative stereotypes frequently leveled against Judeans.[50] That is, Luke's Christians are "Judean" in their descent from Abraham (whether actual or aspirational), their worship of God, their hope in the ancestral promises laid out in scripture, their ethical conduct, and their openness to outsiders; on the other hand, the community's enemies are "Judean" in their resemblance to various antisemitic stereotypes such as clannishness, social disruptiveness, and propensity to violence (Luke 4:29; 11:46–51; 23:18–25; Acts 7:54–58; 9:1; 9:23; 12:1–3).[51] (To be more precise, perhaps we should not say that Gentile Christians are "Judean" by virtue of their derivation from Abraham, but rather "Israelite" [or Israel-adjacent]—because for Luke, Israel is comprised of not only Judeans but other Israelites, such as Anna of the tribe of Asher, and, perhaps, Samaritans.)[52]

Luke's stated intention for his gospel is that his audience "may have certainty concerning the things you have been taught" (Luke 1:4). To do this, Luke must reassure them that the promises and prophecies laid out in Israel's scriptures *do* properly concern Jesus, and that these promises *are* properly their heritage—whether or not they happen to be Judeans by birth. In his gospel, Luke figuratively sets the stage (or, perhaps, prepares the pedestal) on which believers will eventually stand upon, in Acts. Christ-believers are poised to assume an honorable, peaceful, and law-abiding place among the peoples of the Roman empire—an assertion partially made by way of contrast

Introduction xvii

to the rabble-rousing, disruptive behavior of their opponents, whether Judeans (Acts 13:50, 14:19; 17:5–8) or gentiles (Acts 16:19–23; 19:23–40).[53]

But how exactly does Luke understand this identity? What title might he inscribe upon the pedestal that these mixed-origin Christians will occupy? Does he imagine that they actually push (non-Christian) Judeans from their position, so that it might simply still read, ΕΘΝΟΥΣ ΙΟΥΔΑΙΩΝ ("Race of the Judeans")? Or are the gentile Christians merely Judean*ish*—would they perhaps be better described by some other title, such as ΕΘΝΟΥΣ ΙΣΡΑΗΛΙΤΩΝ ("Israelites")?[54] Luke does not, in the end, commit himself to so specific a label for Christ-believers. But whatever else they might be called, Luke suggests that even gentiles who follow "The Way" are the ΤΕΚΝΑ ΑΒΡΑΑΜ, "children of Abraham" (Luke 3:8, Acts 13:26), stones who have been quarried "out of the nations" (εξ εθνων; Acts 15:14, 23) joined to "a people" (λαος) for God's name (Acts 15:14).[55]

NOTES

1. Consider Jonathan Hall's famous statement that in classical antiquity, "The criteria of ethnicity are phrased in the form of a yes or no question—normally, 'can you, or can you not, claim descent from *x*?'" Hall, *Ethnic Identity in Greek Antiquity* (New York: Cambridge University Press), 24–25. Although this somewhat oversimplifies the matter, descent *was* a primal, powerful notion in ancient conceptions of race/ethnicity.

Unless otherwise noted, all New Testament passages are my translation.

2. R. R. R. Smith, "The Ethne from the Sebasteion at Aphrodisias," *The Journal of Roman Studies* 78 (1998): 51; Martinez-Vasquez, 89; Davina C. Lopez, *Apostle to the Conquered: Reimagining Paul's Mission* (Minneapolis, MN: Fortress, 2007), 45.

3. Christopher Stroup, *The Christians Who Became Jews: Acts of the Apostles and Ethnicity in the Roman City.* (New Haven, CT: Yale University Press, 2020), 51. On "ethnic genealogies" generally, see Hall, *Ethnic Identity*, 42–43; Hall, *Hellenicity: Between Ethnicity and Culture* (Chicago, IL: University of Chicago Press, 2002), 25–29.

4. These male faces may themselves have been masculine personifications of the same *ethnos*.

5. The figure which once stood atop this base, presumably a female personification of the race, is now missing. *Judeans*: Throughout this book, I will use "Judeans" to denote the race whose homeland was Judea, rather than "Jews"; see chapter 1 for discussion.

6. I tend to favor the arguments of Shelly Matthews in assigning Luke–Acts a date sometime within the first quarter of the Second Century, although a range of anywhere from 85 to 130 would not trouble my discussion of Luke's racial reasoning. cf. *Perfect Martyr*, 5–6.

xviii   *Introduction*

7. I proceed under the general understanding that Luke–Acts is a composite work in two volumes, with both a preliminary preface (Luke 1:1–4) and a secondary preface in the next volume (Acts 1:1–5), after the manner of some other ancient multi-volume works (e.g., Philo *Moses* 1.1.1–4, 2.1.1; Jos. *Apion* 1.1.1–5, 2.1.1–7; *Ant.* 13:1ff and 14.1ff; Artemid., *Oneiro.* 2.1; Chariton, *Chaereas and Callirhoe* 5.8; Polybius, *Hist.* 4.1; etc.). The level of unity we should ascribe to these volumes, especially when it comes to genre, is a site of ongoing debate among scholars. This debate need not trouble the present study on ethnicity in Luke's thought. I shall primarily engage with the gospel in the current work, and when I do engage with Acts (primarily in chapter 5), it is with the understanding that, whatever the literary relationship between two works may be, the author's ethnic reasoning will be consistent across the two.

8. *"Christianity"* and *"the Way":* I alternate between both terms ("Christian/-ity" and "the Way") throughout this work to refer to early Jesus-believers, both those within Luke's narrative and those within its implied audience. Admittedly, Luke seems to prefer "the Way" to "Christian," presenting the latter as an outsider's label for the group (Acts 11:26; 26:28), not adopted by believers themselves. I will nevertheless use both because the label "Christian" is easily understood today to stand for the group which Luke is referring to. cf. Matthews (*Taming the Tongues of Fire*, xiv) for her observation that if one dates Luke relatively later (perhaps within the first decades of the second century), the term is less anachronistic—although, as she clarifies, this does not necessarily mean that the separation between "Christianity" and Judaism has been fully accomplished by the time of Luke's writing.

9. Of course, Luke also belongs to the then-emerging Christian genre, "gospel," but of other contemporary literature, it most closely resembles a *bios*/biography.

10. For "racial reasoning," see Denise Kimber Buell, *Why This New Race: Ethnic Reasoning in Early Christianity* (New York: Columbia University Press, 2005).

11. For the suggestion that Luke uses Jews to "think with," see Shelley Matthews, *Perfect Martyr: The Stoning of Stephen and the Construction of Christian Identity* (Oxford: Oxford University Press, 2010), 34.

12. Throughout this book, I will alternate between the terms "race" and "ethnicity" to highlight the fact that neither word perfectly corresponds to the ancient notions of peoplehood which underlaid such terms as *ethnos, genos,* and *laos* (or the Latin *gens*).

13. See chapter 1 for elaboration on the *ethnos*-conscious method. I originally articulated and employed this approach in *Race in John's Gospel: Toward an Ethnos-Conscious Approach* (New York: Fortress Academic, 2019).

There is, to be clear, nothing wrong with using the insights of the social sciences as the primary lens by which to read the text; different insights emerge from the application of different methodologies. The approach we will follow *here*, however, privileges *ancient* discussions and theories about race.

14. Hall, *Ethnic Identity*, 19–25; Denise Eileen McCoskey, *Race: Antiquity and Its Legacy* (Oxford: Oxford University Press, 2012), 2–5, 23–33; Philip F. Esler, *Conflict and Identity in Romans, The Social Setting of Paul's Letter* (Minneapolis, MN: Fortress, 2003), 57; David G. Horrell, *Ethnicity and Inclusion: Religion, Race, and*

Whiteness in the Construction of Jewish and Christian Identities (Grand Rapids, MI: Eerdmans, 2020), 69–74.

15. Hall, *Ethnic Identity in Greek Antiquity* (1997); Benjamin Isaac, *The Invention of Racism in Classical Antiquity* (Princeton, NJ: Princeton University Press, 2004); McCoskey, *Race: Antiquity and Its Legacy* (2012); Mary T. Boatwright, *Peoples of the Roman World* (Cambridge: Cambridge University Press, 2012); Erich S. Gruen, *Rethinking the Other in Antiquity* (Princeton, NJ: Princeton University Press, 2011); cf. Shelly P. Haley, "Be Not Afraid of the Dark: Critical Race Theory and Classical Studies," in *Prejudice and Christian Beginnings*, Laura Nasrallah and Elisabeth Schüssler Fiorenza, eds. (Minneapolis, MN: Fortress, 2009), 27–49; Jeremy McInterney, ed., *A Companion to Ethnicity in the Ancient Mediterranean* (Oxford: Wiley-Blackwell, 2014).

16. Denise Kimber Buell, *Why This New Race: Ethnic Reasoning in Early Christianity* (New York: Columbia University Press, 2005). Buell's book primarily interrogates the racial reasoning of *post*-canonical Christian literature, but it inspired New Testament scholars to bring the same questions to scripture.

17. For examples, see: Paul's letters: Cavan Concannon, *"When You Were Gentiles": Specters of Race and Ethnicity in Roman Corinth and Paul's Corinthian Correspondence* (New Haven, CT: Yale University Press, 2014); Caroline Johnson Hodge, *If Sons Then Heirs: A Study of Kinship and Ethnicity in the Letters of Paul* (New York: Oxford University Press, 2007); Davina Lopez, *Apostle to the Conquered*, 2008; Sze-Kar Wan's "To the Jew First and also to the Greek," in *Prejudice and Christian Beginnings,* Laura Nasrallah and Elisabeth Schüssler Fiorenza, eds. (Minneapolis, MN: Fortress, 2009), 129–157; Love Sechrest, *A Former Jew: Paul and the Dialectics of Race* (New York: T&T Clark, 2009). Gospels: Dennis Duling, "Ethnicity, Ethnocentrism, and the Matthean *Ethnos*," *Biblical Theology Bulletin* 35.4 (2006): 127–129; Markus Cromhout, *Jesus and Ethnicity: Reconstructing Judeans Ethnicity in Q* (Eugene, OR: Wipf & Stock, 2007); Andrew Benko, *Race in John's Gospel: Toward an Ethnos-Conscious Approach* (New York: Fortress Academic, 2019); Rodolfo Galvan Estrada III, *A Pneumatology of Race in the Gospel of John: An Ethnocritical Study* (Eugene, OR: Pickwick, 2019); Stewart Penwell, *Jesus the Samaritan: Ethnic Labeling in the Gospel of John* (Boston, MA: Brill, 2020); Love Sechrest, "Enemies, Romans, Pigs, and Dogs: Loving the Other in the Gospel of Matthew," *Ex Auditu* 31 (2015): 71–105. Acts: Cynthia Baker, "From Every Nation Under Heaven," in *Prejudice and Christian Beginnings,* Laura Nasrallah and Elisabeth Schüssler Fiorenza, eds. (Minneapolis, MN: Fortress, 2009), 79–100; Eric Barreto, *Ethnic Negotiations: The Function of Race and Ethnicity in Acts 16* (Tübingen: Mohr Siebeck, 2010); Aaron Kuecker, *The Spirit and the 'Other': Social Identity, Ethnicity and Intergroup Reconciliation in Luke–Acts* (New York: Bloomsbury, 2011); and Christopher Stroup, *The Christians Who Became Jews* (New Haven, CT: Yale University Press, 2020). To this list we might add Gay Byron, who like Buell is primarily focused on post-canonical Christians in her book *Symbolic Blackness and Ethnic Identity in Early Christian Literature* (New York: Routledge, 2002), although she *does* briefly consider the Ethiopian Eunuch of Acts 8:26–40 (pp. 109–115).

xx   *Introduction*

18. J. Daniel Hays, *From Every People and Nation: A Biblical Theology of Race* (Downer's Grove, IL: Intervarsity Press, 2003), 161.

19. compare Luke 1:5–25 // Gen. 15:1–18:16, 21:1–7. See chapter 3.

20. Hall, *Ethnic Identity in Greek Antiquity*, 25.

21. cf. Denise Kimber Buell, *Why This New Race?*, 37–41.

22. On Abraham as convert, see e.g., Philo, *Abr.* 13.67, 15.70, 42.245; *Jubilees* 12:1–14.

23. Tacitus, *Hist.* 5.5.2; 1 Macc. 2:19; 3 Macc. 1:3; Josephus *A.J.* 18.141; Philo, *Mos.* 1.147; *Virt.* 20.102–103; *Spec.* 1.52–53, 1.317, 3.315–317.

24. *Jubilees* 12:1–14; *Apoc.Abr.* ch.'s 1–8; Philo, *Abr.* 13.63,67, 15.70, 42.245.

25. Horrell, *Ethnicity and Inclusion*, 262–273.

26. Ibid., 83–89, 274–277.

27. E.g., 1 Maccabees invokes Abraham as a reason to hold fast to ancestral customs even when persecuted (1 Macc. 2:19–22; 2:50–61). Similarly, Tobit invokes Abraham in support of endogamous marriage (Tob 4:12).

28. As we shall see in subsequent chapters, Luke signals in Luke–Acts that followers of the Way should expect to be accused of having abandoned their kinfolk, their ancestral customs, and in a word, their race. These accusations can be leveled against gentiles (Acts 19:23–28; 16:20) as well as Jews (Luke 11:2–3; Acts 18:12–17; 21:20–24, 28; 23:).

29. "Intellectual genealogies" fostered a sense of commonality and kinship, including philosophical schools, medical schools, and also early rabbinic schools; Caroline Hodge also cites notions of "spiritual" kinship between those who value the same virtues (Philo, *Virt.* 187–227; Plut., *On the Fortune of Alexander*, 329B–D). See *If Sons, Then Heirs*, 38–41. The language of "ascriptive descent" as opposed to "subscriptive descent" is mine, and will be explored in chapter 1.

30. For example: Noah (17:24–27, 30); Abraham (1:54–55; 1:72–75); Moses (24:44; Acts 7:37); David (1:32, 69; Acts 2:25–31); the prophets (1:70; 24:44; Acts 26:22–23); Simeon and Anna (2:25–38).

31. See citations above; Jesus is the "horn of salvation" promised to David (1:69) and the fulfillment of the oath sworn to Abraham (1:73). But Luke *also* affirms that Jewish scriptures had foretold that this salvation would extend to the *ethnē*. Consider Luke 4:23–27, which cites Elijah's miraculous assistance of the widow at Zarephath, and Elisha's healing of the Syrian, Naaman; or consider 3:4–6, which frames John the Baptist's ministry in light of Isa. 40:3–5 (adding significantly more of the passage than Matthew, including the prophecy that "all flesh shall see the salvation of God.") In Acts, James' speech to the Jerusalem Council interprets the inclusion of some gentiles within "a people for his name" is intrinsic to the restoration of "the fallen tent of David" foretold by the prophets (Acts 15:13–18).

32. Regarding the word "race": chapter 1 will briefly address issues of terminology. For example, the question of whether to use "Judean" or "Jew" for this period is much discussed among scholars. I tend to favor "Judean" when writing from an ethnos-conscious point of view, for reasons I will make clear in chapter 1. I will also alternate between both "race" and "ethnicity" when discussing race in antiquity, so

Introduction xxi

as to guard against the implication that any modern word perfectly captures what the ancients meant by such words as εθνος, γενος, *natio*, *gens*, גוי, or עם.

33. cf. Benko, *Race in John's Gospel,* 14–22.

34. Josephus, *Ant.* 14:8–10. Giving the lie to Herod's genealogical claims to the very best Jewish lineage, Herod's critics disparage him as a ἡμιουδαιος "half-Judean" (*Ant.* 14.403). See Shaye Cohen, *The Beginnings of Jewishness: Boundaries, Varieties, Uncertainties* (Berkeley, CA: University of California Press, 1999), 13–24.

35. Hall, *Ethnic Identity in Greek Antiquity; cf.* Hall's *Hellenicity.*

36. 1 Macc. 2:19–22; 2:50–61; Tob. 4:12.

37. Throughout this book, I will use "Judaism" to mean the entire distinctive culture and way of life of ancient Judeans, not "only" the religion of the Judeans (as if this could somehow be abstracted from the rest of their identity). The first documented appearances of this word in 2 Maccabees (2:21; 8:1; 14:38) . . . "Judaism" is implicated in kinship (8:1), hopes for national sovereignty and self-determination (2:20; 14:39–42), loyalty to the Judean homeland (2:21–22; 8:3), distinction between Judeans and "barbarians" (βαρβαρα; 2:21) or "the nations" (εθνη; 14:38), and adherence to ancestral laws (2:22; 8:1)—as well as what might be thought of as merely "religious" concerns. *Judaismos* seems to stand for an entire cultural system assumed to be normative for *Judaioi.*

Shaye Cohen remarks:

> In this first occurrence of the term, *Ioudaïsmos* has not yet been reduced to a designation of a religion. It means rather 'the aggregate of all things those characteristics that make Judaeans Judaean (or Jews Jewish).' Among these characteristics, to be sure, are practices and beliefs that we would today call 'religious,' but these practices and beliefs are not the sole content of the term. (*Beginnings of Jewishness,* 106)

38. Philo describes Abraham as the Judeans' *ethnarch* or *genarch* (ethnic "founder" or racial "originator").

39. See Horrell's excellent *Ethnicity and Inclusion*, esp. 95–135.

40. To be even more precise: an *Israelite* or *Israel-adjacent* identity for gentiles who follow the Way.

41. Cf. Luke 9:51–56; Acts 1:8; 8:1–25; 15:1–3. Consider also the character of Anna, who is "from the tribe of Asher" and therefore a *Northern* Israelite (2:36).

42. For more on Samaritans in Luke–Acts racial imagination, see my forthcoming *Good Samaritans: Samaritan Ethnicity and Evangelism in Luke–Acts,* Andrew Benko and Stewart Penwell. cf. Jacob Jervell, *Luke and the People of God* (Minneapolis, MN: Augsburg, 1972).

43. Luke 3:23–38, which traces Jesus' lineage back past Abraham all the way to Adam, the common ancestor of all humankind, implying that all are related within Jesus' (thoroughly Jewish) genealogy; Luke 3:8, where new "children of Abraham" can be made of even stones, so long as they "bear fruits worthy of repentance."

44. R. R. R. Smith further notes that the subtle differences in their dress and stance "express a range of subtle differences of character and degree of civilization" ranging from "within the fully civilized centre of the empire to different kinds of outlying and

xxii   *Introduction*

barbarian peoples." Smith, "Simulacra Gentium: The Ethne from the Sebasteion at Aphrodisias," 60. See also Lopez, *Apostle to the Conquered*, 45–46.

45. A significant difference between the two, of course, is that Luke's ethnic project is somewhat contradictory. Whereas the Aphrodisian complex links Carians with Romans and contrasts Carians with various *other* races, Luke wants to simultaneously construct a Judean (or perhaps better, Israelite) identity for all Christians, while also contrasting them with (the majority of the) Judeans!

46. See, for example, Luke 23:18–25; 21:20–22; Acts 7:54–58; 9:1; 9:23; 12:1–3.

47. In Denise Kimber Buell's terms, the former constructed "Jew" as a *fixed* category, while the latter allowed some *fluidity* in the construction. See Buell, *Why This New Race?*, 37–41.

48. Consider the "worthy" Centurion who "loves our *ethnos*" and "built our synagogue" (Luke 7:4–5); this character, much revised from the version we find in Matthew, stands in line with the φοβουμενοι and σεβομενοι τον θεον of Acts (e.g., Acts 10:2, 22; 13:16; 16:14; 18:7).

49. Sometimes, it was Abraham who was thought to have introduced innovations to other nations, but it could as easily be Moses or others. We shall consider several of these traditions in subsequent chapters.

50. Cf. Matthews, *Taming the Tongues of Fire*, 68–70.

51. We might, more carefully, say that Luke's Christians are "Israelite" in these ways, not specifically "Judean." Luke's conception of Israel is flexible enough to encompass both Judeans *and* Samaritans—and now, by their belief in Christ, gentiles as well.

52. Anna, Luke 2:36. Regarding Samaritans, consider the Merciful Samaritan (10:29–37) who rightly displays the sort of mercy to one's (ethnic, Israelite) neighbor required by Torah (Lev 19:17–18); consider also Jesus' command to a *Samaritan* leper, "Go, show yourselves to the priests" (Luke 17:14), as well as the Judean and Samaritan "brothers" in Antioch, who collectively understand gentiles as a different group from themselves (Acts 15:3).

53. "As typical of a minority group that is seeking a safe place under empire, Luke attempts to secure a place for his own people by targeting another minority group as unworthy of such security" (Matthews, *Taming the Tongues of Fire*, 55).

54. See Jason Staples' excellent and thoroughly researched *The Idea of Israel*, especially its final chapter, for the point that the concept of "Israel" was wider and more expansive than "*Ioudaios*" in Second Temple Judaism. Staples suggests that with the influx of gentiles into the movement, Christianity quickly became "a competing form of Israelism" (p. 348).

55. All tables throughout the book are created by the author.

Chapter 1

Ethnos and Racial Fluidity
in Antiquity

For my eyes have seen your salvation,
which you have prepared before the face of all peoples (λαων),
a light for revelation to the races (εθνων),
and for glory to your people Israel. —Luke 2:30–32[1]

When Mary and Joseph bring their newborn to the Temple "in order to do for him according to the custom of the law" (2:27; cf. 2:22, 24), a prophet named Simeon greets the infant. Although he had been eagerly awaiting the "consolation of Israel" (2:25), Simeon perceives that Jesus will be revealed to *all* the races of the world, not just his own. His words echo Isaianic "light to the nations" oracles (Isa. 42:6–7, 49:6–7, 51:1–5), which themselves foretell that the salvation of Israel will involve the gentiles (εθνη/גוים).[2]

Simeon's prophecy signals the importance of race in Luke's gospel. But it also raises questions. If the salvation of "the Lord's Christ" (2:26) will reach beyond Israel, will Israel still receive the lion's share of these blessings? Will the "consolation of Israel," or the "redemption of Jerusalem" anticipated by the prophet Anna (2:38), still take the form of political/military vindication—the sort of nationalistic hopes frequently projected onto the messiah?[3] How can a *Judean* messiah be "appointed for the *falling* and rising of many in Israel" (2:34)? Will the gentiles witness these "falls"—or, indeed, experience rises and falls of their own? More basically, who are these "peoples" (λαων) that Jesus is prepared in the presence of, and what does it mean to belong to a people, Israel or otherwise? What are these "*ethnē*" who will see him as a light—and for that matter, how should we translate this word into English? Shall we try out "nation," or "race"—or even "ethnicity," given its connection to the Greek *ethnos*? Should we render it "gentile," as a general term for non-Israelite races, as the word was sometimes used in contemporary Judean sources?[4]

1

2   *Chapter 1*

The Song of Simeon encapsulates, in miniature, the juxtaposition of Israel/ gentile found throughout these initial chapters of Luke. On the one hand, the story is populated by prototypical Judeans of exemplary lineage and piety. On the other hand, we have several reminders of the multi-ethnic context of the wider Roman οικουμενη. The narrative chronology of these early episodes is anchored using the Greco-Roman convention of describing dates in terms of current rulers (1:5, 2:1–2, 3:1–3).[5] The birth of John the Baptist takes place "in the days of Herod, king of Judea" (1:5)—Herod, that half-Idumean, half-Arab client of Rome, who built up not only the Temple in Jerusalem, but also temples to Rome and Augustus in Caesarea (a city he had renamed in the emperor's honor). Thus, the tale of Zechariah and Elizabeth, those model Israelites of impeccable lineage (1:5b) and prototypical religious observance (1:6),[6] abuts reference to Herod, an Idumean "demi-Jew" (ἡμιουδαιος)[7] whose lavish demonstrations of loyalty to Rome raised questions about the sincerity of his commitment to Judaism.[8] Similarly, the birth of Jesus to prototypically Judean parents happens at the same time that "a decree went out from Caesar Augustus, that all the inhabited world (οικουμενην) should be registered" (2:1)—further described as "the first registration, when Quirinius was governor of Syria" (2:2). The geographical references to the *Judean* homeland in the following verses (Galilee, Judea, and Bethlehem as the "City of David") stand cheek-by-jowl with references to *gentile* geography—neighboring gentile provinces, as well as the entire Roman empire (οικουμενη)—and to the gentiles who ruled these lands.[9] The chronological note which introduces the ministry of John the Baptist is especially detailed, specifying that the word of God came to John the son of Zechariah "in the fifteenth year of Tiberius Caesar," and further triangulating the chronology by mentioning several rulers at various levels of governance, both Judean and gentile (see table 1.1).

Table 1.1   Ethnic/Geographic Narrative Horizons, Luke 3:1–2

Narrative frame (Luke 3:1-2)	Ethnic/geographic horizon
"In the 15th year of the reign of T. Caesar,	Roman emperor / all the empire (οικυμενη, cf. 2:1)
when P. Pilate was governor of Judea,	Roman governor / homeland of Judeans
and Herod was tetrarch of Galilee,	Jud.-Id. ruler / largely Judean region adjacent to Judea
and Phillip his brother was tetrarch	Judean-Idumean ruler /
of the region of Iturea and Trachonitis,	largely gentile region adjacent to Judea
and Lysanias was tetrarch of Abilene,	gentile client ruler / nearby gentile region/city
during the high-priesthood	Priestly Judean clients of Roman governor /
of Annas and Caiaphas,	Jerusalem, Temple
the word of God came to John	A Judean of impeccable priestly lineage (cf. 5:5) /
the son of Zechariah in the wilderness."	an evocative location in the Judean imagination
(near the Jordan River)	(cf. Josh. 3–4; 2 Kgs 2:8,14; Ant. 20:97-98)

Ethnos *and Racial Fluidity in Antiquity* 3

These chronological notes establish a certain ethnic tension very early on in Luke. On the one hand, there is a pronounced emphasis on the prototypical Judean identity of several characters, in terms of their Israelite ancestry,[10] Israelite geography,[11] and adherence to distinctively Israelite customs.[12] On the other hand, there are consistent reminders that these thoroughly Israelite characters are embedded within a broader international stage[13]—wherein the decisions of distant emperors and their client-rulers can disrupt the day-to-day life of Judeans, even in their own land. By the time Jesus begins his public ministry, the audience is already attuned to issues of empire and ethnicity. The reader is primed to expect a dialectic between the local and the international, between ethnic belonging (and its in-group benefits) and an ethnic out-group, and more generally between Israelites and gentiles.[14]

This book reads Luke with an ear attuned to such ethnic considerations. We will raise questions such as: How would Luke's racial reasoning have functioned in its original context(s)? What might an ancient hearer of this gospel have understood it to be saying about peoplehood, about group belonging, about Christian identity? How might it have sounded to a late first-century Judean Christian in Antioch, a Samaritan in Sidon, a God-fearing Greek in Thessalonica, or a Gallic slave in Rome?

To address these sorts of questions, we will need some notion of the meaning(s) of *race* in the ancient world. I call this mode of interpretation an "*ethnos*-conscious approach," because it foregrounds *ancient* conceptions of "race" (as described by such ancient words as *ethnos, genos, gens, and natio*), rather than imposing modern definitions on ancient literature.

PRELIMINARY QUESTIONS

Anyone writing about "race" in antiquity faces the thorny issue of what to *call* it. Should we call it "race," or "ethnicity," or perhaps the considerably vaguer "people?" Would it be better to simply transliterate the ancient words and speak of *ethnos* and *genos* with no recourse to modern terminology?

Ancient Terms: εθνος, γενος, etc.

Neither Greek nor Latin had a technical term that precisely corresponds to our word "race"—nor, for that matter, did Hebrew or Aramaic. Greek words like γενος (*genos*), εθνος (*ethnos*), and λαος (*laos*) could carry meanings roughly equivalent to ethnicity, as could the Latin words *gens, natio,* and *populus*. But these ancient terms were used with considerable imprecision.[15] They could be used as synonyms within the same discourse; alternatively, an author might employ them with distinct connotations in mind for each.[16] Sometimes, the same word may recur later in the same text, now bearing a

4   *Chapter 1*

different meaning—indicating "race" here, "sex" there, and "species" in a third place. Commenting upon these ethnic terms, Teresa Morgan remarks,

> When Greek or Latin writers refer to an ἔθνος, γένος, or *genus*, they may therefore be talking about almost any kind of group, for which any aspect of the term may be important, marginal, or irrelevant. We must accordingly always treat the language or ethnicity or identity, including early Christian identity, with caution. Its terminology is so multivalent that its meaning is likely to be highly specific to the context in which it is used.[17]

This lack of lexical exactitude does not mean "race" did not exist in the ancient mind. Ancient thinkers could and did discuss racial differences and speculate as to why different peoples exist. They just did so without a precisely delineated technical vocabulary.[18]

Laos (λαος) is a bit of a special case. This Greek word had gradually fallen out of common usage after Homer, so when the translators of the Septuagint chose it as their most common translation of the Hebrew עַם (*'am*), it gave the expression an archaic, somewhat technical feel. When we encounter this word in turn-of-era Judean texts, we generally have the biblical people of God in view—a pattern that carries forward into early Christian usage.[19]

"A race, by any other name . . ."

We are still left with the question of what to call this category in English discussion.

Some scholars prefer "ethnicity,"[20] while others make compelling arguments for using "race" in discussions of antiquity.[21] Denise Kimber Buell points out that "ethnicity" is every bit as capable of serving racist rhetoric as the word "race," as demonstrated by the so-called "ethnic cleansings" in Rwanda and the former Yugoslavia. She warns that when classicists rely on the supposedly "less odious" term ethnicity, they may actually obscure racist dynamics antiquity.[22] Following the same reasoning as Shakespeare's quip, "A rose by any other name would smell as sweet,"[23] it seems that "race" by any other name may smell as *foul*—or, be just as thorny. Indeed, Denise McCoskey prefers to use "race" precisely *because* the word forces us to foreground issues of power and oppression.[24]

For this study, I will employ several English words in our discussion of ancient *ethnos*. The ancients themselves did not have one single, technical word for race, and the several words they did use (e.g., *ethnos*, *laos*, and *genos*) had a variety of meanings—none of which corresponded perfectly

Ethnos *and Racial Fluidity in Antiquity*

to either English word. Therefore, I will intentionally use a variety of words (race, ethnicity, people, nation) to discourage the over-identification of ancient *ethnos* with any single modern category.[25] By using several words in rotation, I hope to highlight the *slipperiness* of the phenomenon.

When discussing the historical people of Judea in the antiquity, I will typically use "Judean" rather than the modern term "Jew," as closer to the Greek *Ioudaioi,* better preserving the lexical connection to a homeland, *Ioudaia.*[26]

Race as Social Construct

Anthropologists today understand "race" as a socially conditioned concept.[27] It is a discursively constructed category, not a matter of "what is," but of "what is *said* to be." Race is not a factual essence but "the self-conscious insistence on an image of the organic cohesion of a community, however it may be constructed."[28] As such, the meaning and content of race can shift from time to time, and from place to place. When we read Luke or any ancient text with an eye toward its racial reasoning, we should ask what its contemporary audience would have understood it to be saying. The question becomes: How was race actually understood in antiquity?

In truth, there was no single, authoritative view of "race" in the late first-century Mediterranean world. When Christ-believers began articulating their identity in ethnic terms, there was no singular, authoritative definition of race with which they could interact. Rather, authors chose from among a range of possibilities on how to construct what it means to be "Greek" (or any other race), and how to construct peoplehood in general.[29] However, several key features appear fairly consistently across ancient discussions of ethnicity. We will call these features—widely understood to define the category—the "criteria" of race.

Ancient Sources on of the Criteria of Race

A much-cited passage from Herodotus is frequently a first stop. During the Persian War, the Athenians assured the Spartans that they would not ally with the Medes:

> There were a great many reasons why we should not do this [betray Hellas (Ἑλλάδα) to the Persians], nor wish to. First and greatest, the burning and destruction of the ornaments and shrines of the gods. . . . Secondly, the kinship (συγγενεια) of all Greeks: that is, the same blood (ὁμαιμον) and the same tongue (ὁμογλωσσον), both the shrines of the Gods and shared sacrifices, and the same way of life (ηθεα ὁμοτροπα). (Herodotus, *Histories* 8.144)[30]

6   *Chapter 1*

This dense statement situates several features under the general category of "Greekness" (Ἑλληνικον). *Hellenikon* is composed of (1) common blood, (2) common language, (3) common religion, and (4) common mode of life. If we admit mention of "Hellas" from the previous line, we may add a fifth feature: (5) common territory.[31] The "relatedness (*sungeneia*) of all Greeks" is comprised of all of these; this "kinship" is a socially constructed category, encompassing not only biological but also cultural considerations.

In his *Geography,* Strabo discusses several peoples thought to be related to the Arabians. Regarding the "kinship of the races" (της των εθνων συγγενειας) and their "common characteristics" (κοινοτητος), he explains:

> For the race (εθνος) of the Armenians and that of the Syrians and Arabians exhibit a great sameness of stock (ὁμοφυλιαν), not only in their language (διαλεκτον), but in their mode of life (βιους) and physical build (σωματων χαρακτηρας), and particularly wherever they are close neighbors (πλησιοχωροι). (*Geography* 1.2.34)[32]

Here, several factors define race (εθνος): (1) kinship and "common stock," (2) language, (3) mode of life, (4) physical features, and (5) territory. All of these are among the "common characteristics" (κοινοτητος) that demonstrate the relatedness (συγγενειας) of these three peoples. About a century later, Cicero gives a comparable list of the ties that bind a people together, including blood, family traditions, worship, and language (Cicero *De Off.* 1.53–55).[33]

A similar array of ethnic features can be found in Israel's scripture. In the famous "Table of the Nations" in Genesis, beginning with the sons of Noah, we encounter terms reminiscent of those from Greek sources above:

> These are the sons of Shem, by their tribes (φυλαις),
> according to their languages (γλωσσας),
> their lands (χωραις), and their races (εθνεσιν).

> (Gen 10:31 [LXX] cf. Gen 10:5, 29)[34]

Here we have several ethnic features side by side, defining each people in a multifaceted way: ancestry, kinship (φυλαις), language (a cultural feature), and territory.[35] Or consider this passage from Deuteronomy:

> [8] When the Most High apportioned the nations (גוים/εθνη),
>   when he divided humankind (*lit.* "the sons of Adam"),
> he fixed the boundaries of the peoples (עמים/εθνων)
>   according to the number of the gods (בני אלוהים/αγγελων θεου),[36]
> [9] the LORD's own portion was his people (עמו/λαος)
>   Jacob his allotted share. (Deuteronomy 32:8–9)[37]

Here, geography, way of life (represented by religion), and descent collectively define and differentiate the nations. Each has its land, its gods (part of a distinctive culture), and its ancestors. Humanity's *universal* descent from Adam is contrasted with each race's *particular* descent from a founder—for instance, Israel's descent from Jacob.

We see that a whole slate of features tended to accompany ancient discussions of race. Synthesizing her lexical study of the words γενος and εθνος across nine bodies of Greek-language literature,[38] Love Sechrest notes that territory, government, religion, customs, and kinship are consistent ingredients of peoplehood.[39] Steve Mason nicely sums up the lexical accoutrements of race in the ancient sources, noting that:

> Each *ethnos* had its distinctive nature or character (φυσις, ηθος), expressed in unique ancestral traditions (τα πατρια), which typically reflected a shared (if fictive) ancestry (συγγενεια); each had its charter stories (μυθοι), customs, norms, conventions, mores, laws (νομοι, εθη, νομιμα), and political arrangements or constitution (πολιτεια).[40]

Although a few scholars today insist upon "shared descent" as the *sine qua non* of race in ancient thought,[41] more champion a polythetic view acknowledging multiple criteria.[42] Denise Kimber Buell has argued persuasively for a flexible definition.[43] Race, she says, is variously defined in various contexts, with significant criteria receding or coming to the fore with historical changes. Therefore, she argues, racial discourse always entails some degree of what she calls "fluidity." This fluidity may be demonstrated in change over time, as the meaning of race shifts; it may also be demonstrated in the active competition between different definitions during the very same historical moment.[44]

Buell explains that racial discourses may be mapped on a continuum between fixity and fluidity. Factors like shared descent tend toward the "fixed" pole, constructing race in ways that present it as an essential "given." Factors like religion, culture, and self-definition, by contrast, tend toward the "fluid" end of the spectrum.

> Although ethnicity and race are concepts frequently constructed through appeals to fixity (essences, including lineages and "nature"), they can also be constructed through appeals to malleability. That is, definitions of ethnoracial membership can foreground "achievement" (not merely "ascription"). If seeking to portray ethnicity as attainable, one might stress the centrality of common purpose, common language or education (*paideia*), way of life, or religious practices.[45]

8   *Chapter 1*

To take up this last example: religion as an ethnic criterion highlights the possibility of crossing racial boundaries—as for example in the case of conversions.

Dennis C. Duling doubts "whether *any* feature is so constitutive that there is no 'ethnicity' without it."[46] To describe ancient ethnicity, he constructs what he calls an "outsider's model" that is "imposed upon the available data." It has nine criteria: (1) a name, (2) a myth of common ancestry, (3) shared "historical" memories, (4) phenotypical features, (5) homeland, (6) language, (7) kinship, (8) customs, and (9) religion.[47]

Synthesis: A Three-Criteria Model of Race in Antiquity

For the purposes of this study, I will synthesize the above survey into a simple, three-criteria model for race in antiquity. Race was widely understood as a matter of: (1) common ancestry, (2) common association with a specific land, (3) and common distinctive culture, or "way of life."[48] Several scholars have noted these three basic determinants of ancient ethnicity, although the ways they name them may vary.[49]

A model based upon the three criteria I propose—common descent, common homeland, and common distinctive culture—usefully distills the features most commonly found in ancient discussions of race and has a good deal of heuristic utility when applied to the New Testament.[50] Armed with this model, we might return briefly to our discussion of the early chapters of Luke. We can now observe that these chapters are absolutely stuffed with racial signifiers, establishing the thoroughgoing Judeanness of its characters by means of a thick web of references to Judean ancestry, territory, and way of life (see table 1.2).

Luke's protagonist will be a Judean among Judeans, his unshakable claim to that identity grounded in his birth and upbringing in the Judean homeland, his thoroughly Judean genealogy, and his family's strictly observant lifestyle.[51] We might be forgiven for expecting this story to be one which primarily concerns Judeans! It is all the more striking, then, that gentiles persistently appear at the edges of the narrative—in the evangelist's "peripheral vision," as it were. Gentiles are implicit in the chronological framing notices (1:5, 2:1–5, 3:1–2) but are also squarely in view in Simeon's prophetic song. Jesus has been "prepared in the presence of *all* peoples (παντων των λαων)—a light for revelation to the gentiles (εθνων) and for the glory of your people Israel" (2:32).[52] It seems abundantly clear, even before the outset of Jesus' adult ministry, that ethnicity is a significant concern of this gospel.

Within my tentative model of ancient *ethnos*, the criteria are listed in order of general importance. That is, appeals to ancestry were typically more significant (i.e., likely to define one) than appeals to homeland, which in

Ethnos *and Racial Fluidity in Antiquity*

Table 1.2   Ethnic Markers in Luke 1–3

1. Ancestry / genealogy / descent

Descent from Adam: Jesus' [supposed] genealogy from Joseph to Adam (3:23-38)
Descent from Jacob: "the house (οικον) of Jacob" (1:33; cf. 1:16, 1:54)
Tribal identity: Anna, of the tribe (φυλης) of Asher (1:36); tribe of Levi implied (1:5); Judah (3:33)
Priestly ancestry: "of the division of Abijah" (1:5); "of the daughters of Aaron" (1:5)
Descent from David: Joseph "of the house (εξ οικου) and lineage (πατριας) of David" (2:5; cf. 1:27, 3:31); Jesus "of the house (οικου) of David" (1:69); "throne of his ancestor (πατρος) David" (1:32)
Descent from Abraham: Abraham's σπερματι (1:55); "our ancestor (πατερα) Abraham" (1:73, 3:8)
Generic ancestors: "our ancestors (πατερας)," (1:55; 1:72)
Kinship: relatives (συγγενης) (1:36, 58; 2:44) family naming conventions (1:61)
General reproduction: κοιλια, "womb" (1:31,41,42); "brood" (γεννηματα) of vipers (3:7)

2. Territory / homeland

Judea: the "hill country" (1:39,65); "a town in Judah" (1:39); "wilderness" (1:80, 3:2-4); "the city of David, called Bethlehem" (2:4; 2:11, 15); rulers of (1:5, 3:1); Jerusalem/Temple (1:9ff, 2:25ff; 2:41)
Galilee: "a city of Galilee named Nazareth" (1:26; 2:4; 2:39, 51; as πατρις (4:23); tetrarch of (3:1)
Lands beyond: Syria (2:2); Abilene (3:1); all the "civilized world" (οικυμενη, 2:1)

3. Way of life / culture

customs: "according to the custom (το εθος) of the priesthood" (1:9); "according to the custom (το ειθισμενον) of the law" (2:27); "according to the custom (το εθος) of the festival" (2:42)
the law: "the law of Moses" (1:22); "the law of the Lord" (2:23,24,39; cf. 1:6, 2:27)
religious institutions, priesthood: Zechariah (1:8-23); altar of incense (1:9-11)
religious institutions, prophets: ancient (1:17,70); contemporary (1:67,76; 2:26,36; 3:2)
Temple piety: prayers, fasting (2:37; cf. 1:10); pilgrimage (2:41-42)
circumcision: John circumcised on the eight day (1:59); Jesus too (2:21)
scriptures: Torah study among the "teachers" (2:46-47)
the family: naming conventions (1:61); parental obedience (2:51); family/sexual norms (3:19)

turn was more frequently determinative of race than appeals to culture (see figure 1.1). Within this model, the criteria are also ranked along a scale from fixity to fluidity, from *ascription* to *achievement*. Ancestry was ascribed to an individual at birth and presented itself as a fixed "fact" (although in practice, genealogies were subject to revision). Association with a particular land was somewhat more fluid; people might move far from their ancestral homeland, and it was believed that the environment in which individuals lived changed them over time.[53] Still, the land of one's birth, and the land one's people hailed from, were theoretically "fixed." Lastly, way of life was the most fluid of all: anyone might achieve some level of identification with a different people by adopting their way of life. Such Greek words as παιδεια ("upbringing, culture"), πολιτεια ("constitution, way of living"), and εθος ("custom, tradition") speak to this admixture of ideas and practices, which collectively gave each people its own idiosyncratic way of living—and which collectively helped define them as a distinct people.[54] While it is it much easier to see how one might change their "way of life" than their ancestry, it is still the case that

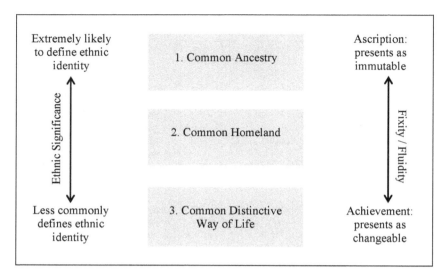

Figure 1.1 A Three-Criteria Model of Race in Antiquity. *Source*: Created by Andrew Benko.

"all three features have the potential to demonstrate mutability."[55] It is to this dynamic that we shall now turn our attention.

FLUIDITY IN ANCIENT CONSTRUCTIONS OF RACE

Having laid out a basic "outsider's model" of *what* ethnicity entailed, it remains to consider *how* the various ethnic criteria were actually invoked for particular rhetorical purposes. We are especially interested in how these three criteria could be used in a "fluid" way, allowing for a shift in identity.[56] Two considerations will be relevant to our discussion: flexibility *within* each criterion, and flexibility *among* the criteria.

(1) *Within the criteria:* In the bulk of the following section, we will consider how each individual criterion could be leveraged in ways allowing for ethnic fluidity, so that individuals (or even whole populations) could undergo shifts in ethnic self-understanding. (2) *Between the criteria*: "Race" was a polythetic construct—that is, it did not always hinge upon the same ingredients in every context. With multiple criteria in play, the very choice of *which* criterion to emphasize, and when, was significant. Ethnic actors could choose which to bring to the fore in any given situation. Even the same author could pick and choose, based on the rhetorical task at hand: Josephus' definition of "Judean"

could emphasize *lifestyle* in order to classify Idumeans as Judeans (*Ant.* 13.257–58), emphasize *descent* in order to exclude the Samaritans (*Ant.* 9:277–290), or emphasize *homeland* to ridicule an opponent who had misrepresented his geographical origins (*Apion* 2.37–38).

Fluidity in Ancestry / Descent

On the surface of it, ancestry is the most "fixed" (stable) of ethnic criteria. The logic of ancestry suggests permanence: one is born (*gennaō*) into a certain family, and one's *gene*alogy is what it is. However, as we shall see, even descent claims could occasionally admit a certain amount of flexibility. Because race is a social construct, not an objective essence, *it is the social recognition of shared ancestry* that matters, not the genealogical "facts" (after all, new "facts" could be generated to support new claims) nor the biological "truth" (in an era before modern DNA testing). Genealogy could be revised on the micro-scale, as individuals staked out ethnic claims based on their family's (supposed) lineage, or revised on the macro-scale, as novel connections were drawn between entire populations.

Ethnic Genealogies

The Persian War (480–479 BCE) was a major moment in the development of Greek ethnic consciousness, with the construction of the "barbarian" as the antitype of "Hellene."[57] Largely spurred on by the identity threat posed by the Persian invasion, various Greek peoples articulated their sense of connection to each other. Many variants of a "Hellenic Genealogy" describe how various Greeks were related, stretching all the way back to the eponymous king Hellen, son of Deukalion.[58] Jonathan Hall calls these myths of origin "a discursive media of ethnic identity":

> Whereas family genealogies allowed individuals to trace their lineage back to three-dimensional characters such as Perseus, Keryx or Eumolpos, ethnic genealogies were the instrument by which whole societies could situate themselves in space and time, reaffirming their identity to appeals to eponymous ancestors such as Doros, Ion, or Dryops, who were at the same time the retrojected constructions of such identity.[59]

These tales could galvanize a notion of ethnic *esprit de corps* among Hellenic races.[60] Such imaginative genealogies continued to inform ethnic thinking well into the Common Era. During the New Sophistic of the second century, an emphasis on Greek classicism gave many Greeks and non-Greeks a kind of "imaginary biology" by which they could construe themselves as related, thanks to the convenient wanderings of many Greek mythological

12   *Chapter 1*

heroes—who could often be invoked as city founders when no appropriate historical agent existed.[61] Sometimes, the proposed connections sound far-fetched to modern ears, tracing shared descent to gods, heroes, or other clearly legendary figures. For example, when the Eobean city of Carystus sought an alliance with a Carian city, Alabanda, in the first century BCE, they claimed that both groups were descendants of Achilles' teacher, Chiron—the centaur![62]

Ethnic genealogies not only *linked* peoples; they often implied a hierarchy. Those races more closely related to the primal ancestor—such as Hellen—were more esteemed. New editions of such myths can show us phases of racial reasoning—the ascendancy of a people as more influential might prompt their "upgrading" to a closer relationship with the founding figure. Sometimes, new peoples could be "grafted in" to these family trees, as existing eponymous ancestors were added to another race's genealogy.[63] During Hadrian's reign, Asian cities of the Panhellenion leveraged (or fabricated) genealogical assertions about their Greek origins.[64] Ties to Athens were especially prized; Aristides remarked,

> For no one would be proud to have Pella or Aegae as his country; there is no Greek who would not wish to have been born an Athenian rather than a citizen of his own city. Not only do private citizens prefer Athens in this way, but also in the case of cities, those who have been actually founded from here and by you would rather boast that they descend from you than possess power equal to yours; *and the others go about seeking somehow to trace themselves back to you.* (Aristides, *Panath.Or.* 334 (emphasis added))[65]

The Greeks did not have a monopoly on this practice. Abraham could serve as a focus for this sort of thinking within Judaism. In Genesis, God promised Abraham, "In you, all the peoples (φυλαι) of the earth will be blessed" (Gen. 12:3 LXX).[66] Scripture relates Israel to various other nations through Abraham, including the Ammonites, the Moabites, the Edomites, and the descendants of Ishmael (Gen. 25:1–18, 36; cf. 1 Chron. 1:28–31).[67] One tradition states that Ishmael's twelve sons gave their names to Arabian tribes (*Ant.* 12.225–26).[68] Extrabiblical accounts made Abraham the ancestor of more nations. Josephus reports that colonies in Troglodytis, Arabia, and Libya had been founded by the sons of Abraham and Keturah (*Ant.* 1.220–21). Cleodemus Malchus, another Judean historian, claimed that Abraham was the ancestor of the Assyrians *and* the Africans.[69] It seems, then, that just as the wanderings of heroes allowed Greeks to propose connections between various races, the famously peripatetic Abraham could do for Judeans. Speaking of Greeks and Judeans, 1 Maccabees even claims Abraham was the ancestor of the Spartans (1 Macc. 12:21)![70]

Early Christ-followers also drew connections via Abraham. Paul's rhetoric provides gentiles with just such a rewritten genealogy in Romans: they are now descendants of Abraham, and brothers of Christ. Like the Hellenic family trees, Paul's "olive tree" (Rom. 11:16–24) constructs ranked relationships between related peoples. Judeans occupy a privileged position, related "more closely" to the root, Abraham, while gentiles-in-Christ occupy an outer position in his "family tree."[71]

Individuals' Genealogies

The genealogy of an *individual* (or individual family) could be used to connect one to a particular race or shore up claims of prestige. This might be motivated by the social esteem associated with an ethnic group or the doors opened by a particular identity. In Seleucid-era Syria, inscriptions left in the gymnasium by newly registered *ephebes* proudly advertised their Greek ancestry—but the onomastic evidence suggests that, in many cases, these individuals have simply invented these claims.[72]

Herod the Great exemplifies another motivation—the use of rewritten genealogy to justify one's *political* position, as well as bolster one's public reputation. Herod the Great belonged to the Idumean segment of the Judean polity; he was a *Ioudaios*, but only in a sense. Herod therefore had his court scribe Nicolas draw up an elaborate, blue-blooded Judaean lineage for himself.[73] There were no official "registers" of Judeans, and oral histories and genealogies were malleable and unreliable. If there were people who could creatively "prove" their ancestors were Greek, Herod could prove his were Judean.[74]

Another political example can be found in the Julian family's claim to descend from the Gods. In the *Aeneid*, which promoted these claims, Vergil associates Augustus with the divine sphere by explaining that he stands in a line that stretched back to Aeneas, the son of Venus, and Hercules, the son of Jupiter (Virgil *Aen.* 8.184–305). Augustus' divine authority as ruler is confirmed—in an epic which likens the new *princeps* to Rome's mythic ancestor.[75] Similar claims were broadcast across various media, such as coinage, inscriptions, and the *Prima Portia* statue of Augustus, where both Venus and her son Cupid appear on the breastplate. These claims were creatively rearticulated by non-Romans for their own ends. In the Aphrodisian Sebasteion, panels depicting the life of Aeneas were likely meant to imply a sort of ethnic tie between the Carians of Aphrodisias (founded by Aphrodite) and the Julian family, descended from Aeneas (son of Aphrodite/Venus).[76] The end result of their artistic schema is a sort of asymmetrical "ethnic genealogy"—not between two races but between one Roman family and the *demos* of one Asian city.

14   *Chapter 1*

Genealogies naturalized the phenomena of likeness within the process of biological descent. This was assumed to connote moral/mental likeness, as well as shore up social position. Because genealogical resemblances are understood to be "natural," they were perceived as self-evident. In this way, relationships of power and hierarchy were also naturalized by such genealogies. Manipulations of genealogy did not, ironically, undermine the logic of immutability on which they depended.[77]

Negotiating Ancestral Claims

Not every genealogical connection, whether corporate or individual, was judged credible. If race is a social construct, a "thing made of words," what matters is not the "truth" of a claim, but its social acceptance (or rejection).[78]

Corporate ethnic claims—what Jonathan Hall calls "ethnic genealogies"—were subject to evaluation, acceptance, or rejection. The relationship between the Samaritans and the Judeans is an instructive example. According to Genesis, all Israelites trace their descent to Jacob (29:31–30:24, 35:16–26, 48:8–49:27). After Jacob blesses his sons, the narrator concludes: "All these are the twelve tribes of Israel" (Gen. 49:28). This much, at least, was unanimously agreed upon by Judeans. Less universally accepted, however, was the *Samaritans'* claim to descend from some of these tribes (particularly Ephraim and Manasseh),[79] and thus, to be Israelites themselves.

This claim was subject to a variety of responses. Many Judeans categorically rejected the idea that Samaritans were Israelites. Their skepticism had some basis in scripture—for example, in an account of the total depopulation of Israel after the Assyrian conquest (2 Kings 17:24–41 // *Ant.* 9.288–91), or in an identification of Samaritans as foreigners who "have no share with" those returning from exile (Ezra 4:1–3; Neh. 2:20, 13:28 // *Ant.* 11.292–347). However, other passages *do* suggest a continuing Israelite presence in the North (2 Chron. 30:2–25, 34:9), or *do* seem to classify Samaritans as belonging to the same race as Judeans (2 Macc. 5:22–23, 6:1–3). The weight of the extant literature, however, leans in the direction of rejection. Josephus is especially dismissive; he characterizes Samaritans as opportunistic liars, ethnic chameleons who only pretend to be related to the Judeans when there is some advantage to it (*Ant.* 9.288–92; *Ant.* 11.323,341–43). Similarly, a fragmentary document from Qumran about Jacob venomously dismisses the Samaritans' claims (4Q371),[80] bluntly stating that no Northern Israelites (personified as "Joseph") remain on the land—and therefore, that latter-day Samaritans who claim to descend from Joseph are liars.[81] (For Luke's *own* assessment of Samaritan ancestry, see my upcoming *Good Samaritans: Samaritan Ethnicity and Evangelism in Luke–Acts.*)

It was not only *collective* genealogies that were subject to scrutiny. *Individuals'* genealogies, along with their ethnic implications, could also be

Ethnos *and Racial Fluidity in Antiquity*

accepted or rejected. Herod's specious genealogy excellently illustrates this phenomenon.

Herod the Great was Idumean by birth. Idumeans were generally considered *Ioudaioi* by virtue of having been brought over to the Judean way of life during the Hasmonean era. "From that time onward," Josephus remarks, "they have continued to be Judeans" (*Ant.* 13.257–58; cf. Strabo *Geog.* 16.2.34).[82] Herod was certainly called a Judean at times. For instance, during a conflict about whether Caesarea was rightfully a "Greek" or Judean city, the resident Judeans argue that the city was theirs because Herod was "born a Judean" (Ιουδαιον γεγονεναι)! Their Syrian opponents even conceded this point, although it clearly did not serve their own argument (*J.W.* 2.266 // *Ant.* 20.173). However, Idumeans could still be thought of as *quasi*-Judeans by those who could boast Judean ancestry (*Ant.* 14:403).[83] The fabrication of a "blue-blooded" Judean lineage reveals that Herod worried that his factual pedigree was insufficient to assure him of an unassailable claim to the epithet *Ioudaios*.[84] It might offend his subjects' sensibilities to be ruled over by, as the Hasmonean claimant Antigonus puts it, "a half-Judean" (ἡμιιουδαιῳ).[85]

Herod's imaginary heritage was traced all the way back to "the leading Judeans who came to Judea from Babylon," suggesting that he was anxious to affirm his Judeanness even in the highly exclusive, lineage-obsessed terms favored by Ezra–Nehemiah—wherein only those who could trace their ancestry to the Babylonian exiles comprised the true Israel (see Ezra 2:59, Neh. 7:61). Shaye Cohen comments, "In American terms, Nicolas is saying that Herod's ancestors arrived on the *Mayflower*."[86] Josephus is having none of it.

> Nicolas of Damascus, to be sure, says that his [Antipater's] family belonged to the leading Jews who came to Judaea from Babylon. But he says this in order to please Antipater's son Herod. (*Antiquities* 14.8–9 [Marcus: LCL])

According to Josephus, Nicolas was an unreliable witness, who always used to write anything Herod wanted to hear (*Ant.* 16.184).[87] Subsequent authors continued to disparage the less-than-fully-Judean nature of Herod's heritage, such as Justin Martyr, who repeats a rumor that Herod was actually an Ascalonite (*Dial. Try.* 52).[88] Clearly, Nicolas' fiction was not universally accepted.

Descent claims, then, whether collective or individual, could be accepted or challenged. Even at the same historical moment, some parties might judge a supposed ancestral connection to be valid, while others might dismiss it as fictitious. This will be important when we turn our attention to Abraham's function in Luke.

16   *Chapter 1*

"Subscriptive Descent" vs. "Ascriptive Descent"

One heuristic for evaluating ancestry was what we might loosely call "family resemblance," as exemplified in the ancient truism, *The son resembles the father.*[89] But the logic of lineal resemblance could function "backwards" as well as "forwards." That is, while an ancestor's character was expected to pass *forward* to his descendants, it was also true that individuals could confirm (or cast doubt upon) their ancestry by their *current* actions.

Furthermore, it might be useful to draw a distinction between "actual" ancestry,[90] and "sense of" ancestry. One might have a symbolic or affective sense of being connected with an ancestor if one admired him greatly, looked to him as a model, and subscribed to his ways. I use the terms "ascriptive descent" and "subscriptive descent" to distinguish these concepts (see table 1.3).

"Ascriptive descent" is simply the descent ascribed to one at birth. This is the default (and most literal) understanding of lineage. It is matter-of-factly attributed to one at birth. Rhetoric emphasizing ascriptive descent, with its notion of literal biological ancestry, tends to imply that race is a "fixed" (stable/unchanging) category. "Subscriptive descent," by contrast, is the *notion* of descent cultivated by *subscribing to* the teachings, lifestyle, habits, and character of an "ancestral" figure. By imitating the model of this ancestor, one embodies a "family resemblance" that demonstrates "spiritual kinship" with them—even if the figure in question is not claimed as one's (biological) forebear.[91] Such ideas were found in a variety of contexts, including philosophical movements, medical schools, and religions, and could evoke the same notions of kinship, loyalty, and consubstantial unity that biological descent did.[92] In contrast to *ascriptive descent*, the invocation of *subscriptive descent* highlights the fluidity of identity—as anyone can choose to follow in the footsteps of an ancestor and so become their "descendant." We will explore this idea further under "Way of Life," below.

Table 1.3   Ascriptive Descent vs. Subscriptive Descent

Ascriptive Descent	Subscriptive Descent
How attributed: Ascribed at birth	Achieved through conduct / identification
How perceived: Presents as natural, fixed	Presents as constructed (naturalized), fluid
Resemblance: Individuals expected to naturally resemble their supposed ancestor; i.e., "the apple doesn't fall far from the tree."	Individuals voluntarily subscribe to the example of the "ancestor," and resemble them by imitating them
Example.: Abraham the "genetic" ancestor of Israelites (4 Macc 18:1), Edomites/Idumeans (Gen 36:9; Mal 1:2; 1 Macc 5:3), and other races (Ant. 1.239-41; Clem. Strom. 5.113).	Abraham the ancestor of those who share his mercy (Besa 32b); Abraham the ancestor of those who share his faith/-fulness (Rom 4:9-18; Gal 3:6-9; Just. Dial. 11:5).

Fluidity in Homeland / Territory

In antiquity, it was commonly held that a land shaped the people who lived there. Environmental theories of race held that the climate, temperature, vegetation, and humidity of a race's homeland directly shaped its character and physique. The environmental theory of race was widely popular for a centuries.[93] A variation on the idea held that a race's *political* environment shaped it. This notion was already discernible in the fifth-century treatise *Airs, Waters, Places* (23:30–41), but was further developed by subsequent thinkers.[94]

Inextricably tied up with environmental theories of race was a belief in the heredity of acquired traits. In antiquity, it was assumed that traits acquired by parents during their lifetimes were passed on to their children (Hip. *De Semine* 11.1; Ps. Hip. *Airs* 13.14–26). The environmental theory, and its constant companion, acquired heredity, continued to be articulated by later thinkers, such as Pliny the Elder (*NH* 2.280, 7:50–52), Seneca (*De Ira* 2.15), and Favorinus (Aulus Gellius, *Noctes Atticae* 12.1.20).[95]

Migration / Relocation

A side effect of the environmental theory was the conviction that migration actually changed people. This is only logical: if the environment produces certain traits in a people, then people who move will take on new traits. Such change was typically conceptualized as a *negative* process: races were not expected to improve, but they might become worse. Livy says that the Gauls had once been good fighters in Gaul but were no longer good fighters in Asia Minor, which had softened them to the level of other Asiatics (38.17.12).[96] He sternly cautions the Romans stationed there to be on guard, for past conquerors had also degenerated in new lands, among lesser peoples.[97]

Change in Political Situation / Cultural Environment

One variant of the environmental theory of race held that a race's *political* environment shaped it. Various countries had historically been under different forms of government; these laws and mores were thought to determine national character over time. Therefore, not only might migration corrupt a people, but a change in governance might.

Domination under foreign rulers was often conceptualized as slavery, and subjugation was thought to warp the national character of pacified peoples. One example might be the Roman impression that Greeks were no longer the noble race they had once been but had become servile and luxurious through long enslavement under foreign empires. Many authors repeat the trope that

18   *Chapter 1*

a subjugated race becomes "servile"—a trait that is then inherited by their children. Cicero (*Ad Quint.* 1.1.16), Josephus (*J.W.* 2.56–58), and Tacitus (*Agric.* 11.5) all suggest that such acquired racial slavishness is permanent, perhaps in as little as one or two generations.[98]

Exposure to another way of life could change one's nature. In cases where this exposure was the result of a sojourn through a foreign land, the environmental theory (based primarily on temperature, climate, and biome) could partially account for this change, but it was also thought that the emigration of foreigners into *one's own land* could cause such changes. For example, it was believed that Asiatic morals had once been corrupted by increased wealth and luxury, and that these, in turn had contaminated their Roman conquerors.[99] Now, the wealth and luxury of the provinces—as well as displaced provincials—flooded the Eternal City, threatening to warp the Romans themselves.

Sense of Connection with a Homeland

An ethnic group was largely defined by its association with a particular country; even individuals who had never been to their ancestral homeland could think of it as "their" land. But what of foreigners who came to identify with another race's territory?[100]

For example, immigrants might gradually come to identify with their new country. Philo notes that Judeans living in the diaspora have a strong sense of connection with their respective lands:

> So populous are the Jews that no one country (χωρα) can hold them, and therefore they settle in very many of the most prosperous countries in Europe and Asia both in the islands and on the mainland, and while they hold the Holy City where stands the sacred Temple of the most high God to be their mother city (μητροπολιν), yet those which are theirs by inheritance (ελαχον) from their fathers, grandfathers, and ancestors even farther back, are in each count accounted by them to be their fatherland (πατριδας) in which they were born (εγεννηθησαν) and reared (ετραφησαν), while to some of them they have come at the time of their foundation as immigrants to the satisfaction of the founders. (*Flaccus* 46)[101]

For these Judeans, "fatherland" is not only the place where one was born (εγεννηθησαν)—the "native land" connotation of πατρις—but also literally the land of their fathers. They inherit their diasporic homelands "from their fathers (πατερων), grandfathers (παππων), great-grandfathers (προπαππων), and ancestors (προγονων) even farther back," and so they are well-justified to consider them their "fatherlands" (πατριδας).[102] These forebears have dwelt in their adoptive countries a long time, indeed, sometimes since "the time of their foundation"; thus they have as firm a claim to their country as anyone. Nevertheless, they still see Jerusalem as the "mother city." The gendered dual-parentage constructed by "fatherland" and "mother city" could imply that the land of one's actual residence (one's "father"-land) might even be the *primary* territorial identification.[103] By the same logic, diaspora Judeans might be viewed as having a hybrid, layered ethnic identity; a Judean like Philo was neither simply a Judean nor simply an Alexandrian, but an Alexandrian–Judean.

Interestingly, this same juxtaposition of πατρις and μητροπολις occurs in Josephus, in an account of the "foundation" of the tribes' homelands. Moses counsels the Israelites that once they have entered into the promised land and won their respective tribal fatherlands (πατριδων), they are to turn their attention to the mother city (μητροπολιν) where the temple would stand (*Ant.* 3:245). The tribes, then, also have a claim to their (respective) lands because their ancestors were there since their foundation. Implicitly, they have the same sort of "dual-enrollment" which Philo describes: they are not merely Israelites, but Israelites *of a particular place.*

What of those who feel attached to another's homeland, not because they have *settled* there, but because they have adopted the *religious* practices of its people? The case of those attracted to Judaism offers an excellent illustration of this phenomenon—especially because this example will be the most relevant to our discussion of Luke. From Luke–Acts, we might cite the Ethiopian pilgrim (Acts 8:26–39), or two centurions who have been generous benefactors to the Judean people (Luke 7:5, Acts 10:2, 22).[104] For a more wide-scale expression of this phenomenon, consider the Jerusalem collection organized by Paul; largely funded by gentiles, it was carried to the metropolis by representatives from various predominately gentile congregations (1 Cor. 16:1–3; Gal. 2:10; 2 Cor. 8–9; Rom. 15:25–27). Indeed, pagans noted and resented the attachment of certain non-Judeans toward Jerusalem. Tacitus complains that "the worst rascals among other peoples, renouncing their ancestral religions (*religionibus patriis*), always kept sending tribute and contributions to Jerusalem, thereby increasing the wealth of the Jews" (*Hist.* 5.1).

Consider the royal family of Adiabene, several of whom converted to Judaism. They lavishly demonstrated their loyalty to Judea and Jerusalem. Josephus reports, "She [Queen Helena] had conceived a desire to go to the city of Jerusalem and to worship at the temple of God, which is famous throughout the world, and to make thank-offerings there" (*Ant.* 20.49). Helena shipped food from Alexandria to Jerusalem during a famine (20.50–52), and King Izates sent funds to Jerusalem's leaders to assist in the relief efforts (20.53). Helena built a palace in Jerusalem (*War* 6.355), and "three pyramids" outside of the city (*Ant.* 20.95). Mishnah *Yoma* 3.10 records that Helena also donated lavish gifts to the Temple, as did Izates' brother Monobazus. After Izates and Helena had both died, "Monobazus sent her bones

20   *Chapter 1*

and those of his brother to Jerusalem with instructions that they should be buried in the three pyramids that his mother had erected at a distance of three furlongs from the city of Jerusalem" (*Ant.* 20.95)[105] Later, Monobazus took part in the Judean Revolt (*War* 2.520), along with Izates' sons (*War* 6.356). Between Helena, Izates/Monobazus, and Izates' sons, we have a record of how three generations of this foreign family all strongly identified with the land of Judea.

Converts to Judaism might have understood *themselves* to be included within scriptural land-promises, with a legitimate stake in the land. Some Qumran documents include the *gēr* ("proselyte") in Israel's land-promises—a strong indication that the *gēr* is now understood as a fellow-Israelite (4Q279, 4Q377). The *gēr* is mentioned in the context of postexilic land return (4Q307; 4Q520), and the promised land of honey (4Q377; 4Q498). Carmen Palmer concludes: "For the Qumran movement, just as for late Second Temple Judaism more generally, the ethnic feature of connection to a land is mutable."[106]

Even some of Herod the Great's extravagant building projects within Judea, particularly his lavish remodeling of the Temple, might be viewed in this light. Early in his reign, Herod built two monuments to emphasize his Abrahamic connections: one at Hebron (linked to the Cave of Machpelah, the traditional site of the burial of the Judean patriarchs; Gen. 23; 25:9; 49:30; 50:13), and one at Mamre (a cultic site linked with Abraham; Gen. 13:18). Because Abraham was accounted the common ancestor of both the Idumeans and Judeans, these sites "allowed Herod to emphasize the unity of Idumaeans and Jews; they were acts of piety to please both and offend neither."[107] With building projects like these, Herod may have been attempting to assert his Judeanness by demonstrating his loyalty to the *land* of Judea.

Fluidity in Culture / Way of Life

Way of life is clearly the place where ancient ethnicity wore its fluidity on its sleeve. Culture / way of life could bring about a shift in one's identity in several ways, including: (1) ethno-cultural umbrellas, such as "Hellenism," (2) religion as a valid ethnic criterion, leading us to discussions of (3) conversion and apostasy, and lastly a discussion of (4) "subscriptive descent," that is, the notion that fictive descent from an ancestor was ratified by following their example.

When purportedly descent-based identities (e.g., "Greek," "Judean") took on a broader referent, expanding their range to include those who shared in the *culture* of the original ethnos, tensions were bound to arise over who had a valid claim to these labels. Blue-blooded Romans might look down on the so-called Julian Latins, who were enrolled as Romans but had a different origin. Those who were Judeans by descent as well as *politeia* could sneer at

Ethnos *and Racial Fluidity in Antiquity* 21

a half-Idumean Herod. Similarly, an Athenian of noble birth might imagine that the term "Greek" applied to her in a very different sense than it applied to a Syrian who had adopted Hellenistic customs. As if in agreement with these ancient ethnic gatekeepers, some contemporary scholars would not acknowledge *cultural* self-definition as "ethnic" in character, either.[108] However, many other scholars have laid out compelling reasons to admit a wider view of ethnicity's meaning in antiquity.[109]

Ethno-cultural Umbrellas: Hellenism, Judaism, Romanitas

With the rise of the Macedonian empire, notions of Hellenism came to emphasize shared language, religion, and way of life—and to comparatively de-emphasize descent. We have already read Herodotus' dense statement from *Histories* (8.144), which constructed "Greekness" according to several factors, including descent, language, religion, and "way of life." By 380 BCE, Isocrates observed that

> The name "Greek" (το των Ελληνων ονομα) seems no longer to connote the race (or "birth," γενους) but the mental attitude (διανοιας), and people are called "Greeks" who share our culture (παιδευσεως) rather than our common origin (*or* "common nature," κοινης φυσεως). (Isocrates, *Panegyricus* 50)[110]

Increasingly, as Hellenism became a world culture, others could *become* Hellenes by adopting this way of life.[111] As cultural praxis gained ascendancy in defining Greeks, ambiguities emerged. Did "Greek" practice really make one Greek? Did such practice manifest an underlying "Greekness" which already existed?[112]

Career opportunities, social benefits, or legal status could sometimes accrue to those willing to embrace a Greek identity. This is amply documented in Hellenistic Egypt, where many ethnic Egyptians employed Greek names on certain kinds of documents—often for tax benefits. These names are usually a matter of "additive" or "hybrid" ethnicity, but in some cases, the new identity seems to completely overshadow the old. Such was the case with a second-century Egyptian man named "Nektsaphthis, son of Petosiris," who ended his life known as "Maron son of Dionysios, a Macedonian of the caoectic cavalry."[113] Similarly, Josephus sneers that Apion, "born in an Egyptian oasis, more Egyptian than them all, as one might say, disowned his true country and falsely claimed to be an Alexandrian, thereby admitting the ignominy of his race" (*Contra Apion* 2.29).[114]

Greeks could themselves be tempted to adopt the way of life of *other* nations. During the Peloponnesian Wars, the very period when the notion of collective "Greekness" was being catalyzed by the encroachment of the Persians/Medes, a Spartan named Pausanias was accused of "Medizing" (e.g.,

22   *Chapter 1*

abandoning Spartan ways in favor of Μηδισμος, "Medism"). He was charged with showing "contempt of the laws [of his native Sparta] and imitation of the barbarians . . . all the occasions on which he had in any way departed from the prevailing customs (των καθεστωτων νομινων)." In Greek, ethnic -ιζω/-ισμος constructions denoted patterns of *behavior*; in this case, a Greek was understood to have left behind his own ancestral ways and embraced those of the Medes. During the same conflict, when the Thebans were accused by Plataeans of "Medizing," they in turn accused *them* of "forsaking *their* ancestral traditions (παραβαινοντες τα πατρια)" by "going over to the Athenians (προσχωρεω προς Αθηναιους)" (Thucydides 3.61.2). The Thebans counter that the Plataens' earlier embrace of Athenian ways had been a *similar* abandonment of their own ancestral traditions! They concluded: "So, as concerns our involuntary Μηδισμος, and your *voluntary* Αττικισμος, this is how we explain things" (Thucy. 3.64.5).[115]

A somewhat analogous process surrounds *Romanitas*, but less overtly ethnic in character. Roman identity almost always included a sense of shared culture and governance, rather than (or in addition to) lineage. The Romans' own mythic origins were porous and heterogeneous. This also reflected the historical situation prior to Roman hegemony when over forty language groups existed in Italy. Earlier an ethnic term, "Latin" came to be used as a legal status granted to some allies. "Roman," too, was a legal status, denoting citizenship and shared law. But some sense of "innate" or racial Romanness existed. Quintilian drew a conceptual distinction between those who were Roman by birth and those who were Roman by citizenship (*Inst.Or.* 8.1.3).[116] Nevertheless, it is clear that the label could describe those who adopted Rome's way of life and won citizenship, not only those "born" to it.

A similar, but less pronounced, shift took place with the term "Judean." During the Hasmonean period, "Judea" was both a country and a district within that country. The Hasmoneans adopted a Greek view of *politeia* that gave them a model for naturalizing conquered peoples, establishing Judaism as a counter-Hellenism, "a citizenship and way of life open to people of diverse origins." The residents of other regions within Judea—such as Idumaea or Peraea—could also be described by the name *Ioudaioi*, but were also understood to constitute *ethnē* of their own.[117] Both "Judean" and "Hellene" became ethnic/racial categories that could serve as overarching "umbrellas," under which multiple races might be grouped. *Hellenismos* emerged as an umbrella category in reaction to the aggressive expansion of the Persians; *Ioudaismos* emerged as an umbrella category explicitly in juxtaposition to Hellenism and in the context of (Hasmonean) imperial expansion. Neither label precluded other ethnic self-understandings.[118] For example, under Hasmonean expansion, Idumeans and Itureans became Judean in a sense, but retained their own distinctiveness. Ptolemy, a biographer of Herod, writes that Idumeans are *called* Judeans because they have been conquered and forced to observe their customs, but Judeans "are so originally and naturally."[119] Apparently, Idumaeans, even though politically and religiously Judean, could have their credentials questioned.[120]

People might even be considered "Judean" simply for associating with Judeans, especially at meals. Judeans lived together in ethnic neighborhoods in many cities. In Ephesus (48 BCE), and empire-wide after 70 CE, Judeans were legally defined by adherence to Judean laws and customs. At least to outsiders, Judaism was most distinctive and recognizable in the observance of Judean practices.[121] Cassius Dio shows some bafflement regarding some who are called Judeans, but are not by birth: "I do not know how they obtained this appellation, but it applies also to other people, even if they are of alien descent (αλλοεθνεις), who adopt their customs (τα νομιμα)" (Dio 37.17.1)[122] *Politeia,* as "constitution, way of life, or citizenship," was a mutable facet of identity—but it could sway which ethnic labels were applied to individuals.[123] Both Philo and Josephus refer approvingly to outsiders who become insiders, by adopting the *politeia* of the Judeans."[124]

Race and Religious Practice

We have already argued that "way of life" was a significant factor in the construction of ancient ethnicity, but a word must be said about *religion* in particular. Modern definitions of "religion" (both in casual parlance and the social sciences) tend to treat the category as a discrete facet of identity, distinct from such considerations as race, nationality, class, gender, etc. Such an understanding of religion is, almost by definition, unrelated to the construction of "race."

However, this modern understanding of religion—as something separable from cultural, ethnic, political, and family identities and practices—is not appropriate for the ancient world.[125] If we are to discuss "religion" at all for this period (and not, for example, "religious practice"), we must understand it differently. Ancient religion was not a stand-alone phenomenon.[126] Teresa Morgan explains that "divine-human relations are so structural to ancient societies, so integrated into every other aspect of life from family, to civic life, to politics, that they cannot be abstracted out."[127] As we shall see, ancient "religion" was implicated in a number of other domains—many of which we have already noted are *racial* in character.[128] For instance, we have already encountered Herodotus' affirmation that "the kinship (συγγενεια) of all Greeks" is partially comprised of the fact that they share "the shrines of the Gods and shared sacrifices, and the same way of life" (*Hist.* 8.144). Greek religion, then, is integral in the construction of Greekness.

People were generally expected to continue in the practices "inherited" from their ancestors. Paula Fredricksen quips that in antiquity, "gods run in

24 *Chapter 1*

the blood."[129] "Gods attached to particular *peoples*; 'religion' ran in the blood. . . . Ethnicity expressed 'religion' (acknowledging the anachronism of both terms for our period), and religion expressed 'ethnicity.'"[130] Steve Mason describes how the various epiphenomena of religion were embedded in each people's distinctive identity:

> An ancient *ethnos* normally had a national cult (τα θεια, τα ιερα, θρησκεια, θεων θεραπεια, *cura / cultus deorum, ritus, religio*) involving priests, temples, animal sacrifice. This cannot be isolated from the *ethnos* itself, since temples, priesthood, and cultic practices were part and parcel of a people's founding stories, traditions, and civic structures.[131]

Because each nation had their own ancestral gods and practices, honoring the gods was a matter of *ethnicity* as well as piety.[132]

This does not mean that religion was fixed at birth. Rather, both descent and religious practice were flexible dimensions of ancient identity construction.[133] What modern social scientists might call "conversion," then, could have implications for how one's ethnic identity was understood.[134] This may have been *especially* true in the case of conversions to or from "Judaism."[135] Steve Mason explains, "Shocking though it may seem, we consistently find both *Ioudaioi* and outsiders understanding 'conversion' as in fact movement from one *ethnos* to another, a kind of change of citizenship."[136] The Judeans' monotheism meant that full conversion forced proselytes to leave behind their former practices, an abandonment often viewed by gentiles as "atheism" (αθεοτης).

Conversion could have simultaneous "constructive" and "deconstructive" effects upon the convert's ethnicity. One man's *prosēlytos* ("incomer") is another's *apostatēs* ("deserter").[137] On one hand, conversion "constructs" the proselyte's ethnic identity as thoroughly joined to a new people, as she adopts their ancestral practices. On the other hand, the apostate's conversion "deconstructs" her pre-existing ethnic identity. These two concomitant results (ethnic identification and ethnic alienation) are the twin effects of conversion—the two "sides of the coin" in the racial reasoning of proselytism/ apostasy.

In the following sections, we will first review the "constructive" ethnic function of conversion, as the proselyte becomes identified with a new people. Then, we will consider the "deconstructive" ethnic implications of conversion, as the apostate's abandonment of ancestral customs alienates her from her (former) people.

i. Constructive Effect of Conversion: The Proselyte Is Added to the People

Jewish scripture already contained examples of foreigners who joined themselves to Israel.[138] The closer we get to the date of Luke–Acts, the more evidence accumulates that *some* Judeans, at least, understood that gentiles could truly become Judeans if they adopted their customs and way of life. Josephus testifies that Judean identity is available to those who fully adopt the Judean way of life (*Ag.Ap.* 2.210).[139] He boasts that Judeans in Antioch attracted "multitudes of Greeks" to their religious ceremonies, "and these [Greeks] they had in some measure incorporated into themselves" (*War* 7.45).[140]

Gentiles' attraction to Judaism was also rhapsodized by Philo:

> Throughout the world of Greeks and barbarians, there is practically no state which honours the institutions (νομιμα) of any other... We may fairly say that mankind from east to west, every region (χωρα) and race (εθνος) and city (πολις), shew aversion to foreign institutions (ξενικων νομιμων), and think that they will enhance the respect for their own by shewing disrespect for those of other countries. It is not so with ours. They attract and win the attention of all, of barbarians, of Greeks, of dwellers on the mainland and islands, of peoples (εθνη) of the east and the west, of Europe and Asia, of the whole inhabited world (οικουμενην) from end to end. (*On Moses* 2.4.18–20.)[141]

Here, Philo celebrates the sweeping appeal of the Judean ways—an appeal supposedly unique in world history.[142] Philo lays out an almost "imperial" vision for Judaism, rivaling Rome its creation of a world culture, spanning the entire οικυμενη, colonizing others with its institutions. In fact, if Judeans' circumstances were to improve, "I believe that each nation would abandon its peculiar ways (όιμαι τα ιδια), and, throwing overboard their ancestral customs (πατριοις), turn to honouring our laws alone" (*On Moses* 2.7.44).[143]

How did natural-born Judeans regard gentiles drawn to their faith? According to Philo, Moses commanded Israel to regard a proselyte as "one of their own":

> Having laid down laws for members of the same nation (όμοεθνων), he holds that incomers (επηλυτας) too should be accorded every favour and consideration as their due, because abandoning their kinsfolk by blood (γενεαν την αφ' αιματος), their country (πατριδα), their customs (εθη) and the temples and images of their gods, and the tributes and honours paid to them, they have taken the journey to a better home . . . He commands all members of the nation to love the incomers, not only as friends and kinsfolk (συγγενεις) but as themselves both in body and soul . . . so that they may seem to be the separate parts of a single living being which is compacted and unified by their fellowship in it. (*On the Virtues* 20.102–103)[144]

26   *Chapter 1*

In this passage, Philo describes a rich transition encompassing the various phenomena associated with ethnicity.[145] David Horrell comments, "Clearly, 'religion'—or religious practice—is inextricably bound up in the various dimensions of what it entails to disidentify with one people and identify with another, in effect a process of both ethnic and religious reidentification."[146] Rabbinic sources will later reinforce this general impression, explaining that the convert is to be regarded as "Israel in all respects" (*y. Eruv.* 6.2).[147] This identification may be so absolute, precisely *because* "the convert divests himself entirely from his original non-Jewish identity."[148]

Let us return to the royal family of Adiabene, for example. In the mid-first century CE, Josephus tells us, "Helena, queen of Adiabene, and her son Izates changed (μετεβαλον) their way of life (τα εθη τον βιον) to that of the Judeans" (*Ant.* 20.17).[149] This happened after a Judean merchant taught Izates and his wives "to worship God after the manner of Judean ancestral ways" (ὡς Ιουδαιοις πατριον ην); meanwhile, Helena had already been "brought over to their laws" (εις τους εκεινων μετακεκομισθαι νομους) by a different Judean (20.34–35). When Izates learned that his mother was "very much pleased with Judean ways (εθησιν)," he determined to fully convert (μεταθεισθαι). As Izates understood it, this change had to include circumcision; he reckoned that he would not be "genuinely Judean" (βεβαιως Ιουδαιος) until taking this step (*Ant.* 20.38). We have seen that after conversion, Helena and Izates were thoroughly oriented toward Judea and Jerusalem, even arranging to be buried there.[150] In sum, their case study entails a thoroughgoing shift in identity, touching upon ancestry, ancestral practices, homeland, and way of life. Steve Mason notes that their story

> brims with the standard language of *ethnos*, law, and custom. . . . Josephus does not speak of a 'religious conversion,' but rather of adopting or going over to *foreign laws, customs, and ways,* and that language is precisely what lends the story its force.[151]

In conversion, Izates had become a "genuine Judean" (βεβαιως Ιουδαιος), just as he hoped.[152]

ii. Deconstructive Effect of Conversion: The Apostate Abandons the People

The royal family of Adiabene also shows us conversion's power to *deconstruct* race. Just as conversion could (re)construct a proselyte's ethnic identity in connection with a new people, so too might conversion *deconstruct* their (prior) ethnicity.

Ethnos *and Racial Fluidity in Antiquity* 27

After a Judean named Ananias taught had Izates and his wives "to worship God after the manner of the Judean tradition," Izates decided to get circumcised. But he delayed because others attempted to prevent him (*Ant.* 20:38–41).[153] Several observations are relevant here. (1) The account presumes that by adopting their "ancestral ways" (πατρια/εθη), including circumcision, Izates truly *could* become "really Judean" (βεβαιως Ιουδαιος)—and that he would be recognized as such by others, both Judeans and his own people. (2) There is a pressing fear that after conversion, Izates' countrymen would no longer tolerate his rule over them, as a foreigner. That is, the *identification* of Izates as a Judean seems to go hand-in-hand with his *disidentification* from his own people.[154] (3) Note that it is *adherents of Judaism themselves* (Helena and Ananias) who fear what Izates' countrymen would say about his "strange and foreign rites" and "unseemly practices."

We are left with a strange situation: Izates' own instructor in Judaism is the one who warns him *not* to fully adopt it! Ananias tried to argue that a gentile might worship the God of Israel and be "zealous for the ancestral-ways of the Judeans," without being circumcised. When Izates later *does* undergo circumcision,

> they were immediately seized with consternation and fear beyond measure that . . . the king would risk losing his throne, since his subjects would not submit to government by a man who was a devotee of foreign practices, and that they themselves would be in jeopardy since the blame for his action would be attributed to them. (*Ant.* 20.47)

This likely speaks to the complex reality of many gentiles who were attracted to Judean practices but were also anxious about the backlash from their own people should they convert. Both such gentiles *and* the Judeans they were in contact with might have an interest in articulating "compromise" positions such as the one Ananias proposed.[155]

Many gentiles did, in fact, react strongly against their erstwhile confederates who became Judeans. Conversion was perceived as a problem by gentiles, from the Adiabenian to the Roman, *precisely because it was perceived as a betrayal of one's own ethnos.*[156] Many viewed Judeans as antisocial "atheists" for their refusal to participate in the worship of the gods. For example, a relative of Domitian, Flavia Domitilla, was accused and convicted of "atheism (*atheotēs*, αθεοτης), a charge on which many others who drifted into Jewish ways (ηθη) were condemned" (Cassius Dio, *Roman History* 67.14.1–2).[157] The specter of good Romans "drifting off into the way of the Judaeans (των Ιουδαιων ηθη)" caused some real anxiety among elites, at the end of the first century CE (cf. Cassius Dio 68.1.2).[158] It was observed that

28   *Chapter 1*

converting to Judaism alienated people from their former observances, their
ancestral traditions, and even their families.

> Whatever their origin, these rites are maintained by their antiquity: the other
> customs (*instituta*) of the Jews are base and abominable, and owe their persis-
> tence to their depravity. For the worst rascals among other peoples, renouncing
> their ancestral religions (*religionibus patriis*), always kept sending tribute and
> contributions to Jerusalem, thereby increasing the wealth of the Jews . . . Those
> who are converted (*trangressi*) to their ways follow the same practice [circumci-
> sion], and the earliest lesson they receive is to despise the gods (*deos*), disown
> their country (*patriam*), and to regard their parents, children, and brothers as of
> little account. (Tacitus, *Histories* 5.5)[159]

With numerous references to a homeland, kinship, and way of life, Tacitus is
clearly using the "stuff" of race to describe how converts to Judaism betray
their own people.[160] Tacitus was not alone; many gentile authors discussed
conversion in ways which suggest a shift in ethnicity.[161]

Early Christians could also be seen as "atheists" for their refusal to honor
the gods (*Mart.Pol.* 9.2). In a letter to Trajan, Pliny the Younger opines that
this pernicious new superstition might still be checked. He feels optimistic,
now that Christianity is being persecuted: "The temples by now almost
deserted have begun to be thronged and sacred rites long neglected are being
resumed and on every side the flesh of sacrificial victims is being sold, which
up 'til now very rarely found a purchaser" (*Ep.* 10:96–97).[162] Christianity
echoed and continued Judaism's legacy of drawing people away from their
own household observances, ancestral traditions, and the social religious rites
which integrated them with their civic communities—but without even the
measure of respect Judaism was afforded for its great antiquity.

For their own part, Judeans describe apostates from Judaism as if they, too,
have abandoned them—often in terms strongly suggestive of ethnic change.
The Hellenistic crisis during the reign of Antiochus IV (175–164 BCE) is
certainly recounted in such terms—those who voluntarily pursued a program
of Hellenization cultivated new ethnic identities for themselves but lost their
Jewishness in the process. These apostates "joined themselves to the *ethnē*"
(1 Macc. 1.15) "in order to be Greeks" (*Ant.* 12.241). In so doing, they had
"abandoned their ancestral laws" (*Ant.* 12:240), "disdaining the honors their
ancestors had prized" (2 Macc. 14:15) (see table 1.4).

Antiochus subsequently pursued a campaign of enforced homogenization
throughout his entire empire, with expressly ethnic goals: "The king wrote to
all his kingdom that all should be one people (λαον ἑνα), and that all should
give up their particular customs (νομιμα)," to which not only "all the *ethnē*"
but also "many from Israel" acquiesced (1 Macc. 1:41–43).[163] Judeans were
pressured to "change over (μεταβαινειν) from the laws of their ancestors

Ethnos *and Racial Fluidity in Antiquity* 29

Table 1.4 Hellenization as Racial Shift, in Seleucid Judea

		1 Maccabees 1:12-15	Antiquities 12.240-241	2 Maccabees 4:10-15
deconstruction	of Jewishness	"…they abandoned the holy covenant…"	"…to abandon their ancestral laws (πατριους νομους) and way of life (πολιτειαν)," "giving up πατρια…"	"…disdaining the honors prized by their ancestors (πατρωους)…" e.g. neglecting daily sacrifices
		"…they removed the marks of circumcision…"	"…they concealed the circumcision of their private parts…"	- no mention of surgical epispasm (cf. Celsus, *Med.* 7.25)
construction of	Greekness	"…they yoked themselves to the gentiles," observed ordinances (δικαιωματα) and customs (νομιμα)…	"…to adopt the Greek way of life (πολιτειαν)" … "they imitated the practices of foreign nations (αλλοεθνων)"	"…shifted to the Greek way of life (χαρακτηρα)," "an extreme of Hellenization (Ἑλληνισμου) in the adoption of foreign ways…"
		"…they built a gymnasium in Jerusalem…"	"…to build a gymnasium in Jerusalem…"	"Jason delighted in establishing a gymnasium right by the citadel."
		literal trans.: "…they 'gave themselves foreskins'…"	"…so as to be Greeks (ειεν Ἑλληνες) even when unclothed"	the games mentioned (discus, wrestling) typically played naked

(των πατρων νομων) and no longer to live (πολιτευεσθαι) by the laws of God (τοις του θεου νομοις)." In Jerusalem, "they could neither observe the sabbath nor the festivals of their ancestors (πατρωους εορτας), *nor even confess themselves to be Judeans* (Ιουδαιον ὁμολογειν ειναι)" (2 Macc. 6:1,6; cf. *JW* 1.34).[164] Although each account has its own particular emphases, these two Maccabean books and Josephus all describe the "religious" changes imposed by Antiochus as full of *ethnic* consequences.

As with the "voluntary" Hellenizers of the 170s BCE, Judean literature often described apostates as if they had undergone a racial shift. The most notorious examples were high-profile Judeans, who achieved a measure of real status as officials while pursuing policies that actively harmed Judeans. In 3 Maccabees, we hear of a certain "Dositheus, known as the son of Drimylus, a Judean by birth (το γενος Ιουδαιος) who later changed his religion (μεταβαλων το νομιμα) and apostatized from the ancestral traditions (των πατριων δογματων)" (3 Macc. 1:3).[165] One apostate, Tiberius Julius Alexander, was Philo of Alexandria's nephew. He became a prominent Roman administrator and advised Titus during the Judean Revolt.[166] Around the same time, the Judeans of Antioch were troubled by an apostate named Antiochus (*War* 7.47–51).[167] Antiochus successfully demonstrated his loyalty to the Greeks of Antioch by worshiping as a Greek, and he proposed this as a "test" for the rest of the Judean community. Those who refused were massacred. The city appointed Antiochus himself, with Roman troops under his command, as a sort of "enforcer" to police the Judean community (*War* 7.51–53).[168] In leaving behind one well-defined cultural-religious system (Judaism) for another (Hellenism), Antiochus had "completely broken with his tradition and in all essentials become a Greek."[169] In each of the three cases outlined above, other Judeans saw the apostate as doing much more

30   *Chapter 1*

than just "dabbling" in another culture; instead, apostasy was felt to comprise a near-total realignment of identity.

Early rabbinic literature aligns with this view. Various passages affirm the eventual punishment of apostates in Gehenna (*t. Sanh.*13:4–5; *b. Rosh Hash.* 17) or posits the equivalence of apostates with non-Jews (e.g., *t. B. Metz* 2). One of the clearest expressions of this attitude is the blunt statement, "the apostate is a non-Jew in all respects" (*y. Eruv.* 6.2). Sacha Stern comments:

> In a sense the apostate is the mirror image of the convert: just as the latter is "Israel in all respects," so the apostate is a "non-Jew in all respects." However, the apostate differs from the convert in that the latter divests himself entirely from his original non-Jewish identity, whereas the apostate retains his basic identity as Israel, even though it is seldom referred to.[170]

Stephen Wilson cautions that this *continuing* Israelite identity "may be technically correct but is substantially insignificant." Whenever someone is called an "apostate Israelite" (*Israel mumar*) in rabbinic discourse, the term "Israel" is not a positive statement about that person's *current* identity, but rather a way of saying what a person *used to be*.[171]

Some Judeans reflected sympathetically on what gentile proselytes had given up, aware that in the process of joining themselves to Israel, they had also made a break with their own people.[172] Conversion created significant social dislocation for converts; their family, relations, and associates did not always react well to their abandonment. Philo notes that "The incomer (επηλυτῳ) has turned his kinfolk (συγγενεις) . . . into mortal enemies" (*Speg. Leg.* 4.178).[173] Therefore, in compensation for what they have lost, Moses commands Israel to accept such proselytes "not only as friends and kinsfolk (συγγενεις) but as themselves both in body and soul" (*Virt.* 103). This passage pushes the very limits of what might reasonably be called "fictive" kinship: there is a sense of almost organic factuality to the new relationship. If a race is a grouping of people who share the consciousness of organic cohesion, the proselyte is indeed, as the rabbis would later put it, "Israel in all respects."

As we have seen, apostasy could have what we might call a "deconstructive" effect upon the identity of the apostate. To the extent that apostasy could shatter (or at least disrupt) one's ties to one's family, relatives, ancestors, ancestral customs, homeland, and political loyalties—one's *ethnic* identity was destabilized. The fallout from such a shift, in a time when family was the base constitutive unit of society, was tremendous. The intensity of love enjoined toward Judean proselytes (*Virt.* 103; *Spec. Leg.* 1.51–53; *Legat.* 210–11) hints at the profundity of their estrangement from their families of origin—so that their "adoptive" people must embrace them all the more.[174]

Similar social dislocation was experienced by at least some early Christ-believers.[175] Consider Paul's discussion of familial estrangement within partially Christian households (1 Cor. 7:12–16), or Luke's (12:51–53; 18:28–30).[176] Paul's repeated emphasis on intense solidarity, effusive love, and solicitous care within the *ekklēsia* suggests that the church is an emotional surrogate for some of its members, now estranged from their (former) friends and non-Christian family.[177]

While anthropologists sometimes employ the term "fictive kinship" to describe such patterns, I prefer "*constructed* kinship." *Fictive* could wrongly imply that such relatedness is merely "honorary" or illusory, despite the fact that ancient sources speak about such bonds as if they were entirely natural, cohesive, and organic.

iii. Constructed Kinship and Subscriptive Descent

The modern term "fictive kinship" is misleading because discursively constructed kinship can seem very real to the actors themselves. Carmen Palmer uses "non-cosanguinal kinship" to describe these bonds, "against the notion that any kind of brotherhood that is not cosanguinal from birth must be merely fictive."[178] For our discussion, I will use "constructed kinship," in acknowledgment that this bond is a social construct, a "thing made of words and deeds"—but no less socially "real" for all that.

Philo recognized that proselytes

> have left their country (πατριδα), their kinsfolk (συγγενεις) and their friends (φιλους) for the sake of virtue and religion. Let them not be denied another citizenship (πολεων) or other ties of family (οικειων) and friendship (φιλων), and let them find places of shelter standing ready for refugees to the camp of piety. (Special Laws 1.52).[179]

The household of God replaces the family the convert has lost. In fact, Philo views the kinship of faith as *more* authentic than that of biology:

> For Moses alone, it is plain, had grasped the thought that the whole nation (εθνος) from the very first was akin (συγγενειαν) to things divine, a kinship most vital and a far more genuine tie than that of blood (αἱματος), and, therefore, he declared it the heir (κληρονομον) of all good things that human nature can contain. (*Virtues* 79)[180]

By describing the joining of Judean and convert in terms of close family bonds, Philo effaces any ethnic distinction between the two. Erich Gruen comments: "Philo signifies that kinship in its purest sense eclipses any relationship by blood, a metaphorical notion that removes it from the bounds of

32   *Chapter 1*

a descent group."[181] A passage in *On the Special Laws* makes this point even more plainly:

> As for these kinships (συγγενειαι), as we call them, which have come down from our ancestors (εκ προγονων) and are based on blood-relationship (αφ' αίματος), or those derived from intermarriage (επιγαμιας) or from similar causes, let them be cast aside if they do not seek earnestly the same goal, namely, the honour of God, which is the indissoluble bond of all the affection which makes us one. For those who are so minded will receive in exchange kinships (συγγενειας) of greater dignity and sanctity. (*Special Laws* 1.317)[182]

Relatedness itself is redefined: in Philo's conceptualization of συγγενεια, "the metaphorical trumps the physical."[183] The so-called kinships based on blood or marriage can be broken, but the "better kinships" received in exchange are "indissoluble."

Philo describes the Essenes in such terms. They hold that "Nature, like a mother, has borne (γεννησασα) and reared (θρεψαμενη) all as genuine brothers (αδελφους γνησιους), not just so-to-speak, but in actual reality (οντας οντως)," creating a state of relationship rightly described as kinship/συγγενεια (*Every Good Man* 79).[184] For this reason, even childless (ατεκνοι) old men among them are regarded as parents and honored by a numerous (πολυπαιδες) and close-knit (ευπαιδες) family (*Hypothetica* 11.13). This regard for community elders is a form of *family* piety: "Reverence and regard is given to elders like that which real children (γνησιων παιδων) give to their parents (γονεων)," including material support in their later years (*Every Good Man*, 87).[185] Josephus also describes the Essenes' practice of property sharing in terms of kinship, so that "all, like brothers, enjoy a single patrimony" (*War* 2.122).[186] It demonstrates just how *real* constructed kinship was for those involved, that it frequently entailed *economic* responsibilities—just as "real" family did.

We do, indeed, find such constructed kinship in the Dead Sea Scrolls. Within the "D" community at Qumran, the *gēr* ("convert") who joins the community has become a "brother," creating non-consanguinal kinship between all members of the community, even those who would formerly have been classified as gentiles. In the *Damascus Document*, the fact that *gēr* are "brothers" seemingly categorizes them, too, as the "seed of Israel" (CD 13.20).[187] In various Dead Sea Scrolls, "father" and "mother" appear as honorary titles (4QD^a 7.1.13b–15).[188] The *mevaqqer* of the community assumed many of the traditional roles of the father.[189] This community leader is described as both mother *and* father:

> You have made me a father for the sons of kindness, like a wet-nurse to the men of portent; they open their mouth like a chi[ld on the breast of its mother,] like a suckling child in the lap of its wet-nurse. (1QH^a 15.20–22)

Ethnos *and Racial Fluidity in Antiquity*

The leader has indeed "given birth" to the community (11.1–18). This conceptualization of the leader may be meant to fill the void left by detachment from one's biological parents—a detachment which is itself held up as an ideal in various passages (e.g., 1QH^a 17.29–36).[190] This undermining of biological family loyalty, paired with father–son language, fosters "filial" submission among the rank-and-file, and simultaneously allows followers to define themselves as legitimate members of an honorable family.[191]

Various other groups also used familial in-language, as is richly attested in both literary and epigraphic evidence. "Brotherhood" (φρατρες) was a frequently used term for voluntary associations, and "brother" for those who belonged to them.[192] Palmer notes, "Upon joining cultic associations, members appear to assume a notion of shared kinship in a socially constructed manner."[193] For example, three inscriptions associated with the Mithras cult from Rome employ various kinship terms to describe its members, including "fathers," "brothers," and "sisters" (*CIL* XIV 4315, *CIL* VI 727, *CIL* VI 377).[194] An early third-century gravestone from the Bosporan region was inscribed: "Those gathered around the priest, Valeris son of Neikostratos, and the father (*patēr*) of the synod, Kallistos the younger, and the rest of the members of the synod honored their own brother (*adelphos*), Symphoros son of Philippos" (*CIRB* 104 = *PH* 182821).[195] In a dedicatory inscription from Macedonia, one Claudius Tiberius Polyarmos, "father of the synagogue in Stobi," who donated rooms and furnishings to the holy place, asserts his continuing authority *and that of his descendants* over these spaces (*CIJ* 694).[196] Such constructed kinship language was pervasive in early Christian communities, as testified by Paul's letters,[197] and the Pastoral Epistles (1 Tim. 5:1–2).[198]

A phenomenon related to such "constructed kinship" is a sense of relatedness to one's teachers, and going back further, to the movement's founder. In some groups, members might consider the founding figure their "father," or ancestor. Again, I call such thinking "*subscriptive descent*"—the conviction that one descends from the group's "founding father" by self-conscious adherence to their teachings, example, or way of life.[199] Such thinking could be found within various philosophical schools, which frequently had an almost religious veneration of their founder (e.g., Plut. *Adv.Col.* 1117B; Lucr. *De rerum natura* 5.8).[200] Philosophical movements actually shared this feature with ethnic groups: they revered their founding figures and connected latter-day members to them by complex lineages tracing the transmission of ideas from teacher to student, down through the generations, in a kind of intellectual genealogy.[201]

One particularly clear articulation of this logic can be found in the Hippocratic Oath. Medical students swore

> To hold my teacher in this art equal to my own parents (ισα γενετησιν εμοις); to make him partner in my livelihood (βιου κοινωσεσθαι); when he is in need

34   *Chapter 1*

of money to share mine with him; to consider his family (γενος) as my own brothers (το εξ αυτου αδελφοις ισον), and to teach them this art, if they want to learn it, without fee or indenture; to impart precept, oral instruction, and all other instruction to my own sons (υιοις εμοις), the sons of my teacher (τοις του εμε διδαξαντος), and to indentured pupils who have taken the physician's oath, but to nobody else. (*Oath* 7–15)[202]

Here, the pupil vows to regard his teacher as his own "father." This father/ teacher has passed on the teachings of his *own* father/teacher, and he *his*, so on and so on—all the way back to Hippocrates, the "ancestor" of the line.[203] Enduring social relations and duties are created by this transmission, mirroring those in biological families—including the obligations of support for one's "parents," and instruction of one's "children."

Denise Kimber Buell laments that the "intellectual genealogies" in ancient sources do not get the analytical scrutiny they deserve. Perhaps these procreative and filial metaphors for education have become so naturalized in our *own* academic habits that they seldom elicit comment.[204] Regarding the function of citation in modern scholarship, Keith Hopkins quips, "Foot-notes acknowledge and reinforce academic kinship ties; perhaps this is their principle function."[205] Buell says:

This metaphorical description of citation defines the transmission of knowledge as a biological and political process whereby a teacher or intellectual movement transmits to a student both an essence (the content of or the approach to knowledge) and a right to lay claim to that essence. While the new life produced or represented by the student must be recognized by its progenitor as an authentic offspring, the offspring participates in this process by positioning her or himself as legitimate, through careful citation of and allusion to her or his alleged intellectual heritage.[206]

The metaphor of "descent" and "inheritance" from one's forebears is thoroughly embedded in early Christian discourse, as well.[207] Clement's contemporary Alexander of Jerusalem wrote:

This proved to be the will of God . . . that the friendship that comes to us from our ancestors [*progonoi*] should remain unshaken. . . . For we know as fathers [*pateres*] those blessed ones who went before us, with whom we shall be before long: Pantaenus, truly blessed and my master, and the holy Clement, who was my master and profited me, and all others like him. Through these I came to know you, who are the best in all things, and my master and brother. (Alexander of Jerusalem (in Euseb. *Eccl.Hist.* 6.14.8–9))

Ethnos *and Racial Fluidity in Antiquity*

This letter drafts a genealogy of successive teachers and students, from Pantaenus to Clement, and finally to Origen and Alexander in the same "generation." The rhetorical function of this quote for Eusebius is just as telling: Eusebius cites it as evidence of an unbroken "lineage" of authoritative teaching stretching back in time to the apostles.[208] Like Eusebius, subsequent Christians often reinscribe such thinking; A. Cleveland Cox rhapsodizes that

> It is delightful to trace the hand of God from generation to generation, as from father to son, interposing for the perpetuity of the faith. We have already observed [in the previous volumes] the continuity of the great Alexandrian school; how it arose, and how Pantaenus begat Clement, and Clement begat Origen. So Origen begat Gregory, and so the Lord has provided for the spiritual generation of the Church's teachers, age after age, from the beginning.[209]

We have seen, then, that each of the major ingredients of race in the first century—common ancestry, common homeland, common way of life—could function in slippery ways, expanding or contracting to admit (or exclude) individuals from the groups delineated by them. For a concise list of some of the ways that ethnic criteria could function in a "fluid" manner, see table 1.5.

The Polythetic Nature of Race

As we have seen, race is polythetic in nature. [210] The boundaries of each ancient *ethnos* were amorphously drawn around a loose cloud of (presumably) shared attributes. Each people had its common ancestors (πατερες), ancestral traditions (πατρια), and fatherland (πατρις); each had its sense of kinship (συγγενεια) and shared nature (φυσις), whether based on the presumption of common blood (ὁμοαιμα) or on a common way of life (ηθεα ὁμοτροπα, βιος)—the latter comprised of such things as charter stories (μυθοι), laws (νομοι), constitution (πολιτεια), customs and mores (εθη, νομιμα), religious practices, and language (γλωσσα).[211] Contrary to the claims of those who insist that *ethnos* must have some stable core attribute (usually

Table 1.5   Sources of Fluidity in Ancient Constructions of Race

Ancestry / Descent	Homeland / Territory	Culture / Way of Life
• ethnic genealogies	• migration / relocation	• ethno-cultural umbrellas
• individual genealogies	• environmental theories	• conversion
• subscriptive descent	• orientation to a new land	• constructed kinship

36   *Chapter 1*

ancestry),[212] actual ancient actors capitalized on its very flexibility, in order to make particular points, depending on the rhetorical context. [213]

Specific ethnic identities were also discussed with a good deal of flexibility. The meaning of "Greek" was, as we have already seen, a moving target. Irad Malkin notes, "In attempting a response to the question 'Who is a Greek?' [most ancient writers] would play with acceptable conventions, choosing to emphasize particular aspects or even invent new ones."[214] Similarly, scholars increasingly acknowledge the multivalency of ancient Judean ethnicity; when a Judean invoked ethnicity as a form of differentiation, its actual content was "variable, negotiable, and contestable."[215] The same might be said of all ancient peoples:

> What it meant to be—or to be regarded as—Greek, Jewish/Judean, or Epidauran, Thessalian, Cyprian, or Tarsian in antiquity, or to be English, Cornish, Chinese, Malaysian, or Avambo today, cannot be answered or understood merely by checking a standard list of ethnic characteristics, but only by looking at the particular set of discourses and practices operative in relation to any of those identities and the ways in which they are claimed, attributed, or contested.[216]

An assessment of one's ethnic identity was always embedded in discourse and variable by context.[217] Sometimes the inconsistent attribution of ethnic labels caused puzzlement, consternation, or objections. Consider, for example, John the Seer's excoriation of those who "say that they are Judeans, but are not,"[218] or Isocrates' bemused observation that people are now called "Greek" who do not share their birth (γενος), but only their attitude (διανοιας) and education (παιδευσις).[219] It seems that if we wish to ask what these ethnic labels "really" meant, we must qualify the question with, "to *whom*?" and "in what context?"[220]

In other words, the *choice* of how to define the construct of race is itself a form of racial reasoning; authors could pick and choose, stressing different defining criteria for different occasions. One could emphasize seemingly "fixed" ethnic criteria to differentiate and exclude, or emphasize more "fluid" criteria to include others. Neither approach was "incorrect," in that both drew from among the commonly agreed-upon variables which made up race.

Ancient authors who wished to erect a firm boundary around an *ethnos* might emphasize the criterion of ancestry. The insistence on ancestry as *the* single qualifying (or disqualifying) attribute of membership trades on the seemingly "fixed" character of birth: after all, one cannot choose one's parents, nor change them.[221] Some Judeans emphasized lineage for gatekeeping purposes. Ezra–Nehemiah advocates an exclusionary vision of Judean/Israelite identity—predicated on genealogy, and impermeable to gentiles. Families who were unable to prove their ancestry were therefore *also* unable

Ethnos *and Racial Fluidity in Antiquity* 37

to demonstrate that they belong to Israel (Ezra 2:59, Neh. 7:61). Similarly, *Jubilees* understands Israel as a genealogical status, rather than a ritual or moral status. The boundaries of "Israel," therefore, cannot be altered—and these boundaries cannot accommodate the inclusion of gentiles.[222]

By contrast, many ancient sources admit the possibility that outsiders *could* come to be identified with a new people. Lifestyle is the most obvious way in; anyone can adopt the culture of another race and so "become" a part of that people. Of course, those born into that race—some of whom may identify *descent* as a crucial part of the equation—might challenge or at least qualify the extent to which these *nouveau* members "really" belong to their people.[223] But others might readily acknowledge these former foreigners as "kin." To a lesser extent, homeland could function this way—one could always move to a new land, as Ruth did with Naomi (Ruth 1:16–17). Environmental theories of race held that the *ethnos*-shaping effects of a new home might act quite quickly, and be passed on to children. Even without relocating, individuals might become strongly oriented to another people's "fatherland" (as was the case with the royal family of Adiabene).[224]

"Race," then, could be permeable or impermeable, fluid or fixed. Nor did one have to choose one approach and stick to it in every case. Authors used one view here and another there, as the situation warranted. Ancient ethnic actors, then (as now), displayed "double discursive competence," able to apply *essentialist discourses* here to construct race as fixed and *processual discourses* there to construct race as flexible.[225] One telling example is Josephus, who draws upon whatever view of race best suits him within any given passage. He emphasizes *way of life* and *geography* to include Idumeans under the rubric "*Ioudaios*,"[226] but emphasizes *ancestry* elsewhere to disparage Herod (also an Idumean!) as a "half-Judean,"[227] and to deny that Samaritans are Israelites in any sense (despite sharing the Northern Israelite's culture, language, religious practices, and homeland).[228]

Summarizing the slipperiness of ancient *ethnos*, Teresa Morgan describes it as "the 'queer' of its day":

> What modern scholars call "ethnic" terms in the Hellenistic world are highly complex. At once meaningful and vacant signs, absolute and relative categories, they are as definitive as a person's skin and as layered as their clothes. They are complex not least of which because they act simultaneously as outsider and insider terms: used by governments to classify and rank individuals and groups and by individuals and groups to switch identities, accrete them, perform multiple affiliations simultaneously, and in the process reinvent them. Ancient ethnicity, one might suggest, is the 'queer' of its day: A set of labels designed to define, differentiate, and discriminate, which are taken over by those to whom they apply, and then resisted, subverted, reworked, embraced, abandoned, and

38 *Chapter 1*

celebrated in a conversation that ranges far beyond what states or dominant social groups control.[229]

RACE IN ANTIQUITY: CHAPTER CONCLUSIONS

The various scholars and ancient sources surveyed in this chapter show that there was no singular, definitive view on what race was, or how it was constructed. Instead, a fluid, or flexible, view of race, best fits what we find in ancient sources themselves. No one definition (or criterion) seems to fit all discussions of differences between peoples, or all cases of racial rhetoric.

However, we must have *some* sense of what we are dealing with, so it is necessary to at least sketch out the rough contours of what race meant in antiquity. We will therefore proceed with a model sketched out along the following lines: *(1) A three-criteria model:* the ancients generally seemed to construct ethnicity in terms of shared descent from a common ancestor, common association with a particular land, and a common way of life. *(2) A fluid model:* all three of these general criteria could be deployed in flexible ways, which allowed for the creative realignment of ethnic identity. Even the rhetorical choice of *which* criteria to emphasize in any given context could leverage specific constructions of race, which allowed for more—or less—permeability.

We will have this basic model of race in mind as we move on to discussions of Abraham and ancestry—first, in Judaism generally, and then in Luke's gospel. As we shall see, both allowed for a surprising degree of "fluidity" in their construction of ethnic identity—even in regards to one's relatedness to Israel's primordial father.

NOTES

1. My trans. *N.B.:* I generally do not employ Greek diacriticals when presenting Greek text—such diacriticals being, after all, a later addition not found in the earliest manuscripts. For clarity, I *do* preserve the rough breathing mark (') and the iota subscript.

2. Cf. also Isa. 60:3 and Acts 13:47. The resonance between Simeon's song and these prophetic traditions will be further explored in chapter 3. *N.B:* as with my omission of Greek diacriticals (as a later scribal innovation, not found in the earliest manuscripts), I do not include vowel marks or other Masora when representing Hebrew words.

3. Examples of this expectation of a nationalistic/militaristic messiah are found in *2 Bar.* 40:1–3, 72:1–6; *1 En.* 90:9–27; *Pss.Sol.* 17:21–24; *3 En.* 45:5; *4 Ezra* 12:31–33; *4QFlor.* 1.7–19; *4Q458* fr.2, col.2; *4Q285* frag. 7 // *11Q14* frag.1, col.1; Jos. *War* 2.261–63; *Ant.* 17:269–285; *Tg.Neof.Gen.* 49.10–12; *Tg.1Sam.* 1.10.

Ethnos *and Racial Fluidity in Antiquity* 39

4. On the plural *ethnē* frequently corresponding to the Hebrew *goyim*, a pattern which continues into early Christian usage, see Skarsaune, "Ethnic Discourse in Early Christianity," in *Christianity in the Second Century: Themes and Developments*, James Carleton Paget and Judith Lieu, eds. (Cambridge: Cambridge University Press, 2017), 252.

5. This also mirrors a *Judean* pattern; in some of the later prophets, the text might note which *foreign* king was in power when "the word of the LORD came to" them (e.g., Hag 1:1, 2:1, 20; Zech 1:1, 7, 7:1). cf. Fuller, *The Restoration of Israel*, 220 N 96).

6. More broadly, their religious prototypicality and their faithful adherence to the traditions of the ancestors are demonstrated in Zechariah's service in the Temple according to his prescribed role in society (1:8–11), even completing his allotted time of service after he became mute (1:23)—as well as by the couple's striking resemblance to Sarah and Abraham. See chapter 3.

7. Josephus, *Antiquities* 14.403.

8. Herod's theater featured armored trophies mimicking the motif of *simulacra gentium* (images of the nations), representing races now incorporated into the empire. Some Judeans understood these trophies to violate the prohibition of images (*Ant.* 15:281). Herod introduced fighting with wild animals (15:274) and a law that sold housebreakers into slavery (16.1), which many considered violations of Torah. Judeans worried he was violating their law (15:365) or "introduction of practices not in accord with custom, by which their way of life would be totally altered . . . as an enemy of the whole nation" (*Ant.* 15:283). cf. Matthew Thiessen, *Contesting Conversion: Genealogy, Circumcision, & Identity in Ancient Judaism & Christianity* (Oxford: Oxford University Press, 2018 [2011]), 102.

9. Nothing certain regarding this "Lysanias the Tetrarch" has been found in other sources. *See* François Bovon, *A Commentary on the Gospel of Luke,* Hermeneia (Minneapolis, MN: Fortress, 2002–2012), 1:119–120; Culpepper, *Luke,* NIB, 80. Abilene was originally part of Iturea and was in the first century a part of the province of Syria, so we may have Iturean and/or Syrian ethnicity invoked here.

10. Judean ancestry in Luke 1—3: See Luke 1:5,16, 27, 32, 33, 36, 54, 55, 72; 2:5; 3:8.

11. Judean geography in Luke 1—3: See Luke 1:5, 26, 39, 65, 80; 2:4, 39, 51; 3:1–4.

12. Judean culture/customs in Luke 1—3: See Luke 1:6, 9–11, 22; 2:21, 23–24, 27, 39, 41–42.

13. This serves Luke's interest to situate the Way within the wider οἰκουμένη. Gilbert comments, "The importance of Jesus and the church is not limited to a single people or region, for 'this was not done in a corner' (Acts 26:26)." Laura Nasrallah remarks, "In this brief sentence Luke's geographical imagination spills from Paul's mouth." (Gilbert, "The List of Nations in Acts 2," 520; Nasrallah, "The Acts of the Apostles, Greek Cities, and Hadrian's Panhellenion," *JBL* 127.3 (2008): 533).

14. The inclusion of both Israelite and "pre-Israelite/gentile" ancestors in the genealogy of Jesus (3:23–38) is in line with this general motif—of broad ethnic horizons which encompass both Israelites and gentiles. See chapter 5.

40   *Chapter 1*

15. Love Sechrest offers a host of key synonyms for γενος or εθνος, including *populus* ("people"), *tribus* ("tribe"), *natio* ("birth, breed, kind, race"), *civis* ("citizen"), λαος ("people"), φυλη ("tribe"), and πολις ("city, government"). Sechrest, *A Former Jew*, 58; cf. Mary Boatwright, *Peoples of the Roman World* (New York: Cambridge University Press, 2012), 12.

16. McCoskey, *Race*, 30; Hall, *Ethnic Identity in Greek Antiquity*, 36. Commenting on the somewhat distinct semantic fields of the two words, Oskar Skarsaune notes that while humanity as a whole is frequently called a *genos* (because all human beings presumably descend from one ancestor), humanity in general is never referred to as one human *ethnos*, "because *ethnos* is by nature a differentiating term." Skarsaune, "Ethnic Discourse in Early Christianity," 252.

17. Teresa Morgan, "Society, Identity, and Ethnicity in the Hellenic World," in *Ethnicity, Race, Religion: Identities and Ideologies in Early Jewish and Christian Texts, and in Modern Biblical Interpretation*, Katherine M. Hockey and David G. Horrell, eds. (New York: T&T Clark, 2018), 25.

18. Hall, *Hellenicity*, 18; Boatwright, *Peoples of the Roman World*, 12.

19. Christians took to applying *laos* to themselves as well—a lexical imitation of the LXX fitting their own claim to be God's chosen "people." Skarsaune, "Ethnic Discourse in Early Christianity," 252–253. See also "λαος" in the *TDNT*, 32–45, 51–57.

20. Jonathan Hall concedes the frequent "covert synonymy" between the two terms, but still prefers to use the term "ethnicity" in his own books on ancient Greece, doubting that "race" has yet "shed enough of its toxic connotations" to re-enter social scientific discourse (Hall, *Hellenicity*, 14–15). cf. UNESCO, "The Scientific Basis for Human Unity," *UNESCO Courier* 3 (1950): 8; Muddathir Abdel Rahim, Georges Balandier, et al., "UNESCO Statement on Race and Racial Prejudice," *Current Anthropology* 9.4 (1968): 270–272.

Philip Esler similarly sees "race" as too caught up in the pseudo-scientific racism of the 19th/20th centuries; thus, it is anachronistic to speak of "race" in antiquity, but acceptable to speak of "ethnicity." (Esler, *Conflict and Identity in Romans* [Minneapolis, MN: Fortress, 2003], 9, 51–53.) Implicitly, Esler's position treats "ethnicity" as a socially conditioned category flexible enough to admit different shades of meaning, but treats "race" as a term that can only mean one thing.

21. Denise Kimber Buell identifies several assumptions implicit in Hall's position: (1) that the two terms are sufficiently distinct, (2) that "ethnicity" is appropriate for historical analysis but "race" would be an anachronism, and (3) that "race" is a noxious term due to its connection with rac*ism*. She rebuts: 1a) "Race" and "ethnicity" are used with considerable inexactitude, both in their contemporary context *and* in their application to antiquity. 2a) *All* of our terms are anachronistic when applied to antiquity. 3a) The avoidance of "race" does *not* avoid the noxiousness of "rac*ism*." (Buell, *Why This New Race*, 18–20). cf. Denise McCoskey, *Race: Antiquity and its Legacy*, 28–31.

22. Buell, *Why This New Race*, 14.

23. *Romeo and Juliet*, Act II, Scene II.

24. McCoskey, *Race*, 31.

Ethnos *and Racial Fluidity in Antiquity* 41

25. Rodolfo Estrada III, largely subscribing to Buell's position, also alternates between "race" and "ethnicity" in *A Pneumatology of Race in the Gospel of John: An Ethnocritical Study* (Eugene, OR: Pickwick), cf. 17–19. David Horrell notes that our choice of *modern* terms (and modern analytical categories) can distort our understanding of *ancient* issues. Horrell, "Race, Ethnicity, and Way of Life," 47.

26. For discussion, see Benko, *Race in John's Gospel*, 12–14. See also Caroline Johnson Hodge's response to Cohen's position (*If Sons then Heirs*, 12–15); John M. Barclay, "Ἰουδαιος: Ethnicity and Translation," in *Ethnicity, Race, Religion: Identities and Ideologies in Early Jewish and Christian Texts, and in Modern Biblical Interpretation*, Katherine M. Hockey and David G. Horrell, eds. (New York: T&T Clark, 2018), 47; Philip F. Esler, *Conflict and Identity in Romans*, 63–65; Philip F. Esler, "The Social World of Early Judaism," in *Early Judaism and its Modern Interpreters*, Matthias Henze and Rodney A. Werline, eds. (Atlanta, GA: Society of Biblical Literature, 2020), 58–59.

Steve Mason cites the "universal tendency of ancient non-Christian authors to discuss the Ἰουδαιοι alongside other εθνη" (rather than alongside cults); early Christians, by contrast, *did* sometimes discuss "Ioudaioi" in contrast to various cults (Mason, "Jews, Judaeans, Judaizing, Judaism," 489). Shaye Cohen's preference for "Jew," on the argument that *Ioudaios* increasingly came to denote a "religion" rather than a "people," is therefore difficult to defend (*Beginnings of Jewishness*, 69–71). Philip Esler notes that Cohen's preferred usage treats "religion" as if it were separable from its matrix of kinship, politics, and economics ("Social World," 70–71). Markus Cromhout concurs: "To switch from 'Judean' to 'Jew' based on a so-called shift to a more 'religious' significance is arbitrary at best. . . . Cohen's argument cannot be accepted since for first-century Judeans, ethnicity—here particularly ethnogeographic identity—was inseparable from religious identity" (*Jesus and Identity: Reconstructing Judean Ethnicity in Q* [Eugene, OR: Cascade, 2007], 2–3). Steve Mason, explicitly grounding his discussion in ancient (not modern) constructions of identity, similarly concludes that the Judeans were an *ethnic* identity ("Jews, Judaeans, Judaizing, Judaism," 460–484).

27. Hall, *Hellenicity*, 14.

28. A definition put forward by David Konstan, although he employs "ethnicity" rather than "race": see Konstan, "Defining Ancient Greek Ethnicity," *Diaspora* 6.1 (1997): 108; cf. Hodge, *If Sons, Then Heirs*, 21.

29. Buell, *Why This New Race*, 37; cf. McCoskey, *Race*, 25.

30. My translation.

31. The Spartans' plea to the Athenians had been based almost entirely on the notion of co-territoriality:

> We on our part are sent by the Lacedaemonians to entreat you to do nought hurtful to Hellas (Ἑλλαδα) and accept no offer from the foreigner (βαρβαρου). That were a thing unjust and dishonourable for any Greek (Ἑλληνων), but for you most of all, on many counts; it was you who stirred up this war, by no desire of ours, and your territory was first the stake of that battle, wherein all Hellas is now engaged. (Herod, *Histories* 8.142 [Godley, TX: LCL]).

Remarking on this passage, Teresa Morgan cautions, "Modern historians would refine Herodotus mainly by emphasizing what Herodotus often illustrates, that

42   *Chapter 1*

not every dimension is in play in every context." Morgan, "Society, Identity, and Ethnicity in the Hellenic World," 23–45; cf. Gruen, "Christians as a 'Third Race'," 236–237.

32. My translation.

33. "There are a great many degrees of closeness or remoteness in human society. To proceed beyond the universal or our common humanity, there is the closer one of belonging to the same people (*gentis*), tribe (*nationis*), and tongue (*linguae*), by which men are very closely bound together. . . . The bonds of common blood (*sanguinis*) hold men fast through good-will and affection; for it means much to share in common (*communia*) the same family traditions (*monumenta maiorum*), the same forms of domestic worship (*sacris*), and the same ancestral tombs (*sepulcris*)." (Cicero, *De Officiis* 1.53, 55 [Miller: LCL])

34. My translation.

35. Wongi Park and Mark McEntire similarly note that these three texts delineate four ways that human beings are categorized: (1) in their lands, (2) by their languages, (3) according to their tribes, and (4) in their nations. They remark, "If this text is doing ethnic identification, it is doing it in a multifaceted way." McEntire and Park, "Ethnic Fission and Fusion in Biblical Genealogies," 35–36. The same list of features occurs at Gen. 10:5 (enumerating the descendants of Japheth) and again at 10:29 (the descendants of Ham).

36. 4Q37 [4QDeutj] differs from the MT here, which instead reads "the number of the children of Israel." Both the LXX and Qumran versions feature "sons/angels of god/s," agreeing on this point against the MT.

37. NRSVue.

38. Mostly written between 100 BCE and 100 BCE: The Jewish Apocrypha, Diodorus Siculus, Dionysius Halicarnassus, Josephus, Philo, the Septuagint, and the New Testament. Sechrest acknowledges that "the Septuagint technically stands outside of the period of interest," but explains, "I included these documents because these were very important in the early Christian thought-world" and those of Second Temple Judeans. Sechrest, *A Former Jew*, 61.

39. Note that Sechrest finds overlapping, but slightly different, semantic fields for εθνος and γενος, and slightly different concept-statistics for Judean vs. non-Judean usage. Sechrest, *A Former Jew*, 61–92, 106.

40. Mason, "Jews, Judaeans, Judaizing, Judaism," 484.

41. Most notably, Jonathan Hall, who insists that shared ancestry was the single most significant determinant of race in antiquity (*Hellenicity*, 15), identifies *two* major criteria (shared descent, shared homeland), with descent as the non-negotiable one (*Ethnic Identity in Greek Antiquity,* 20). In a later book, Hall adds a third criterion ("a shared sense of history") to the mix (*Hellenicity,* 9–10, 20–25).

42. David Konstans heaps strong praise upon Hall, but wonders, "what is gained by restricting the notion of ethnicity to the idea of shared descent?" He muses:

> It would seem more useful to admit a latitudinarian conception of ethnicity, according to which an emphasis on genealogy was one strategy among many for asserting identity, whether local, such as Athenian, or global, such as Greekness as a whole. Ethnicity might be construed, then, as the self-conscious insistence on an image of the organic cohesion

Ethnos *and Racial Fluidity in Antiquity* 43

of a community, however it may be constructed. ("Defining Ancient Greek Ethnicity,"
108–109)

Dennis Duling rebuts Hall:

Not every analysis of ethnicity stresses every one of these cultural features [a common
proper name, myths of ancestry, shared historical memories, phenotypical features,
homeland, language, kinship, customs, and religion]. Furthermore, the Constructionist
critique of Cultural Primordialism's 'objectivism' raises the important question whether
any feature is so constitutive that there is no 'ethnicity' without it. ((Duling, "Ethnicity,
Ethnocentrism, and the Matthean *Ethnos*," 127). cf. Baumann, *The Multicultural Riddle:
Rethinking National, Ethnic and Religious Identities* (New York: Routledge, 1999),
90–95; Buell, *Why This New Race?*, 6–9, 40–41; Hodge, *If Sons, then Heirs*, 21–22)

43. Buell argues that racial criteria are only emphasized as definitive in a particular historical moment, and to a particular purpose. Buell, *Why This New Race*, 39.

44. Ibid., 6–7.

45. Buell, *Why This New Race*, 41.

46. Emphasis in original. Duling, "Ethnicity, Ethnocentrism, and the Matthean
Ethnos," 127. For discussion of *polythetic* vs. *monothetic* constructions of ethnicity,
see Barclay, "Ἰουδαῖος: Ethnicity and Translation" 49.

47. Duling, "Ethnicity, Ethnocentrism, and the Matthean *Ethnos*," 127–129;
cf. Cromhout, *Jesus and Identity,* 93–96. Later, Markus Cromhout adapts Duling's
basic model for his own work on Judean ethnicity. Combining this model with New
Perspective insights about the symbolic universe of Judeans, he constructs a model of
Judean ethnicity which incorporates Duling's criteria, branching up from the *habitus*
of Israel's covenantal practices and situated under the "sacred canopy" of divine election. Cromhout, *Jesus and Identity,* 98–107.

48. Here, "Way of life" replaces and enlarges Hall's "common sense of shared
history" (*Hellenicity*, 9–25). To be sure, a sense of shared history would be one *facet*
of a distinctive common culture, but other phenomena could fall under this heading
as well. Cult and religious practices would fall into this category, as might such considerations as language or mode of governance. Which of these are accorded ethnic
significance at any given moment varied.

49. Kennedy et al.'s sourcebook of ethnicity-related classical texts includes
groupings on Genealogical, Environmental, and Cultural theories of race (the authors
also gather "Genetic" theories under their own heading, rather than grouping them
under "genealogical"). Carmen Palmer lists kinship, land, and common culture as
"markers of [late Second Temple Judean] ethnic identity." David Horrell's recent
Ethnicity and Inclusion includes chapters on ancestry/kinship, common way of life,
and homeland/territory. cf. Carmen Jane Heather Palmer, *Converts in the Dead Sea
Scrolls: The Gēr and Mutable Ethnicity* (Boston, MA: Brill, 2018), 129, revised from
her dissertation "Converts at Qumran: The *Gēr* in the Dead Sea Scrolls as an Indicator of Mutable Ethnicity" (Toronto: St. Michael's College of the Toronto School of
Theology, 2016), 155; David Horrell, *Ethnicity and Inclusion* (Grand Rapids, MI:
Eerdmans, 2020); Kennedy, Roy, and Goldman, *Race and Ethnicity in the Classical
World: An Anthology of Primary Sources in Translation.*

44   *Chapter 1*

50. David G. Horrell's recent *Ethnicity and Inclusion* underscores these same three criteria, devoting an entire chapter to how each of them function in Jewish and Christian racializing practices; (Grand Rapids, MI: Eerdmans, 2020), chapters 4–6.

51. Members of Jesus' family have "blue-blooded" Judean pedigrees ascribed to them with (presumably traceable) genealogies. Joseph is of the house (οικος) and lineage (πατριας) of David (2:5); Zechariah a priest of the division (εφημερια) of Abijah (1:5), and Elizabeth (and presumably her relative, Mary) are "daughters of Aaron" (εκ θυγατεροων Ααρων). By contrast, the Idumean king Herod is a "half-Judean" with no such lineage, who must have such credentials invented by his court scribe.

52. Consider also the prophecy from Isaiah applied to John the Baptist (Luke 3:4–6), where Luke has expanded the verses cited by Mark (1:2–3 // Isa. 40:3–4) to include the oracle that "all flesh will see the salvation of God" (Luke 3:6 // Isa. 40:5).

53. For example, a Roman living in Asia Minor must remain vigilant, lest that his temperate surroundings render him "Asian," that is, soft and luxuriant.

54. Jonathan Hall identifies a partial list of Greek words used to describe what we might call "culture" in antiquity, including *diaita* (daily way of life), *nomoi* (laws, regulated norms), *ethea* (dispositional habits), *paideia* (education). Hall, *Hellenicity*, 18.

55. Carmen Palmer, *Converts in the Dead Sea Scrolls*, 129 // Palmer, "Converts at Qumran," 156.

56. For further discussion of racial "fixity" and "fluidity," see Ann Stoler, "Racial Histories," 198; Buell, *Why This New Race?*, 6–10.

57. Hall, *Hellenicity*, 175.

58. Ibid., 25–27.

59. Hall, *Ethnic Identity in Greek Antiquity*, 41.

60. Ibid., 38.

61. Swain, "Polemon's *Physiognomy*," 197.

62. Teresa Morgan, "Society, Identity, and Ethnicity in the Hellenic World," 31.

63. Hall, *Ethnic Identity in Greek Antiquity,* 42–43, 48.

64. Nasrallah, "Acts, Greek Cities, and Hadrian's Panhellenion," 547–548.

65. Trans. Behr, qtd. in Nasrallah, "Acts, Greek Cities, and Hadrian's Panhellenion," 549.

66. cf. the LXX of Gen 18:18, "all the *nations* (εθνη) of the world will be blessed in him"; or Gen. 22:18, "In your descendants (*or* "seed," σπερματι) shall all the εθνη of the earth be blessed."

67. See chapter 2, "The Rock from Which You Were Hewn."

68. Jae Won Lee, "Paul and Ethnic Difference in Romans," in *They Were All Together in One Place? Toward Minority Biblical Criticism,* Randall C. Bailey, Tat-siong Benny Liew, and Fernando F. Segovia, eds. (Atlanta, GA: Society of Biblical Literature, 2009), 151–152.

69. Jos. *Ant.* 1.239–241; cf. Clem. *Strom.* 5.113 and Eus. *PE* 12.13.40.

70. We will discuss such Abraham traditions in greater detail in chapter 2.

71. Hodge, *If Sons, Then Heirs*, 33, 146–147.

72. Teresa Morgan, "Society, Identity, and Ethnicity in the Hellenic World," 31.

73. Cohen, *Beginnings of Jewishness*, 23.

Ethnos *and Racial Fluidity in Antiquity*

74. Ibid., 50–52.

75. Sabine Grebe, "Augustus' Divine Authority and Vergil's Aeneid," *Vergilius* 50 (2004): 57–58, 60–62.

76. Christopher Stroup, *The Christians Who Became Jews: Acts of the Apostles and Ethnicity in the Roman City* (New Haven, CT: Yale University Press, 2020), 51; for other Roman families who also traced their lineage to Aeneas, see T. P. Wiseman, "Legendary Genealogies in Late Republican Rome," *Greece & Rome* 21.2 (1974): 153.

77. Hodge, *If Sons, Then Heirs*, 20–21.

78. As Jonathan Hall puts it, "The genealogical reality of such claims is irrelevant; what matters is that the claim for shared descent is consensually agreed." *Ethnic Identity*, 25.

79. The Samaritans "say they are related to them [Judeans] and trace their line back to Ephraim and Manasseh, descendants of Joseph" (*Ant.* 11:341); Samaritans on the island of Delos refer to themselves as "Israelites" in two separate inscriptions (Pummer, *Samaritans*, 92–94; Kartveit, *Origins of the Samaritans*, 216–218); a Samaritan woman mentions "our ancestor Jacob" to Jesus in John (4:12; cf. 4:20).

80. "10Moreover, Joseph was carried off into lands he had not kn[own . . .] 11among a foreign nation, dispersed into all the world. All their mountains were desolate of them, [. . .] and fools [were liv]ing [in their land,] 12fashioning for themselves a high place upon the high mountain, so as to arouse Israel's jealousy. They spoke [insulting] wor[ds against] 13the sons of Jacob, saying horrifying things, even blaspheming the tent of Zion. They told lies against them, 14spoke every sort of untruth, intending to enrage Levi, Judah, and Benjamin with their words." ((4Q371); in Wise, Abegg, and Cook, *The Dead Sea Scrolls*, 423)

81. cf. Sir. 50:25–26; Matt. 10:6. See also Benko, *Race in John's Gospel*, 96–99, and forthcoming *Good Samaritans: Samaritan Ethnicity and Evangelism in Luke–Acts*, Stewart Penwell and Andrew Benko.

82. Michal Marciak, "Idumea and Idumeans in Josephus' Story of Hellenistic–Early Roman Palestine," *Aevum* 91.1 (2017): 181.

83. Cohen further clarifies that Herod is not "half-Judean" in the sense of having one Idumean parent and one Judean one; his mother is *Arabian* (*J.W.* 1.181, *Ant.* 14.121). Rather, he is "half-Judean" because his father is "half-Judean"—that is to say, Idumean. Cohen, *Beginnings of Jewishness,* 17–19.

84. Ibid., 17; Thiessen, *Contesting Conversion*, 98.

85. This is precisely the point Antigonus makes to the Romans: "It would be contrary to their own notion of right if they gave the kingship to Herod, who was a commoner and an Idumean, that is, a half-Jew (ἡμιουδαιος)" (*Ant.* 14:403 [Marcus:LCL]); for further discussion of the ἡμιουδαιος (which is a *hapax legomenon* in extant Greek literature), see Thiessen, *Contesting Conversion*, 99.

86. Cohen, *Beginnings of Jewishness,* 17.

87. "For since he [the historian Nicolas] lived in Herod's realm and was one of his associates, he wrote to please him and to be of service to him, dwelling only on those things that redounded to his glory, and transforming his obviously unjust acts into the opposite or concealing them with the greatest care." (*Ant.* 16.184 [Marcus: LCL])

46   *Chapter 1*

88. Sextus Julius Africanus repeats the tradition that Herod is an Ascalonite, cited in Eus. *Ecc.Hist.* 1.7.11.

89. cf. Hodge, *If Sons, then Heirs,* 22–25, for discussion of this expectation.

90. i.e., at least, "putative" ancestry—what was held to be "factual" in one's genealogy.

91. The anthropologist Anthony Smith distinguishes between "genealogical" myths of descent and "ideological" myths of descent. The latter do not historical figures invoked as *literal* ancestors, but more as "leaders" or models. "According to Smith, 'ideological' myths of descent simply provide a sense of 'spiritual kinship' with the ancestors, triggering the vague acknowledgment of an underlying consubstantiality." Hall, *Hellenicity,* 15.

92. See "Constructed Kinship and Subscriptive Descent," later in this chapter.

93. Supporters of the environmental theory of race included the fifth-century Pseudo-Hippocrates (*Airs, Waters, Places*), Polybius (*His.* 4.21), Posidinus (qtd. in *Diodorus* 3.34.8), Diodorus, and Vitruvius *(De Arch.* 6.1.3–11). cf. Isaac, *Invention of Racism,* 60–69, 82–85.

94. Including Aristotle (*Pol.* 1327b, 1285a), Cicero (*De lege agr.* 2.95.5), Strabo (*Geo.*2.3.7; 14.2.16). cf. Benko, *Race in John's Gospel,* 25–27; Isaac, *Invention of Racism,* 70–73, 88–92.

95. Isaac, *Invention of Racism,* 74–82.

96. Ibid., 90.

97. "The Macedonians who rule Alexandria in Egypt, who rule Seleucia and Babylon and other colonies spread all over the world, have degenerated into Syrians, Parthians and Egyptians; Massilia, situated among the Gauls, has taken over some of the characteristics of its neighbors; what have the Tarentines preserved of that hard and terrible Spartan discipline? Whatever grows in its own soil, prospers better; transplanted to an alien soil, it changes and it degenerates to conform to the soil which feeds it. . . . You, by Heracles, being men of Mars, must take care and escape as quickly as possible the amenities of Asia: such power have these foreign pleasures to smother vigor of character, so powerful is the impact of contact with the way of life and customs of the natives." (Livy 38.17.12,16; qtd. in Isaac, *Invention of Racism,* 307)

98. Ibid., 81–82; 189–190.

99. Florus wrote, "It was the conquest of Syria which first corrupted us, followed by the Asiatic inheritance. . . . The resources and wealth thus acquired the morals of the age and ruined the State, which was engulfed in its own vices as in a common sewer" (Florus, *Epitoma* i 47.7). cf. Sallust *Cat.* 11.5; Pliny *NH* 33.148; Cic. *Pro Mur.* 13. (Isaac, *Invention of Racism,* 305–309).

100. Consider, for example, Hadrian's lavish gifts to Greece and Asia Minor.

101. Colson, LCL. cf. Philo *Embassy to Gaius,* 281–290. For discussion of both see Baker, "From Every Nation Under Heaven," in *Prejudice and Christian Beginnings: Investigating Race, Gender, and Ethnicity in Early Christian Studies,* Laura Nasrallah and Elisabeth Schüssler Fiorenza, eds. (Minneapolis, MN: Fortress, 2009), 86–91.

102. "Great-grandfathers" (προπαππων) is oddly missing from F. H. Colson's translation (LCL).

103. Baker, "From Every Nation Under Heaven," 87.

104. Both will be discussed in chapter 5.

105. Feldman: LCL.

106. Carmen Palmer, *Converts in the Dead Sea Scrolls,* 139–141 // "Converts at Qumran," 169–172.

107. Richardson, *King Herod,* 61–62, cit. in Thiessen, *Contesting Conversion,* 101.

108. E.g., Shaye Cohen renders *Ioudaios* as "Judean" when it is used as an "ethnic/geographic" label, distinguishing this from a "religious" use, which he translates as "Jew" (*Beginnings of Jewishness,* 71–82); he thus clearly excludes religion/culture from his definition of ethnicity. Benjamin Isaac's definition of "race" hinges upon essentialism, so he *automatically* excludes anything which allows for change. Jonathan Hall reads Isocrates' *Paneg.* 50 (which admits cultural "ingredients" within Hellenism) as an indication that "Greek" is now being used in a *non*-ethnic sense— unsurprising, given Hall's insistence on a *monothetic* understanding of the ethnicity (with putative descent as the non-negotiable ingredient).

Other scholars, who admit a *polythetic* sense of race/ethnicity in antiquity, read this same passage as evidence that cultural practices were gaining increasing significance in defining ethnicity. Philip Esler comments on Isocrates' words: "The transition from ancestry to culture and language does not solemnize the disintegration of Greek ethnicity, but simply represents an alteration in the cultural indicia by which the boundaries of the group are negotiated." Esler, *Conflict and Identity,* 57; contra Hall, *Hellenicity,* 208–210; cf. McCoskey, *Race,* 63.

109. See especially the arguments of Buell and Hodge cited above, and the discussion of "Race and Religion" below.

110. Norlin: LCL; cit. in McCoskey, *Race,* 63.

111. Cohen, *Beginnings of Jewishness,* 132.

112. McCoskey, *Race,* 63.

113. We can actually track the evolving ethnic self-presentation of this individual, over time, from different records. "Nektsaphthis" from Kerkeosiris, who is called "Maron son of Dionysios, formerly known as Nektaphthis son of Petosiris" in a document dated to 118/117, appears later as "Maron son of Dionysios, Macedonian of the caoectic cavalry"—the latter being an elite military classification originally limited to those of Macedonian descent (Teresa Morgan, "Society, Identity, and Ethnicity in the Hellenic World," 33–34).

114. Thackeray: LCL. Josephus is also aware that some Egyptian Judeans have been classified as "Alexandrians" or "Macedonians," labels which signify Greekness (*Apion* 2.37–38). However, this is not an abandonment of their race, as Apion's claim is (2.28–30); they are called this by virtue of their having lived in Alexandria since its founding (2.38), whereas indigenous Egyptians have not had this status extended to them (2.71–72).

115. Mason, "Jews, Judaeans, Judaizing, Judaism," 462–463.

116. Cohen, *Beginnings of Jewishness,* 69–71.

48   *Chapter 1*

117. Cohen, *Beginnings of Jewishness*, 127, 138, 72–73.

118. Baker, "From Every Nation Under Heaven," 91–98.

119. Cohen, *Beginnings of Jewishness,* 18, 60.

120. *1 Esdras* 8:66 inserts Idumeans into Ezra 9:1's list of nations which the Israelites should separate themselves from, and the "Animal Apocalypse" of 1 Enoch deems the descendants of Esau (the Edomites) categorically different from the descendants of Jacob—i.e., as wild asses rather than sheep (Thiessen, *Contesting Conversion,* 90, 94–95; Cohen, *Beginnings of Jewishness*, 24).

121. Cohen, *Beginnings of Jewishness,* 53–59.

122. qtd. in Isaac, *Invention of Racism*, 460.

123. Cohen, *Beginnings of Jewishness*, 126.

124. Josephus speaks of the Idumeans' conversion to the Judean *politeia* (*Ant.* 12.142), and Philo's speaks of proselytes who have "come to a new and God-loving *politeia*" (*Spec.Laws* 1.9.51). Cohen, *Beginnings of Jewishness*, 126.

125. Horrell, *Ethnicity and Inclusion,* 83–89. The application of the modern category of "religion" to antiquity has also been criticized for its emphasis on personal "belief" or inner sentiment—perhaps not as crucial an ingredient of *ancient* religion as that assumed by modern usage, in which "religion" is nigh-synonymous with "faith."

126. Esler, "The Social World of Early Judaism," 59.

127. Teresa Morgan, "Society, Identity, and Ethnicity in the Hellenic World," 39.

128. Esler, *God's Court*, 15.

129. Paula Fredricksen, "Mandatory Retirement: Ideas in the Study of Christian Origins Whose Time Has Come to Go," *SR* 30 (2006): 232.

130. Paula Fredricksen, "What 'Parting of the Ways'? Jews, Gentiles, and the Ancient Mediterranean City," in *The Ways That Never Parted: Jews and Christians in Late Antiquity and the Early Middle Ages*, Adam H. Becker and Annette Yoshiko Reed, eds. (Tübingen: Mohr Siebeck, 2003), 39.

131. Mason, "Jews, Judaeans, Judaizing, Judaism," 484.

132. Stroup, *The Christians Who Became Jews,* 21–22.

133. Horrell, "Religion, Ethnicity, and Way of Life," 45.

134. Horrell, *Ethnicity and Inclusion*, 144.

135. Based on her exhaustive survey of the semantic fields of εθνος and γενος in turn-of-the-era Jewish usage, Love Sechrest argues that religion was even more prominent in how Judeans conceptualized ethnic/racial identity than it was for gentiles.

> The prominence of religion in this model of Jewish identity also results in a greater porousness of ethnic and racial bonds. . . . When religion is pre-eminent in identity, acts of what we would call 'religious conversion' amount to a change in race or ethnicity. (*A Former Jew,* 102; cf. 102–105)

David Horrell concurs that "being a *Ioudaios* is . . . an ethnic identity that one could adopt through the process of becoming a proselyte, or whose traditions one could take on to various degrees." (David Horrell, "Religion, Ethnicity, and Way of Life," 46). Love Sechrest further cites Philo *Virt.* 103–104, *Spec. Laws* 1.309, 317–318, *Agr.* 4–6; and Jos. *Apion* 2.210, 261 (*A Former Jew*, 102–104).

Ethnos *and Racial Fluidity in Antiquity* 49

136. Mason, "Jews, Judaeans," 491.

137. cf. the BDAG entry on προσηλυτος, suggesting the sense of one who has "come over" or "come in" (from προς + ηλθον or ελευσις). Cf. also entries for αποστας (deserter, rebel) and αποστασια, meaning "rebellion against" or "abandonment."

138. The Moabite Ruth is an obvious example, telling her Israelite mother-in-law, "your people (עם/λαος) shall be my people, and your God shall be my God" (Ruth 1:16). Matthew Thiessen further cites: (1) Esther 8:17, where many of the gentiles (εθνων) were circumcised and "Judaizing" (ιουδαιζον) out of fear of the Judeans; (2) Judith 14:10, where Achior the Ammonite is circumcised and "added (προσετεθη) to the house of Israel"; and (3) the three Hasmonean rulers who compelled non-Judeans to adopt Judean practices—John Hyrcanus with the Idumeans (*Ant.* 13.257–258; *War* 1.63; Strabo *Geogr.* 16.2.34), after which they were considered "Judeans," Aristobolus with the Itureans (*Ant.* 13.318–319), and Alexander Jannaeus, who destroyed Pella because it refused to comply (*Ant.* 13.397). Thiessen, *Contesting Conversion,* 68; cf. also Stroup, *The Christians Who Became Jews,* 84–85.

139. Josephus, *Against Apion* 2:210. Regarding the "foreigner" (αλλοφυλος), Philo's Moses is most welcoming:

> To all who desire to come and live under the same laws with us, he gives a gracious welcome, holding that it is not birth (γενος) alone that makes up familial-cohesion (οικειοτητα), but agreement in the principles of how to live (του βιου νομιζων) (my translation). (cf. Stroup, *The Christians Who Became Jews,* 85; Mason, "Jews, Judaeans," 510)

140. Thackeray: LCL.

141. Colson: LCL, with emendations after the Greek. Note the density of terms related to race: "*ethnē*," "Greeks," "barbarians," and references to geography and way of life.

142. Philo further claims the LXX was translated to reach *gentiles*, not primarily for use by Greek-speaking Judeans! "Some people, thinking it a shame that the laws should be found in half only of the human race, the barbarians, and denied altogether to the Greeks, took steps to have the translated"—*On Moses* 2.5.27 [Colson: LCL].

143. Colson: LCL.

144. Colson: LCL.

145. Esler, *God's Court,* 17; Mason, "Jews, Judaeans, Judaizing, Judaism," 491; David Horrell, "Religion, Ethnicity, and Way of Life," 49–50. Horrell cites *Spec.Leg.* 1.52 as further evidence of conversion's racial implications.

146. Horrell, "Religion, Ethnicity, and Way of Life," 50.

147. Stephen D. Wilson, *Leaving the Fold: Apostates and Defectors in Antiquity* (Minneapolis, MN: Fortress, 2004), 132.

148. Sacha Stern, *Jewish Identity and Rabbinic Writings* (Leiden: Brill, 1994), 109; qtd. in Wilson, *Leaving the Fold,* 131–132.

149. My translation: in the LCL, Louis H. Feldman translates τα Ιουδαιων εθη τον βιον μετεβαλον as "were converted to Judaism," which might overlook that this "change" involved their entire way of living, not merely their "beliefs."

50 *Chapter 1*

150. "Now she [Helena] had conceived a desire to go to the city of Jerusalem and to worship at the temple of God, which is famous throughout the world, and to make thank-offerings there" (*Ant.* 20.49). Mishnah *Yoma* 3.10 relates that she donated a golden candlestick and a golden tablet engraved with scripture to the Temple, and Izates' brother Monobazus later donated golden handles for temple vessels. When Helena learned of a famine in Judea, had food shipped in from Alexandria, and Izates sent funds to Jerusalem's leaders (Ant. 20:50–53). Helena also built a palace in Jerusalem (*War* 6.355). Later, after Izates and Helena died, "Monobazus sent her bones and those of his brother to Jerusalem with instructions that they should be buried in the three pyramids that his mother had erected at a distance of three furlongs from the city of Jerusalem" (*Ant.* 20.95) [Feldman: LCL].

Monobazus (Izates' brother) later took part in the Judean Revolt (War 2.520), as well as Izates' sons, who then sued for protection after Titus' victory (*War.* 6.356);

151. Mason, "Jews, Judaeans," 506, emphasis in original.

152. Horrell, "Religion, Ethnicity, and Way of Life," 50.

As a sort of epilogue, other members of this family eventually converted. "Izates' brother Monobazus and his kinsmen . . . became eager to abandon their ancestral religion (τα πατρια εθεσι) and to adopt the practices of the Judeans" (*Ant.* 20.75). It was Monobazus who sent his mother's and brothers' bones to be buried in Jerusalem, as per their wishes (*Ant.* 20.95). During the Jewish Revolt, Romans taunted the Judeans that they could not expect help from any others, unless perhaps from their "kinsmen (ὁμοφυλους) in Adiabene" (*War* 2.388); it is striking that proselytes are described, even sarcastically, as "fellow-tribesmen!" Monobazus and Izates' sons *did* take part in the revolt (*War* 2.520). We have here, then, three successive generations of the royal family of Adiabene, who after conversion, demonstrated an enduring sense of Judean ethnicity, even through adversity and war.

153. "[38]When Izates had learned that his mother was very much pleased with the customs of the Jews (τοις Ιουδαιων εθεσιν), he was zealous to convert (μεταθεισθαι) to these himself; and since he considered that he would not genuinely be Judean (βεβαιως Ιουδαιος) unless he was circumcised, he was ready to act accordingly. [39]When his mother learned to his intention, however, she tried to stop him by telling him that it was a dangerous move. For, she said, he was a king; and if his subjects should discover that he was devoted to rites that were strange and foreign to themselves (ξενων και αλλοτριων αυτοις εθων), it would produce much disaffection and they would not tolerate the rule of a Judean (Ιουδαιου) over them. [40]Besides this advice she tried by every other means to hold him back. He, in turn, reported her arguments to Ananias. He, in turn, reported her arguments to Ananias. The latter expressed agreement with the king's mother and actually threatened that if he should be unable to persuade Izates, he would abandon them and leave the land. [41]For he said that he was afraid that if the matter became universally known, he would be punished, in all likelihood, as personally responsible because he had instructed the king in unseemly practices (απρεπων εργων). The king could, he said, worship God even without being circumcised if indeed he was devoted to the ancestral ways of the Judeans (ζηλουν τα πατρια των Ιουδαιων). [42]He told him, furthermore, that God Himself would pardon

Ethnos *and Racial Fluidity in Antiquity* 51

him if, constrained thus by necessity and by fear of his subjects, he failed to perform this rite." (Josephus, *Antiquities* 20.38–41. LCL: Feldman, with emendations)

154. Horrell, "Religion, Ethnicity, and Way of Life," 50.

155. One is reminded of Aramean general Naaman, who after determining worship only the Lord, begged one allowance: his civic/religious duty required him to bow in the temple of Rimmon, when his master leaned on his arm—a concession that Elisha grants (2 Kings 5:17–19). One wonders what compromises the "faithful" centurion of Luke 7:1–10 had to regularly make in the course of his duties; yet the delegation of Judean elders who approach Jesus on his behalf testify, "He is worthy of having you do this for him, for he loves our people."

156. For this point, see Mason, "Jews, Judaeans," 510. Furthermore, the influence of Judeans upon the body politic was sometimes seen as subversive. Stroup says Judeans were often considered "scandalously bad citizens" (*Christians Who Became Jews,* 33). Quintilian describes the Jews as being a textbook example of "a nation (*gens*) which is pernicious for others" (*Institutio Oratoria* III.7.21), and Diodorus Siculus states "they never will eat nor drink with any other nation, or wish them any prosperity" (*Lib.Hist.* 34.1). Juvenal claims they refuse to extend even basic acts of human kindness to others, such as giving directions to the nearest water source, except to fellow Judeans (Juvenal, *Satires* XIV.103–104). Where such attitudes prevailed, siding *with* the Judeans might easily be seen as siding *against* one's own people.

157. "At this time the road leading from Sinuessa to Puteoli was paved with stone. And the same year Domitian slew, along with many others, Flavius Clemens the consul, although he was a cousin and had to wife Flavia Domitilla, who was also a relative of the emperor's. The charge brought against them both was that of atheism (αθεοτης), a charge on which many others who drifted into Jewish ways (ηθη) were condemned. Some of these were put to death, and the rest were deprived of their property" (Cassius Dio *Roman History* 67.14.1–2; cf. Suetonius, Domitian 12.1–2). qtd. in Wilson, *Leaving the Fold,* 102–103. Wilson surmises political reasons for this trial; we are dealing with Roman aristocrats whose defection would be seen as a serious state matter, especially since Flavius and his wife were the parents of Domitian's designated heirs.

158. Mason, "Jews, Judaeans," 510.

159. Moore: LCL.

160. Mason, "Jews, Judaeans," 509.

161. Horace, *Sat.* 1.9.68–70; Petronius, *Sat.* 102.14; Epictetus, *Discourses* 12.2; Juvenal *Sat.* 14.96–106; Tacitus *Hist.* 5.5.1–2; Suetonius, *Domitian* 12.2. See Cohen, *Beginnings,* 24–49; and Stroup, *The Christians Who Became,* 161 N89.

162. Whitaker: LCL. cf. Wilson, *Leaving the Fold,* 78–82.

163. NRSV.

164. Similarly, in nearby Ptolemais, Judeans were compelled to "change over (μεταβαινειν) to the customs of the Greeks (προαιουμενους επι τα Ἑλληνικα)" under pain of death (2 Macc. 6:9).

165. NRSV, with Ιουδαιος emended to "Judean." We are not given access to Dositheus' motivations, but he seems to be well placed in a foreign ruler's court, so it

52 *Chapter 1*

is possible that his conversion was fueled by social/political ambition. He may be the same Dositheus mentioned in a papyrus as scribe in the court of Ptolemy Eurgetes I and "the priest of Alexander and the gods "Adelphoi" and the gods "Euergetai" (*CPJ* 127)." See Wilson, *Leaving the Fold*, 28–29.

166. Tiberius Julius Alexander's privileged upbringing would have regularly exposed him to the culture and patterns of the Hellenistic aristocracy. He was likely educated in the gymnasium, which would entail some serious religious compromises, but was nevertheless often the first step toward social advancement for Alexandrian Jews (Wilson, *Leaving the Fold*, 29–30). Regarded as a skeptic by Philo himself (*Prov.* 1 and 2; *Anim*), he later became prominent in Roman administration: he was, successively, *epistrategos* of Thebaid (42 CE), procurator of Judea (46–48), a high-ranking officer (63), and governor of Egypt (66–69). During this last period, he suppressed a Jewish uprising in Alexandria and subsequently served as Titus' second-in-command during the siege of Jerusalem. Josephus describes Alexander somewhat neutrally in the *Jewish War* (ca. late 70), perhaps aware that he, too, could be accused of siding with the Romans during the revolt; it is only in the later *Jewish Antiquities* that Josephus remarks dryly that Tiberius Alexander "did not keep his ancestral practices (πατριοις εθεσιν)" (*Ant.* 20.100). Barclay, "Deviance and Apostasy: Some applications of deviance theory to first-century Judaism and Christianity," in *Modelling Early Christianity: Social-Scientific Studies of the New Testament in its Context*, Philip F. Esler, eds. (New York: Routledge, 1995), 119–121.

167. "When hatred of Jews was everywhere at its height, a certain Antiochus, one of their own in number and highly respected for the sake of his father, who was chief magistrate of the Jews in Antioch, entered the theatre during an assembly of the people and denounced his father and the other Jews, accusing them of a design to burn the whole city to the ground in one night; he also delivered up some foreign Jews as accomplices to the plot. . . . Antiochus further inflamed their fury; for thinking to furnish proof of his conversion (μεταβολης) and of his detestation of Jewish customs (των Ιουδαιων εθη) by sacrifices after the manner of the Greeks, he recommended that the rest should be compelled to do the same, as the conspirators would thus be exposed by their refusal." (*The Jewish War* 7.47, 50–51 [Feldman: LCL])

168. We may never know exactly what motivated Antiochus' wholesale "conversion" (i.e., defection). Perhaps he was motivated by hopes for citizenship or career necessities (Magnus Zetterholm, *The Formation of Christianity in Antioch,* 76). Stephen Wilson suggests that seeing the Judean Revolt winding down, Antiochus was convinced that the Judeans were politically doomed, and decided there was no need for him to go down with the ship (*Leaving the Fold,* 28).

169. Zetterholm, *The Formation of Christianity in Antioch,* 76.

170. Sacha Stern, *Jewish Identity and Rabbinic Writings* (Leiden: Brill, 1994), 109; qtd. in Wilson, *Leaving the Fold*, 131.

171. Wilson, *Leaving the Fold*, 132.

172. Josephus frequently uses the word "abandon" (καταλειπο/καταλυω) in his descriptions of what converts leave behind, taking things like "ancestral laws" or

Ethnos *and Racial Fluidity in Antiquity* 53

"ancestral worship" (πατριοι νομοι /πατριοι θρησκεια) as its direct object (e.g., *Ant.* 12.269, 364, 384–385). cf. Wilson, *Leaving the Fold*, 24–25.

173. The passage is a veritable thicket of racial markers—kinship, which has been severed, and various cultural changes, figuratively described as a shift in *geography*:

> The incomer has turned his kinfolk (συγγενεις), who in the ordinary course of things would be his sole confederates, into mortal enemies, by coming as a pilgrim to truth and the honouring of One who alone is worthy of honour, and by leaving the mythical fables and multiplicity of sovereigns, so highly honoured by the parents and grandparents (γονεις και παπποι και προγονοι), and all the blood relations (οι αφ'αίματος) of this immigrant to a better home (αποικιαν). (*Spec.Leg.* 4.178 [Colson: LCL]. *See* Barclay, "Deviance and Apostasy," 133 for discussion)

174. Horrell, "Religion, Ethnicity, and Way of Life,"

175. It is likely that many Judeans saw Paul as having turned his back on them. In Acts, Torah-observant Judeans accuse Paul of teaching people to "abandon (*apostasian*) the teachings of Moses" (Acts 21:21). Much later, Eusebius testifies that the Ebionites viewed Paul as an apostate from Judaism (Eus. *Hist. Eccl.* 3.27.4). Wilson, *Leaving the Fold*, 50.

176. Barclay, "Deviance and Apostasy," 133.

177. Intense, familial love is enjoined for all within the *ekkēsia* throughout Paul's letters: see 1 Thess. 4:9–10; Phil. 1:8–9a, 2:2, 4:1; 1 Cor. 5:13b–15, 13:1–13, 16:14; 2 Cor. 2:1–10; Philem. 8–20; Gal. 5:13; Rom. 12:10, 13:8–10.

178. Carmen Palmer, *Converts in the Dead Sea Scrolls*, 164–165 // "Converts at Qumran," 194, 206.

179. "Thus, while giving equal rank to all in-comers (επηλυταις) with all the privileges which he [Moses] gives the native-born (ευπατριδαις), he exhorts the old nobility to honour them not only with marks of respect but with special friendship and more than ordinary goodwill. And surely there is good reason for this; they have left, he says, their country (πατριδα), their kinsfolk (συγγενεις) and their friends (φιλους) for the sake of virtue and religion. Let them not be denied another citizenship (πολεων) or other ties of family (οικειων) and friendship (φιλων), and let them find places of shelter standing ready for refugees to the camp of piety." (Philo, *Special Laws* 1.52 [Colson: LCL])

180. Colson: LCL.

181. Erich S. Gruen, "Philo and Jewish Ethnicity," in *Strength to Strength: Essays in Honor of Shaye J. D. Cohen*, Michael L. Satlow, ed. (Atlanta, GA: SBL: Brown Judaic Studies, 2018), 186, 194.

182. Colson: LCL; cf. *Rewards* 152.

183. Gruen, "Philo and Jewish Ethnicity," 186.

184. My translation.

185. *Every Good Man* above, my translation. Consider also Philo's *Hypothetica* 11.13:

54 *Chapter 1*

The old men too even if they are childless (ατεκνοι) are treated as parents of a not merely numerous (πολυπαιδες) but very filial family (ευπαιδες) and regularly close their life with an exceedingly prosperous and comfortable old age; so many are those who give them precedence and honour as their due and minister to them as a duty voluntarily and deliberately accepted rather than enforced by nature. [Colson: LCL]

186. Thackeray: LCL.

187. Palmer, *Converts in the Dead Sea Scrolls*, 130–131, 136 // "Converts at Qumran," 157, 165. Thus, just as later rabbis would categorize the convert as "Israel in all respects" (*y. Eruv.* 6.2), so did least some of the communities who left behind the Dead Sea Scrolls.

188. Jokiranta and Wassen, "A Brotherhood at Qumran?," 185.

189. Fatherly prerogatives usurped by the community leader include the examination of new members (CD 13.12–13), supervising member's business transactions (CD 13.15–16 // 4QDa 9.3.1–4), and oversight of marriage and divorce (4QDa 9.3.4–6). Jokiranta and Wassen, "A Brotherhood at Qumran?," 186; cf. Wassen 2005, 160–164, 202–205.

190. Jokiranta and Wassen, "A Brotherhood at Qumran?," 183–184, 193.

191. Jokiranta and Wassen, "A Brotherhood at Qumran?," 202; cf. 192, where the authors propose that the metaphor of sonship may invoke various aspects of "sonship's" domain, including 1. quality / origin, 2. submission / obedience, and 3. honor. They conclude, "Thus, *son-ship terminology can stress the unity of members through common, fictional origins, through common obligations, or common honorable status*" (italics in original).

192. E.g., *IKyme* 39 = PH268310; Aristotle, *Eudemian Ethics* 7.1241b.24–26; *TAM* V.2 1148; *PLond* VII 2193 = *NewDocs* I 5; Artemidoros *Oneirocritica* 4.44, 5.82; cf. esp. cf. esp. *TAM* V.2 1148 From Thyatira, . . . "The children and the members of the brotherhood (*phratores*) set up this monument. If anyone knocks down or vandalizes this monument." For full quotes, see Richard S. Ascough, Philip A. Harland, and John S. Kloppenborg, *Associations in the Greco-Roman World: A Sourcebook* (Waco, TX: Baylor University Press, 2012).

193. Palmer, "Converts at Qumran," 192, cf. 214.

194. Palmer, *Converts in the Dead Sea Scrolls*, 172–174 // "Converts at Qumran," 202–204.

195. Ascough, Harland, and Kloppenborg, *Associations in the Greco-Roman World*, 65.

196. Cf. two inscriptions which mention "fathers" (*patēr*) of synagogues, in Rome, *JIWE* II 288 and *JIWE II* 576; Ascough, Harland, and Kloppenborg, pp. 45, 214–215. For similar usage by non-Judeans, see *CIRB* 1277, which references a "father (*patēr*) of the synod," or *IG* XIV 1084, an inscription left by an association of those who sang paeans in Rome, which mentions one "Embes, prophet and father (*patēr*) of the order." For further discussion of many of these, see also Palmer, *Converts in the Dead Sea Scrolls*, 167–182 // "Converts at Qumran," 196–213.

197. Paul is fond of "brother" (with variants, over 100 times in the Pauline corpus), and describes Phoebe as a sister (Rom 16:1). He also speaks of "relatives" (Rom. 16:7, 11). However, he more typically describes *himself* as a "father" (1 Cor. 4:15),

Ethnos *and Racial Fluidity in Antiquity* 55

"old man" (Phlm 9), or even "mother/nurse" (1 Thess. 2:7–12)—thus implying a "generational" distinction between himself and others. This may illustrate something we saw in the DSS as well—the "familialization" of hierarchy. In some cases, however, "parental" language might refer not to authority, but merely affection or lines of teaching—consider Rufus's mother, who Paul says "has been a mother to me as well" (Rom. 16:13). See Jokiranta and Wassen, "A Brotherhood at Qumran?," 195 FN 60 & 61; and Palmer, *Converts in the Dead Sea Scrolls*, 160 // "Converts at Qumran," 191.

198. 1 Timothy enjoins his audience to treat older members as fathers and mothers, younger members as brothers and sisters (1 Tim. 5:1–2).

199. As opposed to "ascriptive descent" [which is simply ascribed at birth], subscriptive descent is achieved by *subscribing* to the ways of the founder and thereby showing one's self to be the founder's "descendant."

200. David Sedley, "Philosophical Allegiance in the Greco-Roman World," 97–119 in *Philosophia Togata*, Miriam Griffin and Jonathan Barnes, eds. (Oxford: Clarendon, 1989), 97; Loveday Alexander, "Paul and the Hellenistic Schools," 71–72; Loveday Alexander, "IPSE DIXIT: Citation of Authority in Paul and in the Jewish and Hellenistic Schools," 108–115.

201. Teresa Morgan further notes that although the Stoics are not generally regarded as an "ethnicity," Stoic cosmopolitanism might, by its own logic, be understood in these terms. Morgan, "Society, Identity, and Ethnicity in the Hellenic World," 39.

202. Jones: LCL.

203. Sarah Pomeroy suggests that the oath may reflect the "ordinary situation" within professions, whereby a master's pupils would in fact normally be his own sons (Sarah B. Pomeroy, "Some Greek Families," 157). While this is not unlikely, it is therefore all the more telling that the oath *does* consider situations where this is not the case and directs such a student to treat such a teacher as "equal to his own parents"—creating a bond characterized not only by filial affection but filial duty, including the obligation to share resources, and familial duties to his (natural) children. *See* Pomeroy, "Some Greek Families: Production and Reproduction," in *The Jewish Family and Antiquity*, Shaye J. D. Cohen, ed. (Atlanta, GA: Brown Judaic Studies), 157. See also Alexander, "Paul and the Hellenistic Schools," 74.

204. Denise Kimber Buell, *Making Christians: Clement of Alexandria and the Rhetoric of Legitimacy* (Princeton, NJ: Princeton University Press, 1999), 6.

205. Keith Hopkins, "Seven Missing Papers," in *Parenté et Stratégies Familiales dans l'Antiquité Romaine. Actes de la table ronde des 2—4 octobre 1986* (Paris, Maison des sciences de l'homme), Jean Andreau and Hinnerk Bruhns, eds. (Collection de l'École Française de Rome 129; Palais Farnèse: l'École Française de Rome, 1990), 624; qtd. in Buell, *Making Christians*, 5.

206. Buell, *Making Christians*, 5–6.

207. Consider even the classification of these early writings as "The Church Fathers" or "Patristics." We might also cite the use of familial terms *abba* and *amma* among the "desert fathers" of early Egyptian monasticism. Another clear example of this thinking is apostolic succession: later Christians asserted an unbroken lineage of bishop to bishop, in a "genealogy" stretching back to one of the apostles.

56 Chapter 1

208. Buell, "Origen Stories," 7.

209. A. Cleveland Coxe, "Introductory Note to Gregory Thaumaturgus," in *Ante-Nicene Fathers. Volume 6*, Alexander Roberts and James Donaldson, eds. (Peabody, MA: Hendrickson, 1994 [1886]), 3.

210. John Barclay writes, "It is only possible to use the term 'ethnicity' for the ancient phenomena if we are clear that this is a *polythetic*, and not a *monothetic*, category. The difference is this: a monothetic category must have at least one element that is necessary for inclusion in the category, some common feature without which a phenomenon cannot be included. Polythetic, on the other hand, means 'relating to or sharing a number of characteristics which occur commonly in members of a group or class, but none of which is essential for membership of that group or class' (*Oxford English Dictionary*). One would expect clusters of characteristics, or 'family resemblances', but there is no single item which is the sine qua non of membership in that category, 'essential' either as necessary or as 'of the essence'." (Barclay, "Ιουδαιος: Ethnicity and Translation," 49)

211. For a similar list, see Steve Mason, "Jews, Judaeans, Judaizing, Judaism," 484.

212. Jonathan Hall insists that ethnicity *must* be monothetic so that it can be a clear-cut, "objective" category within social scientific discourse, with the same meaning across all eras (Hall, *Hellenicity,* 12). This insistence is based upon his prioritization of the category's "heuristic utility"—he deems a flexible category too vague to be "useful." Such an argument, however, defines terms based on *what we want them to do*, rather than *how they were actually used in primary sources.*

213. David Horrell insists, "Ethnicity was not a stable or singular categorization but a field of identity in which a person might claim, or be given, different 'ethnic' labels in different times and contexts" ("Religion, Ethnicity, and Way of Life," 44). cf. Dennis Duling's doubts "whether *any* feature is so constitutive that there is no 'ethnicity' without it" ("Ethnicity, Ethnocentrism, and the Matthean *Ethnos*," 127).

214. Irad Malkin, "Introduction," in *Ancient Perceptions of Greek Ethnicity,* Irad Malkin, ed. (Cambridge, MA: Harvard University Press, 1990), 6.

215. Teresa Morgan, "Society, Identity, and Ethnicity in the Hellenic World," 26–27.

216. Horrell, "Religion, Ethnicity, and Way of Life," 44; cf. a similar assertion in Teresa Morgan, "Society, Identity, and Ethnicity in the Hellenic World," 37.

217. Horrell, "Religion, Ethnicity, and Way of Life," 44.

218. Rev 3:8–9 and 2:9.

219. Isocrates, *Panegyricus* 50.

220. Barclay, "Ιουδαιος: Ethnicity and Translation," 46.

221. Under certain circumstances, some of the "cultural stuff" of ethnicity might also have such a gatekeeping function. One obvious example is circumcision—especially in the minds of those Judeans who saw *eighth-day* circumcision as the only acceptable form, to be accounted true Israelites. As grown men could not go back in time and be circumcised as infants, this represented another insurmountable barrier to becoming Judean.

222. Matthew Thiessen, *Contesting Conversion,* 67–68, 83.

Ethnos *and Racial Fluidity in Antiquity* 57

223. e.g., Isocrates on who is really "Greek," or Josephus' denigration of Herod's claims. Even in Acts—which arguably affirms the power of conversion to change one's identity—it remains possible to distinguish proselytes from those actually born as Judeans (Acts 2:10, 6:5, 13:45). Josephus draws a distinction between those who are "Judean" by virtue of culture and practice (Idumeans, Pereans, etc.) and the "natural-born (γνησιος) people (λαος) of Judea itself" (War 2.43, 46–47 // Ant. 117.254, 257–58). See "γνήσιος" in the LSJ: the word derives from γενος, and thus can mean not only "genuine, actual, real" but specifically "native, legitimate by birth, belonging to a race."

224. Consider also the Idumeans who call Jerusalem their "mother city" (*War* 4.273–275), or the Ethiopian in Acts 8:26–39.

225. On the "double discursive competence" of ethnic actors, see Baumann, *The Multicultural Riddle*, 90–95; cit. in Hodge, *If Sons, Then Heirs*, 21–22.

226. Jos. *Ant.* 13.257–258, 319; *Ant.* 17.254–258 // War 2.43–47; War 4.273–275.

227. Jos. *Ant.* 14.403.

228. Jos. *Ant.* 9.288–292; 10.183–184; 11.341; cf. also 4Q371 lines 10–14.

229. Teresa Morgan, "Society, Identity, and Ethnicity in the Hellenic World," 38. Gifford Rhamie similarly asserts that "notions of ethnicity as refracted through such terms like . . . ὁ λαος, το εθνος (τα εθνη) and γενος are not biologically ascribed, but are floating, composite signifiers that are contingent on land, religious life, relationships and collective peoples." Rhamie, "Whiteness, Conviviality and Agency: The Ethiopian Eunuch (Acts 8:26–40) and Conceptuality in the Imperial Imagination of Biblical Studies," PhD Dissertation (Canterbury: Canterbury Christ Church University, 2019), 188–189.

Chapter 2

"The Rock from Which You Were Hewn"

Abraham in Judean Racial Reasoning

Look to the rock from which you were hewn,
   and to the quarry from which you were dug.
Look to Abraham your father
   and to Sarah who bore you;
for he was only one person when I called him,
   and blessed him, and loved him, and multiplied him. —Isaiah 51:1b-2 [LXX]

Delivered during the Babylonian Exile, Second Isaiah's striking oracle calls Israel to look to Abraham, "the rock from which you were hewn," as a pledge that God would vindicate them. This arresting image—that of having been quarried from the patriarch—was particularly fitting for Abraham, whom God had promised, "I will surely multiply your offspring (σπερμα) like the sand on the shore" (Gen. 22:17; cf. Gen. 13:16). A rock is a fitting metaphor, for what *is* sand, but so many grains of stone? And what *is* Israel, but a chip off the old block, Abraham?

Judeans had long looked to Abraham as their definitive ancestor, the prototype and progenitor of their people. Israelites frequently described themselves as the "seed (זרע/σπερμα) of Abraham."[1] Thus, the intended audience of the Second Isaiah's oracle, those who look to "your father Abraham," are Judahites/Judeans; God calls them "my people" (λαος) who "know righteousness, the people in whose heart is my Law" (Isa. 51:4, 7a). These Judeans are reminded of God's twin promises to Abraham: progeny (51:2) and land (51:3). These promises, given to Abraham in the past, stand as surety for the prophet's *current* oracle of hope—precisely because it is addressed to Abraham's descendants.

However, the prophet reveals that the restoration of Israel will have consequences for *other* races as well. God says,

60 *Chapter 2*

Listen to me, listen, my people (λαος), and kings, give ear to me;
> for a law will go out from me, and my justice will be a light for the nations (εθνων).

My righteousness draws near, and my salvation goes out like light,
> and on my arm the nations (εθνη) will hope;
> the islands wait for me, and they will hope for my arm. (Isaiah 51:4–5 [LXX])

Somehow, the promises vouchsafed to Abraham (and inherited by his latter-day descendants, now in Babylon) have ramifications for the other races of the earth. God's restorative justice will be a "light for the nations," a phrase Luke borrows twice.[2]

By the Second Temple period, Judeans had a rich tradition of using Abraham in their racial reasoning.[3] Discussion of Abraham may be considered "racial" because it almost always touched upon the three most constitutive elements of race in the ancient world: shared ancestry, shared homeland, and shared distinctive way of life. (1) Regarding *ancestry*: Abraham was universally hailed as the ancestor of the Judeans—even his name (אברהם, "father of a multitude") invokes his role as father/ancestor.[4] Narratives about Abraham frequently mention his "offspring/descendants"[5] or refer to him as an "ancestor." (2) In terms of *homeland*, Abraham was often mentioned in the same breath as God's promise to give his descendants the land of Canaan—so that the homeland of his latter-day descendants might aptly be called "the land of Abraham" (Tob. 14:7). 3) Regarding *way of life,* Abraham was understood in many ways to have been the pioneer of the Israelite constitution (πολιτεια) and way of life (εθη), the recipient of a covenant with God—a covenant sealed by circumcision (Gen. 17).[6]

Some even opined that the "Hebrews" owed their very name to Abraham. Artapanus supposes that Hebrews were "named for Abraham (καλεισθαι δε αυτοις απο Αβρααμου)," seemingly based upon their shared *b* and *r* sounds.[7] Aulus Claudius Charax of Pergamum, whose 44-volume history was widely read in antiquity, agrees: "This [Hebrews] is the name Jews get from Abraham, as Charax says."[8]

Abraham featured heavily both in Judean musings about themselves, and about their relationship to other peoples. This is understandable, given the biblical account itself. Abraham received promises which established a unique relationship between God and one particular people (Gen. 12:2; 17:7–8, 19, 21; 15:1–21)—but at the same time, God informed the patriarch that he would be the "father of many races/gentiles (εθνων/גוים)" (Gen. 17:4–6).[9] Beyond that, God promised that "all the races of the earth" (τα εθνη της γης) would be blessed through his descendants/σπερματι (Gen. 22:18; cf. Gen. 12:3, 18:18).[10] Other scriptural mentions of Abraham demonstrate that he was an ideal figure to think with when contemplating *both* Israel's unique identity *and* Israel's place among the nations.[11] The rich and layered deposits of Abraham traditions in scripture became resources that later Judeans could excavate for their own ends—mining selectively those veins which best suited their views and recutting what they found to fit whatever argument they were crafting. Thus, although all Second Temple Judeans understood themselves to have been hewn from their ancestor Abraham, various authors creatively shaped this rock to buttress their own understandings of themselves and their relationship to others.

This chapter will survey some of the diverse ways Abraham was used during the Second Temple period to construct Judean identity.[12] In many ways, Abraham was the bedrock from whom Judean identity was hewn. But there are many things sorts of things one can build, of rock. When it comes to the Judeans and the *ethnē*, is Abraham a bridge, or a wall? Broadly speaking, we will find two divergent sets of answers to the related questions: 1) *Who* belongs to Abraham? and 2) *To whom* does Abraham belong?

We will divide our survey of Abraham traditions into two categories, based on what is implied about the relationship between Judeans and non-Judeans. (1) Abraham-as-wall: First, we will survey some ways in which Abraham was invoked to assert that Judeans are *distinct* from other races and perhaps possessed of an exclusive status or privilege because of this fact. In many of these sources, the patriarch emphatically "belongs" to the Judeans, and to none else. We will call these "exclusivist" Abraham traditions, in that they excluded others, drawing firmer boundaries between "us" and "them." (2) Abraham-as-bridge: Second, we will survey ways in which Abraham was invoked to suggest *connections* between Judeans and others; we will call these "inclusivist" Abraham traditions. These could range from the expansion of biblical traditions about Abraham's many descendants, to the creative assertion that Abraham was also the ancestor of other contemporary races, or tales of Abraham's supposed cultural influence upon them. In a few cases, a sort of "honorary" descent from Abraham was even suggested, based on following his example—that is, what we have been referring to as "subscriptive descent."

"OUR FATHER ABRAHAM"—EXCLUSIVIST USES OF ABRAHAM

In rabbinic Judaism, Abraham is referred to as *Abraham Abinu* (אברהם אבינו), or "our father Abraham." In the Talmud, this phrase signifies both that Abraham is the biological progenitor of the Jews, and that he was the "father" of the Jewish way of life (i.e., Judaism); thus, his "fatherhood" might be stretched to include those who have adopted his ways and thus

62   *Chapter 2*

been adopted into his lineage (proselytes).[13] Many ancient Judeans, however, understood *"our"* more restrictively—"Our father Abraham" in that
he was distinctly, and *exclusively*, the father of (lineal) Israel. In this section, we will review some ways Abraham could be invoked in an ethnically
"exclusivist" way.

Abraham traditions could be leveraged as a sort of "wall" between Israel
and the nations (*ethnē*), differentiating Judeans from all others. Sources
also drew distinctions *among* Abraham's various descendants, between the
"favored" and legitimate line (Israel), and the other miscellaneous branches
of the family tree (Ishmaelites, etc.). For many Judeans, it was only the former—Israel, and the latter-day Judeans—who could meaningfully be called
the σπερμα Αβρααμ, or "seed/descendants" of Abraham. Members of *this*
people could expect to derive benefits and blessings from their Abrahamic
heritage; other scattered by-blows could not. Even some exhortations to follow Abraham's example (what we have been calling "subscriptive descent")
could serve exclusivist purposes. For some authors, following Abraham's
example was crucial not because it could "graft" outsiders into his family
tree, but because *failure* to do so might jeopardize a Judean's inheritance.
Emulation of the patriarch could also be conceptualized as a form of ethnic
differentiation—reinforcing that Israel must not be like "the nations."

Ascriptive Descent—Israel *Distinguished* from Other Abrahamic Races

Ascriptive descent is the sort of ancestry simply ascribed at birth—that is,
based on (presumptive) physical descent—shared blood and its (presumed)
conferral of consubstantial likeness. In Genesis, God had promised Abraham
that he would be the father of "many nations" (Gen. 17:4–6; cf. Sir. 44:19,
Jub. 15:6–8). Accordingly, Judean literature attributed biological descent
from Abraham to a number of peoples. This hearkens all the way back to
the biblical account. There is Isaac, of course, ancestor of the Israelites and
Edomites. There is Ishmael, whose sons were "twelve princes, according to
their tribes (אֻמָּה/εθνη)" (Gen. 25:12–18; cf. 1 Chron. 1:28–31);[14] Judean traditions identified the Arabians as his descendants (*Jub.* 20:12–13; Jos. *Ant.*
1.214).[15] The Midianites and other ethnic groups descend from Abraham
and Keturah (Gen. 25:1–6), and the Edomites descend from his grandson
Esau (Gen. 36). Furthermore, Genesis traces the Ammonites and Moabites
back to Lot and his daughters, making them at least cousins of Abrahamic
peoples (Gen. 19:30–38). This proliferation of races fulfills God's promise,
"I will increase you exceedingly, and I will make you into nations (εθνη/
גּוֹיִם), and kings shall come from you" (Gen. 17:6).[16]

"The Rock from Which You Were Hewn"   63

Although ancient Judaism acknowledged that some other races bore an ancestral connection to Abraham, what was the *significance* of this connection? Generally, Judeans held that they had a firmer claim upon the patriarch than these other peoples: *they* were his legitimate descendants, and he was "theirs" in a sense not true of other races.

The Hebrew Bible itself relates that there is a "chosen" and favored lineage of Abrahamic descent, as opposed to "illegitimate" or less esteemed lines. When mothers appear in accounts of Abraham's children, one of their functions is largely to *differentiate their children*—to highlight Sarah as the "right" mother, but Hagar or Keturah as the "wrong" mothers. That is, the mothers serve to divide their children into more- or less-valued groups. God explains to Abraham that his offspring (σπερμα) shall be reckoned through Isaac, Sarah's son (Gen. 21:12); however, God "will *also* (και) make a great nation (εθνος) of the son of that slave woman, because he is your σπερμα" (Gen. 21:13).[17] Ishmael seems to be "Abrahamic" in a lesser, secondary sense. God later gives Hagar her *own* promise regarding Ishmael's offspring, which mirrors the promise God gave Abraham (Gen. 21:18). By the time Ishmael's twelve sons are enumerated later, the narrator is careful to designate Ishmael as *Hagar's* child (25:12–18)—not Abraham's! Hagar has been consistently identified as an Egyptian, and Ishmael takes an Egyptian wife; thus, when he dies and is gathered to "his people" (γενος), it seems more likely that this refers to the Egyptians, rather than Abraham's folk. Similarly, the phrasing of 1 Chronicles 1:32–33 suggests that Keturah's children can primarily be identified as *hers,* not Abraham's. Genealogically, Keturah's children are bracketed off from the "proper" lineage of Abraham's descendants who inherit the promise (Gen. 18:10).[18]

Poetic sources frequently employ Hebrew parallelism to indicate that it is specifically *Jacob* (and his offspring) who should be identified as the "seed of Abraham":

Similar parallels across the Hebrew Bible convey that "offspring of Abraham" should be understood as a term for *Israel alone*—despite the fact that Genesis explicitly acknowledges that others descend from him. Although

Table 2.1 "Jacob" as "Seed of Abraham"

| But you, Israel, my servant,
    Jacob, whom I have chosen,
      the offspring of Abraham, <br> my friend...

              – Isaiah 41:8 | O offspring of his servant
 Abraham,
    children of Jacob,
    his chosen ones...

         – Psalm 105:6[i] |

---

[i] both passages NRSV.

64   *Chapter 2*

there are technically multiple lines of Abrahamic descent, some are more generally reckoned his "children" than others. This calls to mind Jonathan Hall's discussion of the function of "ethnic genealogies" in antiquity. Ethnic genealogies connect races by common descent from a shared ancestor, but they also create *ranked* relationships—that is, certain branches of the family tree might be considered somehow "closer" to an ancestral founder.[19]

Many later Judean sources elaborate upon the "exclusivist" tendencies of scriptural genealogies, asserting that Israel was in some way better or more favored than other branches of Abraham's family tree.[20] Significantly, extant Judean sources reserve the designation σπερμα Αβρααμ ("Abraham's seed/ descendants") for Isaac and ultimately Jacob, and those descended from them.[21] One particularly clear instance of this motif is found in *Jubilees*. The angels who meet Abraham at Mamre explain this:

> [16]And we returned in the seventh month and we found Sarah pregnant before us. And we blessed Abraham and we announced to him everything which was commanded for him: that he would not die until he begot six more sons and he would see (them) before he died. And through Isaac a name and seed would be named for him. [17]And all the seed of his sons would become nations. And they would be counted among the nations. But from the sons of Isaac one would become a holy seed and he would not be counted among the nations, [18]because he would become the portion of the Most High and all his seed would fall (by lot) into that which God will rule so that he might become a people (belonging) to the LORD, a (special) possession from all people, and so that he might become a kingdom of priests and a holy people. (*Jubilees* 16:16–18)[22]

This passage is quite explicit: among the sons of Abraham, Isaac is genealogically unique. The other six are "counted with the gentiles," but Isaac is not. Subsequently, only *one* of Isaac's own sons would become the foretold "holy seed," "a treasured people," "a kingdom, a priesthood, and a holy people." Vanderkam comments, "The burden of their message is that, even with the arrival of more sons who presumably would have been circumcised, Isaac would be the one through whom Abraham would have a name and seed."[23] Later, Abraham himself acknowledges that among his grandsons, *Jacob* is the one predicted by these angelic messengers (*Jub.* 19:16).

In 3 Maccabees, the "*sperma* of Abraham" means Judeans. The priest Eleazar prays:

> O King mighty in power, Almighty God Most High who governs all creation with mercy, watch over the descendants of Abraham (Αβρααμ σπερμα), over the children of the consecrated Jacob, your consecrated portion, a people (λαον) who are perishing as foreigners in a foreign land (ξενη γη ξενον). (3 Maccabees 6:2–3)[24]

"The Rock from Which You Were Hewn"   65

Many of the terms mirror those from Jubilees 16, above. Here, "descendants of Abraham" stands in direct parallel construction with "the children of hallowed Jacob," making it clear that these are one and the same—and that this label applies *only* to them. The *Psalms of Solomon* 9 also narrowly identifies the *sperma Abraam* as the latter-day Judeans:

> [8]And now, you are God and we are the people (λαος) whom you have loved;
> look and be compassionate, O God of Israel, for we are yours,
> and do not take away your mercy from us, lest they set upon us.
> [9]For you chose the descendants of Abraham (το σπερμα Αβρααμ) above all the nations (εθνη),
> and you put your name upon us, Lord, and it will not cease forever.
> [10]You made a covenant with our ancestors (πατρασιν) concerning us,
> and we hope in you when we turn our souls toward you.
> [11]May the mercy of the Lord be upon the house of Israel (οικον Ισραηλ) forevermore. (*Psalms of Solomon* 9:8–11)[25]

It is only the Judean "us" of the psalm, the "house of Israel," who comprise the *sperma Abraam*—the people (*laos*) God has loved. This distinguishes them from the nations (*ethnē*), who lurk ominously at the edges of the psalm, ready to "set upon us" if God's mercy were removed (9:8c). Various Judean writings echo the conviction that it is only specifically *Jacob's* line who are Abraham's *sperma* (e.g., *Jub.* 36:6–9; *T.Levi* 8:15), and for this reason, Judeans can also be called the "seed of Jacob" as a near-synonym (*4 Ezra* 8:16, 9:30; *Jub.* 19:23).[26]

Even Philo of Alexandria, who was very willing extend Judean identity to proselytes, describes the specific line of descent traced through Jacob as a new epoch in the history of humankind (Abr. 12.56).[27] Just as Adam the "earth-born" was the common ancestor of primal humanity, and just as Noah became the father of a "new race of humanity," so is Abraham—*through Jacob*—the father of the holy εθνος of Israel.

Excursis: Abraham in the "Animal Apocalypse" of 1 Enoch

The "Animal Apocalypse" (*1 Enoch* 85–90) represents various peoples as different species of animals, constructing an almost "ontological" gap between Judeans and gentiles. This retelling of world history might be described as a racial "fall narrative," with a distinct pattern, repeated twice: (1) *cattle of various colors* (red, black, and white) signal the differentiation of distinct lineages;[28] (2) *numerous animal species* appear, who are unlike their parents; (3) *fear* and *violence* increase, so that (4) some *cry out,* followed sometime later by (5) the coming of a snow-white animal who *becomes a human being* (see table 2.2). Each iteration of this cycle leads to greater diversity—and this

66   *Chapter 2*

Table 2.2   Pattern of Racial Speciation in *1 Enoch*

Fall Narrative 1: Adam to Noah	Fall Narrative 2: Noah to Moses
85:3-8 black / red / white = Cain / Abel / Seth	88:9 white / red / black = Shem / Japheth / Ham
86:4 elephants, camels, and asses	89:10-12 fifteen species + two more
86:5—86:1 All of the cattle feared them and were terrified of them. And they began to bite with their teeth and to swallow and gore with their horns. Then they began to devour those cattle.	89: 11 And they began to bite one another... 89:15 And the wolves began to fear them and to oppress them until they were destroying their young...
86:1 the earth cries out	89:15-16 the sheep cry out
88:1 (Noah) ...born a bull but became a man... 88:9 ...that white bull that had become a man.	89:36 that sheep (Moses) became a man... 89:38 that sheep had led them, and become a man...

diversity leads to greater suffering. In the "Animal Apocalypse," then, race is understood as a *problem*. Without so many distinct *genē*, there would not be such violence.

Before the primeval flood, humanity was represented as cattle. After the flood, these cattle "began to beget wild beasts and birds," including lions, leopards, wolves, dogs, hyenas, wild boars, foxes, conies, pigs, falcons, vultures, kites, eagles, and ravens, "but among them a white bull was born," Abraham (*1 Enoch* 89:10).[29] The sons and grandsons of Abraham "speciate" further: Isaac is a white cattle like his father, but Ishmael is a wild ass (89:11; Gen. 16:12).[30] Esau is a wild boar, but Jacob is a white sheep—signaling the end of the Sethite/Shemite line (white cattle) and the beginning of the Israelite line (sheep).[31] Jacob is like Abraham, another white "clean" animal; Abraham's *other* descendants are differentiated from him by color, cleanness/impurity, and domesticity/wildness. (A similar tradition in *Jubilees* 37:18–24 "naturalizes" the enmity between Esau and Jacob by likening it to the instinctive enmity between various wild/predatory animals—including a boar—and the clean/domestic animals they prey upon.)[32] After Jacob, there is no further "speciation" of Israelites into other animals: from this point in *1 Enoch*, race is a fixed trait.[33]

The text assigns taxonomical categories to various groups of peoples who were understood as similar in some way, creating "classes" of related species/races (see table 2.2). Interestingly, the offspring of the giants are unclean but tame animals.[34] Wild birds, who enter the narrative relatively late, are widely understood to represent various Hellenistic peoples.[35] "Class" likely represents some putatively *shared quality* of these related races. The fact that gentile races are represented as unclean and predatory, for example, implies something about their acceptability to God, *and* their relationship with Israel (who are sheep, a prey species).[36] Edomites and Ishmaelites are represented as *wild* breeds of animals that it is *possible* to domesticate (the donkey and

"The Rock from Which You Were Hewn" 67

the pig). Perhaps this implies that they *ought* to be able to get along with Israelites, who are, after all, their distant kin, and yet they frequently fail to do so[37] (see table 2.3).

Interestingly, the apocalypse does not consign gentiles to a state of genealogical impurity forever. In the last days, long after the last of the antediluvian "cattle" have died out, a new snow-white bull will be born (a messiah), after which "all the beasts of the field and all the birds of the sky" and "all their kindred" will themselves be transformed into snow-white cattle (*1 Enoch* 90:37–38). These new cattle, then, are gentiles who have once again been incorporated into the righteous lineage of Abraham (who, recall, was a white bull). Perhaps surprisingly, Judeans *remain* Judeans (white sheep, representing the Israelite line); but gentiles are restored to the Sethite/Abrahamic type of humanity.[38] However, this restoration will have to wait until the eschaton. Effectively, *1 Enoch* 85–90 envisions a fundamental racial gap between Judeans and others, as insurmountable as the difference between species—at least until the end of the age.

Abrahamic Blessings for (Just) the Judeans

We have seen that, in the minds of some Judeans, their race was uniquely descended from the patriarch, despite the existence of other nations whose ancestry also stretched back to Abraham.[39] But we are tempted to ask: "So what?" Why does a "special" sort of connection to Abraham matter? Other than the simple delineation of boundaries—tracing out exactly where the line between "us" and "them" is drawn—what difference does this make? As we shall see, Judeans held that a closer tie to Abraham actually *did* make a great deal of difference; Judeans were the recipients of various blessings and benefits because of their special standing. Frequently, a number of attributes—covenant, circumcision, land, status as God's chosen—were collectively understood as Israel's *particular* inheritance from Abraham.[40] Certain blessings were popularly expected to convey his latter-day descendants, the Judeans; these blessings were not always limited to the twofold promises of

Table 2.3   Types of Races/Species in the Animal Apocalypse

Type of race	"Genus"	Species
Primordial humanity, Israelites	Clean, tame animals	Cattle, sheep
Giant-hybrids	Unclean, tame animals	Elephants, camels, asses
Pre-Hellenistic gentiles	Unclean, wild animals	Lions, leopards, wolves, etc.
Non-Israelite Abrahamic races	Unclean, feral but domesticable	Wild-asses, wild-boars
Hellenistic peoples	Unclean, wild birds	Eagles, kites, ravens, etc.

68   *Chapter 2*

progeny and land (Isa. 51:1–2). God could be relied upon to save/redeem the Judeans, for the patriarch's sake.[41] Some authors added other elements, such as the idea that Abraham might intercede for the souls of Israelites, even after their death.

Judean sources overwhelmingly treated God's covenant with Abraham in Genesis as pertaining only to the children of Jacob. Pseudo-Philo relates that God gave Abraham the promise of land, the covenant, and an "everlasting seed" through *Sarah*, specifically—not through or to any of his other descendants (*L.A.B.* 8:3).[42] *Jubilees* expands upon this idea, not only affirming that Abraham's seed will be synonymous with Jacob's seed (*Jub.* 19:16), but even explaining *why this should be so*. Isaac instructed his sons Jacob and Esau to imitate their grandfather (*Jub.* 36:6).[43] They must "perform righteousness and uprightness upon the earth so that the LORD will bring upon you everything which the LORD said he would do for Abraham and for his seed" (*Jub.* 36:3) including the promise of numerous progeny (36:6b). Isaac cautions them that if either of them fails, "his seed will be destroyed from under heaven" (36:9).[44] In *Jubilees'* retelling of Genesis, Esau and his sons do exactly this (*Jub.* 37)—leaving Jacob as the sole inheritor of the Abrahamic promises. From this point on, "everything which the LORD said he would do for Abraham and for his seed" (*Jub.* 36:3) will be done exclusively for Jacob's descendants, *not* Esau's.[45]

When it comes to promises inherited by the "descendants/זרע/σπερμα" of Abraham (land and becoming a great nation),[46] these descendants were overwhelmingly understood *narrowly*—that is, as Israelites, and after the loss of the Northern tribes, as Judeans. This is clearly an "exclusivist" tendency in Abraham traditions. Adding the covenant—or making the covenant the requirement for receiving these blessings—excludes even other races who could be understood as descended from Abraham, in a "lesser" way.

But there is another exclusivist trend related to God's covenant with Abraham, although it is largely observable only as an absence. Mladen Popović searches Second Temple period Judean literature for discussion of God's promise to "bless the nations" through Abraham, as found in Genesis 12:3 and 22:18, but to little avail. A reception of such passages is largely lacking, even where one would expect to find it.[47] *Sirach* 44:21, which *does* repeat the "blessing of the nations" formula from Genesis 22:18, narrows the scope of this blessing from "all the races of the earth" (כל גוים הארצ) to just "the races" (גוים/εθνη). This phrasing de-emphasizes the universality of such blessings; perhaps Ben Sira has only in mind nations who physically descend from Abraham, such as Ishmaelites?[48] Popović concludes that "the theme of Abraham and the blessing of the nations was not a major issue in early Jewish texts."[49]

"The Rock from Which You Were Hewn"   69

Another particularist tendency was the trope of Abraham-as-intercessor. Abraham was expected to "watch over" his descendants (the Judeans) in a special way, perhaps as an intermediary between them and God. A postbiblical tradition arose that Abraham might intercede personally for his children, even after their death. This notion was likely inspired by the Genesis account of Abraham bargaining with God on behalf of Sodom (Gen. 18:22–23). If Abraham had dared interpose himself between God and the wicked residents of Sodom, how much more would he do so for his own offspring! Because Abraham was a "friend" of God,[50] God would hearken to these prayers (*Test. Ab.* rec.A 14:1–15). Various Judean texts anticipate that Abraham will be active in the afterlife, or the eschatological kingdom of God, receiving the righteous or otherwise celebrating God's victory.[51]

Sometimes, other ancestors join in such intercessions. The three patriarchs together (Abraham, Isaac, and Jacob) were thought to intercede for the living (Philo *Q.Gen.* 44, *De Execr.* § 9, *Rewards* 166; *T.Lev.* 15:4; Jos. *Ant.* 1.), or even for righteous souls after their death, "on account of his own people" (*Sib.Or.* 2:331; cf. *3 En* 44:7–10).[52] At the eschatological judgment, "Abraham, Isaac, and Jacob will rejoice" to see the vindication of the righteous, on that day when "the Lord will rejoice in his children" (*T.Lev.* 18:12–14; cf. *T.Jud.* 25:1).[53]

Subscriptive Descent—Abraham's Children follow Abraham's Ways

Some Judean literature, then, viewed Abraham the ancestor of only one specific lineage, for all intents and purposes: the Israelites. Abraham's name could be invoked as one prayed for his (Judean) descendants (2 Macc. 1:1–6; 3 Macc. 6:2–3; *Pr.Manasseh* 1:8; *Add.Esth* 13:15–17). Indeed, Abraham himself would intercede for them, much as he had for the inhabitants of Sodom in his own day (cf. Gen. 18:22–33). In such texts, the need to imitate the patriarch's example was often emphasized. Abraham could be invoked to call Judeans to cleave to their ancestral traditions; sometimes this was paired with the notion that his descendants would derive *no* benefits or blessings from their genealogical status, if they failed to hold fast to his example.

We see such thinking as early as Ezekiel 33. Some of the Exiles are cocksure they must inevitably re-inherit the land: "The inhabitants of the waste places in the land of Israel are saying 'Abraham was one man and yet he gained possession of the land, and *we* are many; the land is surely given to us to possess'" (Ezek. 33:24).[54] However, the prophet quickly disabuses them of the assumption, because unlike Abraham, *they* look to idols, eat food with the blood in it, and defile their neighbors' wives. God asks in exasperation,

70 *Chapter 2*

"Shall you then possess the land?" (33:25–26). The answer—despite the fact that they *are* Abraham's descendants—is a firm "no" (33:27–29).

Jubilees retrojects this logic all the way back to Abraham's own lifetime, explaining the relative standing of Esau and Jacob by reference to their conduct. Extensively reworking the source for this story (Gen. 25:24–27), *Jubilees* 19 characterizes Jacob as civilized and literate, and Esau as uncouth and hotheaded.[55] Therefore, "Abraham saw the deeds of Esau, and he knew that in Jacob should his name and seed be called" (*Jub.* 19:16). Abraham refers to Jacob as "my son," as if he has formally adopted him.[56] In this retelling, it seems that *worthiness* supplements genealogy to "legitimate" patrilineal descent. Esau and Jacob are both Abraham's grandsons, but Esau's conduct is unworthy of the patriarch (19:16a). Abraham calls Jacob "my stead on the earth" (21:17), who will inherit the promises first given to him (19:21b–23).[57] Esau was unworthy to receive these promises, but Jacob is worthy.[58] This theme in *Jubilees* mirrors a tendency in some Qumran texts to blame the nations for their own exclusion: they, like their ancestors, are full of sin, perpetuating the cycle of selection and rejection.[59]

Abraham could be summoned as an argument-in-miniature for avoiding too-close associations with gentiles, and for endogamy. Tobit instructs Tobias:

> Beware, my son, of every kind of fornication. First of all, marry a woman from among the descendants of your ancestors (του σπερματος των πατερων σου); do not marry a foreign (αλλοτριαν) woman, who is not of your father's tribe; for we are the descendants of the prophets (υιοι προφητων). Remember, my son, that Noah, Abraham, Isaac, and Jacob, our ancestors of old, all took wives from among their kindred (αδελφων). They were blessed in their children, and their posterity (σπερμα) will inherit the land. (Tobit 4:12)

Notice how thickly this passage bristles with the terminology and logic of ethnicity—even "way of life" is implied, both in adherence to ancestral example, and in the unspoken (but common) concern that exogamous marriage leads to idolatry.[60] The precedent set by the patriarch supports Tobit's intentions for his son—an endogamous marriage—and it is strongly implied that the blessing Abraham received in his own progeny was linked to this endogamy.[61] Of course, one must overlook Abraham's involvement with Hagar (an Egyptian) to derive this "lesson" from his example![62]

In Genesis, God attests that "Abraham obeyed my voice, kept my charge, my commandments, my statutes, and my laws" (Gen. 26:5). Some Judeans took this a step further, speculating that Abraham had kept the entire Torah, even before it was written down![63] Therefore, Abraham could be invoked to encourage contemporary Judeans to adhere to the law and Judaism. Because

"The Rock from Which You Were Hewn" 71

customs served as identity markers, heightening ethnic distinctiveness, this may be seen as an "exclusivist" function of Abraham. That is, these traditions construct the patriarch as the unique ancestor of a unique people; his "ways" become a sort of border delineating the difference between Judeans and everyone else. Although appeals to Abraham along these lines can be found in many places (e.g., 1 Macc. 2:50–52; 2 Macc. 1:2–4; *Sir.* 44:20)[64] the clearest, most extended use of this trope is probably 4 Maccabees.

Throughout 4 Maccabees, Abraham is the model for latter-day Judeans. The book is set during the reign of Antiochus IV, when many Judeans were forced to abandon traditional religious practices upon pain of death. The author insists that as "children of Abraham" (οἱ παιδες Αβρααμ), Judeans must be ready to "die nobly for their piety" rather than "feign a role unbecoming to us" (4 Macc. 6:17–22). Turid Seim comments, "Their relation to Abraham is mobilized as an argument against cowardice and lack of self-control, and it serves an exhortatory and didactic function. The terms employed reflect a language rooted in concepts of genetic descent and kinship."[65] In 4 Maccabees, lineal descent from Abraham *does* matter, but it must be activated by adherence to his example; Abraham is more "significant as archetype rather than ancestor."[66] His genetic descendants may "disqualify" themselves, as it were, and lose their status.[67] Despite the liberal application of torture, Antiochus "was by no means able to compel the Jerusalemites to adopt foreign ways (αλλοφυλησαι) nor to change their ancestral customs (πατριων εθων)" (18:15).[68]

In 4 Maccabees, it is not only ascriptive descent (attributed at birth) which matters, but also subscriptive descent (being Abraham's "child" by way of imitation). The author coins novel words from Abraham's name to convey this.[69] The eldest of seven martyred brothers is a "great-souled and Abrahamic (Αβραμιαιος) youth" (4 Macc. 9:21).[70] The brothers' heroic mother is an "Abrahamitess" (Αβρααμιτις, 18:20), which may indicate that "she is a woman concerned with what Abraham stands for."[71] Upon their martyrdom, these "Abrahamic children" (Αβραμιαιοι), along with their "Abrahamitic" mother, are brought into the "chorus of ancestors" (πατερων χορον). Because they share not only Abraham's *descent* but his *characteristics,* these heroic martyrs are "gathered" to their ancestors (18:23).[72]

Notice that imitation of Abraham functions largely in the negative, here: although some Judeans might imperil their Abrahamic standing by failing to live up to his example, there is no hint that gentiles might emulate Abraham and so become his "children." Josephus also holds that Israelites must follow Abraham's ways—best expressed in the Torah entrusted to Moses—or jeopardize their status as Abraham's children (*Ant.* 4:2–6; 5:107, 113).[73]

We have already mentioned the trope that Abraham might intercede for individual Judeans, likely inspired by Abraham's intercession for Sodom

72   *Chapter 2*

(Gen. 18:22–23). In that story, God initially considered *hiding* his intentions toward Sodom from Abraham (18:17), but allows Abraham to know about it beforehand, so "that he may charge his children and his household after him to keep the way of the LORD by doing righteousness and justice, *so that the LORD may bring about for Abraham what he promised him*" (18:17–19).[74] Sodom thus constitutes a warning to Abraham's own descendants; the implication is that if they also fail to act righteously, they will *not* receive the blessings God intends for them. It is also notable that Abraham's intercessions fail in Sodom's case—specifically, because not even ten righteous people could be found there. In the very tale which inspired later "intercession" traditions, a modicum of "worthiness" was neccesary, in order to benefit from Abraham's prayers.

Some subsequent "Abrahamic intercession" traditions incorporate this element. In *4 Ezra*, despite God's promise to "never forsake" Abraham's descendants (*4 Ezra* 3:15), he still requires obedience from them in order to *receive* his blessing (3:20–22).[75] Abraham's descendants, it seems, have a "double inheritance"—an "evil heart/root" from Adam and "the law" from Abraham (cf. 3:19). If Judeans follow the "wrong" ancestral example and do not produce good "fruit," then they can expect to be "delivered into the hands of your enemies" just as Jerusalem was (3:27). But not *all* Judean traditions held that failure to follow Abraham's example could jeopardize the assistance his children were entitled to.[76]

Summary: Abraham as Wall

Many Abraham traditions, then, could serve to divide Judeans from other races, stressing not only their *distinctiveness*, but also their *privilege* in the economy of God's blessing. As we have seen, Abraham could fulfill this function in several different ways: *(1) Appellation:* Judeans generally limited their understanding of who was a "descendant/child (σπερμα) of Abraham" to themselves. Therefore, this Abrahamic label was a mark of difference between them and others. Perhaps, some speculated, even the name "Hebrew" derived from Abraham. *(2) Ascriptive Descent:* Most gentile races, of course, claimed no connection to the patriarch. Judean sources acknowledged that a few other races might trace their descent to Abraham, but often emphasized that these others had not been chosen to receive the Abrahamic blessings. Meaningful Abrahamic descent was often restricted to Israelites. *(3) Subscriptive Descent:* Lastly, Abraham could be invoked as a sort of "argument in miniature" to hold fast to the Judean way of life—an exhortation to "be like Abraham." Judeans should hold fast to these traditions which (supposedly) stretched all the way back to the patriarch. Some went so far as to affirm that Abraham "kept the entire Torah even before it was

"The Rock from Which You Were Hewn"   73

revealed" (*m.Qiddushin* 82a 10), retroactively making him the "first Judean,"
as it were.

"A BLESSING TO THE NATIONS"—INCLUSIVIST
USES OF ABRAHAM

Abraham traditions did not *always* erect walls between Judeans and gentiles.
Sometimes, the patriarch was discussed in ways which suggested *connections* between them. Broadly, we will break these up into (1) traditions
about ascribed genealogical descent from Abraham, (2) legends constructing cultural connections *not* based on descent, and (3) subscriptive descent
traditions, often appealing to Abraham as the archetypal convert, suggesting
that gentiles might follow Abraham's example and so become his "spiritual
offspring."

Ascriptive Descent—Israel's Kinship to Other Abrahamic
Races

In Genesis, God tells Abram that his descendants will be as numberless as the
stars in the heavens of heaven, or the sand on the seashore (Gen. 15:5, 22:17).
God renames him "Abraham" (אברהם, "father of a multitude")[77] because he
will be "extremely fertile," the "ancestor of a multitude of races" (πατερα
πολλων εθνων, Gen 17:5–6). Abraham's son by Hagar becomes the father of
the "twelve [Ishmaelite] princes, according to their tribes (אמה/εθνη)" (Gen.
25:12–18; cf. 1 Chron. 1:28–31), just as Jacob later becomes the father of
the "twelve tribes (שבט/φυλας)" of Israelites. The Midianites descend from
Abraham's children by Keturah (Gen. 25:1–6; 1 Chron. 1:32–33), and the
Edomites descend from his grandson Esau (Gen. 36:8–9). The Ammonites
and Moabites can be traced back to Lot and his daughters, making them at
least distant cousins (Gen. 19:30–38).

References to Abraham's descendants from the Hebrew Bible create an
"ethnic genealogy"—a series of connections between races based upon their
purported descent from a shared ancestor (see figure 2.1). According to classicist Jonathan Hall, in the ancient world such genealogies speak to both the
degree of relatedness, and the *ranked* valuation of the "related" races.[78] Such
ethnic genealogies also suggested how members of these races "ought" to
treat each other, based upon these supposed genealogical connections. The
relationship of the Israelites and Edomites is an instructive example. Because
Esau and Jacob had been brothers, the nations of Edom and Israel are also
"brothers" (Num. 20:14; Amos 1:11; Obad. 1:10), and their treatment of each
other ought to include some sense of mutual obligation, or at least tolerance

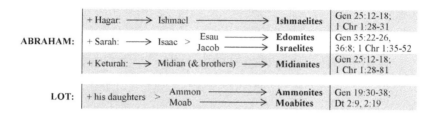

Figure 2.1 Abraham's Ethnic Genealogy (Bible). *Source*: Created by Andrew Benko.

(Dt. 2:4–5; Dt. 23:7). Their shared genealogical connection to Abraham, then, generated (and may have originally been generated *by*) a sense of relatedness between these two neighboring peoples.

Ethnic genealogies may change over time to describe the shifting relationships between races. Hall explains,

> If we accept the view that ethnicity is not a primordial given, but is instead repeatedly and actively structured through discursive strategies, then clearly myths of ethnic origins are among the very media through which such strategies operate. They function as cognitive artefacts which both circumscribe and actively structure corporate identity, so that whenever the relationships between groups change, then so do the accompanying genealogies. What enables us to trace this genealogical restructuring is precisely the appearance of mythical variants—that is, the occasional survival or earlier elements which coexist, albeit uncomfortably, alongside later elements.[79]

As an example of such restructuring, we might cite Sheba and Dedan, two descendants of Ham (Gen. 10:7), who later reappear as grandsons of Abraham (Gen 25:1–6).[80] Reconfigurations of genealogy could reflect shifts in relations between peoples and conversely could generate expectations upon how the "related" peoples should get along. Again, take the Edomites and Israelites. Their supposed relatedness engendered a sense of "family betrayal" during periods of conflict—elevating it beyond "sibling rivalry" to outright fratricide (Num. 20:15–21; Amos 1:11; Ps. 137:7). Turn-of-the-era Judeans explicitly identified the Idumeans of their own day as the biblical Edomites (e.g., *Ant.* 2.3–6).[81] Herod the Great built two monuments related to Abraham in Idumean territory (at Hebron and Mamre), likely hoping to remind his kingdom's Idumeans and Judeans of their shared Abrahamic heritage.[82] During the Judean Revolt, a sense of kinship (συγγενεια) seems to have partially motivated the Idumeans' disastrous "assistance" to a besieged Jerusalem (*War* 4.224–353).[83] We can see that the Pentateuchal traditions

"The Rock from Which You Were Hewn"

about Israel and Edom's "brotherhood" could be adapted, invoked, or challenged, as later events warranted.

Ethnic genealogies could be expanded, affirming novel connections between races by "grafting in" new branches of the ancestral family tree. Inspired both by biblical allusions to Abraham's "innumerable" descendants (Gen. 15:5, 22:17; Sir. 44:19) and by a shifting political landscape, Second Temple Judeans proposed various additions to Abraham's family tree. Some began to affirm that Abraham had not only taken Lot under his wing (cf. Gen. 13:1–12, 14:14–16), but formally *adopted* him as a son—a move which would bring Moabites and Ammonites more firmly into the ranks of Abrahamite races (*Ant.* 1.154, 205; *Jub.* 12:30).[84] The Septuagint Greek of 1 Chronicles 1 amends certain names among the descendants of Ishmael to suggest these included the founders of the Idumeans and Itureans, among others: Dumah (דומה) has become Idouma (Ιδουμα), and Jetur (יטור) becomes Iettour (Ιεττουρ).[85]

A common Second Temple tradition traces the Arabs to Ishmael (*Jub.* 20:12–13; Jos. *Ant.* 1.214).[86] Apollonius Molon, a Carian active in Rhodes in the first century BCE, relates a somewhat garbled version of this motif, demonstrating that some non-Judeans were aware of at least the broad outlines of the Abrahamic family tree—including both biblical and postbiblical elements:

> After taking two wives, one, a local (and) a relative, the other, an Egyptian (and) a slave, he had twelve sons by the Egyptian, who, departing for Arabia, divided up the land among themselves and were the first to rule as kings over the people of that country. As a result of this, (even) in our day there are twelve kings of the Arabians, having the same names as them (i.e., Abraham's sons). From his wife, he had one son whose name in Greek was Gelos (Laughter). Abraham died of old age. From Gelos (=Isaac) and his native wife there were born eleven sons and a twelfth, Joseph, and from him, in the third generation, Moses.[87] (Apollonius Molon, qtd. in Josephus)

Sometimes these proposed ethnic linkages went well beyond what was found in the Bible. The Judean historian Cleodemus Malchus greatly expands the account of the children of Katura (Keturah), whom Abraham instructed to move away and "found colonies" (*Ant.* 1.239). In a bit of highly creative etymology, several of Abraham's sons become the eponymous ancestors of far-flung races: Abraham's son Sures/Assuris (Σουρης/Ασσουρις) gives his name to Assyria (Ασσυρια), and his sons Apheras (Αφερας) and Japhras (Ιαφρας), who settled in Libya, give their names to the city of Aphra and to the entire country of Africa (Αφρικα)! Most incredibly, Malchus claims that the Greek hero Herakles (i.e., "Hercules") married Aphranes' daughter, making Abraham the great-great-grandfather of Sophon, the eponymous ancestor

76   *Chapter 2*

of a "barbarian" tribe of Numidia, the Sophakes (*Ant.* 1.239–41; cf. Clem. *Strom.* 5.113 and Eus. *PE* 12.13.40). Cleodemus Malchus himself was from North Africa (Libya). In describing Abraham's sons as military leaders in Africa, he portrays Abraham as a commanding general, perhaps justifying the Judean presence in Libya.[88]

The Maccabean literature proposes an even more imaginative addition to the family of Abraham: the Spartans! King Arius I of Sparta supposedly wrote to the high priest Onias I,[89] after making a surprising discovery in Sparta's records (table 2.4).

This discovery, likely wholly fictitious, supposedly kicked off a decades-long correspondence between the Spartans and Judeans. These letters were supposedly sent during a period of intense international diplomacy, when the fledgling Hasmonean state was cultivating ties to various nations.[90] The upshot of these documents is that the Spartans and Judeans share a common ancestor in Abraham—exactly the sort of "discovery" likely to aid the Hasmoneans as they forged ties with others. The Spartan letters capitalize upon the perceived authority of the written word (official archives, written letters, and public readings of the same) to "prove" that the Spartans and Judeans are related (see table 2.5).

Historically, it is unlikely that the Spartans would have actually proposed such a genealogical connection. Arius would not have needed kinship ties to initiate a political alliance, and for that matter, it is doubtful that a third-century Spartan would have known about of Israel's legends to invent one! A more plausible explanation is to regard the entire correspondence as a Judean fabrication—a matter of cultural creativity, assimilating Greeks into their own mythos. The letters functioned to elevate the status of the Judeans by the claimed connection with a respected Greek people, who were widely regarded as a yardstick for Hellenistic achievement. Simultaneously, the letters assert Israelite self-sufficiency (cf. *Ant.* 13.167 // 1 Macc. 12:8–9). The Judeans do not actually *need* anything from the Spartans, but only wish to

Table 2.4 The "Discovery" of the Spartan/Judean Connection

It has been found in writing concerning the Spartans and the Jews that they are brothers (Σπαρτιατων και Ιουδαιων ότι εισιν αδελφοι) and are of the family of Abraham (εκ γενους Αβρααμ). – 1 Maccabees 12:21 [NRSV]	We have come upon a certain document from which we have learned that the Jews and Lacedaemonians are of one race (ένος ειεν γενους Ιουδαιοι και Λακεδαιμονιοι) and are related by descent from Abraham (εκ της προς Αβρααμον οικειοτητος). It is right, therefore, that you as our brothers (αδελφους) should send to us to make known whatever you may wish... – Antiquities 12.225[i]

---

[i] Marcus: LCL.

"The Rock from Which You Were Hewn"
77

Table 2.5 The Spartan—Judean Documents

Document:	Significant Contents:	Source(s):
Archival record found Spartan archives	"It has been found in writing" that Spartans and Judeans are brothers (αδελφοι) of the family (γενους) of Abraham.	1 Macc 12:21
Letter 1 King Areus of Sparta to high priest Onias, ca. early third century	After the record of the Spartan/Judean connection rediscovered, Areus inquires after the Judeans' welfare, and offers to share resources: "Your livestock and your property belongs to us, and ours belongs to you."	1 Macc 12:19-23 // Ant. 12.225-27 (Jos. wrongly thinks it is Onias the III, not I.)
Archival record found Jerusalem archives	Letter 1, sent "in time past," rediscovered in Jerusalem's archives, prompting composition of Letter 2.	1 Macc 12:7
Letter 2 Jonathan Hyrcanus to the Spartans, ca. 144 B.C.E.	Calls Spartans "our brothers" (αδελφοι) and is meant to "renew our family ties (αδελφοτητα) and friendship with you." The Judeans do not need any assistance; but they remember their "brothers" in their prayers.	1 Macc 12:5-18 // Ant. 13.166-70
Archival record filed Spartan archives	"A copy of their words" (the Judean envoys'? Letter 2?) filed in Sparta's "public archives" to "record them."	1 Macc 14:23
Letter 3 Spartans to Simon, high priest, ca. 142 BCE	Grieved that Jonathan has died, the rulers of Sparta greet "the Judean people, our brothers" and the new High Priest Simon, and they "renew their friendship."	1 Macc 14:16-23 // Ant. 13.170
Archival record filed Jerusalem archives	Copy of Letter 3 on "bronze tablets"; with "a copy of this" (Letter 2, or the words of the Judean envoys?) appended	1 Macc 14:18, 23

renew the ties of friendship (1 Macc. 12.13–15). *2 Maccabees* implies that Jason of Cyrene knew this of genealogical/diplomatic tradition, when he appealed to the Spartans for help on account of their "kinship" (συγγενεια). Perhaps the notion was circulating among Judean intellectuals at least around the turn of the second century BCE (2 Macc. 5:8–9).[91] Across all sources, the relevant texts brim with ethnic and kinship terms, such as *ethnos* (εθνος), race/birth/family (γενος), kinship (συγγενεια), brothers (αδελφοι), brotherhood (αδελφοτητος), and relatedness (οικειοτητος).

From this survey of later traditions, we might synthesize an expanded ethnic "family tree" for Abraham, linking him to a larger number of races (see figure 2.2). It would seem that Second Temple Judeans were not content to stick to the *biblical* list of races Abraham founded. This demonstrates a limited willingness to extend a stake in Abraham to other races, perhaps fostering a sense of kinship or cooperation with them.

Cultural Connections—Abraham among the Nations

The ascription of shared descent to other races was not the only way Judeans used Abraham to suggest connections between themselves and others. After all, Abraham was more than the father of his own nation(s)—God promised that he would be a blessing to *other* nations (table 2.6)

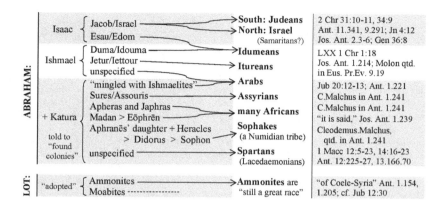

Figure 2.2 Abraham's Ethnic Genealogy (Expanded). *Source*: Created by Andrew Benko.

Table 2.6 The Nations Blessed in Abraham

Genesis 12:2-3	Genesis 18:18
I will make of you a great nation, and I will bless you, and make your name great, and you will be a blessing; I will bless those who bless you, and curse the one who curses you; and all the tribes (משפחת/φυλαι) of the earth will be blessed in you.	Abraham shall become a great and mighty nation, and all the nations (גוי/εθνη) of the earth will be blessed in him.

But how exactly are other races "blessed in Abraham?"[92] Although Genesis 12:2–3 itself was relatively neglected in Second Temple discussions of scripture,[93] a number of creative legends *did* elaborate upon Abraham's sojourns in other lands—and about his supposed contributions to these nations' culture, history, and achievements. Abraham was a natural subject for retrojecting Judean ethnic pride into the histories of other nations, because his wide travels brought him to so many different lands.[94] These tales might be viewed as attempts to speculate on how Abraham directly or indirectly "blessed the nations." They imply links between Abraham's own descendants, and the descendants of the peoples he "blessed" with his wisdom.

We have already alluded to the traditions passed down by Cleodemus Malchus, which not only posit Abraham as the *ancestor* of various peoples, but also imply that he cast a long *cultural* shadow across North Africa. He instructed Keturah's sons to "go out and found colonies" there, and his sons (and he himself?) were military heroes in Africa's distant past (*Ant.* 1.239–41; cf. Clem. *Strom.* 5.113 and Eus. *Pr. Ev.* 12.13.40).

"The Rock from Which You Were Hewn" — 79

Pseudo-Eupolemus expands the Genesis narratives of Abraham's travels.[95] The patriarch becomes a sort of "cultural pioneer," who mastered the wisdom of the Chaldeans and imported it to other countries. Not only did the patriarch teach the Phoenicians astrology—he was also a successful general, negotiator, and a favorite of the local ruler (Eus. *Praep.Ev.* 9.17.3–5). Upon migrating to Egypt, Abraham similarly introduced the Egyptian priests living in Heliopolis "both to astronomy and to the other sciences" (*Praep. Ev.* 9.17.18).[96] Artapanus echoes this claim and adds that Abraham tutored Pharaoh "Pharethothes" himself (qtd. in *Praep.Ev.* 9.18.1).[97] These Abraham traditions implicitly make the case that Judeans are culturally superior to both indigenous Egyptians and Egypt's ruling Greco-Macedonian elites.[98] It is likely that Pseudo-Eupolemus, Cleodemus Malchus, and Artapanus were all Judeans, as all three clearly utilize (but embellish) biblical accounts of the patriarch.[99] Margaret Williams argues that these accounts were likely written by and for *diaspora* Judeans, noting that they ignore the land of Canaan (latter-day Judea), but instead focus on Egypt, Libya, or Phoenicia—all areas densely populated by Judeans in the Hellenistic period.[100]

Many repeat the trope of an astrologically inclined Abraham. Josephus relates that it was the Chaldeans (among whom Abraham was raised), not the Egyptians, who originated astronomy. He depicts Abraham as the ideal sage, the proto-scientist who taught the Egyptians the science for which they would become famous (*Ant.* 1.67–68).[101] Philo adds that, unlike his Chaldean neighbors, Abraham realized that there were limits to what astrology alone could reveal (*Cher.* 1.4; *Abr.* 70).[102]

Judean legends of the patriarch's exploits seeped into gentile awareness, so that a few gentile sources echo these tales. Berossus, a fourth-century Babylonian historian, calls him "the just and great man versed in celestial lore who lived among the Chaldeans in the tenth generation after the flood" (*Ant.* 1.158). Hermippus of Smyrna, a scholar who spent his professional life at the Museum in Alexandria (3rd c. BCE), also wrote about Abraham. Drawing on stories circulating in Egyptian–Judean circles, he reports that the "most wonderful Abraham" (ὁ θαυμασιωτατος Αβραμος) had been an authority in astrology. Pagan authors from the Roman period, if they knew of Abraham at all, knew and admired him as an astrological expert. Vettius Valens, a well-known second-century CE authority on astrology, writes "The most wonderful Abramos has shown us about this position [regarding travel] in his books (εν τοις βιβλοις αυτου)." Abraham has become not only a *teacher* of astrology, but an author of books on the subject! Valens is citing Hermippus here, suggesting that the tradition of Abraham as an astrological author circulated in Alexandrian academic circles from the third century BCE. Such admiration by gentile authors demonstrates the success of diaspora Judeans in publicizing the achievements of their patriarch.[103]

80   *Chapter 2*

Another tradition linked Abraham with the city of Damascus. Nicolaus of Damascus (1st c. BCE), tutor to the children of Cleopatra and Marc Antony and later the court scribe of Herod the Great, seemingly knew a Damascene–Judean tradition that Abraham had once dwelt in Damascus.[104] He depicts him as a kind of "proto-Hellenistic monarch," invading Syria from Chaldea and capturing it with an army, then ruling from Damascus as a king.[105] He further reports that "the name of Abraham is still celebrated in the region of Damascus, and a village is pointed out that is called after him Abraham's Abode" (*Ant.* 1.160).[106] Pompeius Trogus, a Romanized Gaul writing in Rome around the turn of the era, also depicts Abraham as a kingly ruler of Damascus. Trogus describes Abraham as an indigenous ruler rather than an invader, citing a source which states "*Iudaeis origo Damascena*"—the Judeans originated in Damascus (*Hist. Phil.* 36:2.1). According to Trogus, after he died, his son "Israhel" (i.e., Israel) ruled Damascus after him (*Hist. Phil.* 36:2.3). Seemingly, what started as a local tradition in Damascus, likely among Judeans themselves, has become an established trope in Greco-Roman literature about the Judeans.[107]

We see, then, that Judeans could and did creatively expand upon tales of Abraham's travels among the nations to wonder how he might have left his mark upon far-flung cultures. These traditions imagined deep, historically grounded links between Judeans and others, and they bolstered the Judeans' sense of self-esteem in the international arena. Whether or not these accounts were originally meant to be taken literally (rather than as a form of playful fiction), *later* authors echo them at face value. And although they certainly originated among Judeans, gentile authors were becoming aware of these traditions by the first century c.e.

Subscriptive Descent—Abraham, "Father" of Converts

Even if one did not physically descend from Abraham, might one look to him as one's "ancestor" in another sense? Some discussions of the patriarch suggest those who subscribe to his example might call him "father." This possibility is heavily implied in some Second Temple traditions characterizing Abraham as the archetypal convert; the possibility is made explicit in a few sources.

Many accounts elaborated upon God's call to Abram to "go out from your land (γης) and your kindred (συγγενειας) and your father's house (οικου του πατρος σου) to the land I will show you" (Gen. 12:1), often characterizing this migration as a rejection of his own family's idolatry. The *Liber Antiquitatum Biblicarum* offers a colorful example of this trend. In this work, Pseudo-Philo anachronistically inserts Abraham into the story of the Tower of Babel (Gen. 11:1–9), which is also confused with the tale of the fiery furnace (Daniel 3).

"*The Rock from Which You Were Hewn*" 81

In this creative reworking of scripture, Abraham's refusal to add bricks to the tower is interpreted as a refusal to take part in idolatry, for which he is hurled into the fire (*L.A.B.* 6.1–18). Here, Abraham is presented as a heroic resister of idolatry: God observes, "When all those inhabiting the land were being led astray after their own devices, Abraham believed in me and was not led astray" (*L.A.B.* 23.5).

Jubilees retells Genesis 11:20–12:5, with particular emphasis on Abraham's rejection of the pagan environment of his upbringing. His great-grandfather Serug grew up in the idolatrous culture which proliferated after the flood: he worshiped idols and taught his son Nahor the astrology of the Chaldeans (*Jub.* 11:7–8), a demonic science given to humanity by the fallen Watchers (8:3). When Abraham speaks out against the idols which his father crafts, his father silences him, and his brothers are angry with him (*Jub.* 12:8). Eventually, he rises at night and burns his father's idol-crafting studio to the ground (12:12), after which he flees. Thus, Abraham breaks with three generations of idolatry and "demonic" astrology in his own family—Serug, Nahor, Terah (and a fourth generation, if you count his brothers). His family was deeply involved in this culture: Terah was an idolatrous priest, and Haran is sufficiently involved in the cult that he ran back into the burning temple to rescue his gods, dying in the attempt.[108]

Nickelsburg suggests that *Jubilees'* treatment of Abraham's rejection of the Chaldeans' religion could represent older traditions which predate the work. Both *Jubilees* and the *L.A.B.* relate that Abraham was involved with a fiery conflagration, somehow related to his rejection of idolatry. Philo's later discussion about Abraham's upbringing and migration have elements which resemble these; perhaps all three derive from common traditions.[109] According to Josephus, Abraham left Ur because his careful astronomical observations had allowed him to infer the existence of God, and this radical notion caused "the Chaldeans and all the other peoples in Mesopotamia" to rise up against him.[110] Abraham then decided to leave their land and settled in Canaan (*Ant.* 154–57). This parallels the account in *Jubilees*; raising the possibility of a shared source which underlies both.[111]

As discussed in chapter 1, conversion could be understood to *deracinate* individuals, in both senses of the word: (1) It "uprooted" them from the matrix of family, ancestral traditions, and occasionally even homeland, which made up race, and therefore (2) "de-racialized" converts to some extent, as they became abstracted from the very things which defined ethnicity. The Abraham traditions mentioned above prominently feature the hallmarks of race—descent, kinship, culture, worship, and territory—and how Abraham's connection to all these is stretched past the breaking point. But perhaps no other source so clearly conveys the idea of Abraham's ethnic shift as Philo.

82   *Chapter 2*

In his treatise *On Abraham*, Philo writes:

> Under the force of an oracle which bade him leave his country (πατριδα) and kinsfolk (συγγενειαν) and seek a new home . . . he hastened eagerly to obey. . . . Yet who else would be likely to be so firm and unmoved of purpose as not to yield and succumb to the charms of kinsfolk (συγγενων) and country (πατριδος)? The desire of these may be said to be born (συγγεγενηται) and grow with each of us and is a part of our nature as much as or even more than the parts which unite to make us whole. (*On Abraham* 63)[112]

The things Abraham walked away from—relatives, homeland, home—exert a powerful influence over us and might be thought of as an "inborn" part of our very nature. They are intrinsic to who we are—an almost irresistible aspect of identity. Nevertheless, Abraham left them behind, becoming a man without a people:

> And so, taking no thought for anything, either his fellow-clansmen (φυλετων), or wardsmen, or schoolmates, or comrades, or blood relations on father's or mother's side (των αφ' αίματος όσοι προς πατρος η μητρος), or country (πατριδος), or ancestral customs (αρχαιων εθων), or community of nurture or home life, all of them ties possessing a power to allure and attract which it is hard to throw off, he followed a free and unfettered impulse and departed with all speed. (*On Abraham* 67)[113]

Making the existential decision to cast off everything that once defined him, Abraham becomes the archetypal first convert, setting the pattern for future converts to be joined to God's people by devoting themselves wholly to God.[114]

Philo comes close to explicitly calling such changes as a shift in *race*. He says that Abraham, having been raised according to their astrological creed, "remained a Chaldean for a long time" before abandoning those practices (*Abr.*70)—indicating that he was *no longer* a Chaldean afterward. Others who followed Abraham's example underwent similar transformations. Like Abraham, Sarah "showed her wifely love by numberless proofs, by sharing with the severance from his kinsfolk (συγγενων), by bearing without hesitation the departure from her homeland (οικειας)" (*On Abraham* 245).[115] Sarah in turn praises Hagar,

> My handmaiden, outwardly a slave, but inwardly of free and noble race (ευγενη), proved and tested by me for many years from the day when she was first brought to my house, an Egyptian by birth (γενος), but a Hebrew by her rule of life (προαιρεσιν). (*On Abraham* 251)[116]

"The Rock from Which You Were Hewn" 83

By becoming like Abraham, they have been changed like Abraham.[117] Hagar was able to *choose* to be a Hebrew; her willing adherence to their way of life "outstripped ancestry."[118] In Philo's reckoning, all three have undergone a radical racial shift: Abraham and Sarah are no longer Chaldeans, and Hagar is no longer Egyptian. They have taken on new racial identities on account of their radical abandonment of familial ties, religious observance, and home. Philo describes proselytes as similarly leaving family, homeland, and idols, suggesting that they, too, experience a transformation like Abraham (*Virt.* 20.102–103; *Spec.Leg.* 1.52).

Later on, Christian sources would begin to explicitly ascribe "kinship" with Abraham to converts. Citing passages from Genesis, Paul affirms that "those who believe are descendants (σπερμα) of Abraham" (Gal. 3:7) who is the "father (πατηρ) of all who believe" (Rom. 4:11–12, 16–17). Paul is the first known author to explicitly redefine the "us" to whom Abraham belongs, proposing that one might become Abraham's seed *without* first becoming a Judean by conversion.[119] Recall that Abraham could be viewed as the "prototypical gentile convert," whose turn from idolatry and astrology toward God made him an ideal model for gentiles. Like Abraham, Paul's gentile audience has "turned" (επιστρεφω) to God from their former "slavery" to idols (Gal. 4:8–10; 1 Thess. 1:9). Paul's rejection of their former habit of "observing special days, months, seasons, and years" (Gal. 4:10) would line up nicely with traditions about Abraham's reflection upon calendrical/heavenly observations and his eventual rejection of astrology.[120] Even later Christians, like Justin Martyr, would take up Paul's assertion that those who share Abraham's faith are his children—the very children promised to Abraham in Genesis (*Dial.* 119).[121]

In John 8, during a heated exchange between Jesus and "the Judeans who had believed in him," descent from Abraham is contested and redefined. Jesus' opponents assert, "Abraham is our father," to which Jesus replies, "If you were Abraham's children, you would be doing the works Abraham did. But now you seek to kill me, a man who has told you the truth which I heard from God. Abraham didn't do this" (John 8:39–40). As with Paul, the meaning of Abraham's "paternity" is redefined through the lens of Christ-devotion. But notice *how* it is redefined: it is by "doing the works Abraham did." The logic of subscriptive descent is behind all this: those who subscribe to the patriarch's ways are his children, and those who fail to, are not. As Neyrey puts it: "A true son of Abraham will prove to be a chip off the old block by imitating his father, who offered hospitality to strangers from heaven; false sons 'try to kill me.'"[122]

In the (second century?) *Testament of Isaac,* God greets Abraham as he is brought to heaven, hailing him with the words: "Excellent is your lineage!" (*T.Isaac* 6.7). We learn *who* exactly comprises this lineage as the passage

84   *Chapter 2*

continues. Abraham, begging God's leniency for departed souls, haggles God down to a "bare minimum" necessary to win salvation, such as prayers of repentance (*T.Is.* 6.9–23). Only those who do the required acts will be given to Abraham "as a son in my kingdom" (6:18).[123] Because the *Testament of Isaac* contains traces of Christian revision, this affirmation may or may not belong to the earliest (Judean) layers of the text.[124]

Some rabbinic sources characterize Abraham as the father of proselytes, or otherwise relate his experience to theirs.[125] Proselytes repeated, for themselves, the "existential decision of Abraham."[126] As noted earlier, some rabbinic traditions affirmed that Abraham had been the first to know and keep Torah—which could imply his relatedness to all who keep Torah *today*: Karl Kuschel writes,

> If Abraham knew and observed the Torah in the form of the natural law, is he then not also the model for all those who, while not yet Jews, are spiritually close to Judaism? . . . In other words, if people give up all immoral actions, believe in God as the creator of all things and thus open themselves to the spirit and truth, then they are like Abraham; then they are Abraham's descendants.[127]

Jacob Neusner notes that within the Mishnah, "The proselyte has no past, no pre-Israelite family whatsoever, for he becomes fully Israel as a child of Abraham and Sarah; his offspring enter the community of Israel without any distinctions whatsoever" (cf. *Yev.* 22a).[128] We begin to encounter the idea that conduct may create a filial relationship with Abraham:

> For it is written, And [He will] show thee mercy and have compassion upon thee, [teaching that] whoever is merciful to his fellow-men is certainly of the children of our father Abraham, and whoever is not merciful to his fellow-men is certainly not of the children of our father Abraham. (*Besa* 32b)[129]

Summary: Abraham as Bridge

Some Abraham traditions, then, could serve to suggest connections between Judeans and other races. Abraham could not only stand as a "wall" to police identity boundaries but as a bridge, spanning the gap between "us" and "them." A few of these "inclusivist" uses of Abraham included: (1) *Ascriptive Descent:* Abrahamic ancestry could be expanded or extended beyond the groups named in the Hebrew Bible to suggest ethnic ties between races—constructing what Jonathan Hall calls "ethnic genealogies." (2) *Cultural Connections:* Many traditions creatively suggested the patriarch had made significant contributions to the cultures of other nations, implying at least some connection between their latter-day descendants and Judeans. Simultaneously, these

"The Rock from Which You Were Hewn" 85

tales allowed Judeans to understand themselves as an integral and honorable, part of the wider world. (3) *Subscriptive Descent:* Some traditions began to suggest that following Abraham could have an effect on a gentile's ethnic identity, or even allow them to be reckoned a "child of Abraham." Although several sources which apply this label to converts are relatively late (being either Christian or rabbinic), they may represent a willingness on the part of at least some earlier Judeans to attribute a degree of "constructed kinship" with Abraham to gentile proselytes.

CHAPTER CONCLUSIONS: ABRAHAM IN SECOND TEMPLE JUDAISM

From this survey, we can discern one final dimension to the ethnic significance of Abrahamic ancestry. While biological descent from Abraham carried a great deal of weight, shared blood was not the whole story. Judeans drew significant distinctions between themselves and other races understood to derive from Abraham *based on whether they inherited the promises and the covenant given to Abraham.* Whether or not a given son (and his descendants) received a blessing, and whether he explicitly inherited the covenant, defined some races as favored, holy, and in a sense "closer to Abraham" than others. Put bluntly: Isaac inherits—Ishmael (and the Ishmaelites) do not; Jacob inherits—Esau (and the Edomites) do not. Later Judeans commented extensively on the supposed differences between these sons (and the races they founded).[130] In other words, when it comes to Abraham, "inheritance"— inheritance of the promises, the covenant, and the land—is of racial significance, alongside biological descent.

This will become an important consideration in our reading of Luke's gospel in the coming chapters. There, we will encounter cases where, although someone's literal (biological) descent from Abraham is not questioned, they will nevertheless inherit no benefits from this connection (Luke 3:8; 13:28; 16:25).

"Look," the prophet cries, "to the rock from which you were hewn" (Isa. 51:1). But what is to build, with such a rock? We have seen that the son of Terah could serve two very different functions in Judean racial reasoning. Broadly speaking, these can be divided into "exclusivist" and "inclusivist" trajectories. Some used Abraham as a "wall" bolstering the boundary between Judeans and gentiles; the patriarch becomes a mark of distinction, "*our* (but not *their*) father." Other sources lay the Rock of Abraham horizontally, a "bridge" which connects us to them, a shared foundation upon which

86   *Chapter 2*

some sense of common identity might be built. Both of these trajectories were evident during the same periods—indeed, one can frequently discern traces of both "inclusivist" and "exclusivist" thought within the same text.

In Luke's day, then, both tendencies were in circulation and available for the author to consider. What, then, would Abraham signify in the Third Gospel? It is to this question that we turn our attention in the next chapter, beginning with the Infancy Narratives (Luke 1–2).

NOTES

1. For instances of "σπερμα Αβρααμ," as a stand-in for "Israelites/Jews," see Isa. 41:8, Ps. 105:6, 2 Chron. 20:7; *L.A.B.* 23:5; *Sir.* 44:21; 3 Macc. 6:2–3; 4 Macc. 18:1; *Pss.Sol.* 9:9; cf. *T.Lev.* 8:15. This usage hearkens back to God's promises to Abraham in Genesis: "So [numerous] will your seed be" (Gen. 15:5), "To your seed I will give this land" (12:7; 15:18), and "I will establish my covenant between me and you, and your seed through their generations as an everlasting covenant, to be your God, and your seeds' God after you" (17:7). God further clarifies that this everlasting covenant is conveyed not to *all* descendants of Abraham, but to *Isaac's* "seed" specifically (Gen. 17:19).

2. Luke uses the same phrase "a light for the nations" (φως εθνων) in Simeon's prophetic description of Jesus' future significance (Luke 2:32), as well as within Paul's description of his own ministry (Acts 13:47).

3. While this is surely true of Samaritans, who claimed to descend from several of the Northern Israelite tribes, this chapter will primarily focus on Abraham's function in *Judean* racializing discourse. I have made this choice both because of the relative paucity of extant Samaritan sources from the period, and because, despite Luke's interest in Samaritans, its general point of view is still much closer to Judean than Samaritan.

4. This is the folk etymology for his name in Genesis: "And you shall no longer be called Abram (אברם), but your name shall be Abraham (אברהם), for I make you the father (אב) of a multitude (המון) of nations (גוים)" (Gen. 17:5, *JPS* trans.). The wordplay here hinges on combining "father" (אב) with the first two letters of "multitude" (המ) to arrive at Abraham's name (*BDB*, 4).

5. E.g., Isa. 41:8; Ps. 105:6; *L.A.B.* 23:5, 3 Macc. 6:2, Sir. 44:21, *Pss.Sol.* 9:9.

6. Also relevant to "way of life," Abraham's personal ethics and character were understood to be exceptional (Gen. 17:1; Neh. 9:8; Isa. 41:8; 2 Chron. 20:7).

7. qtd. in Eus. *Praep. Ev.* 9.18.1. Margaret Williams, "Abraham in Contemporary Greek and Latin Authors," in *Abraham in Jewish and Early Christian Literature*, Sean A. Adams and Zanne Domoney-Lyttle, eds. (London: T&T Clark, 2019), 173 N 47.

8. "Εβραιοι. ούτως Ιουδαοι απο Αβρααμωνος ώς φησι Χαραξ." (qtd. in Stephanus Byzantius, *Lex. s.v. 'Εβραῖοι =GLAJJ*, Vol. 2, 335). Cf. Margaret Williams, "Abraham in Contemporary Greek and Latin Authors," in *Abraham in Jewish and*

Early Christian Literature, Sean A. Adams and Zanne Domoney-Lyttle, eds. (London: T&T Clark, 2019), 178.

9. This promise—that Abraham would become the father of *many* nations—begins to come true almost immediately in the narrative, as his son Ishmael becomes the father of a new race with twelve tribes (Gen. 17:20, 21:18, 25:12–18), and his grandson Esau becomes the father of the Edomites (Gen. 36:9–19); consider also the "two nations" in Rebekah's womb (Gen. 25:23). Implicitly, his children by his concubine Keturah also went on to found nations in "the east country" (Gen. 25:1–6).

10. This promise—that "all the nations of the world" shall be blessed in Abraham's descendants—seems to convey along the Isaac–Jacob line of descent only. It is said of Isaac's offspring in Gen. 26:4b, and of Jacob's offspring in 28:14b. It is *this* lineage specifically that will be a blessing to the nations.

11. Abraham narratives consistently concern ethnicity. God freely chose Abraham from among the nations (Gen. 12:1–2, Josh. 24:2–3, Neh. 9:7–8, Isa. 41:8–9), and as his descendants, the Israelites are therefore God's particular people (Exod. 6:3–8, Deut. 29:10–15). Indeed, "seed of Abraham" (σπερμα Αβρααμ) could function as another name for Israel, as a race (Isa. 41:8, Ps. 105:5). God's remembrance of Abraham could stand as assurance that God vindicates Israel in the sight of the nations (Exod. 2:23–25, 3:16–20, 2 Kings 13:23, Isa. 51:1–3, Mic. 7:18–20; or have mercy on Israel Exod. 32:11–14, Lev. 26:40–45). It seems that only the Abraham–Isaac–Jacob line inherits the covenant between God and Abraham, and with it the twin promises of descendants and land (Exod. 6:8, 32:13, Lev. 26:42, Deut. 1:8, Ps. 105:8–15 // 1 Chron. 16:13–22). However, Abraham's descendants will *not* possess the land if the people break the covenant, and other peoples might then defeat them (Lev. 32:11, Deut. 6:10–15, Deut. 30:19–20, Ezek. 33:23–29). This raises the issue of competition between races for limited goods (e.g., land): God's favor toward Abraham's descendants can sometimes involve God's relative *disfavor,* or the dispossession, of other peoples (Exod. 33:1–3, Deut. 6:10,18–19, 9:4–5, 2 Chron. 20:7, Ps. 47). In contrast with this "dispossession" motif is the less frequently repeated notion that the nations will be blessed in Abraham's descendants (Gen. 18:18, Gen. 12:3; 18:18; 22:18; Isa. 51:1–5).

12. "Second Temple period" here is a bit of convenient (but somewhat inaccurate) shorthand. In truth, the following discussion will mention a few documents whose composition *postdates* the destruction of the Temple, but which contain ideas relevant to Luke's general milieu.

13. Jon Douglas Levenson, *Inheriting Abraham: The Legacy of the Patriarch in Judaism, Christianity, and Islam* (Princeton, NJ: Princeton University Press, 2012), 3.

14. The LXX of 1 Chronicles slightly amends certain names among the descendants of Ishmael to suggest these included the founders of the Idumeans and Itureans, among others. Dumah (דומה) has become Ιδουμα, and Jetur (יטור) becomes Ιεττουρ. Cf. Matthew Thiessen, "Paul, the Animal Apocalypse, and Abraham's Gentile Seed," in *The Ways that Often Parted: Essays in Honor of Joel Marcus*, Lori Baron, Jill Hicks-Keeton, and Matthew Thiessen, eds. (Atlanta, GA: SBL, 2018), 65 FN 2.

88   *Chapter 2*

15. Thiessen, "Paul, the Animal Apocalypse, and Abraham's Gentile Seed," 65–66.

16. This is, for example, Josephus' interpretation of this multiplication of Abrahamic peoples. Josephus recounts God's promise that Abraham's "race (γενος) would swell into a multitude of nations (εθνη), with increasing wealth, nations whose race-founders (γεναρχαις) would be held in everlasting remembrance." (*Ant.* 1.235). To illustrate the partial fulfillment of this promise, Josephus rehearses the names of Abraham's sons and grandsons by his wife Keturah and relates that Abraham sent these out "to found colonies (αποικιων)" far and wide. Of these, some settled in Troglodytis, some in Arabia Felix, and some in Africa (*Ant.* 1.238–239).

17. Zanne Domoney-Lyttle states, "Sarah received that promise, and only a son born from her can receive Abraham's status and promises;" *in* "Abraham in the Hebrew Bible," in *Abraham in Jewish and Early Christian Literature*, Sean A. Adams and Zanne Domoney-Lyttle, eds. (London: T&T Clark, 2019), 27.

18. Zanne Domoney-Lyttle, "Abraham in the Hebrew Bible," 27.

19. Hall, *Ethnic Identity in Greek Antiquity,* 43. McEntire and Park discuss the phenomenon of ethnic fissure in Abraham's line, in "Biblical Genealogies," cf. 36–37.

20. *E.g.,* "The sons (υιοι) of Hagar, who seek for understanding on the earth, / the merchants of Merran and Teman, / the mythologizers and the searchers for understanding, / have not learned the path of wisdom, / nor remembered her paths" —*Baruch* 3:23; my trans.

21. Matthew Thiessen, "Paul, the Animal Apocalypse, and Abraham's Gentile Seed," 66.

22. Wintermute, *TOTP* v.2. For another translation, see James C. VanderKam, *Jubilees: A Commentary in Two Volumes*, ed. Crawford Sidnie White (Minneapolis, MN: Fortress, 2018), 527.

23. James C. VanderKam, *Jubilees: A Commentary,* 539. The same logic is evident in Philo's discussion of the sons of Abraham—all but Isaac "failed to show sound judgment and, as they reproduced nothing of their father's qualities, were excluded from home and denied any part in the grandeur of their noble birth" (*Virtues,* 207).

24. my trans.

25. trans. R. B. Wright, *TOTP* v. 2.

26. van der Lans calls this a "more exclusive" genealogy of Abraham. "Belonging to Abraham's Kin," 309.

27. "While Moses represented the first man, the earth-born (γηγενη), as father (πατερα) of all that were born up to the deluge, and Noah who with all his house alone survived that great destruction because of his justice and excellent character in other ways as the father of that new race of humanity (καινου γενους ανθρωπων) which would spring up afresh, the oracles speak of this august and precious threesome [Abraham, Isaac, and Jacob] as parent of one species (ειδους) of that race, which species is called 'royal' and 'priesthood' and 'holy nation' (εθνος) . . . called in the Hebrew tongue Israel." (Philo, *On Abraham* 12.56. Colson: LCL)

"*The Rock from Which You Were Hewn*" 89

28. The white/red/black cattle correspond to Shem/Japheth/Ham respectively, according to most scholars (Olson, *All Nations Shall Be Blessed,* 163). Nickelsburg argues against the majority, to identify Ham with the red bull and Japheth with the black (*1 Enoch,* 1.376). Tiller argues there is no way to know for sure, but if black continues to have the most negative connotations, the black bull is most likely Ham (*Commentary on the "Animal Apocalypse,"* 267).

29. cf. Leviticus 11:5–14, where most of these species are designated unclean.

30. Ishmael will be "a wild ass of a man—his hand against everyone and everyone's hand against him" (Gen. 16:12).

31. Esau's species is transparently pejorative; Judeans regarded swine as notoriously unclean animals (Lev. 11:7; Deut. 14:8). See Nickelsburg, *1 Enoch,* Hermeneia, 1.377; and Tiller, *Commentary on the "Animal Apocalypse,"* 274.

32. cf. "If a boar changes his hide and his bristles (and) makes (them) soft as wool, and if he brings forth horns upon his head like the horns of a stag or sheep; then I will observe fraternity with you. . . . And if the wolves make peace with lambs so as not to eat them or assault them, and if their hearts are (set) upon them to do good, then peace will be in my heart for you. 22 And if the lion becomes a friend of the ox, and if he is bound with him in a single yoke, and he plows with him and makes peace with him, then I will make peace with you" (*Jub.* 37: 20a, 21–23a [TOTP]). See also *T.Asher* 2:1–10, 3:1–5, which likens different categories of animals to those who embody certain behaviors.

33. As Matthew Thiessen puts it: "From Jacob's generation onward, one's ethnic identity is something inherited and immutable. It runs in the blood and cannot be overcome. Once a gentile, always a gentile. Once a Jew, always a Jew." Thiessen, "Paul, the Animal Apocalypse, and Abraham's Gentile Seed," 67–69.

34. Perhaps this suggests that they are capable of only disordered communal life (they are, after all, depicted as violent and cannibalistic), or that they are under the thrall of the wrong masters (the nephilim, rather than God).

35. Charles, *Commentary,* 2.248; Tiller, *Commentary on the "Animal Apocalypse,"* 36; Nickelsburg, *1 Enoch,* 1.395–396; see especially Olson, *All Nations Shall Be Blessed,* 136–143. Olson remarks: "The An. Apoc. appears to recognize an essential ethnic sameness running through all of the Greek kingdoms from Alexander to the Seleucids" (241). In scientific terms, they belong to a new "class" (avians rather than mammals). In the biblical taxonomy, they belong to a distinct division of living creatures: birds "fly above the earth" (Gen. 1:20), and beast animals move across the ground (1:24–25). The "beasts of the field" and "birds of the sky" are two separate classes of creatures in both texts (Gen. 1:30; *1 En.* 89:10a). Charles similarly remarks: "The new world-power—that of the Greeks, i.e., Graeco-Egyptian and Graeco-Syrian—is fittingly represented by a different order of the animal kingdom, namely, birds of prey" (2.248).

36. Throughout the remainder of the "Animal Apocalypse," the sheep are frequently victimized by the gentiles/wild beasts (89:13–21, 42, 55–57; 90:2–4, 11–13, 16) who prey upon them. cf. Nickelsburg, *1 Enoch* 1.377–378.

37. See below for more on the possible connotations of "wildness."

90   *Chapter 2*

38. Thiessen, "Paul, the Animal Apocalypse, and Abraham's Gentile Seed," 70–71.

39. Most of these authors would also include the descendants of the northern Israelite tribes in this favored sort of descent from Abraham. Whether *Samaritans* were so reckoned, however, was another question.

40. E.g. Micah 7:20; *Sir.* 44:20–23; *L.A.B.* 8:3.

41. E.g. Isa. 29:22–24, 41:8–10; Jer. 33:25–26; Mic. 7:20; *Add.Esth.* 13:15–17 [LXX]; *Sir.* 44:19–23; *Azariah and the 3 Jews* 1:12.

42. And God appeared to Abram, saying,

> To your seed I will give this land, and your name will be called Abraham, and Sarai, your wife, will be called Sarah. And I will give to you from her an everlasting seed, and I will establish my covenant with you. (*L.A.B.* 8:3 [trans. Harrington: *TOTP* v.2])

43. Several of God's promises to Abraham are rehearsed here:

> Remember ye, my sons, the LORD God of Abraham your father, and how I too worshipped Him and served Him in righteousness and in joy, that He might multiply you and increase your seed as the stars of heaven in multitude, and establish you on the earth as the plant of righteousness which will not be rooted out unto all the generations for ever. (*Jub.* 36.6); Wintermute: *TOTP*.

44. Wintermute: *TOTP*.

45. In another passage, Abraham essentially "adopts" Jacob as not only his grandson, but his *son* (*Jub* 19:16). He so closely identifies Jacob with himself that "he shall be in place of me" in future generations:

> And he [Abraham] said to her [Rebecca], "My daughter, guard my son Jacob because he will be in place of me upon the earth and for a blessing in the midst of the sons of men and a glory to all the seed of Shem because I know that the LORD will choose him for himself as a people who will rise up from all the nations which are upon the earth. (*Jub* 19:17-18).

46. Land (Gen. 12:7, 13:14–15, 17:7–8) and greatness/numerousness of progeny (Gen. 13:16, 15:5, 17:17).

47. Popović identifies only *Jubilees* 12:23 and 27:23, *Sirach* 44:21, and Philo, who "deals with Gen 12:3 in his characteristic manner"—which is to say, idiosyncratically, at least considering the other Judean sources. Popović, "Abraham and the Nations," 86–87; cf. van der Lans, "Belonging to Abraham's Kin," 307.

48. Popović, "Abraham and the Nations," 86.

49. Popović adds, the "universalistic tendency [in early Christian texts], to mention the inclusion of other nations in the blessings promised to Abraham, is largely absent from early Jewish texts that transmit Abraham traditions." Perhaps the theme of the blessing of the nations receives such scanty treatment in Judean sources because of the stereotypically negative role the nations play in most Judean apocalyptic or eschatological texts, as the archenemy of Israel ("Abraham and the Nations," 88–89, 102–103).

"The Rock from Which You Were Hewn" 91

50. Abraham is God's "friend" (Isa. 41:8, 2 Chron. 20:7; Philo *Abr.* 273; *Ap. Abr.* 10:5), in *Ap.Zeph*, all three patriarchs are greeted as "friends" in an eschatological vision (9:4). Abraham is "blameless" before God (Gen. 17:1); his heart is found "faithful" by God (Neh. 9:8).

51. For this last point, Siker cites 4 Macc. 13:17, *T.Lev.* 18:14, *T.Jud.* 25:1, *T.Ben.* 10:6, *T.Abr.* 10:1 (Siker, *Disinheriting the Jews: Abraham in Early Christian Controversy,* 25–26).

52. *Sibylline Oracles 2* has clearly passed through Christian hands: the "righteous" ones who intercede include "the virgin," seemingly a reference to Mary. But this is a Christian coloration of an earlier Judean tradition—that the righteous might intercede on behalf of departed souls. *4 Ezra,* by contrast, seems to be aware of such "intercession" traditions but flatly denies that there can be any intercession for the souls of the deceased after judgment (*4 Ezra* 7:102–115).

53. In one source, it is instead *Moses* who acts as "the advocate of Israel, who bent his knees day and night in prayer to make intercession for his people" (*Ass.Mos.* 11.17, 12.6).

54. cf. Ezek. 11:15.

55. cf. esp. *Jub.* 19:13–14. James C. Vanderkam, *Jubilees: A Commentary,* 594–595.

56. Vanderkam remarks: "'My son' may mean no more than that he is a descendant of Abraham, but the expression makes it sound as if the patriarch has adopted his grandson." Ibid., 596.

57. Further indications of Jacob's special lineal status abound: Although *all* Semitic races were thought to descend from the eponymous Shem, only Jacob shall be "the glory of the whole seed of Shem" (*Jub.* 19:17). And, although all living human beings could be understood to descend from Adam, Seth, Enos, Mahalalel, Enoch, and Noah, it is *Jacob* who is actually "worthy" of these ancestors, and it is in *his* line that the names of these ancestors are blessed (*Jub.* 19:24; cf. 22:12).

58. This special place for Jacob clearly fits *Jubilees'* overall tendency to stress the separation of the Judean people from others—not even other "Abrahamic" peoples are properly Abrahamic. Vanderkam argues that Jubilees was written during the Maccabean period, as a part of an effort to resist Hellenization—a likely context for such promotion of Judean distinctiveness. See also Susan Docherty, "Abraham in Rewritten Scripture," in *Abraham in Jewish and Early Christian Literature,* Sean A. Adams and Zanne Domoney-Lyttle, eds. (London: T&T Clark, 2019), 60–63.

59. Matthew P. Van Zile, "The Sons of Noah and the Sons of Abraham: Origins of the Noahide Law," *Journal of the Study of Judaism in the Persian, Hellenistic, and Roman Period* 48.3 (2017): 398.

60. See esp. Hosea, although this trope is nearly ubiquitous in the HB.

61. Géza G. Xeravits, "Abraham in the Old Testament Apocrypha," in *Abraham in Jewish and Early Christian Literature,* Sean A. Adams and Zanne Domoney-Lyttle, eds. (London: T&T Clark, 2019), 27.

62. Furthermore, the use of Abraham to reinforce endogamy stumbles when it comes to Esau—who, after all, was no less the product of endogamy than Isaac!

92   *Chapter 2*

63. Philo claims that Abraham kept "the divine Law and divine commands" during his own lifetime, tutored by "unwritten nature" to keep the (as-yet) "unwritten statute" (*Abr.* 275–276). Early rabbis affirmed that "Abraham kept the entire Torah even before it was revealed" (*m.Qiddushin* 82a:10; *b.Yoma* 28b:9). See also (Sir. 44:20; *Jub.* 6:19–23; 12:27; *2 Bar.* 57:1–2; CD 3:1–3). Siker, *Disinheriting the Jews*, 23, 205 N 51; van der Lans, "Belonging to Abrham's Kin," 310–311.

64. We might also add Josephus' description of Lot who was "benevolent to strangers" (περι τους ξενους φιλανθρωπος) when visited by the angelic visitors because "he had learned the lesson of Abraham's kindliness (χρηστοτητος)" toward the three angels who visited at the Oak of Mamre (*Ant.* 1.200).

65. Turid Karlsen Seim, "Abraham, Ancestor or Archetype? A Comparison of Abraham-Language in 4 Maccabees and Luke–Acts," in *Antiquity and Humanity: Essays on Ancient Religion and Philosophy*, Adela Yarbro Collins and Margaret M. Mitchell, eds. (Tübingen: Mohr Siebeck, 2001), 30.

66. "The significance of descent is not appropriate unless they show themselves to be Abrahamic. Typology takes over and leads a new vocabulary, and Abraham is significant as archetype rather than as ancestor." Ibid., 31.

67. van der Lans, "Belonging to Abraham's Kin," 310.

68. My trans.

69. Turid Seim notes, "Traditional terms of descent are converted to honorific awards of Abraham-like conduct . . . [creating] a varied set of Abrahamitic terms." "Abraham, Ancestor or Archetype?," 35.

70. Calling the young man "Abrahamic" "may indicate a move from kinship terms implying descent . . . to terms of characterization which primarily ascribe Abraham's qualities" (Ibid., 30).

71. Ibid., 41.

72. Ibid., 42.

73. Spilsbury, *The Image of the Jew in Flavius Josephus' Paraphrase of the Bible*, 217; van der Lans, "Belonging to Abraham's Kin," 312.

74. Emphasis added.

75. "Yet you did not take away their evil heart from them, so that your law might produce fruit in them. For the first Adam, burdened with an evil heart, transgressed and was overcome, as were also all who were descended from him. Thus the disease became permanent; the law was in the hearts of the people along with the evil root; but what was good departed, and the evil remained." —*4 Ezra* 3:20–22.

76. Pseudo-Philo strongly emphasizes that God gives Abraham the promise to bless his descendants because of *his own obedience*; once given, this promise is unshakable (*L.A.B.* 6.1–18; 18.5–6; 23.4–6; 32.1–4; 40.2.). Thus, the promise *was once* conditional in that it depended upon Abraham's original fidelity, but *is now* unconditional in the sense that his descendants' infidelity cannot overturn it (*L.A.B.* 30.7, 32.4).

77. *BDB*, 4.

78. Hall, *Ethnic Identity in Greek Antiquity*, 43.

79. Ibid., 41.

"The Rock from Which You Were Hewn" 93

80. McEntire and Park, "Ethnic Fissure and Fusion in Biblical Genealogies," 47.

81. Consider the LXX rendering of 1 Chronicles 1:30–31, where Ishmael's son Dumah (דומה) becomes Ἰδουμα (Idumea). Thiessen, "Paul, the Animal Apocalypse, and Abraham's Gentile Seed," 65, esp. FN 2.

82. The Cave of Machpelah, the traditional site of the burial of the Judean patriarchs (Gen. 23; 25:9; 49:30; 50:13); Mamre was a cultic site long linked with Abraham (Gen. 13:18). See P. Richardson, *Building Jewish in the Roman East* (Waco, TX: Baylor University Press, 2004), 279; and Richardson, *Herod: King of the Jews* (Columbia, SC: USC Press, 1996), 61–62.

83. A company of Idumeans is incensed that one party of the besieged Judeans will not "entrust to their kinsmen (συγγενεσι) the protection of the mother city (μητροπολεως)" and allow them to enter (Josephus, *War* 4.274), further describing themselves as "fellow-tribesmen" (ὁμοφυλων) who wish to defend their "common fatherland" (κοινης πατριδος) (*War* 4.276–281). When they finally manage to enter and fighting breaks out, many Judeans implore them by their common "kinship" (συγγενειαν) to spare them (4.311).

84. See also *Sifre Numbers* 42, which affirms that the Lord "lifted his face" (נשא פנים) to Lot, on account of his friend Abraham. Rosen-Zvi, "Pauline Traditions and the Rabbis: Three Case Studies," *HTR* 110:2 (2017): 189.

85. Thiessen, "Paul, the Animal Apocalypse, and Abraham's Gentile Seed," 65 FN 2.

86. Ibid., 66.

87. Molon in Eusebius' *Praep.Ev.* 9.19. Eusebius is quoting Polyhistor, who in turn is citing Molon. Translation from Williams, "Abraham in Contemporary Greek and Latin Authors," 170.

Seemingly neutral on the surface, Molon's account might be somewhat negative. He exaggerates the rapid reproduction of Abraham and his offspring, skipping a generation when attributing twelve children to Abraham by the unnamed Hagar, and another dozen to Gelos/Isaac. This may reflect Greco-Roman stereotypes on the Jews' *polyandria* and alarming reproductive rate. Molon's anti-Judean bias *is* attested in other sources; for example, his slander of Moses (Jos. *Apion* 2.145) and his comment that Judeans are "the most incapable of all barbarians, and are consequently the only people who have contributed no useful invention to civilization" (*Apion* 2:148). (These quotes after Thackeray: LCL, but modifying Thackeray's translation of αφευστατους). For discussion, see Williams, "Abraham in Contemporary Greek and Latin Authors," 170–172; and Jeffrey Siker, "Abraham in Graeco-Roman Paganism," *JSJiPHRP* 18.2 (1987): 192.

88. Williams, "Abraham in Contemporary Greek and Latin Authors," 175.

89. Josephus, for his part, mistakenly believes Arius wrote to Onias III, but the chronology would make little sense in this case.

90. The order of these documents is a bit convoluted in 1 Maccabees. They actually begin when Jonathan Hyrcanus sends a letter to the Spartans, to which is appended a supposedly *older* letter sent by the Arius, king of the Spartans (which itself refers to an *even older* record found within Sparta's archives). So, at least "on camera," it is really *Jonathan Hyrcanus* who initiates this series of letters, and his

94   *Chapter 2*

claim to have "found" Arius' letter (which would have been written a full century earlier) might be regarded with healthy suspicion.

91. Erich S. Gruen, *The Construct of Identity in Hellenistic Judaism* (Boston, MA: De Gruyter, 2016), 156, 164–166.

92. Both Genesis 12:3 and 18:18 promise that all the races of the earth shall be blessed *in Abraham himself,* unlike the variant of this tradition in Genesis 22:18 (where the nations of the earth will gain blessing "in your offspring [σπερμα])." The latter seems to make the descendants of Abraham (likely understood as the Israelites alone) the instrument of blessing, whereas for the earlier two, the blessing proceeds from Abraham directly.

93. Mladen Popović, "Abraham and the Nations," 86–97; cf. van der Lans, "Belonging to Abraham's Kin," 307.

94. Jared W. Ludlow, "Abraham in the Old Testament Pseudepigrapha: Friend of God and Father of Fathers," in *Abraham in Jewish and Early Christian Literature*, Sean A. Adams and Zanne Domoney-Lyttle, eds. (London: T&T Clark, 2019), 44–45.

95. Pseudo-Eupolemus is preserved in fragmentary form in Eusebius' *Preparation for the Gospel.*

96. Williams, "Abraham in Contemporary Greek and Latin Authors," 174; cf. also Ludlow, "Abraham in the Old Testament Pseudepigrapha," 44.

97. Ludlow, "Abraham in the Old Testament Pseudepigrapha," 44.

98. Williams, "Abraham in Contemporary Greek and Latin Authors," 173–174.

99. Gruen, *Heritage and Hellenism: The Reinvention of Jewish Tradition* (Berkeley, CA: University of California Press, 1998), 146–153; Williams, "Abraham in Contemporary Greek and Latin Authors," 173.

100. Williams, "Abraham in Contemporary Greek and Latin Authors," 173.

101. Abraham is cast in the model of the enlightened philosopher, bringing clarity and insight to a floundering people:

> For seeing that the Egyptians were addicted to a variety of different customs (εθεσι) and disparaged one another's practices (νομιμα) and were consequently at enmity with one another, Abraham conferred with each party and, exposing the arguments which they adduced in favour of their particular views, demonstrated that they were idle and contained nothing true. Thus, gaining their admiration at these meetings as a man of extreme sagacity, gifted not only with high intelligence but with power to convince his hearers on any subject which he undertook to teach, he introduced them to arithmetic and transmitted to them to the laws of astronomy. For before the coming of Abraham the Egyptians were ignorant of these sciences, which thus travelled from the Chaldeans into Egypt, whence they passed to the Greeks. (*Ant.* 1.166–168 [LCL])

For discussion, see Michael Avioz, "Abraham in Josephus' Writings," in *Abraham in Jewish and Early Christian Literature,* Sean A. Adams and Zanne Domoney-Lyttle, eds. (London: T&T Clark, 2019), 98, 107.

102. Ludlow, "Abraham in the Old Testament Pseudepigrapha," 44.

103. Williams, "Abraham in Contemporary Greek and Latin Authors," 168–169, 172–177.

104. Whether or not Nicolaus was himself a Judean is unknown, but certainly possible. What is sure is that he was, himself, thoroughly Hellenistic in outlook.

105. Williams, "Abraham in Contemporary Greek and Latin Authors," 169.

106. qtd. in Williams, "Abraham in Contemporary Greek and Latin Authors," 168–170.

107. Ibid., 177. On Trogus, see also Siker, "Abraham in Graeco-Roman Paganism," *JSJiPHRP* 18.2 (1987): 168–170, 176, 193.

108. Nickelsburg, "Abraham the Convert," 153–156.

109. Ibid., 157, 162–163.

110. Michael Avioz, "Abraham in Josephus' Writings," 107.

111. Nickelsburg, "Abraham the Convert," 161.

112. Colson: LCL.

113. Colson: LCL.

114. Gruen, "Philo and Jewish Ethnicity," 193; cf. Karl-Josef Kuschel, *Abraham: A Symbol of Hope for Jews, Christians, and Muslims* (London: SCM Press, 1995), 44; Kamudzandu, *Abraham Our Father: Paul and the Ancestors in Postcolonial Africa*, 84–87.

115. Colson: LCL.

116. Colson: LCL.

117. Josephus adds that Lot, too, emulated Abraham's example. Lot was "benevolent to strangers" because "he had learned the lesson of Abraham's kindliness" (*Ant.* 1.200).

118. Gruen, "Philo and Jewish Ethnicity," 187. Similarly, Philo characterizes Tamar as a foreigner (αλλοφυλος) from Syria, who has left behind her idols and entered a life of piety (*Virt.* 220–222).

119. Rosen-Zvi, "Pauline Traditions and the Rabbis: Three Case Studies," 169–194, 173.

120. Nickelsburg, "Abraham the Convert," 168–170.

121. Justin Martyr boldly asserts that Christians are Abraham's seed, and constitute a race in a sense unique from any identifiable earthly race (including ones which biologically descend from Abraham):

Therefore we [Christians] are not a people to be despised, nor a barbarous race, nor such as the Carian and Phrygian nations; but God has even chosen us, and "He has become manifest to those who asked not after Him.". . . For this is the nation which God of old promised to Abraham, when He declared that he would make him a father of many nations; not meaning, however, the Arabians, or Egyptians, or Idumæans, since Ishmael became the father of a mighty nation, and so did Esau; and there is now a great multitude of Ammonites. . . . God called Abraham with His voice by the like calling, telling him to quit the land wherein he dwelt. And He has called all of us by that voice, and we have left already the way of living in which we used to spend our days, passing our time in evil after the fashion of the other inhabitants of the earth; and along with Abraham we shall inherit the holy land, when we shall receive the inheritance for an endless eternity, being children of Abraham through the like faith. (Justin Martyr, *Trypho* 119 [Coxe: TAF 1]. cf. Skarsaune, "Ethnic Discourse in Early Christianity," 257–258. cf. Eusebius, *Eccl. Hist.* 1.4.12–14)

122. Neyrey, *The Gospel of John,* 161.

123. Stinespring: TOTP.

124. Stinespring, "Introduction to the Testament of Isaac," TOTP 1.904.

125. e.g., Suk. 49b; Yev. 22a; Mishpatim § 18; Mekhlita de-Rabbi Ishmael, Nezikin 18; Gen. R. 39.14, 43.

126. Karl-Josef Kuschel, *Abraham: A Symbol of Hope for Jews, Christians, and Muslims* (London: SCM Press, 1995), 49.

127. Ibid., 44.

128. Jacob Neusner, "Was Rabbinic Judaism Really 'Ethnic'?," *CBQ* 57.2 (1995): 281–305, 288 N 12. Neusner's understanding of "ethnicity" seems predicated upon *physical* (biological) descent as its *sine qua non*; under this definition of the construct, the rabbis' willingness to classify proselytes as Abraham's children "can only mean that Israel forms not an ethnic category, but a supernatural one" (289). For this project, we have already proposed a broader understanding of ancient race/ethnicity, not wholly dependent upon any one criterion, not even descent (see chapter 1). This more expansive understanding would modify the sense of Neusner's observation to: "this can only mean that Israel forms not (only) a biological ethnicity, but a supernatural one."

129. qtd. in Stewart Penwell, *Jesus the Samaritan: Ethnic Labelling in the Gospel of John* (Boston: Brill, 2019), 128 FN 158.

130. Consider the discussion in *Jubilees* on why Abraham favored Jacob, practically adopting him as "another son" while spurning his other grandchild, Esau.

Chapter 3

"Our Ancestor Abraham"

Abraham in the Infancy Narratives

He was the son (as was supposed) of Joseph, the son of Heli, the son of Matthat, the son of Levi, the son of Melchi, the son of Jannai, the son of Joseph . . .
. . . the son of Jacob, the son of Isaac, the son of Abraham, the son of Terah . . .
. . . the son of Enos, the son of Seth, the son of Adam, the son of God.

—Luke 3:23–24, 34, 38

In Luke Chapters 1–2 (and in the genealogy of 3:23–38), Luke presents his
account of Jesus' origins. The story is heavily seasoned with Abrahamic
flavors, peppered with both direct and indirect references to the patriarch.
So many mentions of the patriarch so early in the gospel show that Luke is
keenly interested in this central pillar of Judean ethnic identity.[1] The family of
Jesus is described as prototypical descendants of Abraham, who recognize in
the births of Jesus and John the fruition of God's promises to their founding
father. This child will enlighten even the gentiles (1:72–73; 2:32), fulfilling
God's promise: "In your descendants (σπερματι), all the races (εθνη) on earth
will be blessed" (Gen. 22:18 // Gen. 26:4).[2]

ABRAHAMIC STOCK: THE FAMILY OF
JESUS IN LUKE 1–2

After a brief dedicatory forward (Luke 1:1–4), Luke's gospel opens with a
description of the parents of John the Baptist:

[5]It came to pass during the days of Herod, King of Judea, that there was a
certain priest named Zechariah, of the priestly division of Abijah; and his wife
was from the daughters of Aaron, and her name was Elizabeth. [6]And they were
both righteous in God's eyes, walking blamelessly in all the commandments and

97

98   *Chapter 3*

regulations of the Lord. ⁷But they had no child, because Elizabeth was infertile, and both of them were getting on in years. (Luke 1:5–7)

As we saw in chapter 1, this introduction to Jesus' extended family is laden with racial markers, including ancestry (descent from Abijah and Aaron), common history (Israel's covenantal history), and shared distinctive culture ("walking in all the commandments and ordinances of the Lord").[3] Zechariah and Elizabeth both belong to priestly lines; and Elizabeth has fulfilled the customary expectation that the daughter of a priestly family will marry a priest.[4] In their piety and lineage, both are prototypical exemplars of Israelite identity.[5]

Elizabeth and Zechariah (Luke 1:5–7) are patterned after Sarah and Abraham in Genesis (Gen. 16:1, 18:11).[6] Scholars have noted numerous allusions to Abraham, in their story.[7] Even Luke's diction self-consciously echoes the Septuagint Greek version of the Genesis account [see table 3.1]. Their situation, as described in 1:7, echoes that of other various childless couples in Hebrew Scriptures, but the resemblance to Sarah and Abraham is particularly strong (Gen. 16:1; 18:11).[8] Even their names suggest that they are awaiting the consummation of the patriarch's hopes: Zechariah ("the Lord has remembered") and Elizabeth ("my God's oath") will see the promises to Abraham coming true before their very eyes (1:41–45, 54–55, 72–75).[9]

Allusions to ancestors are an evocative way of activating ethnic identity. This latter-day couple's words and actions are imbued with Abrahamic gravitas; we have, as it were, "Sarah and Abraham" before our eyes again, in this generation. It is not just that they are filled with the Holy Spirit (1:15, 41, 67)—they are *also* prototypical representatives of Abraham himself. Therefore, when they (and their son, John) invoke the more "inclusivist" trajectory of Abraham traditions (Luke 3:8; 1:73–79), they do so with the authority of quintessential insiders.[10] These are no "fringe" Israelites, would-be Judeans staking a claim on traditions that may or may not really belong to them— these are "Hebrews born of Hebrews," as Paul would say (cf. Phil. 3:4–6). And similarly to the way Paul invokes his own unimpeachable ethnic credentials to establish his authority to incorporate *others* into his ethnos (Gal. 1:13–16), Luke leverages this family's prototypicality to assert their authority to extend Abrahamic blessings to *non*-Judeans.

Mary and Joseph are prototypical Israelites as well. It is noted several times that Joseph is "of the house and lineage (πατριας) of David" (Luke 2:5, 1:27, 3:31); therefore, Jesus is as well (1:32, 1:69). Because Mary is Elizabeth's "relative" (συγγενης), she should also be numbered among the daughters of Aaron (1:7), hailing from priestly lineage. Jesus' parents are also beacons of Judean piety, in full observance of the laws, as was true of Zechariah and

"Our Ancestor Abraham"

Table 3.1   Abraham and Sarah, Zechariah and Elizabeth

Elizabeth and Zechariah, Luke 1—2	Sarah and Abraham, Genesis 12—21 [LXX]
…were righteous (δικαιοι) before (εναντιον) God, walking blamelessly (αμεμπτοι) in all the commandments of the Lord. - 1:6	I am God; be well-pleasing before (εναντιον) me, and be blameless (αμεμπτος) – 17.1 [and "righteousness," cf. 15:6, 18:19]
…had no child (τεκνον), because Elizabeth was barren (στειρα)… – 1:7a	And Sara was barren (στειρα), and had not had a child (ετεκνοποιει) – 11:30; cf. 15:1
…were both getting on in years (προβεβηκοτες εν ταις ημεραις αυτων).– 1:7b	…were old (πρεσβυτεροι), getting on in years (προβεβηκοτες ημερων) –18:11
Don't be afraid (μη φοβου), Zechariah – 1:13a	Don't be afraid (μη φοβου), Abram – 15:1
Your wife (ή γυνη σου) Elizabeth will bear a son for you (γεννησει υίον σοι), and you will call his name (και καλεσεις το ονομο αυτου) John. – 1:13b	Your wife (ή γυνη σου) Sarah will bear a son for you (τεξεται σοι υίον), and you will call his name (και καλεσεις το ονομο αυτου) Isaac. – 17:19
How will I know (κατα τι γνωσομαι)… -1:18	How will I know (κατα τι γνωσομαι)…? - 15:8
…this, for I am an old man (πρεσβυτης), and my wife is getting on in years (προβεβηκυια εν ταις ημεραις αυτης)? – 1:18b	Shall a child be born to a hundred-year-old, and shall Sarah, who is ninety, bear?" – Gen 17:17, cf.18:13

Elizabeth.[11] Both couples circumcise their sons on the eighth day (Luke 1:59, 2:21) as Abraham did for Isaac (Gen. 21:4)—and as God's covenant required of his descendants (Gen. 17:12–14).

Luke has described both couples, then, in thoroughly Abrahamic terms. Genesis has provided the "pigments" for Luke's portrait of these model Judeans. They amply demonstrate their Abrahamic identity—in terms straight out of God's mouth:

> [7]I will establish my covenant between you and your descendants (σπερματος) throughout their generations (γενεας) for an everlasting covenant, to be your God and your descendants' after you. . . . [9] And you shall keep my covenant, and your descendants (σπερμα) after you in their generations. [10]This is my covenant which you shall keep, between me and you and your offspring after throughout their generations: You will circumcise every male among you. (Gen. 17:7, 9–10 [LXX])

In Luke 1–2, these four certainly keep God's covenant "in their generation." In Genesis, God further said,

> For I have chosen [Abraham] that he may order his sons and his house (οικω) after him—and they will keep the ways of the Lord, to enact righteousness and justice, that the Lord may bring upon Abraham everything that he promised him. (Gen. 18:19)

100 *Chapter 3*

Here, it is *especially in keeping the covenant*, taught by Abraham to his "house" and those after him, that one is recognizable as Abraham's descendants, his σπερμα. In scrupulously keeping that covenant, Mary and Joseph, like Elizabeth and Zechariah, are marked as Abraham's own.[12] When the sons of these families—Jesus and John—eventually reimagine what it means to belong to Abraham, they do so as thoroughly vested sons of Abraham, themselves.

THE SONGS OF ELIZABETH AND MARY (LUKE 1:39–56)

After Gabriel tells Mary she will have a son, she visits her relative (συγγενης) Elizabeth, who is now six months pregnant (Luke 1:39–40). When Mary greets her, Elizabeth is filled with the Holy Spirit and cries out:

> [42b]Blessed are you among women, and blessed is the fruit of your womb (ὁ καρπος της κοιλιας σου)! [43]And why is this happening to me (και ποθεν μοι τουτο)—that the mother of my lord should come to me? [44]For behold, when the sound of your greeting came to my ears, the baby leapt (εσκιρτησεν) for joy in my womb (εν τη κοιλια)! [45]And happy is she who believed that there would be a fulfillment of the things spoken to her by the Lord. (Luke 1:42b–45)

John leaps for joy and greets his cousin Jesus, even within the womb.[13] This detail would have reminded alert listeners of two other babies, leaping within a *single* womb:

> [21]And Isaac prayed on behalf of Rebecca his wife because she was barren. And God listened, and Rebecca his wife conceived (*lit.* "received in her womb," ελαβεν εν γαστρι). [22]And because the children were leaping (εσκιρτων) in her [womb], she said, "If it is to be like this, why is this happening to me (ἱνα τι μοι τουτο)?" (Genesis 25:21–22 [LXX])

Like Rebecca, Elizabeth is στειρα, "barren" (Luke 1:7, Gen. 25:21) until God intervenes. Both tales involve babies "leaping" (σκιρταω).[14] Σκιρταω's semantic range is flexible enough to describe both John's joyful leaping and the distressing thrashing of Isaac and Esau.[15] Both feature the question "Why has this happened to me?" in response to fetuses kicking. Although Elizabeth more strongly resembles *Sarah*, Luke supplements this comparison with yet another of Israel's founding matriarchs.[16]

Mary responds with her famous exclamation, the *Magnificat* (or "Song of Mary," 1:46–56). For our purposes, we are most interested in her reference to

"Our Ancestor Abraham" 101

Abraham toward the end, but we might note briefly that the bulk of the hymn concerns the mercy God shows to the poor, the lowly, and the hungry—and God's concomitant humbling of the rich, the arrogant, and the rich (1:46–53). This situation of reversal plays out both in Mary's personal situation (1:46–49) and in the national situation of Judea generally (1:50–53). Raymond Brown and others have suggested that the hymns of Luke 1–2 fit the general sensibilities of Judean *Anawim* piety.[17] "Anawim," initially denoting the poor, eventually expanded its meaning to encompass those on the fringes of society in some way or another—the poor, but also widows, orphans, those with chronic illnesses or unclean spirits, the impure, and those who were social outcasts for other reasons.

Mary links her status-reversal with God's promises to Abraham:

[54]He has come to the aid of his servant (παιδος) Israel,
in remembrance of his mercy,
[55]just as he spoke to our ancestors (πατερες),
to Abraham and his descendants (σπερματι) forever." (Luke 1:54–55)

The hymn does not identify particular promises to Abraham; instead, Mary asserts that God is fulfilling the promises to Abraham in a general sense,[18] and she aligns Abraham with those of low degree: the "hungry" and "those of low estate," over and against the rich (πλουτουντας) and the powerful (δυναστας) (1:52–53).[19] According to Mary (and Luke), Abraham is implicated in the gospel's ethic of concern for the poor; he is conscripted as a spokesman for the *Anawim* piety of marginalized Israelites. Implicitly, there are some in Israel who are indicted by this word, just as there are implied to be *some* in this generation of Israel who do not "fear God" (1:50).

But how does *racial reasoning* inform this hymn? Mary does not connect Abrahamic promises to gentiles. When she mentions ethnicity directly, it is to rejoice that God "has come to the help of his child/servant (παιδος) Israel" (1:54), synonymous in her mind with Abraham's σπερματι (1:55). The end of her song echoes Isaiah 41:

[8]But you, my child (παις) Israel, whom I have chosen,
offspring of Abraham (σπερμα Αβρααμ) whom I loved:
[9]You whom I took from the ends of the earth
and I called you from its lookouts,
And told you, "You are my child (παις),
I have chosen you and not cast you off." (Isa. 41:8–9 [LXX])[20]

In this oracle, God's special love for Abraham stands surety for the blessings which God's own "child" (παις), Israel, will receive. Micah 7:20 similarly explains that God's faithfulness to the pledge made to Abraham is fulfilled in his faithfulness to

102   *Chapter 3*

"Jacob" (Israel), and Israelites of Micah's day can call Abraham and Jacob "our ancestors."[21] Mary similarly invokes Abraham in a fairly "exclusivist" way, applying the blessings promised to Abraham *to Judeans.*

However, the song does contain *hints* of expansive possibilities—especially because those Israelites whom God will bless are those on the margins, those overlooked by respectable Judean society. Even marginal Israelites, whom blue-blooded elites might sneer at as unable to produce a "proper pedigree" stretching back to those returning from exile, will be swept up in these blessings. As I will argue in my forthcoming book *Good Samaritans,* this includes Samaritans, whom most Judeans did not acknowledge as fellow Israelites.[22] We may also have an *indirect* mention of non-Israelites, as "those who fear [God]" in verse 50; recall that Luke employs the term "God-fearer" for gentiles associated with the synagogue.[23] Still, we must concede that the "Song of Mary" reflects a strong in-group bias. Mary's longed-for correction of unjust resource distribution reflects her sense of the entitlement of those *within* Israel, who are currently disenfranchised—it does not explicitly announce that those blessings will be distributed *beyond* Israel.

Mary's song of salvation, then, does not announce its full scope. To be sure, Luke *does* strongly affirm in-group love; but in-group love which exists as an end to itself is a distortion of Israel's privileged identity.[24] There is no explicit mention of the Spirit's involvement in Mary's song, unlike the exclamations of Elizabeth (1:41) and Zechariah (1:67), not to mention the preaching of their son John (1:15) or the ministry of Jesus (3:22). Kuecker argues that for Luke, it is the Holy Spirit that enables characters to turn toward the ethnic other. Perhaps, without such in-*spir*-ation, Mary's hymn lacks a more expansive racial horizon.[25]

THE SONG OF ZECHARIAH (LUKE 1:67–79)

After John is named, Zechariah prophesies, "filled with the Holy Spirit."[26] Although the song is occasioned by the birth of his own son, he *first* praises God for the "horn of salvation" being born in David's house (1:69)—that is, Jesus (1:27,32). This birth is the fulfilling of what was spoken through the mouths of the prophets (1:70):

> [71] Salvation from our enemies (εχθρων),
>   and from the hand of all who hate us,
>   [72] to show mercy to our fathers/ancestors (πατερων)
>   and to remember his holy covenant (μνησθηναι διαθηκης ἁγιας αυτου),
>   [73] the oath (ὁρκον) which he swore (ωμοσεν)

"Our Ancestor Abraham"   103

to our ancestor Abraham (Αβρααμ τον πατερα ἡμων), to grant us
[74] that we, being delivered from the hand of our enemies (εχθρων)
might worship him fearlessly
[75] in holiness and righteousness before him all our days. (Luke 1:71–75)

Racial factors are front-and-center, especially the repeated references to ancestry (including Israel's archetypal progenitor, Abraham). The cultural ingredients of race (history, tradition, way of life) are also represented, in references to worship and covenant. The "holy covenant" that God remembers (1:72b) stands in apposition to "the oath he swore to our father Abraham" (1:73); thus, we have the *Abrahamic* covenant in mind here, not the covenant God gave through Moses.[27]

At first blush, Abraham seems to serve a rather proscribed, ethnocentric function here: the content of the promise is that "we (Judeans) will be freed from our enemies" (εχθροι, vss. 71 and 74), who are by implication non-Judeans, that is, gentiles.[28] This would constitute a fairly exclusivist use of the patriarch—Abrahamic blessings are for "us," over and against "them." Indeed, some of Luke 1:72–73's biblical echoes express an antagonistic stance toward other races.[29] It seems that at least some of the scriptural intertexts for this passage suggest an "exclusivist" Abraham—the Abraham whose blessings are peculiarly the possession of Israel.

However, Luke 1:72–73 echoes other verses, and not all of them limit Abraham's blessings to ethnic Israel. Verse 1:73 closely mirrors God's pledge to Isaac in Genesis 26 (table 3.2)

The verbal parallel is clear, despite the shift in pronouns. The broader context of Genesis 26 asserts Abraham's significance to *all* peoples:

[3]Sojourn in this land, and I will be with you and I will bless you, for to you and your seed (σπερματι) I will give all this land, and I will establish my oath (ορκον) which I swore to your father Abraham (ωμοσα Αβρααμ τῳ πατρι σου). [4]And I will increase your offspring (σπερμα) like the stars of heaven, and I will give your offspring all these lands; and in your offspring (σπερματι) all the nations of the earth (παντα τα εθνη της γης) will be blessed. (Gen. 26:3–4)

Table 3.2   The Oath Sworn to Father Abraham

Luke 1:73	Genesis 26:3
...the oath (ὁρκον) which he swore (ὁν ωμοσα) to our father Abraham (προς Αβρααμ τον πατερα ἡμων)	... my oath (τον ὁρκον μου) which I swore (ὁν ωμοσα) to your father Abraham (τῳ Αβρααμ τῳ πατρι σου)

104   *Chapter 3*

We do see some elements of the "exclusivist" tendency in these verses: the blessings that God originally promised to Abraham's descendants are now pledged to "*your* (Isaac's) *sperma*," excluding the descendants of Abraham's other children (e.g., Ishmael). And the promise of "these lands" foreshadows the violent conquest of those lands from others.[30] But in the same breath, we hear a promise for all *ethnē*. Given that Luke's phraseology so closely mirrors Genesis 26:3, we should read Zechariah's song with the next verse's promise ringing in our ears: "In your descendants all the nations of the earth will be blessed" (Gen. 26:4 // Gen. 12:3).

God's promise to Isaac exemplifies why Abraham is such an ambiguous figure, in terms of ethnic reasoning: the source material for the Abraham traditions is itself ambivalent in its stance toward the ethnic other. One the one hand, God's promises to Abraham are for us-*but-not*-them, but they are somehow (and simultaneously) for us-*and*-them. Both of these impulses are at play in Luke's gospel, in the tension between the in-group love of one's own people (so evident in Mary's mention of Abraham, Luke 1:54–55), and the possibility that God might bless *other* peoples through the ethnic particularity of Abraham's children.

But what of those enemies Zechariah mentioned? We might be tempted to count the two references to "our enemies" (εχθροι) as evidence that Abraham really *does* appear in his exclusionary garb here—as the bouncer turning away the riff-raff at the velvet rope; the ancestor who makes Judeans unique, for whose sake God will displace or destroy others. After all, if the hymn's "we" is ethnically marked (as children of Abraham), then these "enemies" are also ethically marked (as gentiles).[31] But annihilation of enemies is not the only shape that "salvation" might take. True, violent destruction is *one* way to be "delivered the hands of one's enemies, free one to worship God without fear." This is certainly the disciples' kneejerk impulse when some Samaritans reject Jesus: "Do you want us to call fire to come down from heaven and consume them?" (Luke 9:53–54).[32] However, *peace* might free one from the fear of enemies, just as effectively. Even merely restraining the "hand" of one's enemies, twice mentioned (1:71–74), would do the trick. We might wonder, then, whether the "deliverance" that Jesus will bring from these enemies should be expected to take a violent/destructive form, or some other path. To put it another way—what sort of "salvation" from one's enemies is most "Christlike" (according to Luke's presentation of Christ)—peace, or annihilation? Jesus' exasperated rebuke of his disciples outside that Samaritan village (9:55) suggests that it is not the latter. After all, Zechariah prophesies that God will soon "guide our feet into the way of peace" (1:75). Although the specific in-group denoted by "our" is Judean, there is no peace unless both sides of a conflict cease hostilities. Peace *for* Israel means peace *between*

"*Our Ancestor Abraham*" 105

Israel and gentiles, "enemies" no longer. Although the words "salvation" or "redemption" frequently had military connotations in Judean writings, Luke methodically de-militarizes these terms with reference to Jesus' ministry.[33] Abraham, then, is invoked here as the Abraham-who-connects, whose blessings spill over to the gentiles, rather than as the Abraham-who-excludes, whose blessings spell destruction for the gentiles.

Having first praised God for the impending arrival of Jesus, the "horn of salvation" from the house of David, Zechariah returns to the situation at hand: the birth of his *own* son. Zechariah addresses the infant John directly, saying

> [76] And you also, child (παιδιον), will be called a prophet of the Most High;
> for you will go before the Lord to prepare his ways,
> [77] to give his people (λαῷ) knowledge of salvation,
> by the forgiveness of their sins. (Luke 1:76–77)

The conclusion of his prophesy returns to what is happening more broadly. John will play a role in this unfolding drama, but he will not be its sole player:

> [78] Through the tender mercy of our God,
> the dawn (ανατολη) from on high will break (επισκεψεται) upon us,
> [79] to shine upon those who sit in darkness and in the shadow of death
> (επιφανει τοις εν σκοτει και σκια θανατου καθημενοις),
> to guide our feet into the way of peace. (Luke 1:78–79)

For those who recognize the scriptural allusions, these verses imply that the scope of God's "salvation" encompasses *gentiles,* as well as Israel. The Bible occasionally described non-Israelites as those sitting in darkness or bondage. Consider two parallel oracles, from Isaiah (table 3.3).

These passages provide several points of contact with Luke 1:76–79. In them, we encounter a servant (παις),[34] whom God called even in the womb (Isa. 49:1–2, 5) and on whom God's Spirit rests (Isa. 42:1), who will be a "light to the nations," a light for those sitting "in darkness."[35] In both Isaiah and Zechariah's song, the salvation of Israel will sweep up the nations as well.[36] In Jesus, the "dawn from on high" will "shine on those who sit in darkness and the shadow of death" (1:78–79)—a category which will include gentiles, just as in Isaiah.[37] Isaiah 61 foresees "light" breaking through the darkness of both Israelites *and* gentiles (Isa. 61:1–3).[38] The Isaianic allusions in Zechariah's song, then, foretell a broad scope for God's impending salvation, which will spill beyond the bounds of Israel to reach the nations.

106   *Chapter 3*

Table 3.3   A "Light to the Nations" in Isaiah

[1] Jacob is <u>my servant</u> (παις); I will lay hold of him. Israel is my chosen; my soul has accepted him. I have placed my spirit upon him; he will bring forth judgment to the nations (εθνεσιν)... [4] He will blaze up (αναλαμψει) and not be crushed, until he has established judgment on the earth; and the nations (εθνη) hope in his name...
 	
    [6b] I have given you as a <u>covenant to the race</u> (γενους), as <u>a light to the nations</u> (φως εθνων); [7] to open the eyes of the blind, to bring out those bound in chains and to bring from prison <u>those sitting in darkness</u> (καθημενους εν σκοτει).
                    – Isaiah 42:1,5,6-7 [LXX]
	[5a] And now the Lord says, who formed me from the womb to be his servant (δουλον)... [6] It is a great thing for you (Heb.: "too small a thing for you") to be called <u>my servant</u> (παιδα) to raise up the tribes of Jacob, and to return the scattered (διασποραν) of Israel. Behold, I will make you <u>a light to the nations</u> (φως εθνων), that you may bring salvation to the ends of the earth.
	    [8b] I will give you [Israel] as a <u>covenant to the nations</u> (διαθηκην εθνων) to establish the earth, and to apportion the uninhabited inheritance, [9] saying to those in chains, "Come out," and to <u>those in darkness</u> (εν τω σκοτει), "Be seen!" – Isaiah 49:5-6,8-9 [LXX]

It is not just scriptural allusions which suggest gentiles here; Luke's *own* use of light/dark imagery also suggests an expansive referent for "those who sit in darkness" (1:79). Paul cites Isaiah when explaining that he is sent to both Judeans and gentiles: "For so the Lord commanded us, saying, 'I have established you as a light to the nations (φως εθνων), that you may bring salvation to the ends of the earth'" (Acts 13:47 // Isa. 49:6). Jesus told him,

> I have appeared to you for this: to appoint you as a servant and witness . . . rescuing you from the people (λαου) and from the races (εθνων) to whom I am sending you, in order to open their eyes, and so that they may turn from darkness (σκοτους) to light (φως). (Acts 26:16–18)

Paul would face dangers "from his people" (εκ του λαου), and "from gentiles" (των εθνων); furthermore, through Paul, Christ would "proclaim light (φως) to both [Israel] (τω λαω) and to the gentiles (τοις εθνεσι)" (Acts 26:23). No Lukan usages of φως, φωτιζω, or φωτεινος imply that this "light" is the exclusive property of ethnic Israel.[39]

In light of all this, those "in darkness" (1:79) must include both gentiles and Judeans. Zechariah prophetically foresees that the same light will enlighten both. These blessings, understood as the consummation of "the oath which he swore to our ancestor Abraham" (1:73), would deliver Judeans from the fear of their enemies (1:71,74)—possibly because those enemies are being transformed into brothers/sisters, by being brought out of the darkness.[40]

"Our Ancestor Abraham"   107

THE SONGS OF SIMEON AND ANNA (LUKE 2:25–38)

When Mary and Joseph bring their infant to the Temple "to do for him according to the custom of the law (κατα το ειθισμενον του νομου)"[41] they encounter a man named Simeon. He is "righteous" and "devout"—words frequently used to describe Abraham. The Holy Spirit had "revealed that he would not see death until he saw the Lord's Christ" (2:25–26). Upon spotting the child, Simeon snatches him up and exclaims:

[29] Master you are now dismissing your servant,
according to your word, in peace;
[30] For my eyes have seen your salvation
[31] which you have prepared before the face of all peoples (παντων των λαων)
[32] a light for revelation to the nations (φως εις αποκαλυψιν εθνων),
and the glory of your people (λαου) Israel. —Luke 2:29–32

Simeon, who has himself been "waiting for the consolation of Israel" (2:25), affirms that this child will do *more* than glorify Israel; he will be revealed to *all* peoples, a light to the *ethnē*. This again echoes the "light to the nations" passages in Isaiah (42:1–7; 49:5–9).[42] As Isaiah affirmed, it is "too small a thing" for this light to shine upon Israel alone; it will extend even to the nations—indeed, even to the ends of the earth (Isa. 49:6).[43] Verse 31 also echoes Isaiah 52:10, "The Lord has bared his holy arm before the eyes of all nations (גוים/εθνων), and all the ends of the earth shall see the salvation of our God."[44] In infancy hymns rife with scriptural allusion, Luke channels Second Isaiah's universal monotheism, and the eschatological vision of the ingathering of both Judeans and gentiles.[45] Presumably, this song causes Mary and Joseph to "marvel" not because of the assertion that Jesus will save Israel (this has already been revealed to them), but because he will even be a revelation to those *outside* of Israel.[46]

Nor will the child's effects upon Israel be unambiguously positive. Simeon tells Mary, "Behold, this one is appointed to the falling and rising of many in Israel; and to be a sign that is opposed, (and a sword will pierce your own soul also), so that the hearts of many may be revealed" (Luke 2:34–35). It seems that this messiah will elevate some and lower others, as Mary herself had already proclaimed (1:52). This raising-or-lowering has to do with what will be "revealed" (αποκαλυφθωσιν) in the hearts of "many," an act of revealing which exposes the inner thoughts of both gentiles and Judeans.[47] Αποκαλυψιν was just used two verses ago in reference to gentiles (2:32a); now it used with Judeans in view. It seems that, just as Jesus will be a light for revelation among the gentiles (2:32), so it will be in Israel (2:34). All hearts will be disclosed—including whether they oppose this sign. Although

108 *Chapter 3*

this thoroughly Judean messiah is indeed the glory *of* Israel, his coming does not augur good fortune for all *within* Israel—all who oppose him, even fellow Judeans, will "fall."[48]

There also happens to be a prophet in the Temple, Anna the daughter of Phanuel. She is of exemplary piety (1:37), and strikingly, she belongs to the tribe of Asher (1:36), one of the Northern tribes of Israel exiled by the Assyrians, seemingly lost to history. Sadly, we do not hear the *content* of her prophesy; this is not the last time Luke will pair male and female prophets, but only relate the direct speech of the man.[49] But her tribe alone speaks volumes; her presence may indicate the restoration of Israel, the regathering of the lost tribes as foretold in Isaiah.[50] In Simeon and Anna, we have paired prophets, representatives of Judah (Simeon) and Israel/Samaria (Anna, of the tribe of Asher). Proleptically, this pair anticipates a restored Israel, gathered together in the Temple and united by their recognition of Jesus.

We might also note that Anna observes not only *some* form of Yahwism, but *Judaism in particular.* Samaritans, who also claimed descent from the Northern tribes of Israel, had their own distinctive form of devotion to the God of Abraham. Their cult centered on Mt. Gerizim, rather than the temple in Jerusalem. But here Anna, of the tribe of Asher, seemingly does not worship God in this way. With her focus on the Temple and the centrality of Jerusalem, she represents exemplary observance of Yahwism *according to the customs of the Judeans.*[51] She may also represent, then, a model of conversion; although she is an Israelite of the tribe of Asher, she is functionally a "Judean" by observance, making her a "child of Abraham" twice over.

Both of these prophetic figures—Anna and Simeon—express a longing for the national salvation of Israel, a significant theme for Luke.[52] Of the two, only Simeon alludes to the involvement of gentiles in this hope—and only Simeon is expressly noted to be accompanied by the Holy Spirit. Simeon's song does, indeed, simultaneously express in-group love and out-group love, and it expresses the hope of blessings to be shared by both.[53] In Anna's case, there is no mention of the Spirit, and her message emphasizes her hopes for ethnic Israel—an expression of in-group bias, love within one's own ethnic group, with no explicit mention that these blessings will apply to non-Israelites. But then, as with Mary, Anna's exclamation is not explicitly prompted by the Holy Spirit, although this may be implied by her identity as a "prophet."[54] Both Zechariah and Simeon, who are explicitly filled with the Spirit (1:67, 2:27), predict that gentiles will be swept up into the salvation to come.

ABRAHAM IN THE GENEALOGY OF JESUS (LUKE 3:23–38)

We will examine Luke's genealogy of Jesus (3:23–38) in greater detail in chapter 5, which deals with the logic of descent/ancestry in Luke–Acts generally (beyond the figure of Abraham). Here, it suffices to note how *Abraham* features in this list. Reading Luke's genealogy alongside Matthew's may be instructive. Matthew makes Abraham the terminal ancestor of Jesus' lineage (Matt. 1:2), the first in sequence and one of only two ancestors whom Jesus is said to be "the son of" (alongside David, 1:1). This is further highlighted by the pattern of fourteen generations between Jesus, the Exile, David, and Abraham (1:17). Matthew's lineage most clearly highlights Jesus' Israelite and royal credentials, via Abraham and David, respectively. By contrast, for Luke, Abraham practically get lost within a list of seventy-seven names, stretching all the way back to Adam, and beyond him, to God.[55] Rhetorically, Luke's positioning the patriarch in the middle of a much longer list *relativizes the emphasis on Jesus' literal descent from Abraham*: it is important, but not all-important.

Furthermore, Luke is somewhat "tentative" about his genealogy for Jesus. He chooses his words carefully when introducing the list, noting that Jesus was "reckoned" (ενομιζετο) to be the son of Joseph, who was the son of Heli, the son of Matthat, the son of Levi, and so on (3:23).[56] So, while Jesus has the same claim to descend from Abraham as any Judean, this *particular* sequence of ancestors leading back to him may or may not represent his exact bloodline. (Indeed, given that the genealogy begins with Joseph, it *cannot* be precise). This is an idealized, notional genealogy for Jesus, the sort of genealogy that Jesus "would have," but the particulars may not matter.[57] The fact that this is only Jesus' "reckoned" genealogy downplays the significance of precisely traced biological descent from Abraham—and it might also call into question the importance of the sort of "default" descent from Abraham which *all* Judeans could claim (a sort of association with Abraham which the Baptist explicitly disparaged). John's statement at Luke 3:8, coupled with Abraham's relative lack of prominence in Jesus' genealogy (3:34), may have a "levelling effect," downplaying the importance of physical descent from Abraham—and potentially, placing Judeans and non-Judeans on equal footing before God.[58] After all, if this is "truly" Jesus' genealogy, then it is "true" on some level *other* than biology.

As discussed earlier, Jesus' connection with Abraham *is* strongly affirmed throughout Luke, but not through sequential lineage. Instead, as we saw, Jesus' relation to Abraham was claimed most emphatically in the Infancy

110   *Chapter 3*

Narratives—both because his immediate family is thoroughly "Abrahamic" in piety and righteousness, and because he is *himself* the culmination of Abrahamic promises. Beyond the sort of "default Judean" descent from Abraham affirmed in the list of 3:23–38 (which, obviously, all Judeans could claim), chapters one and two link him to Abraham by "family resemblance," showing us that his immediate relatives resemble the patriarch, "proving" the connection.

ABRAHAM IN THE INFANCY NARRATIVES: CONCLUSIONS

In his introductory chapters, Luke frames Jesus' story as a continuation of God's covenantal promises to Abraham.[59] Jesus' family of origins are themselves prototypical Israelites of exemplary piety and righteousness.[60] They descend from Abraham not only biologically, but by what we have called "subscriptive descent"—they are model heirs of the covenant of circumcision he passed down to his descendants (Luke 2:21, Gen. 17:10), and they scrupulously hold fast to the traditions of the ancestors.[61] Like the heroes of 4 Maccabees, they are true "sons/daughters of Abraham" not only biologically, but also because they have held fast to Abraham's ways.[62] Simeon and Elizabeth are even described in the same terms which described of Abraham and Sarah, in Genesis.

We might summarize several implications of the Infancy Narratives for Luke's ethnic reasoning: (1) *Resemblance to Abraham:* It was an ancient commonplace that children were expected to resemble their parents. Because Jesus' family is exemplarily "Abrahamic," Jesus (and John) are, as well. Thus, this whole family has credibility when they speak about Abraham, as they frequently do.[63] (2) *Prototypicality and boundary-policing:* Jesus and John, as "prototypical sons of Abraham," have more credibility when they comment upon who *else* might also be reckoned a child of Abraham. Their teachings on this remind us of Judean traditions about how Abraham adopted Lot because of his godliness (*Ant.* 1.154, 205; *Jub.* 12:30), or ruled on which of his sons would be his "sperma" (*Jub.* 19:16), sending others away (Gen. 21:14, *Ant.* 1.239).

In the songs of the Infancy Narrative, we find two general approaches regarding who will benefit from the ancestral blessings. (3) *In-group bias:* Mary and Anna express markedly "in-group" focused hopes; they both express the hope that Israel, understood as Abraham's offspring, will be blessed richly. In and of itself, this inwardly focused hope is not portrayed negatively. (4) *Out-group inclusion:* Simeon and Zechariah enrich this expectation with the understanding that gentiles will be blessed alongside Israel.

"Our Ancestor Abraham" 111

In the words of David Smith, these two display a "non-competitive dual concern for Israel's salvation and the generous extension of that salvation to the world."[64] Such outwardly flowing blessings are *also* the fulfillment of the promises to Abraham (Gen. 12:3, 26:4). Both the exclusivist and inclusivist tendencies in these hymns echo trends in Second Temple traditions, although the former *are* more widely attested in the literature. Luke's gospel does not condemn nor favor either position; both are correct, but either expectation (Abrahamic blessings for Israel, or Abrahamic blessings for the nations) would be deficient without the other.

NOTES

1. Siker comments, "By associating the beginning of his gospel story with Abraham, Luke puts down the deepest roots he can and claims Abraham as a primary link to God's covenant promises with Israel." Jeffrey Siker, *Disinheriting the Jews: Abraham in Early Christian Controversy* (Louisville, KY: Westminster John Knox, 1991), 107–108.

2. cf. Genesis 12:3.

3. See Chapter 1; cf. Aaron Kuecker, *The Spirit and the Other*, 53.

4. Alen Culpepper, *Luke* NIB (Nashville, TN: Abingdon, 1995), 45; David Smith, "Luke, the Jews, and the Politics of Early Christian Identity," PhD Dissertation (Durham, NC: Duke University, 2018), 72.

5. Kuecker, *The Spirit and the Other,* 54–56; Smith, "Luke, the Jews, and the Politics," 73, recently published as *Luke and the Jewish Other: Politics of Identity in the Third Gospel* (Abingdon: Routledge, 2024).

6. Siker, *Disinheriting*, 106; Kuecker, *The Spirit and the Other*, 54

7. Francis Bovon, *Luke,* Hermeneia Commentary (Philadelphia, PA: Fortress, 2002), 1.34; Kuecker, *The Spirit and the Other,* 55 FN 17; cf. Joel Green, *The Gospel of Luke*, New International Commentary on the New Testament, 1997, 53–33; Culpepper, *Luke*, 47.

8. Other "childless couple" allusions, albeit with fewer points of similarity than Sarah and Abraham, include: Manoah and his wife (Judg. 13:2), Hannah and Elkanah (1 Sam. 1:1–2), Rachel and Jacob (Gen. 30:1), and Rebecca and Isaac (Gen. 25:21). *See* Bovon, *Luke* 1.34 FN 24; Culpepper, *Luke*, 45.

9. Culpepper, *Luke*, 45.

10. As we will see below, Luke 1:79 resonates with Isaianic oracles identifying the *gentiles* as "those who dwell in darkness" or the "shadow of death" (Isa. 42:1–7, 49:5–9, 60:1–3). Paired with the invocation of the promises to Abraham in 1:73–75, we likely hear a ghostly echo of God's promise that "the nations/gentiles" would be blessed in him.

11. e.g., customs (1:9, 2:27, 2:42), law (1:6, 22; 2:22–24, 27, 39), pilgrimage and temple piety (2:41–42); circumcision (1:59, 2:21); see table 1.2 from chapter 1.

112　　　　　　　　　　　　　　　　*Chapter 3*

12. In their exacting adherence to Judaism, Jesus' family resembles the "Abrahamic" heroes of 4 Macc; see discussion below.

13. cf. the *Targum* to Ps 68:27: "Praise God, you embryos in the womb, you seed of Israel!" and *Odes Sol.* 28:2 "my heart continually refreshes itself and leaps (σκιρταω) for joy, like the babe who leaps for joy in his mother's womb" (trans. James Charlesworth, *Odes of Solomon* (Oxford: Clarendon, 1973), 108. Cited by Sahlin, *Messias,* 143 N 1.

14. Fitzmeyer, *The Gospel According to Luke,* 1:358; Bock, *Luke* 1:134–135; cit. in Nickolas Fox, *The Hermeneutics of Social Identity in Luke–Acts* (Eugene, OR: Pickwick, 2021), 97.

15. This Greek word can refer to the kicking of a child in the womb, but can encompass both a more playful sense ("skip," "frolic," "be frisky") such as a young animal's innocent joy in physical movement, and a more destructive sense ("thrash about," "be unruly"). *Cambridge Greek Lexicon,* "σκιρταω;" cf. LSJ and *BDAG,* "σκιρταω."

16. For the connection between this episode and Rebecca in Genesis 25, see Fitzmyer, *Luke* 1:358; Bock, *Luke,* 1:134–135.

17. Raymond Brown, *Birth of the Messiah,* 350–355; and Brown, "Gospel Infancy Narrative Research from 1976 to 1986: Part II (Luke)," 660–680. Fitzmeyer, *The Gospel According to Luke I–IX,* is in general agreement with Brown on this; cf. Siker, *Disinheriting the Jews,* 104.

18. Michael Fuller notes that the hymn carefully avoids any mention of the promise of the land—the primary emphasis of the Abrahamic covenant in the Hebrew Bible—but focuses mainly upon the covenant in terms of descendants. Fuller, *The Restoration of Israel:Israel's Re-Gathering and the Fate of the Nations in Early Jewish Literature and Luke–Acts* (Berlin: De Gruyter, 2012), 205.

19. Siker, *Disinheriting,* 105–106; Smith, "Luke, the Jews, and the Politics," 76.

20. My translation. This allusion pointed by Brown, *Birth,* 359; Siker, *Disinheriting,* 105, *et alia.*

21. Micah 7:20: "You will be faithful to Jacob, and show love to Abraham, as you pledged on oath to our ancestors in days long ago." Cit.by Fox, *The Hermeneutics of Social Identity in Luke–Acts,* 102.

22. *Good Samaritans: Samaritan Ethnicity and Evangelism in Luke–Acts,* with Stewart Penwell, forthcoming.

23. "He has mercy from generation to generation on those who fear him [i.e., God, vs. 46]."

"Και το ελεος αυτου εις γενεας και γενεας τοις φοβουμενοις αυτον [θεον]."—Luke 1:50.

Cornelius, "a devout man who feared God (φοβουμενος τον θεον)"—Acts 10:2

"Cornelius, a centurion, an upright man and god-fearing (φοβουμενος τον θεον)"—Acts 10:22.

"In every nation whoever fears him (i.e., God, vs. 34) [ὁ φοβουμενος αυτον] is acceptable."—10:35.

"Men, Israelites and god-fearers (οἱ φοβουμενοι τον θεον) . . ." Acts 13:16.

"Sons of the race of Abraham, and those among you who fear God (φοβουμενοι τον θεον) . . ."—13:26.

Note that Luke gradually replaces the expression with "those who reverence God" [οἱ σεβομενοι τον θεον], seemingly in reference to the same group; cf. Acts 13:43, 50; 16:14; 17:4, 17; 18:7. Mary's assertion (Luke 1:50) is also echoes of one of the Jerusalem Council's rationales for incorporating uncircumcised gentiles: "For Moses, from generations past (γενεας), has had those who proclaim him in the synagogues in every city, being read aloud every sabbath" (Acts 15:21). For discussion of the phrases φοβουμενοι τον θεον and σεβομενοι τον θεον, whether used in reference to interested gentiles (e.g., a synagogue inscription in Aphrodias) or to "god-fearing" Jews (e.g., a synagogue inscription in Miletus), see Judith Lieu, "The Race of the God-Fearers," 484–97. Because the terms were also used of Jews, we cannot be sure that the isolated use of this phrase in the midst of Mary's very in-group focused song actually refers to gentiles.

24. For examples, see Luke 3–4. cf. Aaron Kuecker, *The Spirit and the Other: Social Identity, Ethnicity, and Intergroup Reconciliation in Luke–Acts* (New York: Bloomsbury, 2011), 60.

25. Kuecker may overstate the contrast, however, in claiming Mary's song is the *antithesis* of Luke's vision (*The Spirit and the Other*, 56–61). This is hardly the case; David Smith points out that the song of Mary *shares* the theme of judgment for the proud with Zechariah's explicitly Spirit-fueled song. She shares a passion for a sort of judgment for Israel seen in the Maccabees and the zealots of her own day—judgment on those *within Israel* who are unjust and unrepentant. This sort of "national judgement" would not mean the condemnation of the nation, but rather its reform (Smith, "Luke, the Jews, and the Politics," 78–79).

26. Recall that for Luke, the Spirit is frequently the agent/instrument of the turn toward the ethnic other. Kuecker, *The Spirit and the Other*, 62.

27. Jeffrey Siker notes that Luke anchors this prophesy in numerous passages mentioning God's covenant with Abraham, effectively making the claim that what is taking place *now* (in Jesus, and John) is the fulfillment of what was promised *then* (to Abraham). Siker, *Disinheriting*, 106.

28. More concretely, at least in the geographical context of this tale, these gentile "enemies" are Romans and their political collaborators. In keeping with Luke's overall tendency to avoid painting Romans in a negative light, he avoids naming them as such.

29. For example, in response to the Egyptians' abuse, God "remembered" his covenant with Abraham and freed the Hebrews (Exod. 2:23–25). Micah prophesies that "You will give truth to Jacob, mercy (ελεον) to Abraham, just as you swore to our ancestors (ωμοσας τοις πατρασιν) in former days" (Mic 7:20 [LXX]), but that the nations (εθνη) will be ashamed and lick dust like serpents (Mic 7:16–17). Psalm 105 recounts that when God "remembered (εμνησθη) his eternal covenant (διαθηκης), a word which he commanded to a thousand generations; which he pledged to Abraham, and his oath (ορκου) to Isaac" (105:8–9 [LXX]), two things happened: God brought Israel out of slavery in Egypt (Ps. 105:16–38), and gave

114   *Chapter 3*

them "the land of the gentiles" (χωρας εθνων), Canaan (105:11, 44). See also Jer 11:4–5.

30. As narrated in Joshua and Judges, and retold in numerous examples of the "rewritten scripture" genre.

31. Indeed, Jesus does number Romans (and their legions) among these "enemies," later on (Luke 19:43). cf. Fuller, *The Restoration of Israel*, 205.

32. Remember, of course, that Jesus does not greet this proposed bombardment with hearty approval—he "turned and rebuked" them (Luke 9:55).

33. Fuller, *The Restoration of Israel*, 205.

34. In Isaiah's shifting usage, "child/servant" (עבד/παις) may stand for Israel (44:1–2; 43:1–10; 45:4; 49:3; 42:1 [LXX]), the prophet himself (49:6; cf. 50:4–11), or an ambiguous figure who cannot be decisively identified (52:13–15). Similarly, across the Infancy Narrative, παις may describe Mary (1:48a), Israel (1:54), John (1:59, 76, 80), David (1:69), and Jesus (2:27, 40).

35. In Isaiah 49:8, עם לברית ("covenant people," "people of covenants") has been translated in the plural, becoming διαθηκην εθνων ("covenant to/for the nations"). This suggests a more ethnically expansive understanding of the servant's significance, for a later Hellenistic Judean translator. (In Isaiah 42:6, the same Hebrew phrase has been rendered "covenant to/for the γενους," retaining the singularity of עם.)

36. The Hebrew reading of Isaiah 49:6, attested in both the MT and Dead Sea Scrolls, better captures the widening of the horizon of this light than the Septuagint version. God tells the servant, "*It is too small a thing* that you should be my servant to raise up the tribes of Jacob and to restore the survivors of Israel; I will give you as a light to the nations." cf. Isa. 49:6 in the *BHS* and *The Dead Sea Scrolls Bible,* edited by Abegg, Flint, and Ulrich, 352.

37. For further discussion see Kuecker, *Spirit*, 63–64.

38. "Arise, shine, for your light (אור/φως) has come, and the glory of the LORD has risen upon you. For darkness (חשך/σκοτος) covers the earth, and thick darkness (ערפל/γνοφος) covers the peoples (אמים/εθνη); but the LORD will arise upon you, and his glory will appear over you. Nations (גוים/εθνη) shall come to your light (אור/φωτι), and kings to the brightness (נגה/λαμπροτητι) of your dawn."—Isaiah 60:1–3. Translation is by Joel Green from the Hebrew, but I have removed his italics, and added the Hebrew/Greek of key terms (Green, *Conversion in Luke–Acts,* 100).

39. Φως/φωτιζω/φωτεινος: Luke 2:32; 8:16; 11:33–36; 12:3; 16:8; 22:56; Acts 9:3; 13:47; 16:29; 22:6–11; 26:13, 18, 23. Kuecker, *The Spirit and the Other*, 65 (cf. FN 69). For Joel Green's survey of light/dark imagery in Luke–Acts, see Green, *Conversion in Luke–Acts*, 100–101 (cf. FN 23).

40. Mark Kinzer notes that the double promise that Israel would be "saved from the hand of all who hate us" (1:71, 74) stands in glaring contrast to Judeans' actual historical circumstances at the time of Luke's composition. The disastrous destruction of the Jewish War stands in stark relief to Zechariah's prophesy that God would "save us from our enemies (εχθροι)" (1:71). This promise has not yet been fulfilled, in Luke's day. Indeed, Jesus' own prophetic lament over Jerusalem seems to predict the exact opposite outcome: "Would that you, even you, had known the things that make for peace! But now they are hidden from your eyes. For the days are coming when

your enemies (εχθροι) will hem you in on every side. . . ." (Luke 19:42–43), a clear reference to the siege of Jerusalem. A number of shared words (οφθαλμος, εχθρος, ειρηνη) further suggest that Jesus' words ought to be read alongside the Song of Zechariah, and the Song of Simeon. Kinzer posits that the "falling and rising of many in Israel" (Luke 2:34) may describe a *temporal* sequence: Israel will first "fall" (the Jewish War, specifically the destruction of the Temple and devastation of Jerusalem), but will later "rise"—indeed, Jerusalem itself will, in a sense, participate in Jesus' resurrection. Mark Kinzer, *Jerusalem Crucified, Jerusalem Risen: The Resurrected Messiah, the Jewish People, and the Land of Promise* (Eugene, OR: Wipf and Stock, 2018), 27–34.

41. Why does Luke say "the days of *their* cleansing" (implying that both Mary and Jesus must be purified), when Leviticus only requires the *mother* to be purified after "the days of *her* cleansing" (Lev 12:4)? Some Second Temple sources do witness to the practice of purifying infants along with their mothers (4Q265, 4Q266, and *Jubilees*). Rather than proving Luke's confusion about Judean laws, this detail may in fact imply Luke's familiarity with the halakhic outworkings of those laws during the Second Temple period—and therefore, serve to reinforce the impression of Jesus' family's punctilious piety. *See* Baumgarten, "Purification after Childbirth and the Sacred Garden in 4Q265 and *Jubilees*," in *New Qumran Texts and Studies,* George Brooke and Florentino García Martínez, eds. (Boston, MA: Brill, 1994), 417–427; Smith, "Luke, the Jews, and the Politics," 82–84; and Thiessen, "Luke 2:22, Leviticus 12, and Parturient Impurity," *Novum Testamentum* 54.1 (2012): 16–29.

42. Lexical echoes between the passages in include "light to the nations," "salvation," "eyes," and "servant" (although here Simeon uses the word δουλη, not παις).

43. The Hebrew of both the Masoretic Text and the Dead Sea Scrolls agree on this reading (against the Septuagint). see *The Dead Sea Scrolls Bible*, Abegg, Flint, and Ulrich, 352.

44. Fox, *The Hermeneutics of Social Identity in Luke–Acts*, 113. Isa. 52:10 is also evoked in assertion that the Lord "has shown strength with his arm" (51).

45. Robert Beck, *A Light to the Centurions: Reading Luke–Acts in the Empire* (Eugene, OR: Wipf & Stock, 2019), 32–33.

46. Ravens, *Luke and the Restoration of Israel*, 45.

47. In contrast to this reading, Kinzer (following Tiede, "Glory to Thy People Israel," 27–28), argues that the phrase "the falling and rising of many in Israel" refers not to individuals and their response to Jesus, but to Israel as a whole: it describes a *temporal sequence* of national events—falling (the destruction of the Jerusalem during the war) and rising (a future participation of Jerusalem and Israel as a whole in the salvific effects of Jesus' resurrection). Jesus would thus be a "sign that is opposed" by Israel as a nation, not by individual Israelites. This reading has the benefit of making sense of Jesus' predictions over Jerusalem (Luke 19:41–44), which need not be a contradiction of Zechariah's prophesy, but rather describes a different temporary moment in a sequence. By the time of Luke's writing, Jesus' prediction (Israel's "falling") has already come to pass, but the "rising" predicted by Zechariah has not yet. Kinzer, *Jerusalem Crucified, Jerusalem Risen*, 33–34.

116   *Chapter 3*

While there is definite merit in this reading, it may be an overstatement to divorce all sense of personal-response and personal-judgment from the saying. After all, Jesus is a sign that will be opposed "so that the hearts (καρδιων) of many will be revealed" (2:35b). This focus on the disclosure of what is within *individuals'* "hearts" militates against the claim that the "rising" and "falling" of 2:34 is entirely corporate.

48. But those who "fall" may "rise" again, later; consider the accounts of Paul's vision (Acts 9:4–6, 22:7–9; 26:14–16), with the same terms for "falling" (πτωσιν/ πιπτω) and "rising" (αναστασιν/ανιστημι) as in Luke 2:34, albeit in different lexical forms.

49. Four "prophesying" (yet textually silent!) daughters of Philip (Acts 21:8–9) are paired with Agabus, whose speech is directly quoted (21:10–11).

50. Pao, *Acts and the Isaianic New Exodus* (Eugene, OR: Wipf & Stock, 2016), 115; Fox, *The Hermeneutics of Social Identity in Luke–Acts*, 115.

51. Fox, *The Hermeneutics of Social Identity in Luke–Acts*, 115.

52. Smith, "Luke, the Jews, and the Politics," 80–81.

53. Kuecker, *The Spirit and the Other*, 69–70.

54. Ibid., 70.

55. Siker, *Disinheriting,* 109.

56. Jeremy Punt, "The Politics of Genealogies in the New Testament," *Neotestimentica* 47.2 (2013): 383.

57. Horrell, *Ethnicity and Inclusion: Religion, Race, and Whiteness in the Construction of Jewish and Christian Identities* (Grand Rapids, MI: Eerdman's, 2020), 99.

58. Siker, *Disinheriting,* 109–110.

59. Joshua Jipp, "Abraham in the Synoptic Gospels and the Acts of the Apostles," in *Abraham in Jewish and Early Christian Literature,* Sean Adams and Zanne Domony-Lyttle, eds. (New York: T&T Clark, 2019), 113–114.

60. Isaac Oliver, *Torah Praxis after 70 CE: Reading Matthew and Luke–Acts as Jewish Texts* (Tübingen: Mohr Siebeck, 2013), 435.

61. See figure 1.2 from chapter 1.

62. For discussion of the function of Abraham in 4 Maccabees, see chapter 2.

63. This family cannot seem to *stop* talking about Abraham: consider Mary's reference to the promise made to Abraham and his seed (τω Αβρααμ και τω σπερματι αυτου, Luke 1:55 // Gen. 17:9), the Song of Zechariah (1:68–79), and the covenant granted by God to Abraham our father (προς Αβρααμ τον πατερα ἡμων, Luke 1:73 // Gen. 17:22). See Hartman, "The 'Children of Abraham' in Luke–Acts," *Henoch* 39.2 (2017): 359.

64. Smith, "Luke, the Jews, and the Politics," 88–89.

Chapter 4

"We Have a Father—Abraham"

Abraham as Ancestor and Ethnic Founder in Luke

And he said, "Then I beg you, father (πατερ), send him to my father's house, for I have five brothers; so that he might warn them, lest they also come to this place of torment." But Abraham said, "They have Moses and the prophets; they should listen to them." —Luke 16:27–29

You are the sons of the prophets and [sons] of the covenant that God made with your ancestors (πατερας), saying to Abraham, "And in your descendants (σπερματι) shall all the families (πατριαι) of the earth be blessed." —Acts 3:25

In the parable of the rich man and Lazarus (Luke 16:19–31), a deceased man calls out to "father Abraham" (16:24) from Hades. He begs the patriarch to assist him, or at least his family, as some Judean traditions anticipated he would.[1] Abraham counters that his children shouldn't only focus on how this association can benefit *themselves*; they should consider how to leverage their Abrahamic inheritance to bless *others*, like poor Lazarus (16:25) or even gentiles (cf. Acts 3:25). Because the rich man had failed to show mercy to others during his lifetime, there is little Abraham's mercy can do for him now (Luke 16:26).

This chapter investigates how Abraham functions as ancestor, founder, and benefactor in Luke's gospel, and what this means for the ethnic identity of those who call him "father." The Third Gospel aligns itself with a particular trajectory of existing Abraham traditions—those which suggest that descent alone will not ensure one inherits his blessings, without following in his footsteps.[2] Luke seems to be perfectly aware, however, of another stream within Judaism—one which expected the patriarch's righteousness to overrule his descendants' sinfulness (e.g., *L.A.B.* 30.7, 32.4). Luke rejects this viewpoint and criticizes those who would simultaneously presume upon their standing as Abraham's children, while rejecting his ways (Luke 3:8–9). True to some sources circulating in Luke's day, Abraham's heritage includes repentance, turning to God, hospitality, and mercy (including the extension of blessings to the social "other").[3] Abraham's heirs must keep their progenitor's ways in order to inherit the blessings promised to his descendants (Luke 1:55, 1:72–73) and through them, to others (Luke 1:32; Acts 3:25 // Gen. 12:3, 22:18).

Furthermore, Luke aligns his use of Abraham *with* the subset of Second Temple traditions which leveraged the patriarch to suggest connections between Israelites and other peoples—and, conversely, *against* another trajectory of Second Temple thought that leveraged Abraham to distance Israel from all others. Throughout Luke–Acts, Abraham tends to show up in contexts where Luke asserts that the inclusion of gentiles is part and parcel of God's purposes in Christ—purposes originally announced and vouchsafed to Abraham.[4] Luke invokes Abraham in ways that suggest non-Judean Christians have a legitimate claim upon the patriarch.[5]

In terms of ethnicity, Luke destabilizes one of the base concepts that Judean racial identity was built upon—(biological) ancestry and its benefits. Luke affirms that Judeans are Abraham's children, but he denies that Judeans, simply *as* Judeans, will necessarily inherit the blessings God promised to Abraham's descendants—that is, if their conduct is unbecoming of the ancestor. (As demonstrated in the previous chapter, this idea was already "in the air" in Second Temple Judaism.) Moreover, he suggests that "unAbrahamic" Judeans cannot meaningfully claim to be Abraham's children at all (Luke 3:8), an impression which is corroborated by how ancestry is reconfigured more generally in Luke–Acts (see chapter 5). The seeming bedrock of race, ancestry, is shown to be shifting sand, as Luke suggests that grievous offenses may deracinate sinners from their ancestral roots (Luke 3:7–9, 16:18–31; 13:28).

Judean tradition widely remarked upon how Abraham had left behind his homeland, his family, and their traditions in order to seek the one true God. Luke's gospel poses the problem: if *this* generation has turned their back on Abraham's ways, have "returned to Chaldea" as it were, has the patriarch been left childless—in seeming contradiction to God's promises? Luke's answer (and Q's before him) is "No." If anything is lacking in Abraham's children, God is perfectly capable of appointing *others* to that role (Luke 3:8; cf. 19:40), perhaps in order to fulfill God's promise of descendants to the patriarch (Gen. 15:5; 17:2–3; 22:17). If Abraham is indeed the *patēr* in whom all *patriai* shall be blessed (Acts 3:25), have these included outsiders been somehow adjoined to his own *patria*—at least as distant cousins?

JOHN THE BAPTIST AND THE CHILDREN OF ABRAHAM (LUKE 3:1–22)

Luke 3:1–22 gives us Luke's account of the ministry of John the Baptist. Luke incorporates and expands other synoptic sources to depict John as a

"We Have a Father—Abraham"   119

prototypical "child of Abraham" in the prophetic mold, with the authority to declare what makes one a "child of Abraham." Here, as in Q,[6] Luke challenges those who assume they will receive in-group benefits merely because of their ascribed ancestry—but the Baptist goes further, questioning even his audience's assumption that they can even *claim* this identity.

Luke's Infancy Narratives have gone out of their way to portray John as cut from Abrahamic cloth. His standing as an exemplary "son of Abraham" is in marked contrast to the various political figures mentioned in the geographical/chronological frame of his ministry (3:1–2). These include individuals unrelated to Abraham in any sense (Tiberius Caesar and Pontius Pilate, Lysanias), individuals whose Abrahamic credentials were subject to criticism (such as the Herods),[7] and two elite Judeans (Annas and Caiaphas), whose impeccable lineage and commitment to Judaism[8] might *seem* unimpeachable—at least, to other elites. The Baptist's Judean prototypicality contrasts starkly with these gentiles, compromise-ridden Herods, and Temple-cult collaborators lurking at the fringes of his story. The difference will become even more striking when these forces collude to close in on John (Luke 3:19–20) and eventually, on Jesus.

After the chronological note, Luke sketches out John's mission and location. God's call comes to John in the wilderness, then John goes into "all the region around the Jordan." In Genesis 13, this phrase describes the area near Sodom, and so it subliminally suggests Lot and Abram (Gen. 13:10–12).[9] Luke continues with "the words of Isaiah the prophet":

A voice crying in the wilderness:
prepare the way of the Lord, make his paths straight.
Every valley will be filled in,
and every mountain and hill will be brought low;
and the crooked will be made straight,
and the rough ways made smooth;
and all flesh will see the salvation of God. (Luke 3:3–6 // Isa. 40:3–5 [LXX])

Luke has cited more of Isaiah's oracle than Mark, including the promise that "all flesh" (πασα σαρξ) shall see the salvation of God.[10] To state the obvious, all flesh necessarily includes all *races*. The "crowds" (οχλοι) addressed by the Baptist in Luke (3:7–9) are vaguer, and potentially more ethnically expansive, than Mark's "Judeans/Jerusalemites" (Mark 1:5 // Matt. 3:5) and the "Pharisees and Sadducees" added in Matthew's account (Matt. 3:7a).[11] In Luke, a more diverse audience is further suggested by the presence of various subgroups in the crowd, such as tax collectors (3:12), soldiers (3:14), and partisans of Herod (implicitly, 3:19–20). The soldiers might or might not have been ethnic Romans; they could just as easily be local mercenaries (often Syrians) serving the Herods or the Roman governor.[12] Although the majority of

120   *Chapter 4*

this crowd likely understood themselves as "descendants of Abraham" (3:10), Luke leaves us room to imagine a smattering of non-Judeans among them.

Brood of Vipers (Luke 3:7)

John's opening salvo excoriates the collective identity of those listening, in the most unflattering terms:

> Then John said to the crowds who came out to be baptized by him, "You brood of vipers (γεννηματα εχιδνων)! Who warned you to flee the wrath to come?" (Luke 3:7)

John hurls this insult at the "crowds," whereas in Matthew it is addressed to Pharisees and Sadducees (Matt. 3:7).[13] In Matthew, this is a polemical slur aimed at specific opponents; in Luke, this invective is a broadside fired at a large, heterogeneous (but mostly Judean) group.

This metaphor not only likens the crowds to unclean serpents (Lev. 11:42)—it specifically uses the language of descent to do so: "brood" (γεννημα/-ατα). The Greek *gennēma* relates to *gene*ration (note its resemblance to "bear/beget" *gennaō*), and the word emphasizes the biological processes of reproduction and birth. The term "γεννημα" is particularly appropriate for describing non-human (animal) offspring (cf. *Did.* 13.3); in the New Testament, it is *only* used in reference to a brood of vipers (Luke 3:7; Matt. 3:7, 12:34).[14] Although John is not *literally* claiming his listeners are the spawn of serpents, his choice of metaphor taps into the logic and value of ancestry to impugn their character.

"Brood of vipers" is what we might call a *genetic insult.* Craig Keener notes that in ancient polemic, the shame of one person typically reflected upon their entire family; therefore, genetic insults could be quite effective.[15] One could shame someone by insulting their parents (or legitimacy), as in "Your true father is unknown, given your mother's reputation" (Lysias, *Or.* 10.2, §116).[16] Because descent was so central in ancient constructions of race, calling someone's ancestors "vipers" is also an *ethnic* insult.

Why vipers? In the Hebrew Bible, snakes are frequently associated with danger, treachery, and calamity. Because they "crawl upon their belly," snakes are classified as unclean, as "abominable creeping things" (Lev. 11:42–43). Vipers (אפעה) make only a few appearances in Judean scriptures (Job 20:16; Isa. 30:6; Isa. 59:4–5). By far the most relevant of these for our passage is the latter:

> They rely on emptiness and speak falsehood,
> Conceiving (הרו/κυω) wrong and begetting (ילי/τικτω) evil.

They hatch adder's eggs
and weave spider webs;
He who eats of those eggs will die,
And if one is crushed, it hatches out a viper. (Isaiah 59:4b–5)[17]

This passage, like John the Baptist's pronouncement, draws upon the language of biological generation, both in terms of the subjects' wickedness ("conceiving" wrong and "bearing" evil), and in terms of animal procreation (the wicked "hatch" from eggs). Subsequent verses condemn the "waywardness" of the unrighteous, in terms strikingly reminiscent of the Isaianic prologue to John the Baptist's mission (Luke 3:4–6; cf. table 4.1).

With this scriptural echo in mind, the "brood of vipers" John addresses come into focus. They are John's polar opposites: where he is plainspoken, they "speak falsehood"; where he resists violence, they destroy peace; where he makes crooked paths straight, their ways are crooked. It is their *ways* (ὁδοι) that expose them as "spawn of vipers."

In the *Damascus Document*, Isaiah's "viper" imagery is applied to Jannes and his brother, who rebelled against Moses in the wilderness (CD 5.14).[18] Sometimes the community's present-day enemies are described as serpents: "their wine is the poison of serpents" (Deut. 32:33) is interpreted to mean, "The serpents are the kings of the peoples" (CD 19.22–23).[19] There also seems to have been a tradition, attested in both early Christian and rabbinic sources, that Cain's true father was the serpent in the Garden of Eden, thus ascribing "serpentine" ancestry to his descendants.[20]

Vipers held a nasty reputation in the Hellenistic imagination. Vipers were regarded as an image of terror (Ovid, *Metam.* 4.454, 475, 491–99, 617–20) who might bite one's feet unexpectedly (Aeschylus, *Suppl.* 896–97; Dio Chrysostom, *Or.* 59.3), or even lay in wait inside one's house to suck one's blood (Sophocles, *Ant.* 531–32). Their hostility toward humans made them

Table 4.1   Isaiah 59: the "Crooked Paths" of Vipers

Isaiah 59:7-8 [LXX]	Luke 3:4-6 // Isaiah 40:3-5
"Destruction and misery are in their ways (ὁδοις) and they do not know the way (ὁδον) of peace, and there is no judgment in their ways (ὁδιος); For the paths (τριβοι) they walk along are crooked, and they do not know peace."	"Prepare the way (ὁδον) of the Lord, make his paths (τριβους) straight. Every valley will be filled in, and every mountain and hill will be brought low; and the crooked will be made straight, and the rough ways (ὁδους) made smooth; and all flesh will see the salvation of God."[i]

---

[i] My trans.

122   *Chapter 4*

a natural symbol for moral evil (*Phaedrus* 4.20; *Babrius* 143.5–6). Some of these tropes resonate with similar depictions of venomous serpents in the Hebrew Bible (Job 20.16; Ps .140.4; Prov. 23:32; Jer. 8.17).[21]

More striking were Hellenistic theories about how vipers reproduced. They were popularly thought to eat their way out of their mother's womb, thereby avenging their fathers, who were themselves killed during intercourse (Herod., *Hist.* 3.109).[22] Thus, vipers could figuratively represent "parent-murderers," and the metaphor was used this way in some literature.[23] The ancients widely regarded parent-murder as one of the most heinous of crimes.[24] Recall that the Baptist speaks not only of vipers, but of the "*spawn* (γεννηματα) of vipers," which might recall to mind these widespread theories about their generation and birth.

John's "genetic" insult, aimed squarely at his audience's origins and nature, metaphorically denies their understanding of themselves and calls into question any benefits they might expect to receive based on their status as Abraham's children. At the moment, many of them live more like murderous snakes than like their purported father, Abraham. They are a "brood of vipers" who must *perform* righteousness ("bear fruit worthy of repentance," 3:8) in order to inherit Abraham's benefits.

Sons from Stones (Luke 3:8)

The Baptist has wrong-footed his listeners' sense of identity, insulting their parents/ancestors as "vipers." He goes on to link ancestral identity explicitly with *conduct*, calling even their descent from Abraham into question:

> Therefore bear the fruits worthy of repentance; and don't start telling yourselves, 'We have Abraham as our father/ancestor (πατερα),' for I tell you that God can raise up children for Abraham (τεκνα τω Αβρααμ) from these stones (εκ των λιθων τουτων)! (Luke 3:8)

Luke's version of the saying ("do not *begin* to say to yourselves . . .")[25] suggests either such a response is already on the tip of their (forked) tongues, or that the crowds have indeed *already* begun to grumble. Perhaps, they have started to reject the label "γεννηματα εχιδνων" by affirming their Abrahamic roots.[26]

John demands they "bear fruit," using a common biblical metaphor. Actions actualize identity: these could-be spawn of vipers (and would-be children of Abraham) must *show* themselves to be either one or the other. Some of them have begun to assert "We have a father—Abraham," but verbal protestations are so much hot air. John counters that, if necessary, God can raise up children for Abraham from some nearby stones! This colorful

"We Have a Father—Abraham" 123

hyperbole insists that God can fashion children of Abraham out of any "material" at hand—perhaps, one wonders, even gentiles?[27] A bit of wordplay might underlie the Q saying (Luke 3:8 // Matt. 3:9). If the original phrasing of the saying had been "sons for Abraham," there would have been a pun in the Aramaic, between "stones" (*abnayya*/אבניא) and "sons" (*bennayya*/בניא).[28] If this was originally the case, the pun has been lost in the transition to Greek, as "sons" became "children."

The "stones" here may recall Isaiah 51:[29]

> Look to the rock from which you were hewn, and to the quarry from which you were dug. Look to Abraham your father, and to Sarah who bore you; for he was only one person when I called him, and blessed him, and loved him, and multiplied him. (Isaiah 51:1b–2 [LXX])

As discussed in chapter 2, this oracle offered assurance to Zion of God's impending salvation (Isa. 51:3, 5–6). Their descent from Abraham (and Sarah) stands as surety that God will redeem them, just as surely as God fulfilled his promises to Abraham (51:1–2). God's justice will *also* shine as a "light for the peoples" (Isa. 51:4), but the general thrust of Isaiah's oracle, in its context, is that God's salvation of the Judeans is certain *because* they were quarried from Abraham. Alan Culpepper observes that both this passage and Luke 3:8 go beyond literal biological reproduction, enlisting the *inanimate* to provide children for Abraham. "If, metaphorically, the Israelites are stones hewn from Abraham, then *a fortiori* God can use stones to produce other children to Abraham."[30] But the rhetorical effect is reversed: rather than assuring the "stones" that God will bless them for Abraham's sake, here the "stones" will replace those unworthy to be Abraham's children.

These children from stones may also call Ezekiel to mind.[31] In two nearly verbatim oracles, the prophet proclaims God's plan to replace the people's hearts of stone with hearts of flesh (Ezek. 11:19–20 // Ezek. 36:26–28).[32] Here, "heart of stone" is a negative image, to be replaced by a "heart of flesh" which will follow God's ways. Although the actual word "repentance" (שוב/μετανοια) is not used, the logic of repentance is on full display: a literal "change of heart" enables the Judeans to walk in God's ways. The overall message of these two passages, then, is similar to the overall thrust of John's preaching—a call to repentance. If God can metaphorically replace hearts of stone with hearts of flesh, then God can also turn lifeless stones into living children for Abraham—if Abraham's actual descendants prove too stony-hearted. John's saying may also echo Deuteronomy 32, where God—here himself "the Rock" who is "your father" (32:4–6)—complains against his "degenerate children" Israel: "You were unmindful of the Rock who bore

124 *Chapter 4*

you; you forgot the God who gave you birth" (Deut. 32:18, NRSV), or "the God who *nursed* you" (τρεφοντος) in the Greek.[33]

Although such Judean intertexts provide an informative background to John's "stones" image, there may be other echoes at play. Luke's implied audience includes "god-fearers" like Cornelius (Acts 10:1–8; cf. Luke 7:1–10), familiar with both Judean and Hellenistic traditions. Therefore, Luke's audience may have drawn additional associations from the Greek milieu.[34] There were a number of pagan tales in which human beings were formed from stones, or in some cases, dragon's teeth.[35] Most famous of these was the legend of Deucalion: after the primeval deluge, the sole human survivors, Deucalion and Pyrrha, repopulated the world by tossing stones behind them, which turned into human beings (Apoll., *Bib.* 1.7.2; Statius, *Thebaid* 8.305). Apollodorus's version of the tale even includes a play on words, not unlike the *stones* (*avnayya*) from *sons* (*bennayya*) in the Aramaic underlying Luke 3:8: in this case, *people* (λαος) from *stones* (λαας).[36]

The Baptist's saying about children for Abraham is related to the exhortation at the beginning of the verse: "bear fruit worthy of repentance." Seemingly, some in the crowds are counting on their Abrahamic heritage (and its presumed benefits) but engaging in some very *un*Abrahamic conduct.[37] In figuratively attributing other (serpentine) "parents" to the crowds (if they persist in not bearing fruit), and in challenging their descent from Abraham, John strikes at the very root of Judean ethnic identity—their self-understanding as the σπερμα Αβρααμ. Race was most primally a matter of ancestry—even in cases where this ancestry was fictive, imaginary, or "spiritual" (as in the case of "subscriptive descent"). John the Baptist insults their Abrahamic ancestry,[38] and by extension, their Abrahamic *ethnicity*. Are Judeans who refuse to repent still "children of Abraham?" John implies "no," but stops just shy of saying it.

The insufficiency of genetic descent alone was a commonplace in Mediterranean antiquity. If someone fell short of their ancestors, others might deny that they were "really" their descendants—even if the "genetic" facts were not in question.[39] For example, despite the fact that Polemo had children, Philostratus laments, "With Polemo ended the house of Polemo, for his descendants (γενομενοι), through they were his kindred (ξυγγενεις), were not the sort of men who could be compared with his surpassing merit" (Philostratus, *Vit.Soph.* 1.544).'"[40] We can find similar ideas in a *Judean*-Hellenistic milieu. Philo held that shared faith could create a bond of kinship (συγγενεια) "far more genuine than that of blood" (*Virtues* 79), and that so-called kinships should "be cast aside if they do not earnestly seek the same goal, namely, the honor of God" (*Rewards* 152). Josephus coldly asserts "destruction is just for all who being of the race of Abraham attempt new practices that pervert our normal ways" (*Ant.* 5.113). Clearly, some thinkers held that conduct could either invalidate or confirm one's "genetic" identity. Note that the value of pedigree is not overturned in such discussion; it is rather that especially undeserving descendants might be in some way "bracketed off" from their worthy families, and especially deserving outsiders might be "inserted" into a lineage. A similar logic operates here (Luke 3:8): One's behavior could confirm or invalidate one's Abrahamic pedigree. But Luke would likely disagree with Josephus and Philo, and with most Jews, on how to understand the "example" set by the patriarch!

The Baptist's reconfiguration of Abrahamic descent echoes other New Testament literature.[41] Paul describes his audience's share of the patriarch's "faith," which can have both positive and negative genealogical consequences (Rom. 4:11–12, 16).[42] Positively, Paul holds that sharing Abraham's faith can confirm one as his descendant (Rom. 4:11, 16; cf. Gal. 3:7). By subscribing to his example, or "walking in his footsteps," you make him your father. Negatively, *failure* to do so might call one's descent into question. He implies that Abraham is *not* the ancestor of all "the circumcised" (i.e., Judeans), but only of "the circumcised who also walk in the footsteps" of his faith (Rom. 4:12).[43] Of course, Paul disagreed radically with most Judeans about what Abraham's "faith" comprised—for Paul, this means faith in Jesus and does not require Torah observance, at least not for gentiles.[44]

John 8:33–51 offers an even closer parallel to Luke 3:8.[45] In a heated argument between Jesus and "the Judeans who had believed in him," Jesus' opponents defend their honor by citing their ancestry. They declare, "We are offspring of Abraham (σπερμα Αβρααμ εσμεν) and have never been slaves to anyone" (John 8:33), and further insist, "Our father is Abraham (Ό πατηρ ἡμων Αβρααμ εστιν)" (8:39). This is similar to the crowds' (imagined) rebuttal to John's viperous vitriol (table 4.2).

Their eventual claim, "we have one father—God" (Jn 8:39), is structurally similar to the claim "we have a father—Abraham" in Luke (3:8). The phrase "children of Abraham" (τεκνα Αβρααμ) shows up in both places (Luke 3:8; John 8:39), both times met with skepticism as to whether the claim really

Table 4.2 "Children of Abraham": Q and John

Luke 3:8 // Matt 3:9:	John 8:33, 39-40
We have a father: Abraham. (πατερα εχομεν τον Αβρααμ)	[39]Our father is Abraham. (ὁ πατηρ ἡμων Αβρααμ εστιν) [41]We have one father: God. (ἑνα πατερα εχομεν τον θεον)
...children for Abraham... (τεκνα τῳ Αβρααμ)	[33]We are offspring of Abraham. (σπερμα Αβρααμ εσμεν) [40]If you are children of Abraham... (τεκνα του Αβρααμ)

126   *Chapter 4*

applies. In John 8, Jesus questions the validity of their supposed descent based on his opponents' *behavior*: "If you were Abraham's children, you would be doing the works Abraham did. But now you seek to kill me, a man who has told you the truth, which I heard from God. Abraham did not do this" (John 8:39–40). Rather than resisting Jesus, "Your father Abraham rejoiced that he would see my day" (8:56). For the fourth evangelist, one must do Abraham's works to legitimately claim him as a father. John's Jesus, much like John the Baptist (Luke 3:7–17), destabilizes descent from Abraham, making it contingent upon walking in Abraham's footsteps.[46]

According to the Baptist, Abraham's children must "bear fruit." As we saw in chapter 2, *some* Judean traditions understood God's covenant with Abraham to guarantee benefits for all his (Judean) descendants no matter what (Isa. 51:2–3, Sir. 44:21; *Jub.* 12:22–24; *T.Levi* 15:4), with no sense of dependence upon their own conduct (*L.A.B.* 30.7, 32.4).[47] Luke 3:8, however, is aligned with those traditions which insisted that Abraham's descendants must be worthy of Abraham, in order to be legitimate—traditions which are echoed and amplified in early Christian discourse.[48]

In John's gospel, Jesus' excoriation of the Judean leaders' ancestry was so offensive that they "seek to kill him" (John 8:40). Telling someone they are not really who they say they are is a dangerous business! In John the Baptist's ministry, too, there is a *frisson* of possible violence, as two conceptions of Abrahamic identity clash. On the narrative level, some of those gathered at the Jordan are soldiers. On the figurative level, vipers were associated with malice and patricide. Keener remarks that "Failing to live up to ancestral righteousness was bad enough, but if John's interlocutors are parent-murderers, their claim to descend from Abraham takes on even more hideous overtones."[49] If these crowds are indeed a "brood of vipers," infamous parent-killers, then those vipers will be murderously inclined toward their own claimed "father," Abraham. They might sink their fangs not only into *Abraham's* foot, but into anyone else's who walk in his ways—perhaps even into John's. As it so happens, this occurs in just a few verses: the same political who frame the chronology of this episode (Luke 3:1) are indeed watching John and preparing to strike (3:18–20).

Axes, Trees, Fruit (Luke 3:8–9)

Bear fruit worthy of repentance. . . . Even now the axe is laid at the root (ριζαν) of the trees (δενδρων). Every tree that does not bear good fruit is cut down (εκκοπτεται) and thrown into the fire. (Luke 3:8a, 9)

"We Have a Father—Abraham"   127

John the Baptist has insulted the crowd's genealogical/ethnic honor by (1) calling them a "brood of vipers," and (2) warning them not to presume upon their supposed Abrahamic ancestry. After all, John says, God could produce replacement "children for Abraham from these stones." John now adds a third racial image to the mix: the imperiled tree.

Arboreal imagery was a common metaphor for Israel, in scripture and later tradition. In the Bible, Israel was variously depicted as a fig tree (Jer. 8:13; Hosea 9:10–13; Joel 1:5–7), an olive tree (Hosea 14:5–6, Jer. 11:16–17; Isa. 17:4–6), and a grapevine (Isa. 3:14; 5:1–7, 27:4; Jer. 2:21, 8:13; Ezek. 15:1–8; Hosea 9:10; Joel 1:6–7; Ps. 80:8–16; *4 Ezra* 5:23–30; *2 Baruch* 39:7–8; *4Q433a* frag. 2; *6Q11*). In some iterations of the motif, the tree is threatened with immanent destruction because of unfruitfulness. Jeremiah laments,

> The Lord called your name "a beautiful, shady olive tree." To the noise of its being chopped (περιτομης), a fire was kindled against it; great is the disaster [coming] to you; its branches were made useless. And the Lord who planted you has pronounced evil upon you; according to the evil of house of Israel and the house of Judah, because they did [this] to themselves, provoking me to anger by burning incense to Baal. (Jeremiah 11:16–17 [LXX])

Ezekiel predicts that fire will consume the vine Jerusalem, like grape wood, which is good for nothing except burning (Ezek. 15:1–10). John the Baptist's imperiled trees, in imminent danger of being cut down and burned, call to mind the ethnic trope of the imperiled tree, Israel.

Sometimes, plant metaphors could bear a genealogical sense—not unlike the sense of the English phrase "family tree" (Ps. 127:3; Sir. 40:15). For example, Isaiah uses the image of a tree stump to think genealogically[50]:

> A shoot will come forth from the stump (מגזע/ ριζης) of Jesse,
> and a branch from his roots will bear fruit (יפרה). (Isa. 11:1 [Hebrew])[51]

Ριζα means "root," but can figuratively stand for *any* foundation, including the "stock" from which a family springs.[52] Εκ with the genitive of relationship can mean "born of" or "descended from." So, "from the root" could describe the vegetative budding of a stump *or* reproductive descent from Jesse. The stem which springs from this root will blossom and bear fruit. Furthermore, Jesse's scion will heal the relationship of the branching lineages, Ephraim and Judah (Isa. 11:13).[53]

Philo also employed the image of a tree to discuss lineage, down through the generations. Here, he describes the renowned ancestors of Israel as various parts of a tree:

128   *Chapter 4*

Shem is planted as a root (ῥίζα) of excellence and virtue; and from this root there sprang up a tree (δένδρον) bringing forth good fruit, namely, Abraham, of whom . . . Isaac, was the fruit (καρπὸς), by whom again the virtues which are displayed in labor are sown (κατασπείρονται), the practiser of which is Jacob. (Philo, *On Sobriety*, 65)[54]

Here we have an extended family tree, stretching all the way from root to seed! Each ancestor corresponds to one part: Shem, the roots, Abraham the trunk; Isaac, the fruit, and Jacob, the seed.

Various Judean texts also described Abraham as the "root" of Israel.[55] For example, in *1 Enoch* 93:8–10, "the whole race of the chosen root will be cut off" for sin, followed later by a "plant of righteousness."[56] Ethiopian commentators understand the first reference to be Abraham, the second, Isaac.[57] In *Jubilees* we read: "From him [Abraham] would arise the plant of righteousness for the eternal generations, and from him a holy seed" (*Jubilees* 16:26).[58] In the *Genesis Apocryphon*, both Noah and Abraham receive a vision from God about a tree threatened by destruction, both with genealogical implications.[59] Philo praises Abraham as the root of that virtuous branch, Israel:

For that man [Abraham] is truly a chief of a nation (ἐθνάρχης) and ruler of a family (γενάρχης), from whom, as from a root (ῥίζης), sprang that branch so fond of investigating and contemplating the affairs of our nature, by name Israel. (Philo, *Who is the Heir of Divine Things?* 279)[60]

In Philo's estimation, Abraham is both *ethnarch* and *genarch* of Israel. Since αρχη can denote origin as well as rule, these terms bear a double meaning: Abraham is ruler *and* origin of this ethnos/genos. The patriarch is both source and archetype: his descendants are *from* him, and his descendants are *like* him. Those unlike Abraham are in danger of losing their naturally derived standing in this family tree: unworthy descendants "like stalks of plants are cut away," and in their place, proselytes like "new growths shoot up which supersede the old" (*Rewards,* 152, 172; cf. Romans 11:1, 16–18).[61]

Non-Judeans also used plant imagery to discuss descent. Romans used the Greek loan-word *stemma* (literally "garland") for the linked family portraits displayed in elite houses. Pliny describes them thus: "The pedigree (*stemmata*) of the individual was traced in lines upon each of these colored portraits" (*Natural History* 35.6).[62] Juvenal lambasts a rival with *Stemmata quid faciunt?* ("What avail your pedigrees?") in the opening volley of his eighth satire (*Satires* 8.1).[63] They might speak of "branches" growing from these *stemmata,* talk of family growing from "stock," or describe adoption as grafting, much as the highly Hellenized Philo also did (*De Agr.* 1.6).[64] Plutarch employed the Greek *stemma* (στεμμα) with this same sense, "lineage."[65]

Early Christ-believers leveraged existing Judean ethnic symbols, including plant imagery, in various ways. In Mark, Jesus curses a fig tree on his way into Jerusalem for its failure to yield fruit at the opportune time, causing it to wither (Mark 11:12–25 // Matt. 21:18–22); this story is interpolated with Jesus' cleansing of the Temple, implying the fig mirrors the Temple leadership's failure to "bear fruit."[66] John's gospel reworks the longstanding ethnic metaphor of the people of God as a grapevine, making union with Jesus ("the true vine") the crucial criterion for membership (John 10:1–16).[67] Paul reconfigures the "olive tree" metaphor to allow gentile Christ-believers a place within the people of God:

> [16b] If the root (ριζα) is holy, so are the branches.[17] But if some of the branches were broken off, and you despite being a wild olive were grafted in among them and became a sharer of the root and the oily-sap of the olive,[18] do not boast over the branches; but if you do boast, [remember] you do not support the root, but the root [supports] you. (Romans 11:16b–18)[68]

Arguably, the holy "root" of Romans 11:16 is again Abraham, mentioned just a few verses earlier as a key anchor of ethnic identity (Rom. 11:1).[69] Earlier in the same letter, Paul explained that Abraham is the ancestor of "adherents of the law" as well as "those who share his faith" (Rom. 4:11–18)—that is, both types of branches found on this olive tree. Romans 11:28 further supports this reading; there, Israelites are "beloved on account of the patriarchs" (or "ancestors," πατερας, similarly mentioned in 9:5).[70]

In light of these Judean (and later, Christian) traditions,[71] we might understand Luke 3:8–9 as sprouting from an existing ethnic metaphor. The motif of Israel as some sort of tree was widespread in Judaism, and some sources furthermore identified Abraham as its "root." The Baptist's saying about Abrahamic descent is wedged between his remark about "bearing fruit" (3:8a) and the warning about the ax and the trees (3:9), further suggesting we identify the "root" as Abraham himself. Israel's "trees" collectively spring from one source; but those who fail to bear fruit will be chopped away from the root, severing them from Abraham.[72]

Repentance is a major crop this tree is expected to produce. At the beginning of Luke, John the Baptist exhorts his listeners to "bear fruit worthy of repentance (μετανοιας)" (3:8a); at the *end* of Luke, the disciples are told "that repentance (μετανοιαν) for the forgiveness of sins should be proclaimed in [Jesus'] name to all races (παντα τα εθνη), beginning in Jerusalem" (24:47).[73] Peter later tells the "circumcision party" in Jerusalem how God had given the Holy Spirit to Cornelius and his household, they exclaim, "then God has

130   *Chapter 4*

given even to gentiles (εθνεσιν) the repentance (μετανοιαν) that leads to life"
(Acts 11:18), again echoing the Baptist's exhortation. It seems as if Judeans
are not the *only* ones able to bear this particular "fruit." If Abraham's genealogical descendants might be severed from their "root" for lack of repentance,
might gentiles be added if they *do* repent?[74]

The Baptist's "imperiled trees" call to mind the parable of the barren fig
tree (13:6–9). Luke lacks Mark's account of Jesus cursing a fig tree (Mark
11:12–25 // Matt. 21:18–22), but he does relate this unique parable:

> [6]A certain man had a fig tree which had been planted in his vineyard; and he
> came seeking fruit (καρπον) on it, but found none. [7]And he said to his vine-
> dresser, "Look, for three years now I've been coming seeking fruit on this fig
> tree, and I haven't found any. Cut it down (εκκοψον)! Why should it waste the
> soil?" [8]And he answered him, "Lord, leave it alone this year, until I dig around
> it and put down manure. [9]And if it should bear fruit (ποιηςη καρπον) next year,
> good; and if not, you can cut (εκκοψεις) it down." (Luke 13:6–9)

A connection between this parable and Luke 3:8–9 is suggested not only
by the imagery (a tree threatened with destruction), but by vocabulary:
trees ought to "produce fruit" (ποιεω καρπον) and will be chopped down
(εκκοπτω) if they do not. Narrative context also suggests a connection; both
abut references to Abraham. In Luke 3:8–9, the saying about Abraham is
sandwiched between the injunction to "bear fruit" and the saying about the
axe; in Luke 13, the fig parable is followed immediately by the story of a
"daughter of Abraham" who is healed on the Sabbath (13:10–17).[75] Furthermore, immediately *before* this parable, Jesus exhorted the crowds, "repent, or
you too will perish" (13:5), reminding us of John's "trees," planted within a
sermon about repentance (3:3, 8).

Significantly, Luke 13:6–9 contains not one, but two traditional ethnic
metaphors for Israel: the vineyard[76] and the fig tree.[77] The parable opens with
a vineyard owner, reminding the attentive reader of the vineyard Israel—and
how God vowed to destroy the vineyard, because "I waited for it to produce
a cluster of grapes—but it brought forth thorns!" (Isa. 5:2).[78] In Luke's parable, however, it is one particular tree *within* the vineyard that is threatened
on account of unfruitfulness. Combining two traditional metaphors for the
race of Israel in this way suggests that while the vineyard stands for Israel as
a whole, the fig tree stands for individual Judeans.[79] This recalls the scriptural
trope in which *individuals* are likened to trees, which either flourish or lan-
guish based upon their behavior (Jer. 17:5–7; Ps. 1:3–4; Dan. 4:1–25), a motif
picked up in later Judean literature. Consider this passage from the Armenian
recension of *The Words of Ahiqar*, which strongly resembles Luke's parable:

"We Have a Father—Abraham"   131

> And I spake to Nathan thus: Son, thou hast been to me like a palm-tree which was grown with roots on the bank of the river. When the fruit ripened, it fell into the river. The lord of the tree came to cut it down, and the tree said: Leave me in this place, that in the next year I may bear fruit. (*Ahiqar* 8.25)[80]

Even the narrative context of Luke's fig parable suggests that it concerns individuals. Jesus has just commented upon two groups of Judeans who have suffered misfortunes (the Galileans whom Pilate slaughtered in the Temple, and those who died when a tower in Jerusalem collapsed); he remarked that these were "no worse sinners" than other Galileans or other residents of Jerusalem (Luke 13:1–4). All who were lucky enough to avoid these catastrophes are still in danger—and therefore his listeners should repent (13:5). What seems to be in view here, then, is not the fruitfulness or unfruitfulness of the entire *ethnos*/vineyard, but that of the individuals/trees who make up that *ethnos*. Still, within the narrative of Jesus' parable, the fig tree is situated *within* the vineyard; we therefore hear an echo of God's surprise and consternation that his carefully tended "vineyard" (Israel) is not bearing fruit (Isa. 5:1–2). Like John's image of the trees threatened with chopping/burning, this parable functions as a warning to a mostly Judean crowd: their ethnic identity will not save them from the consequences of their individual actions. They might even find themselves uprooted from that vineyard (removed from Israel?) for their unfruitfulness.

In the parable, the initial intention of the vineyard owner is forestalled by the advice of his vinedresser (13:8–9). God was frequently described as the owner of the vineyard, Israel,[81] who might resolve to destroy that vine for fruitlessness;[82] therefore, the vinedresser's counsel resonates with the biblical motif of God's anger being restrained by the generous request of a spokesperson.[83] This is precisely the sort of intercession Abraham once offered for Sodom (Gen. 18:23–33), and was popularly expected to make for individual souls (Luke 16:24).

To return to Luke 3:8–9, John the Baptist's "trees" which might be slashed and burned hearken back to traditions describing Israel as a tree. Luke has inherited this logion from one of his sources (Q), but his inclusion of a parable about another unfruitful tree threatened with the same punishment (13:6–9) amplifies the resonance of the image. Those trees that do not bear fruit will be "cut down" at the root. Note that although there are many "trees," there is only one "root" (3:8a). Every tree that does not bear fruit will be cut at the "root," Abraham, just as every fig tree that does not bear fruit will be removed from the "vineyard," Israel. We have, in both cases, trees as *individuals* (cf. Luke 6:43–45) who are threatened with being excised from an *ethnic* image (Abraham the root, Israel the vineyard). Also, keep in mind that the "final" weeding of Abraham's garden

132   Chapter 4

is future-oriented and eschatological—whether it be the private eschaton of individual death (16:19–31) or the final eschaton (13:23–30). Until this point, Abraham's wayward children are *threatened* with excision but may yet avoid being "cut off."

What remains to be addressed is what might become of the "gap" left by these removals. Regarding the fig tree, the owner of the vineyard asks, "Ἱνατι και την γην καταργει;" which conveys the sense both of "why should it still be taking up space?" and "why should it be wasting [the nutrients/water in] the soil?" The implication is that, if removed, another plant could make better use of that same space/soil. Might *other* trees be planted in this vineyard? If the vineyard represents Israel, would such a new tree now be "Israel" too? The singular "root" of 3:8 seemingly supports many "trees," some of which are in danger of being cut off and burned; might *another* tree be grafted into the point of excision, as was common in ancient Mediterranean agronomy[84]—and as was sometimes used as a metaphor for adoption (e.g. Philo, *Agr.* 1.6)?[85] Unlike Paul (Rom. 11:16–24), Luke stops short of naming this possibility, but the image itself does raise the question of what might grow from the root after the tree's removal (cf. Philo, *Rewards* 166, 172).

"What then shall we do?"

John the Baptist has warned his audience to "bear fruit worthy of repentance" (Luke 3:8a // Matt. 3:8); but Luke expands upon his source material (Q) to give this vague demand some specific content. The crowds ask John, "When then shall we do?" (3:10). The following verses (11–14) flesh out the otherwise vague "fruits" of repentance. In the crowd are various sorts of elites, invoking harsh Roman imperial realities, particularly those who have surplus wealth to spare (vs. 11), tax collectors (12–13), and soldiers (14). John's answers to the thrice-repeated question "What should we do?" (3:10, 12, 14) explicate both the content of "repentance" *and* proper Israelite identity as a "son of Abraham." As Aaron Kuecker remarks: "If inappropriate claims to Abrahamic descent and inappropriate repentance are antitheses, it logically follows that proper repentance and properly expressed Israelite ethnic identity are two sides of the same coin."[86]

John first demands that those who have wealth must share it with those in need (3:11). Almsgiving and care for the poor was a longstanding mark of Judean piety, and Abraham was understood to have embodied such behavior in his lavish hospitality toward the three angelic visitors (Gen. 18:3–8). According to Josephus, Lot was also "benevolent to strangers" (περι τους ξενους φιλανθρωπος) when these same angelic messengers came to his own house, because "he had learned the lesson of Abraham's kindliness (χρηστοτητος)" during their earlier visit (*Ant.* 1.200). John the Baptist

"We Have a Father—Abraham" 133

instructs wealthy elites[87] to put their wealth to work for others, performing concrete acts of mercy like sharing food and clothing, consistent with Abraham's example (Gen. 18:3–8), the demands of Torah (Exod. 22:25; Deut. 15:7–11), and the resource-sharing of the early disciples (Acts 2:45, 4:32). Later in Luke, it is precisely the failure to show such mercy which explains Abraham's inability to help the rich man in Hades (16:19–26).

Next, John instructs "tax collectors" (τελωναι) to "collect no more than you are authorized to do." (Luke 3:12–13). Tax collectors could abuse their positions and over-collect, lining their own pockets in the process (cf. 19:8). John forbids this practice. John's ethical instructions to various social groups are two sides of the same coin—they apply the logic of neighbor-love both positively (those with wealth must have mercy upon the poor) and negatively (those in positions of authority must not take advantage of others).[88]

John's third command is addressed to soldiers (στρατευομενοι, Luke 3:14). On the narrative level, these soldiers were likely local mercenaries serving the Herods or troops under the authority of the Roman governor. They may or may not have been ethnic Romans themselves, but could just as easily be Syrians, Samaritans, or even Judeans.[89] John instructs them, "Neither extort (συκοφαντησητε) nor browbeat (διασεισητε), but be satisfied (αρκεισθε) with your wages" (Luke 3:14b). The prohibition of "extortion" employs the word συκοφαντεω, encompassing such practices as blackmail, threats, false accusations, and malicious lawsuits.[90]

Judeans were liable to being "shaken down" by soldiers; indeed, John forbids this practice using a word which literally means "to shake violently" (διαστειω).[91] This could take the form of conscription of involuntary labor[92] or seizure of resources.[93] Some of this co-opting went beyond what was technically allowed, as demonstrated by periodic attempts to curtail such abuses. Nor was this only a danger from *foreign* soldiers; during the Judean Revolt, Josephus attempted to forestall the same behavior by *Judean* soldiers, telling soldiers under this command not to extort money from their fellow countrymen "but be satisfied (αρκουμενους) with their rations" (*Life* 244)[94]—using the same word for "satisfied" as in Luke 3:14.[95]

John's instructions about right conduct are unique to this gospel, suggesting that for Luke, these practices demonstrate what it looks like to walk in Abraham's footsteps—or fail to do so.[96] John's elaboration on the "fruits worthy of repentance" comprises a twofold movement, perhaps playing upon the literal sense of the Hebrew word for repentance, *shuv*/שוב ("turn").[97] The crowds must turn *from* all-too-common predatory practices—from abuses which arise from collaboration with the Roman occupiers; from overcollection (producing debt and loss of traditional family land); from extortion; from false accusation and browbeating. At the same time, they must turn *to* those in need—enacting the same mercy they hope to receive from Abraham. John's

134   *Chapter 4*

answers encourage the people to turn beyond themselves: they must be willing to use their privilege to help others (3:11), and they must not abuse their privilege to the detriment of others (3:13–14).[98] This other-concern might reasonably be applied to racialized encounters as well, especially since the issue of descent from Abraham has already been raised (and problematized) by John. Perhaps the ethnic other, too, must not be taken advantage of, and must be given that extra cloak.[99]

John the Baptist on Abrahamic Identity: Summary

Luke introduced us to the infant John as a true son of Abraham; his adult ministry confirms this impression. John the Baptist explicitly addresses the question of who can, and cannot, claim Abraham as "our father"—and why.

If John is indeed the "prophet of the Most High" who "will go before the Lord to prepare his ways" (1:76), then anyone who wants to silence John is working at cross-purposes with God. Herod Antipas, whose father had so ostentatiously broadcast his devotion to Abraham in the form of lavish building projects,[100] does exactly this—arresting and eventually killing the Baptist (3:19–20). Similarly, if the Christ whom John foretold (3:15–17) and baptized (3:21–22) is truly the "mercy promised to our ancestors [in] the oath that he swore to our father Abraham" (1:72–73), then all who conspire to *kill* that Christ are poor sons of Abraham, indeed! By the end of the Third Gospel, this is exactly what the religious leaders skulking on the fringes of the Baptist's story will do (Luke 3:1–2; Luke 22–23). For Luke, Jesus is the fulfillment of ages of Abrahamic expectation; therefore, the Herods' and high priests' lethal collusion—in direct defiance of God's anointed messiah—erodes their standing as children of Abraham.

Therefore, John the Baptist's preaching is subversive of Judean ethnic identity.[101] John undermines the bedrock upon which race was frequently built—ancestry. (1) *Genetic descent* is destabilized, as John calls his audience a "brood" of vipers (3:7), likening them to the spawn of a creature infamous for the parent-murder. He also questions their standing as children of Abraham (3:8), suggesting that God could generate additional (or replacement?) children for Abraham, even from inanimate matter. What we might call *ascriptive descent*, descent which is simply ascribed at birth, turns out to be an uncertain proposition. Conversely, (2) *subscriptive descent* is emphasized, as John warns the crowds to "bear fruit" (3:8a) because every tree that fails to will be cut from the "root," an image sometimes used of Abraham. John elaborates: this "fruit" includes acts of mercy toward the poor (3:11), repentance from exploitative abuses of position (3:12–14), and recognition of the Christ (3:15–18). Meaningful descent from Abraham, then, depends on more than mere biology: listeners must repent and follow the *example* of the patriarch. (3) *Ethnic implications:* Given that "offspring of Abraham" was a functional synonym for "Judeans," the suggestion that some of them might not really be his children amounts to a direct assault on their racial identity. What would it even mean to be a "Judean" without being a child of Abraham? Or what would it mean to be merely a *nominal* child of Abraham, without an inheritance? Would some Judeans, then, find themselves in a position mirroring the less-favored sons in his lineage, such as Ishmael or Esau—notionally related but effectively "cut off?" Would the hypothetical "children" raised from "these stones" *also* be Judeans? Or would they at least be brought into some sort of ethnic relationship to Judeans—as "fellow children of Abraham"—much like the other races that descend from him?[102]

ABRAHAM'S BLESSINGS—FOR WHOM?

The Infancy Narratives (Luke 1–2) have established the Abrahamic credentials of Jesus and John the Baptist and implied that the gospel would be a continuation of the story of God's faithfulness to Abraham and his descendants. However, John's preaching (Luke 3:1–17) has introduced some uncertainty. There is now static on the line; it is no longer clear who will actually benefit from their connection to Abraham—indeed, it is no longer clear-cut who can even claim to *be* a child of Abraham! Luke has reaffirmed Judaism's understanding that Israelites are Abraham's children who will receive the vindication of God's promises to him but questions whether this applies to *every* individual Judean.[103] Some Israelites are unworthy of Abrahamic descent—they are colorfully described as "spawn of vipers." The racial prerogatives and benefits of Abraham's children are affirmed, at the same time the stability of this identity is troubled.

This aspect of Luke's use of Abraham finds an indirect echo in earlier Abraham traditions. When it comes to Abraham, *inheritance matters.* Both the Genesis narrative and subsequent Judean literature assert that there is a qualitative difference between those sons in the Abrahamic lineage who were favored, blessed, or expected to inherit the covenant—and those sons who were not.[104] There was also a qualitative, ethnically significant difference between their *descendants*, that is, the races they founded. Israel is distinct from Ishmaelites and Edomites not only because they descended from different branches of the family tree but because they received the patriarchal blessings, keep the covenant vouchsafed to Abraham, and are thus the people of God. Thus, any question raised in Luke as to whether someone is or is not truly a "legitimate" child (i.e., heir) of Abraham is an *ethnic* consideration— *even in cases when their genetic descent from Abraham is not in question.*

136   *Chapter 4*

In the following section, we will survey further references to Abraham across the gospel. These include: a "daughter of Abraham" healed on the Sabbath (13:10–17); Zacchaeus, a "son of Abraham" who welcomes Jesus into his home (19:1–10); and a parable about a poor man reclining with Abraham after his death—contrasted with a rich "child" of Abraham who is *separated* from them, in Hades (16:19–31). Echoing this last example, Luke reworks a Q pericope about Abraham at the eschatological feast, from which some who expected to be included will be barred, while sundry others "from east and west, and from north and south" are welcomed in (13:24–30). We will consider what these passages imply about the racial identity of those who can, or cannot, be numbered among Abraham's "children" (τεκνα) or "descendants" (σπερμα)—or those who nominally belong to this line, without inheriting any benefits from it.

A Daughter of Abraham (Luke 13:10–17)[105]

While teaching in the synagogue, Jesus encounters a woman who is doubled over with a "spirit of weakness," bent with an infirmity she has borne for almost two decades. That she has long endured symptoms associated with old age suggests that she is "getting on in years" (cf. Luke 1:7)—although this is not explicitly stated. From the fact that she is mentioned without reference to an accompanying man, we may infer that she is unmarried or a widow. Indeed, she is described not as a mother or a wife, but as a daughter: where living family members are lacking, she has Abraham for a father. Although Luke elsewhere notes the involvement of wealthy women in the early Jesus-movement,[106] nothing suggests that this particular woman is of anything but modest means; indeed, it is more likely—given her condition and seeming lack of family—that she is poor. We may safely infer that she is Judean from her presence at the synagogue. This "daughter of Abraham" is one of those poor but pious worshipers of God, living on the margins of Israel—those lacking in resources, relations, or respect—like those described in the Song of Mary. She is one of the *anawim* (faithful poor) of Israel, who will be vindicated as God fulfills the promises to Abraham and his descendants (cf. 1:51–55).[107]

Jesus heals her, which offends the *archisynagōgos* because it is the Sabbath day. Jesus defends his actions with a typical rabbinic *qal-vaḥomer* argument: if Sabbath observance allows for the relatively "light" matter of watering one's livestock, how much more does it allow for the "weighty" matter of saving a woman on the Sabbath (cf. Luke 14:5). Moreover, she is not just any woman but a "daughter of Abraham." Mentioning this may be a simple matter of leveraging shared ethnicity to evoke sympathy: i.e., "She is your kinswoman." But Jesus could possibly be echoing an early rabbinic teaching that insists upon the dignity and worth of each descendant of Abraham. These traditions affirmed that even the poorest Israelites should be reckoned free men, on account of Abraham (*m. Baba Kama* 8.6); and even the lowliest Judean laborers are worthy of as much honor as Solomon, as Abraham's sons (*m. Baba Mezia* 7.1).[108] Such thinking certainly resonates with Mary's confidence that God will exalt the lowly "as he promised to Abraham and his offspring forever" (Luke 1:51–55).

Although references to his sons are commonplace, "daughter of Abraham" (θυγατερα Αβρααμ) is an extremely rare title in the literature of the period.[109] It is found in 4 Maccabees; indeed, there are *several* uncommon expressions about Abraham or other ancestors, common to both 4 Maccabees and Luke–Acts (see table 4.3).

These linguistic similarities do not seem to result from direct literary dependence; beyond these similarities, neither grammar nor word statistics suggest any special proximity of the two writings. Perhaps they were written at roughly the same time; Antioch has been proposed as a possible place of origin for both.[110] We might consider, then, how Abraham functions in 4 Maccabees's racial reasoning, and ask whether we see any resemblance to Luke's thinking.

In 4 Maccabees, the mother of the seven brothers is described as a "daughter of Abraham" (4 Macc. 15:28). This close association goes beyond biology. She is "one in soul with Abraham" (Αβρααμ ὁμοψυχος, 4 Macc. 14:20), "a daughter of the endurance of Abraham" (4 Macc. 15:28). She is an "Abrahamitess" (Αβρααμιτιδος, 18:20) because she shares not only Abraham's blood, but his moral character.[111] In the terms which I use throughout this book: she is his daughter both by ascriptive descent (*ascribed* at birth) and by subscriptive descent (by *subscribing* to his ways). Similarly, her sons are vindicated as Abraham's children in their heroic adherence to Abraham's ways, even in the face of torture. The same logic applies in reverse: the first of the martyred brothers cautions that Judeans who "transgress our ancestral commandments" (τας πατριους εντολας) also "disgrace our forebears" (προγονους, 4 Macc. 9:2–3, 21). He exhorts his brothers, "imitate my example," for if they do not, they will not be "worthy of Abraham" (9:21–23).[112] The third brother makes this point even more explicit:

Table 4.3 Luke and 4 Maccabees: Abraham and the Patriarchs

- a daughter (θυγατηρ) of Abraham	(Luke 13:16; 4 Macc 15:28)
- Abraham lives / is undying "to God"	(Luke 20:37-38; 4 Macc 7:19, 16:25)
- Abraham and the "patriarchs" (πατριαρχαι)	(Acts 7:8-9; 4 Macc 7:19)
- "God of our ancestors" (πατρῳος Θεος)	(Acts 24:14; 4 Macc 12:18)

138   *Chapter 4*

> Do you not know that the same father begot me (εσπειρεν πατηρ) as well as those who died, and the same mother bore me (μητηρ εγεννεσιν), and that I was brought up (ανετραφην) on the same teachings? I do not renounce the noble kinship (ευγενη συγγενειαν) that binds me to my brothers. (*4 Maccabees* 10:2–3)[113]

The "noble kinship" that the brother shares with his family is not only a matter of biology (represented by words for reproduction, σπειρω and γενναω), but also a matter of keeping the teachings in which he was brought up. To abandon the latter would be to renounce the former. This view is echoed by Philo, who affirmed that "so-called kinships" based upon blood are meaningless if invalidated by bad conduct (cf. *Special Laws* 1.317; *Rewards* 152).[114]

Despite the linguistic parallels, the term "daughter of Abraham" functions differently in Luke 13:16. Here, it is a simple observation, not an honorific. Dorota Hartman notes that the heroic mother of 4 Maccabees proved herself Abraham's daughter by her heroic readiness to sacrifice her sons for her faith (4 Macc. 14:20), as Abraham was willing to sacrifice his son (Gen. 22). By contrast, the woman of Luke 13 does nothing in particular to merit comparison with him. She is simply a "daughter of Abraham" as a member of the Judean *ethnos*.[115]

This is an apt observation: there are clearly differences between these two "daughters of Abraham." However, both Seim and Hartman draw conclusions that go well beyond this point. They argue that, unlike the author of *4 Maccabees*, Luke is altogether uninterested in reframing Abrahamic identity. Supposedly, Luke lacks any of the notion of "spiritual kinship" (or "sharing in Abraham's faith"), which govern the redefinition of Abrahamic descent found in other early Christian texts (e.g., Gal. 3:7; Rom. 4:16; John 8:33–40).[116]

I will more fully engage these claims in my discussion of Zacchaeus. But to tip my hand: I partially agree with their position, but object to their reduction of "spiritual descent" ("subscriptive descent") to an all-or-nothing proposition. They suggest that if Judeans do not have to *earn* their identity as children of Abraham, neither can they *lose* it. Instead, I will argue that Luke characterizes some Judeans as insufficiently Abrahamic, not because of something positive which they *failed* to do, but because of something negative which they *did* do.[117]

Seim and Hartman perceptively recognize that Luke *does* attribute "default" Abrahamic standing to Judeans, including the benefits and blessings of this identity. This positive identity (with its concomitant blessings) naturally accrues to Judeans; they need not do anything special to "earn" it. It is in *this* sense that Luke's "daughter of Abraham" can be identified as such. However, although Luke understands Judeans as children of Abraham, individual Judeans can *jeopardize* this identity by engaging in egregiously

"We Have a Father—Abraham" 139

unAbrahamic offenses (Luke 3:8–14). Things which threaten one's standing include: (1) *mercilessness*—when those with the capability to help withhold assistance from those in desperate need, whether hospitality, clothing, food, or healing (3:11; 6:24–25; 16:19–21); (2) *predatory financial practices*, such as the overcollection of taxes (3:13; 19:8b); and (3) *extortion*, whether accomplished by intimidation, false accusations, or threats (3:14; cf. 6:29–30). Furthermore, it seems as though *4) actively resisting Jesus*, God's messiah, may fall into this category (3:15–17; Acts 3:13–15). Although Judeans do not "need to do anything" to be Abraham's children, they can destabilize their status by these behaviors. Luke holds that in these cases, *and in these cases only*, the positive step of repentance is necessary to restore one's rightful inheritance as his child (Luke 3:3, 8; Acts 3:19–20).

In the case of the woman with the bent back, she is accounted a daughter of Abraham simply by default (as a Judean, presumably). She is one of those simple, pious poor who can rejoice that God will fill the hungry and help Israel, as he promised Abraham (Luke 1:53–55).

A Son of Abraham (Luke 19:1–10)[118]

In Jericho, Jesus meets Zacchaeus, an *architelōnos* (chief tax collector), who is wealthy (πλουσιος).[119] This last detail disposes the alert reader to be suspicious of Zacchaeus, for the rich have not fared well in Luke's gospel.[120] But, as it happens, this entire episode is full of ironies and reversals. Zacchaeus seeks to *see* Jesus, but it is Jesus who spots *him*. Zacchaeus is a professional bureaucrat, yet heedless of his dignity, he climbs a tree like a child. Zacchaeus is short, but Jesus must "look up" to *him*. Zacchaeus has elevated himself over one whom he addresses as "Lord."[121] Jesus could surely lodge with someone respectable; instead, he decides to stay with a tax officer—looked down upon as a collaborator by Judeans, and as *nouveau riche* by gentiles.[122] Zacchaeus extends hospitality to Jesus, but only after Jesus invites *himself* to his house. A renowned religious celebrity is staying with a known "sinner," which does not go unnoticed by the villagers who know Zacchaeus' reputation. Although Zacchaeus's hospitality makes him the *host*, the narrative seems to position him as the *client* of Jesus—the patron who singles him out and bestows salvation. In sum, the scene is rife with incongruities, surprises, and reversals—culminating in Jesus' acclamation of this reputed sinner as a "son of Abraham."

In some respects, the story is reminiscent of Abraham's hospitality to the three divine visitors at the Oak of Mamre (Gen 18:1–8).[123] On the level of vocabulary, the pericope shares several words with the Septuagint account, such as "looked up" (αναβλεπω), "hurried" (σπευδω), and "saw" (ιδειν), and the vocative address "lord" (κυριε). Zacchaeus "ran ahead" (προτρεχω) to see

140   *Chapter 4*

Jesus—only one letter away from Abraham's "running out" (προστρεχω) to meet the visitors. The narratives share several elements: a tree, divine visitors, hospitality, a meal, a blessing pronounced, an objection from someone at the edges of the action (Sarah / the crowds), and an elaboration on that blessing. Like Abraham's eager excitement, conveyed by his hurried actions, Zacchaeus joyfully (χαιρων) receives (ὑποδεξατο) Jesus.[124] Philo describes Abraham as "full of joy" (χαρας) as he sped to carry out his reception/ hospitality (ὑποδοχης); his hospitality (φιλοξενον) was a natural outgrowth of his piety (θεοσεβεια). Philo rhapsodizes on the blessedness of a household ordered according to this principle (*Abr.* 107–18). Luke's scene also echoes Lot's hospitality to the same visitors in Sodom (Gen. 19:1–5): both feature divine visitors, who are invited to lodge (καταλυω) at a house (οικος)—an act of welcoming observed with ill will by other townsfolk. Lot's welcome is itself modeled on Abraham's: Josephus comments that Lot was "benevolent to strangers" (περι τους ξενους φιλανθρωπος) because "he had learned the lesson of Abraham's kindliness" (*Ant.* 1.200). Both Abraham and Lot invited these young men to "partake of [their] hospitality" (ξενιαν παρακαλειν; *Ant.* 1.196–200). Zacchaeus, then, resembles his father Abraham in his eagerness to lavish hospitality upon a divine visitor.

With this project's focus on ethnicity, we are especially interested in the racial implications of the label "son of Abraham," and the sense in which it is applied to Zacchaeus. Is this a default status, ascribed simply because Zacchaeus is a Judean? After all, this was the case with a "daughter of Abraham," earlier (Luke 13:16). Or have his actions contributed to this identification? The answers to such questions will largely hinge upon how one understands Zacchaeus' words to Jesus:

> Look, half of my possessions I give (διδωμι) to the poor; and if I have defrauded (εσυκοφαντησα) anyone of anything, I give it back (αποδιδωμι) fourfold. (Luke 19:8)

Zacchaeus solemnizes this declaration by rising to his feet. Much rides upon how we interpret the verbs. "Give" (διδωμι) and "give back" (αποδιδωμι) are in the present tense. Should they be understood as the futuristic present ("I am going to give . . . ") or as the habitual/iterative present ("I regularly give")?[125] To parse out the several possibilities, see table 4.4.

On the narrative level, the first and most literal option makes little sense. Zacchaeus cannot state, "I (this very moment) give half my possessions to the poor," unless we imagine the poor crowded into his dining room, poised to carry off the silverware! The iterative present is a viable option, making Zacchaeus' words a declaration of his normal practice: he gives, and continues to give, generously, and he always richly overcompensates in cases

"We Have a Father—Abraham" 141

Table 4.4 Possible Readings of Luke 19:8

Simple present:	I now give half my wealth to the poor; I now repay...
Iterative present:	I regularly give half my wealth to the poor; I always repay...
Tendential present:	I resolve to give half my wealth to the poor; I am going to repay...
Futuristic present:	I will give half my wealth to the poor; I will repay...[i]

---

[i] cf. Brooks-Winbury, *Syntax of New Testament Greek*, 85-89; what I here call "Simple Present," they refer to as the "Aoristic Present."

of overcollection. In this reading, this declaration would constitute a self-defense—testimony that refutes the crowd's indictment of him as a "sinner" (19:6).[126] Alternatively, we might understand that these words express his resolve to do something in the future: the *intention* is already true now ("I am going . . ."), but its enactment remains to be done (". . . to give").

Our translation will make a great difference to how we understand the situation. If Zacchaeus is already generous and scrupulously fair, then he has nothing to repent of—his testimony about his customary giving would, in fact refute the charge that he is a "sinner." If, on the other hand, these verbs express *future* action, then Zacchaeus is now turning away from the very ways which have made him rich—in a word, *repenting*. The stakes are: Is this "son of Abraham" so simply by birth, or (also) by repentance?

Several factors favor the interpretation that Zacchaeus does, in fact, repent. Firstly, it is hard to make the iterative reading fit the details in the story. Zacchaeus has already been described as "rich," but it is hard to understand how this could be so if he both refuses to leverage his position for personal gain, *and* periodically gives away half his possessions![127] If these factors were both true, his wealth would dwindle until he found himself living near subsistence level. Jesus' response also suggests that Zacchaeus repents: "*Today* salvation has come to this house" (19:9). Zacchaeus had been among the "lost," whom Jesus came to seek and save (19:10). These verses support a reading of διδωμι/αποδιδωμι as the futuristic present.[128] Zacchaeus had been lost, but "today" is saved.

We might also consider the literary context: the pericope is grouped amongst other stories of repentance and salvation, across chapters 15–19.[129] Robert Beck suggests that the story follows a repeating pattern in Luke, in which repentant and non-repentant characters serve as foils for each other (Luke 7:36–50; 15:11–31; 23:39–43).[130] Jesus had just told a story in which a tax collector was a model of repentance (18:9–14), shortly before meeting Zacchaeus.

Notice the points of contact with the Baptist's preaching. John had warned his audience that the children of Abraham must bear fruit worthy

142   *Chapter 4*

of repentance, and the Lukan expansions of John's preaching gave three examples of what such repentance looks like. The details of the Zacchaeus story recall these instructions. Firstly, Zacchaeus resolves to share his surplus wealth with the needy—exactly half, reminiscent of the instruction for those with "two shirts" to share one of them (3:11). Secondly, John explicitly instructed tax collectors (τελωναι) to collect no more than was appointed for them (3:12–13), exactly the scenario described by Zacchaeus (19:8b). Zacchaeus uses the same word for such extortion that John uses in his third set of instructions:

> *John:* "Do not defraud (συκοφανησητε) anyone. . . ." (3:14)
> *Zacchaeus:* "If I have defrauded (εσυκοφαντησα) anyone. . . ." (19:8)

Συκοφαντεω can mean to extort, accuse falsely, or slander, often before officials or in court.[131] Bovon remarks,

> If we take into consideration the way in which duties and taxes were levied, it is probably this precise, legal sense that must prevail here. For when a tax collector did not get what he wanted, he could pursue in court the person who had not paid up and could even be tempted to produce false evidence.[132]

If Zacchaeus has been engaging in such practices, he is a textbook example of those John called to repent.

How or why, then, is Zacchaeus a "son of Abraham?" The interpretation I favor is that Zacchaeus is a son of Abraham both as a Judean and also as one who "bears fruit" worthy of Abraham (3:8–9).[133] That is, Abraham is his "father" both by ascriptive (default, biological) descent and by subscriptive descent. In this reading, Zacchaeus imitates the patriarch, either in his own positive actions (extending Abrahamic hospitality) or in his turning away from past misdeeds (again following Abraham, whose abandonment of his family's idolatry had by this time become an icon of repentance/conversion).[134] Perhaps he is like Abraham in both of these ways.

The alternative is that "son of Abraham" (19:9) is a simple ascription of identity, equivalent to saying Zacchaeus is a Judean.[135] Does Luke lack a notion of "spiritual kinship," such as that found in some other early Christian texts (Gal. 3:7; Rom. 4:16; John 8:33–40)? Hartman believes so, writing, "in [Luke's] writings, hints of the notion that kinship with Abraham is not enough for obtaining salvation are visible only in the Q passages."[136] (As I will argue below, the parable of Lazarus [16:19–31] makes this assertion untenable).[137] Turid Seim similarly remarks:

"We Have a Father—Abraham"   143

Paul uses the Abraham story both in Galatians and Romans to define who is really counted among Abraham's children. For him the notion of Abraham's faith is crucial, even if he dramatically reinterprets it. It is the more remarkable that this feature is missing in Luke–Acts. Luke seems to be preoccupied primarily with Abraham as the receiver of God's election and promise and with the children of Abraham for whom the promise still holds good. . . . Abraham in Luke remains the ancestor of Israel, whose descendants—sons and daughters—are the heirs of the promise given to him and the blessings that flow from it. Luke does not represent a theology of replacement.[138]

Notice that Seim goes far beyond the simple observation that Luke's use of Abraham is distinct from Paul's: no, *any* notion of "spiritual kinship" (or "subscriptive descent") is "missing" in Luke. She also assumes that any sense of subscriptive descent must represent "a theology of replacement," rather than, say, a theology of inclusion-alongside. Because she conflates these two ideas, Seim argues that if one agrees that Luke does not represent a theology of replacement (a statement with which I agree), one must *also* agree that Luke lacks any notion of "spiritual descent" (a statement I would reject). Francis Bovon's reflections are more judicious:

It would probably be misleading to understand descent from Abraham in the Pauline sense of being chosen through belonging to Christ (Gal. 3:6–18; Rom. 4:1–25). Luke had another conception of Israel's identity; in his eyes, the historical Jewish people remained Abraham's descendants. But this people had to show itself worthy of its status; if not, it would lose that privilege. What Jesus had to do, in the case of these "lost" sheep of Israel, was to find them, reestablish them, "save" them, and thus permit them to fulfill the obligations associated with their Jewish identity.[139]

Bovon asserts *both* that Luke sees Judeans as children of Abraham "by default," *and* that they must act like it. For the "lost" sheep of the people, their privileged status is in jeopardy until they are reestablished by repentance.

To be clear, it is my position that Luke holds that a Judean *is* a son or daughter of Abraham, before and apart from any "good works" or deserving behavior. I certainly agree with Seim that "Luke maintains the genetic thrust of the inherited terms."[140] Even this basic acknowledgment is a sadly necessary corrective in the wake of millennia of Christian supersessionism, and the terrible cost it has exacted in Jewish lives through the centuries. However, I would well stop short of saying that Luke has *no* notion of "spiritual kinship" (or, to be more precise, "subscriptive descent"). For Luke, being a "son of Abraham" *both* denotes biological descent *and* assumes concomitant "subscriptive descent"—that is, some level of conduct compatible with Abraham's. In cases where the biological element is lacking, a connection may still be attributed to individuals who are like Abraham (the

144   *Chapter 4*

"stones" of 3:8); but if the second element is lacking, individuals must be reestablished by repentance (3:3, 8a; 19:8) or risk losing their standing (3:8–9, 16:24–26; Acts 3:12–26). Therefore, when Jesus calls Zacchaeus a "son of Abraham," this does, of course, also acknowledge his "genetic" Judean identity (as the Israelite name *Zakkai* suggests); but Luke would still hold that "no DNA test designed to determine one's ancestry could prove that someone was Abraham's child."[141] The proof is in the pudding: Abraham's children will bear fruit that demonstrates repentance (3:9), which is exactly what Zacchaeus does (19:8).

Beyond the question of "repentance," Zacchaeus' other actions recall Abraham. Allan Mitchell argues that Zacchaeus is Abraham's son because of his *positive* actions:

> It is because Zacchaeus has appropriated the example of Abraham that he is a true child of the patriarch, as opposed to those who claim patrimony in name only. . . . To show just how much Zacchaeus was an authentic son of Abraham, Luke appealed to what the patriarch was remembered for in Hellenistic-Jewish and Christian literature: hospitality and justification by works. . . . Therefore, he depicted Zacchaeus in the tradition of Abraham's hospitality and cast him as someone who customarily performed acts befitting justification.[142]

Rather than repentance, Mitchell focuses on hospitality. He does concede, however, that Zacchaeus' purported "self-defense" in 19:8 closely mirrors John the Baptist's instruction on almsgiving and justice (3:10–14)—which was itself embedded within a call to repent.[143]

What, then, of the bent woman, accounted a "daughter of Abraham" with no reference whatsoever to her conduct (Luke 13:10–17)? For Seim and Hartman, the fact that this daughter of Abraham "does nothing special" to earn the label proves that Luke has *no* concept of subscriptive descent. By contrast, Jeffrey Siker suggested that these pericopes present two distinct ways in which people are reckoned "children of Abraham":

> We see here two different but related types of true children of Abraham: those pious individuals on whom God bestows mercy and salvation because they are poor and downtrodden (e.g., the crippled woman) and those individuals who receive God's mercy and salvation because they repent and bear fruits of repentance (e.g., Zacchaeus). Luke, then, uses Abraham to confirm two patterns of the way in which God brings about salvation: through mercy to the pious poor and through the fruitful repentance of sinners. Both are children of Abraham.[144]

Siker astutely notes that when it comes to Zacchaeus, different (or at least, additional) dynamics seem to be in play. However, Siker may overstate the case in ascribing a positive value to being "poor and downtrodden"—as if other Judeans must "do" something *become* to Abraham's children, but the

"We Have a Father—Abraham" 145

poor need not.[145] It may be more nuanced to say that in Luke's economic imagination, it is the *wealthy* who are in particular need of repentance—who are at particular risk of jeopardizing their Abrahamic status. Poor Judeans, by contrast, are (by and large) assumed not to stand in need of such "repentance."

Zacchaeus, then, is a "son of Abraham" in every sense of the term; he proves to be of Abrahamic birth (as a Judean), and by conduct (hospitality and repentance).[146] The "organic" sense of the designation is not overturned, but reinforced, by adding this second element. Luke affirms that Judeans are children of Abraham, but he also holds that they can jeopardize this status by egregiously non-Abrahamic conduct.[147] In the case of such "lost" children, repentance restores them fully to the status that was already their birthright.[148] Zacchaeus is just such a case. Zacchaeus has (re)activated his ethnic identity, his Abrahamic deed confirming his stake in the patriarch.

The Bosom of Abraham (Luke 16:19–31)

In the parable of Lazarus and the rich man (Luke 16:19–31), Jesus vividly illustrates how bad conduct can undermine one's stake in Abraham. We encounter two characters, "a certain rich man" who wore purple and fine linen and feasted every day,[149] and "a certain poor man named Lazarus" who lied at his gate, covered with sores (16:19–21). The name is intriguing, as named characters are unusual in parables. "Lazarus" might strike a Judean listener as a colloquial Greek version of "Eliezer," the name of Abraham's faithful steward and one-time presumptive heir (Gen. 15:3–4).[150]

Lazarus cuts an especially pathetic figure. His mouth waters at the thought of the scraps falling from the rich man's table; he is meanwhile unable to prevent dogs from licking his open sores. The pair are obvious foils, on opposite poles of the ancient Mediterranean's honor/shame binary.[151] Together, they call to mind the Torah's demand to care for the poor (Deut. 14:28–29; 15:1–8)—an imperative which the rich man audaciously flaunts, feasting while a man starves to death on his doorstep.[152]

Both men die and find themselves in radically different positions *vis-à-vis* Abraham: the poor man is carried by angels to Abraham's breast, and the rich man is "far off" from Abraham in Hades (16:22–23).[153] Luke, like the author of 4 Maccabees, holds that Abraham is "alive to God" (4 Macc. 7:19, 16:25, Luke 20:37–28), and that Abraham can be expected to be present and active in the afterlife. Lazarus is now "εν τῳ κολπῳ," an expression which literally means "at his breast," and which could describe those reclining together while dining.[154] Lazarus now enjoys a feast he could only dream of while alive. Seeing them together, the rich man pleads:

146   *Chapter 4*

Father (πατερ) Abraham, have mercy on me and sent Lazarus so to dip the tip of his finger in water and cool my tongue, because I am in anguish in this flame. (Luke 16:24)

Why does he expect Abraham to help him? Perhaps simple kinship inspires the assumption that, as his πατερ ("father/ancestor"), Abraham would naturally get involved.

Beyond this, he might have in mind the popular Judean trope that Abraham would intercede for the deceased, or otherwise assist them.[155] For example, the *Testament of Abraham* describes the patriarch rejoicing over those who enter the narrow gate of heaven and weeping over those who enter the wide gate (*Test.Abr.* 11:9–11; cf. Luke 13:24), and interceding for sinners in a state of suspense (14:5–18).[156] In the *Apocalypse of Zephaniah*, the narrator crosses a sort of Judean equivalent of the River Styx. Unlike the rich man in Hades, to whom Abraham "cannot cross over," Zephaniah is able to "cross over the crossing place" because his name was written in the Book of Life (cf. Luke 9:2). There, he sees the easy rapport Abraham enjoys with God and his angels: they talk "as friend to friend" (*Apoc.Zeph.* 9:4–5). Abraham looked with compassion upon the anguish of the deceased:

[2]As they looked at all of the torments they called out, praying before the Lord Almighty, saying, "We pray unto Thee on account of those who are in all these torments so that Thou might have mercy on all of them." [3]And when I saw them, I said to the angel who spoke with me, "<Who are these?>" [4]He said, "These who beseech the Lord are Abraham and Isaac and Jacob. [5]Then at a certain hour daily they come forth with the great angel. He soundeth a trumpet up unto heaven and another soundeth upon the earth. [6]All the righteous hear the sound. They come running, praying to the Lord Almighty daily on behalf of these who are in all these torments." (*Apocalypse of Zephaniah* 11:2–6)[157]

This account shares some elements with the parable of Lazarus—anguish after death, two parties in seemingly very different parts of the afterlife who see each other from afar, and assistance from the patriarch.

Misled by these popular expectations, the rich man assumes Abraham will assist him in his plight. However, Abraham replies:

Child (τεκνον), remember that you received your good things during your life, and Lazarus likewise, bad things; but now, he is comforted, and you are in anguish. And besides all this, a great chasm has been fixed between us, so that no one who wishes to pass from here to you is able—nor may those from there pass to us. (Luke 16:25–26)

"We Have a Father—Abraham"   147

Called upon as "father," Abraham addresses the rich man as "child." But his response is anything but tender.[158] Abraham does not assist him—neither by fulfilling his request (cool water), nor by interceding with God. Instead, Abraham explains how the man ended up in this state—he had already received his blessings when alive, while poor Lazarus had nothing. Their situation now echoes Jesus' sermon on the plain:

> Happy are the poor, because yours is the kingdom of God.
> Happy are you who are hungry now; because you will be filled . . .
> But woe to you who are rich, because you have received your comfort (παρακλησιν).
> Woe to you who are full, because you will hunger. (—Luke 6:20–21a, 24–25a)

As in these beatitudes, their former and later situations have reversed. In other passages, Abraham *himself* is implicated in Luke's ethic of concern for the poor. The "mercy which God spoke to our ancestors (πατερας), Abraham and his descendants (σπερματι) forever" includes this bit of good news:

> He has filled the hungry with good things (αγαθα),
> and the rich he has sent away empty. (Luke 1:53)

Now, in this parable, Abraham's words to a "child" (τεκνον) remind us of John's orders to would-be children (τεκνα) of Abraham: "Whoever has two tunics, let him share with one who has none; and whoever has food, let him do likewise" (3:8, 11).[159] Abraham is aligned with the gospel's ethic of wealth, of how the rich ought to treat the poor—and just as clearly, *this* man did not treat Lazarus as a child of Abraham should.

Tombstone inscriptions attest that the "bosom of Abraham" was an image used of the anticipated rest and reward of the faithful after death.[160] Jesus' use of "Abraham's bosom," an image of eschatological feasting, is not accidental, given Abraham's reputation as a paragon of hospitality. The rich man had frequently feasted, joyfully, during his own life. Had he been a good son of Abraham, he would have bestowed hospitality upon the stranger at his gate, inviting him to join him. It is fitting, then, that the inhospitable rich man is not invited to feast with the hospitable Abraham (cf. Luke 3:8; 13:24–29).[161]

The rich man seems to assume, on the basis of biological kinship, that he will receive benefits from Abraham. He is his "father"—they are the same flesh and blood. When Abraham says that he cannot help him, the rich man at least tries to extend such benefits to others, also along kinship lines—his own brothers. Again, Abraham declines. There may be a contrast between his "father's house," full of (presumably) similarly unmerciful brothers, and the "father" he has tried to claim, Abraham. Biological claims, it seems, are

148   *Chapter 4*

no guarantee that Abraham will claim you back—if, that is, you have turned your back on his ways.

The biblical punishment of being "cut off" (Hebrew *karet*) aptly describes the state of the rich man in Hades. In Genesis, God told Abraham that any uncircumcised males would be "cut off from his γενους (race, stock, kin)" (Gen. 17:14),[162] and this dire formula becomes the consequence of a *variety* of offenses throughout the Torah.[163] Jacob Milgram explains,

> The other possible meaning of *karet* is that the punishment is indeed executed upon the sinner but only after his death; that is, he is not permitted to rejoin his ancestors in the afterlife... This meaning is supported by the idiom that is its opposite in meaning: *ne 'esaf 'el*, "be gathered to one's [kin, fathers]" (e.g., Num 20:24; 27:13: 31:2). Particularly in regard to the patriarchs, the language of the Bible presumes three stages concerning their death: They die, they are gathered to their kin, and they are buried (cf. Gen 25:8, 17; 35:29; 49:33).[164]

Applying this concept to Luke 16:19–31, Ed Christian argues that *karet* aptly describes the situation of the rich man in Hades. He is "cut off" from Abraham in the afterlife, whereas Lazarus is "gathered to his father" Abraham.[165]

Who then are Abraham's children? What is implied about the racial identity of someone whose ties to the ancestor are attenuated to such a ghostly thinness—receiving no inheritance, expecting no future blessings, and alienated from him after death? Abraham can *still* address this seemingly disowned man as his "child" (τεκνον). Although "child" is still an appropriate address at this point, what does it really mean?

I would suggest that the parable gives us a glimpse of two possibilities for Abraham's natural children—eternal inheritance and "comfort" at his "breast," or being finally "cut off" from him. Both are still "children," but those who refuse to embody Abrahamic mercy, hospitality, and repentance will eventually be estranged from him. Recall that in Judean traditions, the "inheritance" or "noninheritance" of Abraham's children (whether or not they received the patriarch's blessing and the covenant entrusted to him) had *ethnic* significance among these children's descendants—with a relatively higher valuation of races who were his heirs (i.e., Israelites) than those who were not (everyone else). Thinking along these lines, the Judeans who have endangered their relationship with Abraham may continue to have a sort of secondary genealogical standing with him—but this is along the lines of the "offshoots" of Abraham's line who did not inherit the promises and the covenant, like Ishmael and Esau. I suggest that Luke imagines this to be the case: those who turn their backs on Abraham (in Luke's estimation, at least) are reconfigured ethnically as "second-class" relations to the patriarch.[166] If this is the case, Lazarus' name is all the more poignant—the foreigner Eliezer,

"We Have a Father—Abraham"   149

who might have (but did not!) become Abraham's heir in Genesis (15:2–3), is now, figuratively, reclined intimately upon Abraham's bosom. The literal (and social) outsider has been ethnically vindicated; it is hard to imagine how one could be more demonstrably *Judean* than to be resting upon the founding patriarch's breast! At the same time, the seeming insider is now left deracialized, cut off from Abraham.

But, we must remember, the characters in this parable are already deceased. How does avarice effect Judean ethnicity, *before* death? Certainly, unmerciful Judeans can still rightly be called "Judeans" throughout Luke–Acts, and "Israelites." But what about their connection to Abraham? I would argue that, during their lifetime, the "Abrahamic" identity of rich or cruel Judeans is not decisively *severed*—but it is *placed at risk*. Even those Judeans whom Peter held responsible for Jesus' death are addressed as "Israelites" (Acts 3:12) and "brothers" (3:17)—despite defying "the God of Abraham, the God of Isaac, the God of Jacob, the God of our ancestors" (3:13). But they are *at risk* of losing their inheritance in Abraham. Thus, the call to repentance is urgent (Acts 3:19; Luke 3:7–9); those who die without repenting are in real danger of being "cut off from the people" (Acts 3:23), which, in eschatological terms, might be described as being permanently "cut off" from Abraham (Luke 16:22–26) rather than resting "upon his bosom."

Abraham and the Eschaton (Luke 13:23–30, 17:29–32)

The parable of Lazarus and the rich man shares several features with another Abraham-saying—one Luke inherited from the Q source.[167] Shortly after Jesus healed the bent "daughter of Abraham," someone asks him: "Will only a few be saved?" Jesus responds,

> [24]Strive to enter through the narrow gate (πυλης); because many, I tell you, will seek to enter and will not be able to.[25] When once the master of the house has risen and closed the door, and you begin (αρξησθε) to stand outside (εξω) and to knock at the door, saying: "Lord, Lord, open up for us," then he will answer you saying, "I don't know where you come from."[26] Then you will begin to say, "We ate and drank with you, and you taught in our streets."[27] And he will say, "I tell you, I don't know where you come from; get away from me, all you evildoers."[28] There will be weeping and grinding of teeth there, when you see Abraham and Isaac and Jacob and all the prophets in the kingdom of God, and you yourselves cast outside.[29] And people will come from east and west, north and south, and recline at table (ανακλιθησονται) in the kingdom of God.[30] See, some who are last will be first, and some who are first will be last. (Luke 13:23–30)

150   *Chapter 4*

Lazarus's story could almost have been inspired by this logion—a sort of midrashic expansion upon it, as if its ideas have been fleshed out in narrative form. The evangelist did not simply inherit the saying (Luke 13:23–30) passively from his source (cf. Matt. 8:11–12); rather, he elaborated upon it elsewhere. Moreover, Luke's particular version of this saying places somewhat greater emphasis on Abraham than the Matthean parallel (table 4.5).[168]

Luke 13:23–30 invokes several key ingredients of racial identity, such as ancestry, geography, customs, and religion.[169] In terms of geography, the saying mixes the actual with the imagined. People come "from east and west, north and south" (i.e., from "the ends of the earth"), and they stream to a central location where they can draw near to God, perhaps channeling prophesies which anticipate a day when the nations will stream to Jerusalem, and prophesies which foretell the regathering of scattered Israel. However, in this saying it is not the Holy City where they gather, but the eschatological "kingdom of God."[170]

As in the parable of Lazarus, Abraham is "alive before God" (cf. Luke 20:37–38 // Mark 12:26). Here it is "the Lord" who is petitioned, rather than Abraham. Those unable to enter the narrow gate will "*begin to say* (αρξησθε λεγειν), 'We ate and drank in your presence'" (13:26)—reminding us that John scolded the crowds: "Do not *begin to say* (αρξησθε λεγειν), 'We have Abraham as our father'" (3:8). In both cases, people presume upon family connections to win them special treatment; and in both cases, they are disappointed. Dorota Hartman observes, "It is evident that in the passages originating from Q, Abraham is associated with the Judgment, and that mere kinship with the patriarch gives no special benefits."[171]

In the eschaton, there will be inhospitality precisely for those who resented Jesus' hospitality to the marginalized during his lifetime.[172] Those who failed to embody Abraham's famed hospitality will not enjoy his company at the heavenly banquet. Those who can say that they "ate and drank" with Jesus are (mostly) Judeans—but he will say, "I do not know where you come from" (13:27). This language of not knowing whence (ποθεν) they come could have *racial* implications, as well. Origins were extremely salient in constructions of ethnicity; but it is almost as if their geographical origins (from Judea or

Table 4.5   Shared motifs, Lazarus Story and Luke 13:23–30

Shared motifs in Luke 13:23-30 and 16:19-31
- a "gate" (πυλης) at which someone wishes to enter (13:24 // 16:20)
- a contrast between inside and outside (13:25,28 // 16:19-21,26)
- a dramatic reversal, counter to expectations (13:30 // 16:25)
- from a place of torment (13:28 // 16:24b)
- the excluded "see" (13:28 // 16:23)
- unlikely diners "reclining" with Abraham (13:28-29 // 16:22)

"We Have a Father—Abraham"   151

Galilee) as well as their genealogical origins (from Abraham) are wiped away "on that day." They have become not only *eschatological* but *ethnic* "outsiders," cast out into the cold while Israel's celebrated ancestors feast in the kingdom.

But the patriarchs are not the only ones invited to the feast. The image of people gathered from distant lands echoes the widespread expectation that in the end-times, gentiles would stream to Jerusalem (Isa. 2:1–4; 25:6–8; 51:4–6; 59:19; Mic. 4:1–4; Zech. 14:16; Mal. 1:11; Tob. 13:11; 14:6).[173] Those from "east and west, north and south" (13:29) would include gentiles as well as Judeans.[174] Abraham seems to be involved in (or at least, proximate to) not only the exclusion of presumptive insiders, but also the inclusion of former outsiders.[175] To put it another way: Luke associates Abraham with those who enter God's kingdom (even gentiles) and contrasts Abraham with those who have been shut out (even Judeans).[176]

Elsewhere, Jesus teaches that those in the afterlife are "sons of God, being sons of the resurrection" (Luke 20:36). Since Abraham, Isaac, and Jacob are alive before God (20:28; cf. 13:28), they also fall into this category. Therefore, "those who are accounted worthy to attain to that age and that resurrection" (20:35), are, in a sense "related" to Abraham—they are fellow "children of the resurrection" together. The identity of those who walk as children of Abraham in this life will be confirmed in the resurrection life.[177]

This need not represent a "theology of replacement," as if Abraham has rejected his children and adopted gentiles in their place. Rather, it has always been God's explicit intention to bless the nations in Abraham's children (Acts 3:25 // Gen. 22:18). Although Abraham is, *naturally and by default*, the father of Judeans, some of them have gone out of their way to disqualify themselves from his heritage.[178] And although Abraham is *not* the physical father of gentiles, he may become—unnaturally, as it were—related to those who go out of their way to follow him. Those who experience a shift in relationship to Abraham are therefore the exception—Judeans must be *exceptionally* unAbrahamic to jeopardize their heritage in him, while gentiles must be *exceptionally* Abrahamic to be invited into his household.

Abraham's association with eschatological judgment—for gentiles *and* his own kin—is also glimpsed in the apocalyptic material in chapter 17. Luke has expanded the saying about the "days of Noah" (Luke 17:26–27 // Matt. 24:37–39) by adding a similar saying about the "days of Lot," in Sodom (17:29–30, 32). Both biblical allusions concern a time when a group of mixed peoples stood under divine judgment for extraordinarily wicked behavior—whether the entire earth on account of humanity's violence (Gen. 6:5–7), or Sodom on account of its wickedness (Gen. 18:20–21). In both stories, a very

152   *Chapter 4*

few who are not stained by the prevailing wickedness are spared, while the rest are wiped out.

We are particularly interested in Luke's allusion to Sodom (Luke 17:29–32). Abraham interceded for God to spare the city if a minimum of righteous residents could be found there (Gen. 18:22–32). Sadly, not even ten righteous men can be found in the city, but before it is destroyed, God warns Lot, Abraham's nephew (and adoptive son, according to some traditions Gen. 19:12–13; *Ant.* 1.154, 205; *Jub.* 12:30). The city is finally destroyed, but Lot's family makes their escape. However, Luke reminds his reader, Lot's wife turned around and was destroyed as well (Luke 17:32; Gen. 19:26). Several elements of the allusion are relevant for our purposes. By invoking this story, Luke reminds the reader that Abraham had been willing to extend his assistance to righteous gentiles, and that God had been willing to accept them on Abraham's account (had any been found). Luke also reminds the reader that not even all of Lot's own family were spared—and thus, even of Judeans living side by side "on that day," some will be spared and others taken (17:34–35).[179]

ABRAHAM IN LUKE: CHAPTER CONCLUSIONS

In Luke, we get a glimpse of the expected characteristics of the children of Abraham, a "profile" of those who belong to his family:

(1) *The children of Abraham recognize Jesus and praise God*, as the hymns of the Infancy Narrative (Luke 1–2) illustrate. (2) *They repent*, if their sin has led them astray, just as John exhorted (3:8a) and as exemplified by Zacchaeus. Incidentally, Gentiles may also show such repentance (Acts 11:18), as we learn in Acts. (3) *Children of Abraham are generous and hospitable*, as Abraham himself was; again, Zacchaeus embodies this quality (19:5–9), in terms reminiscent of Abraham's hospitality toward the three strangers at Mamre (Gen. 18:3–8). Note that gentiles may *also* embody "Abrahamic" generosity, as, for example the two "unmercenary" centurions (Luke 7:4–5; Acts 10:1–48), who do not abuse their positions to extort money (Luke 3:14), but in fact leverage their wealth to help others. (4) *The children of Abraham are merciful*, as Abraham was (Gen. 18:22–33), unlike a so-called "child" of Abraham who failed to show mercy (Luke 16:19–25). On a related note, (5) *the children of Abraham deserve mercy* (Luke 13:16), as God promised (Luke 1:54–55, 72–73) and as rabbinic traditions insisted.[180]

This profile, combined with the Baptist's warning (Luke 3:8), has ethnic implication. If Judeans fail to live up to it, they are in real danger of being disavowed by Abraham (like Esau in *Jubilees* 19) or disqualified as his children, undermining their ethnic identity. Conversely, if Abraham's children

"We Have a Father—Abraham" 153

are characterized by recognition of Jesus, repentance, generosity, and mercy, what of gentiles who *do* embody these traits? The Third Gospel foreshadows this possibility, and we will encounter several in Acts who fit the bill. From the unlikely material of the *ethnē*, these "rocks," too, have been quarried from Father Abraham (Luke 3:8; Isa. 51:2).

NOTES

1. See chapter 2, above; but see, e.g., *Test.Ab.* rec.A 14:1–15; *T.Isaac* 6:9–23; Philo *Q.Gen.* 44, *De Execr.* § 9; Jos. *Ant.* 1.13, § 3; *Sib.Or.* 2:331; *3 En* 44:7–10; *T.Lev.* 18:12–14; cf. *T.Jud.* 25:1.

2. See chapter 2, above; but see, e.g., Ezek. 33:24–29; *Jub.* 19:13–23, 21:17; 4 Macc. 18:1–5, 20–24; *Ezra* 3:15–27; Jos. *Ant.* 5.113, Philo *Virtues*, 207.

3. See chapter 2.

4. Jeffrey Siker, *Disinheriting the Jews* (Louisville, KY: Westminster John Knox, 1991), 103.

5. Siker goes so far as to say that for Luke, gentiles have a claim upon Abraham "on the same terms as Jews," which may be an overstatement. *Disinheriting the Jews*, 103.

6. Matt. 3:7–10 // Luke 3:7–9; compare John 8:39–40. For this study, I assume the general contours of the "Four Source Hypothesis" (including the existence of some source common to Matthew and Luke, commonly designated "Q"), over and against the Farrer-Goulder hypothesis of Markan priority, followed by Matthew, with Luke using both as sources.

Presuming the Farrer-Goulder position (eliminating "Q") need not disrupt the logic of my discussion overmuch. I am interested in how Luke makes use of, and possibly edits, pre-existing sources, as an indicator of the author's interests and ideas. For passages where a parallel from the supposed "Q" is under discussion, I am interested in how the Lukan text is different from an earlier source. Whether Luke is using Q or Matthew, we are still able to see his particular emphases in the way he reworks and reframes the text.

7. E.g., Josephus *Antiquities* 14.403; see chapter 1.

8. As a reminder, "Judaism" within this discussion denotes "the aggregate of all those characteristics that make Judaeans Judaean," as Shaye Cohen puts it—that is, it is inclusive of (but not limited to) what moderns would label "religion." Cohen, *The Beginnings of Jewishness*, 105–106.

9. Bovon, *Luke,* Heremeneia (Minneapolis, MN: Fortress, 2002) 1.121.

10. Bovon, *Luke*, 1.119; Nickolas Fox, *The Hermeneutics of Social Identity in Luke–Acts* (Eugene, OR: Pickwick, 2021), 117; Smith, "Luke, the Jews, and the Politics of Early Christian Identity," PhD Dissertation (Durham, NC: Duke University, 2018), 94.

11. Bovon, *Luke*, 1.117; Alen Culpepper, *Luke*, NIB (Nashville, TN: Abindgon Press, 1996), 83.

12. Culpepper, *Luke*, 85.

154   *Chapter 4*

13. cf. Matt. 12:34.

14. *Gennēma* derives from γεννάω, to be born, to bear, to beget (See LSJ, γεννημα), and etymologically highlights the natural processes of generation. See Craig S. Keener, "'Brood of Vipers' (Matthew 3.7; 12.34; 23.33)," *JSNT* 28.1 (2005): 6. The word *can* sometimes be used as in equivalent to the Semitic "children of" idiom (e.g., the "sons of the prophets" in 1 Samuel; cf. Judg 1.10, 20 LXX; Sir. 10.18); but had Q merely wished to invoke a plural designation of the John's audience in this way, we would expect a more generic term like υιοι or τεκνα (Keener, "Brood of Vipers," 6–7).

15. As examples of "genetic insults," Keener cites the behavior of wives (Martial, *Epig.* 2.56; Musonius Rufiis 10, Lutz, p. 78, 11. 16–19; Prov. 12.4), daughters (Sir. 42.9–11; 4Q213 frg. 2.18–20), and sons (Xenophon, *Apol.* 31; Plutarch, *Them.* 2.6). Keener, "Brood of Vipers," 3.

16. Conversely, one might claim that an opponent's parents had harmed the Roman state by having the opponent as their child (Ps.-Cicero, *Invective Against Sallust* 5.13). Keener, "Brood of Vipers," 3.

17. *JPS* trans.

18. CD 5.14 // 4Q266 3 II.

19. Michael P. Knowles, "Serpents, Scribes, and Pharisees," *Journal of Biblical Literature* 133.1 (2014): 168–169.

20. John Byron cites, for instance, 1 Jn 3:10–12; Tert. *Patience* 5.15; *Gos. Phil.* 61:5–10; *Tg.Ps.-J.* Gen 4:1; *Pirqe R. El.* 21. Byron, *Cain in Text and Tradition: Jewish and Christian Interpretations of the First Sibling Rivalry* (Leiden: Brill, 2011), 17.

21. Keener, "Brood of Vipers," 6.

22. Aelian, *Nat. an.* 1.24; 15.16; Pliny *Nat.* 10.169–70; Philostr. *Vit.Apoll.* 2.14. Cited by Keener, "Brood of Vipers," 7. cf. also Knowles, "Serpents, Scribes, and Pharisees," 167.

23. Ibid., 167; cf. Keener, "Brood of Vipers," 8 FN 13.

24. cf. Sophocles, *Oed.tyr.* 1440–1441; Cornelius Nepos 15 (Epaminondas), 6, 2; Diodorus Siculus 1, 77, 8; Dionysius of Halicamassus, *Ant. rom.* 8, 80, 1; Seneca, *Clem.* 1, 23.1; Epictetus, *Diatr.* 1, 7, 31–33; Plutarch, *Rom.* 22, 4; Marcus Aurelius, *Med.* 6.34; Apuleius, *Metam.* 10.8; Diogenes Laertius, *Lives* 1.59; 1 Tim 1.9. Nero's matricide was especially infamous (Martial, *Epig.* 4, 63, 3–4; *Sib. Or.* 4.121; 5.30; 8.71). Examples from Keener, "Brood of Vipers," 9.

25. Compare Matthew's "Do not *presume* (δοξητε) to say to yourselves." (Matt. 3:9).

26. Consider a similar polemical situation in John's gospel: when Jesus impugns some Judeans' parentage (John 8:38), they assert their status as "children of Abraham" (8:39).

27. In Turid Seim's reading, the "stones" are the rejected of *Israel* who are "reclaimed" as heirs of the promise—i.e., literal genetic descendants of Abraham, who have been marginalized because of their social location, impurity, or profession. "The children of Abraham are all Jews, but not all Jews are children of Abraham. God is raising up children of Abraham from stones—the disclaimed are reclaimed as heirs of the promise." Turid Karlsen Seim, "Abraham, Ancestor or Archetype?

"We Have a Father—Abraham"

A Comparison of Abraham-Language in 4 Maccabees and Luke–Acts," in *Antiquity and Humanity: Essays on Ancient Religion and Philosophy*, Adela Yarbro Collins and Margaret M. Mitchell, eds. (Tübingen: Mohr Siebeck, 2001), 42. While the saying could allow for this reading, it would lose some of its surprising quality; "stones" (like gentiles, but *unlike* disenfranchised/marginalized Israelites) do not claim to be Abraham's children!

28. There are reports of similar wordplay in other sources; during the siege of Jerusalem, as huge stones catapulted over the city walls, some cried: "the son is coming!" (*War* 5.272). Knowles, "Serpents, Scribes, and Pharisees," 176. For speculation about a possible pun in the original Aramaic, see e.g., T. W. Manson, *The Sayings of Jesus* (Grand Rapids, MI: Eerdmans, 1979; reprint of London: SCM Press, 1957), 40; A. W. Argyle, *The Gospel According to Matthew* (Cambridge: Cambridge University Press, 1963), 36; Robert H. Gundry, *Matthew: A Commentary on his Literary and Theological Art* (Grand Rapids, MI: Eerdmans, 1982), 47; Donald A. Hagner, *Matthew 1–13* (WBC, 33a; Dallas, TX: Word Books, 1993), 50; Knowles, "Serpents, Scribes, and Pharisees," 175–176; Bovon, *Luke*, 1.123; Levine/Brettler, *JANT*, 105 n. 3:10.

29. Bovon, *Luke,* 1.123.

30. Culpepper, *Luke*, 84.

31. "And I will give them a new heart, and I will put a new spirit in them, and I will remove the stony heart from their flesh (την καρδιαν την λιθινην εκ της σαρκος), and I will give them a fleshy heart; so that they might walk in my ordinances, and keep my commandments and do them, and they will be to me a people, and I will be to them a God."—Ezekiel 11:19–20 [LXX], my trans.

32. "And I will give you a new heart, and I will put a new spirit in you, and I will remove the stony heart from your flesh (την καρδιαν την λιθινην εκ της σαρκος), and I will give you a fleshy heart; And I will put my spirit in you, so that you will walk in my ordinances, and keep my judgments and do them. And you will reside upon the land which I gave to your ancestors (πατρασιν), and you will be to me a people, and I will be to you a God." (Ezekiel 36:26–27 [LXX], my trans).

33. Note that the relationship between God "the rock" and Israel is described as a parent–child relationship, using imagery that evokes *both* mothers and fathers: "father" and "begetting" (γενναω), but also nursing (τρεφω) and the "writhing" (חִיל) of childbirth. However, the child's conduct has angered the father; the LORD resolves to punish them severely "because of the provocation of his sons and daughters," "for they are a perverse generation, sons in whom there is no faithfulness." (Deut 32:19, 20b).

34. Robert Beck argues that the implied reader of Luke–Acts is exactly this sort of gentile God-fearer. Even if pagan allusions were not the primary associations intended by Luke, his audience would have noted the "sparks" his rock metaphor struck against their cultural background. (Beck, *A Light to the Centurions: Reading Luke–Acts in the Empire* [Eugene, OR: Wipf & Stock, 2019], 2–23).

35. Humans from stones: Ovid. Metam. 1.393–394, 400–415. From "dragon's teeth": Aeschylus, *Sept.* 412–413; Apollonius of Rhodes 3.1355–57; Apollodorus, *Bib.* 1.9.23; 3.4.1; Ovid, *Metam.* 3.101–130; 7.121–130; *Her.* 6.33; Valerius Flaccus

156   *Chapter 4*

7.76; Seneca, *Med.* 169, 470. Cited by Craig Keener, "Human Stones in a Greek Setting: Luke 3.8; Matthew 3.9; Luke 19.40," *JGRChJ* 6 (2009): 28–29.

36. Keener, "Human Stones in a Greek Setting," 30. See λαας, LSJ.

37. Consider another mention of (potentially) animate stones: Luke 19:40. As Jesus enters Jerusalem, Luke adds a detail not found in Mark or Matthew: "Pharisees from the crowd said to him, 'Teacher, rebuke your disciples!' And he answered, 'I tell you, if these were silent, the stones (οἱ λιθοι) would cry out'" (Luke 19:40). Here, some members of a "crowd" (οχλος) are not bearing fruit. And again, God could raise up stones (λιθοι) to fulfill God's purposes, if others fail to do so. "Stones" again become a potential replacement for parties who are resisting, or at least not participating in, the unfolding intentions of God.

38. This phrase is borrowed from Fox, *Hermeneutics of Social Identity in Luke–Acts*, 118; cf. Meier, *A Marginal Jew* v.2 (New York: Doubleday, 1994), 29.

39. Keener, "Brood of Vipers," 9. On "unworthy" descent, Isaeus laments that one may have excellent ancestors but make dishonorable choices (*Estate of Dicaeogenes* 47). For this point in reference to Luke's version, cf. Fitzmeyer, *The Gospel According to Luke I—IX*, 468; Siker, *Disinheriting the Jews*, 108.

40. Wright: LCL.

41. "As elsewhere in early Jewish-Christian polemic, so in this passage genetic descent from Abraham is insufficient for salvation" (Keener, "Brood of Vipers," 9).

42. "The purpose was to make him ancestor (πατερα) of all who believe (πιστευοντων) while uncircumcised, so that righteousness would be accounted to them as well, and to make him the ancestor (πατερα) of the circumcised who aren't merely circumcised but who also walk in the footsteps of the faith (πιστεως) that our ancestor Abraham had while he was uncircumcised . . . That is why it depends on faith (πιστεως), in order that the promise to all his descendants (σπερματι) may be confirmed, not to those of the law only, but also to those of the faith (πιστεως) of Abraham, who is the father (πατηρ) of us all."—Romans 4:11–12, 16, my trans.

43. Romans 4:16, however, states simply that his descendants include both those who share the faith of Abraham and those "of the law," which seems to ascribe descent from Abraham to Judeans generally (with no other stipulations).

44. cf. 1 Pet. 3:5–6, where the same logic is applied to Sarah. Wives "become her children (τεκνα)" by imitating her.

45. For more on this passage in John and its function within the racial rhetoric of that Gospel, see Andrew Benko, *Race in John's Gospel: Toward an Ethnos-Conscious Approach* (New York: Fortress Academic, 2019), 124–136.

46. One significant difference is that 3:8 is embedded within an exhortation to follow Abraham's example ("bear fruit"); whereas in John, the disjunction between behavior and claim betrays the "Judeans'" actual origins: their father is not God (or in a meaningful sense, Abraham), but the devil (John 8:44). I have argued elsewhere that this passage is not "antisemitic" in the modern sense; John is not attacking Judeans *qua Judeans* (or latter-day Jews). Rather, John's gospel constructs an overarching "cosmological" layer of racial identity—one either is a child of God or the Devil, and these do not map neatly onto what we might call "earthly" races. These particular Judeans' constitutional "inability" to hear Jesus (John 8:43–47) is not attributable to

"We Have a Father—Abraham"   157

their "earthly" ethnicity (Judean), but rather to their "cosmological" race (children of the Devil). See Benko, *Race in John's Gospel*, 124–136.

47. Culpepper, *Luke*, 84.

48. Of course, many of these early Christian sources may themselves be classified as "Judean," albeit in a form incompatible with the emerging rabbinic articulation of Judaism. Paul and Matthew are the most obvious cases, but scholars have also undertaken readings of John and Luke–Acts *within* the context of late first-century Judaism as well.

49. Keener, "Brood of Vipers," 9.

50. Caroline Johnson Hodge, "Olive Trees and Ethnicities: Judueans and Christians in Rom. 11.17–24," in *Christians as a Religious Minority in a Multicultural City: Modes of Interacting and Identify Formation in Early Imperial Rome*, Jürgen Zangenberg and Michael Labahn, eds. (New York: T&T Clark, 2004), 82.

51. *The DSS Bible* translation. The LXX Greek instead has a *blossom* (ανθος) springing from the root, but the reference to "bearing fruit" is in the Hebrew of both the DSS and MT text. See Abegg, Flint, Ulrich, *DSSB*, Isa. 11:1 (including their footnote about the relevant scrolls); and *Biblica Hebraica Stuttgartensia*, Isa. 11:1.

52. Ριζα, *LSJ*.

53. But there may be harsh consequences for others: Ephraim and Judah will conquer neighboring peoples, several of whom are outgrowths of Abraham. These include Moab and Ammon, descended from the eponymous grandsons of Terah, and Edom, the descendants of Esau (Isa. 11:14). This oracle implies that through the work of Jesse's shoot, God's favor rests on the two chosen "branches" of Abraham (Judah and Israel/Ephraim), while his relative disfavor falls upon various "offshoots." We might recall Jonathan Hall's discussion of ancient "ethnic genealogies;" they not only *associate* various races by their derivation from a common ancestor, but also *rank* those races.

54. C. D. Yonge, trans.

55. Richard Bell, *Provoked to Jealousy: The Origin and Purpose of the Jealousy Motif in Romans 9—11* (Tübingen: Mohr Siebeck, 1994), 121.

56. George H. Schodde, translator. *The Book of Enoch: Translated from the Ethiopic with Introduction and Notes.* (Andover, MA: Warren F. Draper, 1882).

57. Raymond Collins, *The Power of Images in Paul* (Collegeville, PA: Liturgical Press, 1989), 214.

58. R. H. Charles, translator. *The Apocrypha and Pseudepigrapha of the Old Testament* (Oxford: Clarendon Press, 1913).

59. Susan Docherty, "Abraham in Rewritten Scripture," in *Abraham in Jewish and Early Christian Literature*, Sean A. Adams and Zanne Domoney-Lyttle, eds. (London: T&T Clark, 2019), 68.

Noah dreams of a cedar, with celestial bodies hacking away at it, and finally an olive tree. The passage in which God interprets his dream is fragmentary, but it seems clear that the cedar represents Noah and various shoots or branches represent his descendants—some "who will be evil" will be subject to "sickle" and "fire" in later days (*Gen.Apoc.* 13:9–14:23). Later, Abraham has a dream of a date palm and a cedar attached to the same root, menaced by men who want to eliminate the cedar

158   *Chapter 4*

and keep the palm; however, the palm objects, "Do not cut the cedar down, for the two of us grow from but a single root." Abraham interprets the dream with his wife, predicting that some Egyptians will want to kill him unless Sarah tells them, "he is my brother" (*Gen.Apoc.* 17:13–22). Cf. Wise et al., *The Dead Sea Scrolls: A New Translation* (San Francisco, CA: HarperSanFrancisco, 2005), 94–100.

We might also mention the *Testament of Abraham,* in which a talking cypress praises God for summoning Abraham to fulfill God's purposes (*Test.Abr.* A 3:1–4).

60. Yonge trans.

61. See also *Rewards* 166, where it becomes clear that the ancestral "root" is the patriarchs—ultimately Abraham. Borgen, "There Shall Come Forth a Man," 348; Staples, *The Idea of Israel*, 257.

62. Pliny the Elder, *The Natural History*, trans. John Bostock. Perseus Online. http://www.perseus.tufts.edu/hopper

/collection?collection=Perseus%3Acollection%3AGreco-Roman (Accessed April 2013).

63. In *Juvenal and Persius.* Ramsay: LCL.

64. Emily Gowers, "Trees and Family Trees in the Aeneid," *Classical Antiquity* 30.1 (2011): 87–118, 89.

65. As, for example, in *Numa* 1.1, where στεμμάτων means "genealogies." Plutarch. *Parallel Lives.* Plutarch. vol. 1. of the Loeb Classical Library edition. 1914.

66. Although this episode distantly echoes scriptural traditions about Israel as a fig tree (Jer 8:13 [MT]; cf. 24:1–10), the parable's context suggests that this "fig tree" is not Israel as a whole, but Jerusalem's religious elites, particularly those ensconced in the Temple.

67. See also John 10:1–16, where John appropriates the longstanding image of Israel as a flock of sheep, redrawing the boundaries of who the "people of God" described by that metaphor are. For John, belief in Jesus is the determining factor. See Benko, *Race in John's Gospel,* 191–198.

68. my trans.

69. So Collins (*The Power of Images in Paul,* 214). Carl Toney reads "root" as either Abraham himself, or the patriarchs in general (Toney, *Paul's Inclusive Ethic: Resolving Community Conflicts and Promoting Mission in Romans 14–15* [Tübingen: Mohr Siebeck, 2008], 142). A variant interprets the root as Abraham, Isaac, and Jacob (Ziesler, *Paul's Letter to the Romans*, 278; Matera, Frank J. *Romans.* Paideia, 269).

70. John Ziesler, *Paul's Letter to the Romans* (Philadelphia, PA: Trinity Press International, 1989), 277; so also Toney, *Paul's Inclusive Ethic*, 142.

71. Again, keep in mind that many of these early "Christian" sources are themselves a form of Judean discourse—albeit expressing a highly idiosyncratic form of Judaism!

72. This is not dissimilar to Paul's olive tree metaphor; some of the tree's natural branches "were broken off because of their unbelief" (Rom. 11:20).

73. Culpepper, *Luke,* 84.

74. cf. Philo *Rewards* 152–172.

75. Just as Mark's intercalation of the cleansing of the Temple nuances the meaning of the cursing of the fig tree (Mark 11:15–25), so perhaps the juxtaposition

"We Have a Father—Abraham"   159

of Luke's fig parable and the healing of "Abraham's daughter" inform one another. Both Mark 11 and Luke 13 feature religious elites who are chastised; but in Luke, their "unfruitfulness" seems to relate to their lack of mercy (13:15–16), rather than mismanagement of the Temple, as in Mark.

76. For Israel as vine/vineyard, see for example: (Isa. 3:14; 5:1–7, 27:4; Jer. 2:21, 8:13; Ezek. 15:1–8; Hos 9:10; Joel 1:6–7; Ps. 80:8–16; *4 Ezra* 5:23–30; *2 Baruch* 39:7–8; *4Q433a* frag. 2; *6Q11*).

77. For Israel as a fig tree, see (Jer 8:13; Hos 9:10–13; Joel 1:5–7; cf. also Jer 24:1–10; *L.A.B.* 37:3).

78. For more imperiled and/or unfruitful trees, cf. Isa. 5:1–7; 17:4–6; 27:4; Jer 8:13; 11:16–17 [17–18 LXX]; Ezek. 15:1–10; Joel 1:6–7; *L.A.B.* 12:8–9, 28:4.

79. cf. also Luke 20:1–19.

80. R. H. Charles, *Apocrypha and Pseudepigrapha of the Old Testament* (Oxford: Clarendon, 1913), 2:775; cit. in Culpepper, *Luke*, 271.

81. Ps. 80:8–14; Ps. 44:1–2; *4Q33*a frag.2; 6Q11; *2 Baruch* 39:7–8; *L.A.B.* 28:4.

82. Jer. 2:21; Isa. 5:1–7; Ezek. 15:1–8; 4 Ezr. 5:23–30; *L.A.B.* 12:8.

83. This last point made by Bovon, *Luke* 2:27.

84. Theophr., *De Causis Plantarum* 1.6.5; Pliny, *Natural History,* 7.24, etc. cf. Toney, *Paul's Inclusive Ethic,* 145; Philip F. Esler, "Ancient Oleiculture and Ethnic Differentiation: The Meaning of the Olive-Tree Image in Romans 11," *JSNT* 26.1 (2003): 109.

85. cf. Boyle, "The Symbolic Value of Grafting in Ancient Rome," *Transactions of the American Philological Association* 140 (2010): 473, 481; Totelin, "Teaching Trees—Tree Teaching: The Ancient Art of Grafting" on Classicalstudies.org (https:// classicalstudies.org/teaching-trees-%E2%80%93-tree-teaching-ancient-art-grafting) accessed 1/1/24.

86. Aaron Kuecker, *The Spirit and the "Other": Social Identity, Ethnicity and Intergroup Reconciliation in Luke–Acts* (New York: T&T Clark, 2011), 73.

87. In a colonized economy in which many are living at or below the subsistence level, *any* surplus would mark one as "rich," at least while any of one's fellow Israelites go hungry. Torah demanded such surplus be shared. Thus, John's first ethical directive (3:11) indicts not only wealthy elites as Herod or the rich man in the Lazarus story (16:19–21) but also more humble Judeans, such as the priest and Levite in the parable of the good Samaritan, who *could* have clothed their brutalized countrymen but chose not to (10:30–32).

88. Ibid., 74.

89. Culpepper, *Luke*, 85.

90. Sycophantēs, a colorful term literally meaning "fig-revealers," originated as a term for informers against illegal exporters of figs (συκον) from Attica ibid., *Luke*, 85; cf. LSJ, συκοφαντεω.

91. The word's concrete meaning concerns literal shaking, disturbing, or unsettling; the figurative sense derived from this ("to intimidate," "to extort money") therefore is aptly translated with the English idiom "to shake down" (as in, for money or information). cf. διασειω, LSJ and *The Cambridge Greek Lexicon*, vol. 1.

160   *Chapter 4*

92. Jos. *War* 3.95; Matt. 5:41; Matt. 27:32//Mark 15:21 "If anyone forces (αγγαρευσει) you to go one mile." Soldiers could forcibly requisition (αγγαρευω) labor, transportation, and lodging from imperial subjects. Warren Carter, *Matthew and the Margins: A Sociopolitical and Religious Reading* (New York: Orbis, 2001), 153.

93. Matt. 5:39–40 // Luke 6:29.

94. cf. *JW* 2.581. Culpepper, *Luke*, 85.

95. This point becomes especially poignant if we imagine that Luke actually has access to Josephus' writing, as Steve Mason and others have suggested. Cf. Mason, *Josephus and the New Testament* (Peabody, MA: Hendrickson, 1992).

96. cf. Alan Mitchell, "Zacchaeus Revisited: Luke 19,8 as a Defense," *Biblica* 71.1 (1990): 172–173.

97. cf. entry on שוב, BDB.

98. Kuecker, *The Spirit and the "Other,"* 74; Jipp, "Abraham in the Synoptic Gospels and Acts," in *Abraham in Jewish and Early Christian Literature*, Sean A. Adams and Zanne Domoney-Lyttle, eds. (London: T&T Clark, 2019), 114.

99. Aaron Kuecker remarks that, for the Baptist, "expressions of ethnic identity that exhaust themselves in in-group bias but have no concern for the 'other' are improper." *The Spirit and the Other,'* 74.

100. P. Richardson, *Building Jewish in the Roman East* (Waco, TX: Baylor University Press, 2004), 279; and Richardson, *Herod: King of the Jews* (Columbia, SC: USC Press, 1996), 61–62.

101. Meier, *A Marginal Jew,* vol. 2, 1994, 30; qtd. in Markus Cromhout, *Jesus and Identity: Reconstructing Judean Ethnicity in Q* (Eugene, OR: Cascade, 2007), 22.

102. Such as Idumeans, Arabs, and (by their own reckoning) Samaritans.

103. As we saw in chapter 2, various other Second Temple sources raised the same question.

104. Consider, for example: *T.Gad* 7:4; *Jub.* 16:30–31; 19:15–31; 20:11–13; Philo *Mut.* 230; *Sobr.* 26; *QG* 3.33, 4.165–174, 201, 206; *Q.Det.* 45–46; *Ebr.* 9–10; Demetrius the Chronographer in *Prep.Ev.* 9:21.1; *2 Esdr.* 3:16; Heb 12:16; *L.A.B.* 32:5. See chapter 2 for more examples and discussion.

105. "10And he was teaching in one of the synagogues on the Sabbath. 11And behold, there was a woman who had had a spirit of infirmity for eighteen years; and she was bent over, unable to straighten all the way up. 12Upon seeing her, Jesus called her over, and he said to her, 'Woman, you are released from your infirmity.' 13Then he laid hands on her; and she was made upright, and she began to glorify God. 14But the head of the synagogue, distressed because Jesus had healed on the Sabbath, said to the crowd, 'There are six days in which work should be done; therefore come on those days to be healed, and not on the Sabbath!' 15Then the Lord answered him, 'You hypocrites, don't each of you untie your ox or donkey from the manger on the Sabbath, and lead it to drink? 16And this woman—a daughter of Abraham (θυγατερα Αβρααμ) whom Satan bound for eighteen years—shouldn't she be freed from this bondage on the Sabbath?' 17And when he said these things, all his enemies were

"We Have a Father—Abraham" 161

disgraced, and the whole crowd rejoiced in all the glorious things done by him.'"
(Luke 13:10–17, my trans).

106. The wealthy Galilean women (Luke 8:1–3), Martha of Bethany (10:38–42), Mary the mother of John Mark (Acts 12:12), Lydia the purple-dyer (16:14–15), and Priscilla (18:1–40) are all wealthy enough to act as patrons, offering house hospitality and/or material support to the movement.

107. Jipp, "Abraham in the Synoptic Gospels and Acts," 115.

108. Raimo Hakola, *Identity Matters: John, the Jews, and Jewishness* (Leiden: Brill, 2005), 118; Roy Harrisville, *The Figure of Abraham in the Epistles of St. Paul* (Lewiston: Edwin Mellis, 1992), 197; Benko, *Race in John's Gospel*, 129.

109. Dorota Hartman, "The 'Children of Abraham' in Luke–Acts," *Henoch* 39.2 (2017): 354.

110. Seim, "Abraham, Ancestor or Archetype?," 29.

111. Hartman, "The 'Children of Abraham' in Luke–Acts," 355. Note also that Eleazar the priest is Aaron's son both by biological descent (i.e., priestly lineage) and subscriptive descent (4 Macc. 7:11–12).

112. cf. 4 Macc. 6:19.

113. NRSV.

114. cf. Gruen's remarks in "Philo and Jewish Ethnicity," 186.

115. As Turid Seim notes: "There are no extra requirements to meet. She is simply regarded as a member of the progeny of Abraham to whom the promise belongs" (Seim, "Abraham, Ancestor or Archetype?," 38–39; cf. Hartman, "The 'Children of Abraham' in Luke–Acts," 355). In terms of diction, Hartman notes that Jesus' insistence that the woman should be "released" (λυω/απολυω, 13:12, 16) recalls not only Simeon's απολυεις τον δουλον σου, δεσποτα (2:29), but Abraham's "Master (δεσποτα), what will you give me? For I am departing (απολυομαι) childless?" (Gen 15:2). Hartman, "The 'Children of Abraham' in Luke–Acts," 354–355.

116. Seim, "Abraham, Ancestor or Archetype?," 36–37; Hartman, "The 'Children of Abraham' in Luke–Acts," 61.

117. Indeed, one might frame 4 Maccabees' view of "spiritual kinship with Abraham" in negative terms, as well: it is *violations* of Abrahamic conduct that deconstruct what is assumed to be a pre-existing identity (4 Macc. 6:19).

118. "1Jesus entered Jericho, and was passing through. 2And behold, there was a man named Zacchaeus, and he was a chief tax collector, and he was rich. 3And he sought to see who Jesus was, but he couldn't on account of the crowd because he was short. 4And running on (προδραμων) ahead, he climbed up a sycamore tree to see him because he was going to pass that way. 5And when Jesus came to the place, he looked up (αναβλεψας) and told him, 'Zacchaeus, hurry down, for I must stay at your house today.' 6He hurried and came down, and welcomed (υπεδεξατο) him with rejoicing. 7Upon seeing this, everyone began grumbling, saying, 'He has gone in to lodge with a man who is a sinner.' 8And standing, Zacchaeus said to the Lord, 'Behold, half of my possessions I give to the poor; and if I have defrauded (εσυκοφαντησα) anyone of anything, I give it back fourfold.' 9And Jesus said to him, 'Today, salvation has come to this house; because he, too, is a son of Abraham! 10For the Son of Man came to seek and to save the lost.'"—Luke 19:1–10, my trans.

162   *Chapter 4*

119. As an αρχιτελωνος, or "chief tax officer," it is possible that Zacchaeus oversees all tax collection in Jericho. Anna Rebecca Solevåg, "Zacchaeus in the Gospel of Luke," *Journal of Literary and Cultural Disability Studies* 14.2 (2020): 225–240, 233; see also Bovon, *Luke* 2.596.

120. Joel Green, *Conversion in Luke–Acts: Divine Action, Human Cognition, and the People of God* (Grand Rapids, MI: Baker Academic, 2015), 109; Culpepper, *Luke*, 357. As a rich *tax collector*, it is most likely that he has lined his pockets by extortion, defrauding his fellow countrymen (cf. Luke 3:13).

121. Green, *Conversion*, 109.

122. Anna Rebecca Solevåg, "Zacchaeus in the Gospel of Luke," 233.

123. cf. Nils Dahl, "The Story of Abraham in Luke–Acts," in *Studies in Luke–Acts*, L. E. Keck and J. L. Martyn, eds. (Nashville, TN: Abingdon, 1966), 150–153; Mitchell, "Zacchaeus Revisited," 169–171.

124. *hupodechomai* "bears all the implications of first-century hospitality." Bovon, *Luke* 2.598.

125. Bovon, *Luke* 2.598–599; Mitchell, "Zacchaeus Revisited," 153–154; cf. Brooks-Winbury, *Syntax of New Testament Greek*, 85–89.

126. Zacchaeus' very name might suggest this: *Zakkai*, "pure" or "innocent." Hartman, "The 'Children of Abraham' in Luke–Acts," 356 N 21.

127. Dennis Hamm also wonders how one could "habitually" give away half of one's possessions; Hamm, "Luke 19:8 Once Again: Does Zacchaeus Defend or Resolve?," *JBL* 107.3 (1988): 433–434.

128. Bovon, *Luke* 2.598–599; Siker, *Disinheriting the Jews*, 112.

129. Siker, *Disinheriting the Jews,* 112. Mitchell ("Zacchaeus Revisited," 161–162) instead argues that the Zacchaeus story "functions differently" from these other blocks of material; for example, they lack reference to "salvation."

130. To fit Zacchaeus into this pattern, Beck somewhat awkwardly pairs him to Jesus' parable of a "repentant" tax collector and a self-righteous Pharisee (Luke 18:9–14). Beck, *A Light to the Centurions*, 25–30.

131. cf. συκοπαντεω, LSJ and BDAG.

132. Bovon, *Luke* 2.599.

133. Siker, *Disinheriting,* 113; Bovon, *Luke* 2.600; Green, *Conversion in Luke–Acts*, 118; Jipp, "Abraham in the Synoptic Gospels and Acts," 115.

134. See chapter 2, above. Beck describes repentance as the "true heritage of Abraham" (*A Light to the Centurions,* 28).

135. Seim, "Abraham, Ancestor or Archetype?," 39–42. It is the case that Luke only explicitly describes characters as "children of Abraham" if this is also true in a literal sense (Hartman, "The 'Children of Abraham' in Luke–Acts," 363–364). We might note, however, Acts 13:26, where Paul addresses both "sons of Abraham" and "god-fearers" as "brothers."

136. Ibid., 363, cf. N 61.

137. Indeed, Hartman goes on in the same paragraph to concede that within this parable, "this bond [kinship with Abraham] is not sufficient in the afterlife and does not grant salvation" ("The 'Children of Abraham,'" 363). It is unclear how she

"We Have a Father—Abraham" 163

squares this observation with her position, stated moments earlier: "notions that kinship with Abraham is not enough . . . are visible only in [Luke's] Q passages."

138. Seim, "Abraham, Ancestor or Archetype?," 36–37, cf. 40.

139. Bovon, *Luke* 2.600.

140. Seim, "Abraham, Ancestor or Archetype?," 42.

141. Joel Green, *Conversion in Luke–Acts,* 110–111.

142. Mitchell, "Zacchaeus Revisited," 168.

143. Ibid., 173–174.

144. Siker, *Disinheriting the Jews*, 113. This idea of the "two types" of children of Abraham is echoed by Green: "In Luke's narrative, Abraham's children are understood in two ways: (1) they occupy society's fringes where they are easily ignored, yet are those to whom God responds with fidelity and mercy (e.g., 16:19–31); or (2) they are those who demonstrate their family resemblance to Abraham through their Abraham-like behaviors, parsed in terms of socioeconomic relations and hospitality (e.g., 3:7–14). As if Luke practiced double-exposure photography, we see both portraits in the one image of Zacchaeus." (Joel Green, *Conversion in Luke–Acts*, 111).

145. Although Mary does assert God's particular *concern* for the poor, "as he spoke to Abraham" (1:55; cf. 6:20–21).

146. Repentance is "Abrahamic" both in Luke's own theological imagination (in material inherited and expanded from Q, Luke 3:7–17), and in Judean traditions comparing Abraham's migration from Chaldea as a rejection of his father's idolatry [see chapter 2].

147. The idea that serious offenses might risk Judeans' "natural" status as children of Abraham is not unattested in Judean literature; it is richly attested in 4 Maccabees, with which Luke shares several key phrases/terms. Recall that Philo held that natural (birth-related) kinships are meaningless if individuals prove unworthy of their lineage (see chapter 2).

148. By contrast, gentiles are by default *not* children of Abraham—although perhaps they may be eligible for this status by exemplarily Abrahamic conduct (3:8).

149. "Feasted" (ευφραινω)—with a root meaning having to do with being glad, enjoying oneself; we might better translate this phrase with the archaic expression "he *made merry* in luxury every day," for the English "make merry" suggests both cheer and drunkenness.

150. Eliezer (אליעזר, "God is help") is only separated from Eleazar (אלעזר "God's help") by one letter; there was some evidence that these names were used somewhat interchangeably in Rabbinic literature, and Josephus collapsed both names into the single Greek name *Eleazaros*. Yoder, "In the Bosom of Abraham: The Name and Role of Poor Lazarus in Luke 16:19–31," *Novum Testamentum* 62 (2020): 2–3, 8–9.

151. This is reflected in a host of secondary contrasts: rich/poor; inside/outside; fed/hungry; richly clothed / covered in sores.

152. Jipp, "Abraham in the Synoptic Gospels and Acts," 116.

153. The sense of "Hades" here may be closer to the Hebrew *she'ol*; the rich man and Lazarus are seemingly areas. For ancient sources, see Hippol. *De universo* 16–33; Tert. *Marc.* 4:34.11–14. Ed Christian, "The Rich Man and Lazarus: Abraham's Bosom, and the Biblical Penalty *Karet* ('Cut Off')," *JETS* 61.3 (2018): 513–519;

164 Chapter 4

Somon and Voinov, "'Abraham's Bosom' (Luke 16:22–23) as a Key Metaphor in the Overall composition of the Parable of the Rich Man and Lazarus," *CBQ* 79 (2017): 615–616.

154. Somov and Voinov, "Abraham's Bosom," 625–627.

155. Philo *Q.Gen.* 44, *De Execr.* § 9, *T.Lev.* 15:4; Jos. *Ant.* i. 13, § 3; *Sib.Or.* 2:331; *3 En* 44:7–10; *T.Lev.* 18:12–14; *T.Jud.* 25:1; cf. *Ass.Mos.* 11.17, 12.6, where it is instead *Moses* who intercedes.

156. These episodes are from the *Apocalypse of Abraham* recension A, circa first or second century CE. See Sanders, "The Apocalypse of Abraham" in *TOTP*; Jared W. Ludlow, "Abraham in the Old Testament Pseudepigrapha: Friend of God and Father of Fathers," in *Abraham in Jewish and Early Christian Literature*, Sean A. Adams and Zanne Domoney-Lyttle, eds. (London: T&T Clark, 2019), 52. This Judean text has been revised by later Christian editors, but the motif of Abraham as intercessor was attested in other Judean literature and is likely part of the Jewish strata.

157. Wintermute [TOTP].

158. Siker notes that Abraham calls the rich man "child," perhaps a cooler, more distant address than the more intimate "son." Siker, *Disinheriting the Jews,* 117.

159. Hartman comments that the situation is "strikingly similar" to that described in Luke 3:8; "The 'Children of Abraham' in Luke–Acts," 362–363.

160. E.g., this gravestone inscription from Egypt: "God of all spirits and all flesh, of the seen and the unseen, who divided his creation according to the secret intention of the soul to the body, and also according to the will of his goodness, and who made it: Lay the souls of your slaves on the breasts of Abraham and Isaac and Jacob (εν κολποις Αβραμ και Ισακ και Ιακωβ)." (Friedrich Preisigke, *Sammelbuch Griechischer Urkunden aus Ägypten* [Strassburg: K. J. Trübner] 1915, entry 2034).

161. Jipp, "Abraham in the Synoptic Gospels and Acts," 117.

162. See γενος, LSJ.

163. Luke adds being "cut off" as a consequence of failure to heed the "prophet like Moses," Jesus (Acts 3:22; contrast Deut 18:15–18).

164. Jacob Milgrom, "The Penalty of *Karet*," Excursus 36, in *The JPS Torah Commentary: Numbers* (Philadephia, PA: JPS, 1989), 405–408; cf. Ed Christian, "The Rich Man and Lazarus: Abraham's Bosom, and the Biblical Penalty *Karet* ('Cut Off')," *JETS* 61.3 (2018): 513–523.

165. Christian, "The Rich Man and Lazarus: Abraham's Bosom, and the Biblical Penalty *Karet* ('Cut Off')," 513–523.

166. Conduct *does* effect one's association with Abraham. Scripture relates that Abraham's sons and grandsons were themselves favored or disfavored for various reasons, often relating to their character (Gen 16:12; 21:9; 25:27–28; 26:34–35; 28:8–9; 32:11; Obad 1:10; Mal 1:2–3a), and the peoples they founded were not only differentiated, but *ascribed different status*, as a result (Gen 17:17–21; 25:23; 27:29, 39–40; 28:1–4, 13–15; 35:11; 36:6–43; Jer 49:7–50:22; Obadiah; Mal 1:3b–5; Ps 83:3–7).

The contrast between these sons' behavior and their resultant status continues in Second Temple literature, especially regarding Jacob/Esau (*T.Gad* 7:4; *Jub.*

19:15–31; 20:11–13; Philo *Sobr.* 26; *QG* 4.165–174, 201, 206; *Q.Det.* 45–46; *Ebr.* 9–10; Demetrius the Chronographer in *Prep.Ev.* 9:21.1; *2 Esdr.* 3:16; Heb 12:16) but occasionally with regard to Isaac/Ishmael (*Jub.* 16:30–31; Philo *QG* 3.33). Pseudo-Philo expands Malachi 1:2, commenting, "God loved Jacob, but he hated Esau *because of his deeds*" (*L.A.B.* 32:5). Consider also Philo's explanation of the different treatment of Jacob and Esau: "Different blessings should set apart different persons: perfect blessings for the perfect, half-way blessings for the imperfect" (*Mut.* 230 [Colson/Whitaker: LCL]).

Other examples abound; see chapter 2 for more.

167. Again, I assume the general contours of the "Four Source Hypothesis," including the existence of a shared source utilized by Matthew and Luke. However, if even we instead imagine direct Lukan access to Matthew, my analysis of the *different use Luke makes of a pre-existing tradition* is still intelligible.

168. Luke, unlike the Matthean parallel (Matt. 8:11–12), emphasizes that those excluded from the eschatological banquet will actually be able to *see* Abraham, Isaac, and Jacob reclining at the table. cf. Siker, *Disinheriting the Jews,* 114.

169. Cromhout, *Jesus and Identity*, 26.

170. or "kingdom of heaven" in the Matthean parallel (Matt 8:12).

171. Hartman, "The 'Children of Abraham' in Luke–Acts," 362.

172. Jipp, "Abraham in the Synoptic Gospels and Acts," 116.

173. Meier, 1994, 314–315; Cromhout, *Jesus and Identity*, 27.

Note that this ingathering of peoples is not always "good news" for the gentiles! In some cases, the nations seemingly come of their own free will to "inquire of the LORD" (Mic. 4:1–3; Isa. 2:3, 60:1–3; Jer. 3:17; Zech. 2:10–11, 8:20–23; Ps. 86:9; Tob. 13:11); but in others, the imagined scene is more akin to defeated nations forced to bring tribute to the capital of their conqueror (Ps. 2:8–10, 60:11–16, 68:30–32, 72:8–11, 15; Isa. 14:1–2, 18:7; Haggai 2:6–8). However, this passage clearly aligns with the more *gentile affirming* of these traditions, because those coming together collectively "recline at table" (13:26).

174. The themes of irony and surprise throughout verses 28–29 (and the reversal of verse 30) would not bite nearly as deeply if it was only a contrast between *diaspora* Judeans "getting in" and *local* Judeans who are "left out."

175. Jipp, "Abraham in the Synoptic Gospels and Acts," 118.

176. Siker, *Disinheriting the Jews,* 115.

177. Ibid., 115.

178. Again, this is a far more modest assertion than the position that Judeans must do something positive to "earn" their status as his children.

179. Luke links the story of Sodom with the current eschatological crisis (perhaps, on the historical level, the devastation of Jerusalem in 70 CE—an event in Jesus' near future and in Luke's not-too-distant past).

180. *m.Baba Kama* 8.6; *m.Baba Mezia* 7.1. cf. Hakola, *Identity Matters,* 118; Harrisville, *The Figure of Abraham in the Epistles of St. Paul,* 197; Benko, *Race in John's Gospel,* 129.

Chapter 5

Whose Ancestors? Genealogical Reconfiguration in Luke–Acts

> The proselyte has won a prize best suited to his merits . . . while the nobly born (ευπατριδης) who has falsified the sterling of his high lineage (ευγενειας) will be dragged down and carried into Tartarus itself. . . . God welcomes the virtue which springs from ignoble birth (δυσγενειας), He takes no account of the roots (ριζας) but accepts the full-grown stem, because it has been changed from a weed into fruitfulness. —Philo, *On Rewards and Punishments,* 152.[1]

> Even now the axe is laid against the root (ριζαν) of the trees! Therefore every tree that does not bear good fruit is cut down and tossed into the fire. —Luke 3:9

We have by this time discussed the constructed and mutable nature of ancient race/ethnicity and seen that culture (particularly religious practice) was a significant ingredient in the "fluidity" of ancient ethnicity—perhaps especially for Judeans.[2] We have surveyed the function of Abraham in Judean identity-discourse and seen that the patriarch could be used to either emphasize differences, or suggest connections, between Judeans and gentile *ethnē*. I have argued that Luke considered all Israelites—Judeans and Samaritans—to be children of Abraham and heirs-apparent to the promises God have to Abraham's descendants.[3] However, Luke has amplified a saying in "Q" which complicates this default identification (Luke 3:8–9) by adding specific ethical content to the sort of "repentance" befitting his children (3:11–16).[4] It turns out that Abraham's presumptive descendants will derive no meaningful status or inheritance solely on the basis of their birth, if they have lived wickedly— nor will they receive the blessings promised to Abraham's *sperma*, if they abandon the ways of their founding father (3:8).[5]

168   *Chapter 5*

This assertion is but one instance of a wider pattern in Luke–Acts, wherein the entire concept of ancestral descent is destabilized. As we shall see in this chapter, the sweep of this pattern extends far beyond Abraham to encompass other ancestors—and even gentiles will be caught up in this rewiring of ancestral connections. In this, we will leave behind discussion of Abraham in particular to focus on the broader theme of ancestry in general. The pattern of genealogical slipperiness is already discernible in Luke, but it is further developed in Acts. Therefore, this chapter will necessarily engage both of Luke's volumes.

Luke suggests that those who actively resist Jesus are meaningfully the descendants, not of Abraham (Luke 3:8), but of those who killed the prophets (11:47, cf. 13:34, Acts 7:52), whatever their "factual" (ascribed) descent may be. Similarly, those who adhere to the model of the patriarchs are *their* descendants, whatever their family. The figure of Abraham plays a part in this, but the trope encompasses a plethora of other ancestral figures—from Israel's past, and even from within gentile races. Because race was so primally linked to descent, this slipperiness in the attribution of *ancestry* also implies a corresponding slipperiness in *racial identity*.

As I will argue in this chapter, Luke sees race as not (only) a matter of ascriptive descent (i.e., that which is ascribed to one at birth), but more importantly a matter of subscriptive descent. That is, you may be understood as someone's descendant if you subscribe to their ways (*ethē*). In chapter 1, we saw a few varieties of this sort of thinking from the ancient world. These included: the "fictive kinship" discourse which constructed relatedness between members of many Greco-Roman associations;[6] "father/son" language applied to those who have "descended" from certain "lineages" of teaching, from teacher ("father") to student ("son") over the course of generations;[7] and descriptions of conversion as a (partial) realignment of one's *ethnic* identity.[8] One might object: *but this sort of kinship is only a metaphor.* However, as we saw in chapter 1, such "metaphorical" relatedness was often quite real to actual social actors, with real-life consequences and behaviors mirroring the sorts of obligations encountered in "real" families. Similarly, Luke's discourse about ancestors creates space for gentile followers of "The Way" to imagine themselves to be aligned with, and indeed children of, Abraham. They are offered a hybridized identity: they have proven to be "Israelites" by adherence to Abraham's faith, while remaining "gentiles" to some degree. This fosters a sense of kinship between Judeans and gentiles, so that they may consider one another "brothers" in not only a cultic, but ethnic, sense.[9] At the same time, Luke understands some genealogical relationships to be strained, or even severed—as for example, unmerciful Judeans' descent from Abraham, or Christ-believing gentiles filiation with the worst figures of past generations. Such a reconfiguration of descent might drive a wedge between people formerly assumed to share a common identity. There is now some ethnic distance between *most* Judeans and those strange few who associate freely with Samaritans and gentiles (in defiance of longstanding tradition; e.g., Acts 10:28). There is now some distance between *most* gentiles and those strange few who have abandoned the gods to worship a barbaric foreign god and his "anointed."

Luke presents this genealogical rhetoric in two general patterns. One pattern looks back, converging on an originating ancestor; the other pattern moves forward chronologically, differentiating forking branches of a genealogical tree. In the first pattern, Luke sketches out a common genealogy for the whole human *genos*, in which all human beings derive from a single ancestor (Adam). Viewed from this angle, genealogy *converges* toward its origin, emphasizing unity. Located somewhere along this shared lineage, all people are at least theoretically related to Christ, to God, and to each other (Luke 3:23–38; Acts 17:24–31). In the other pattern, Luke looks forward, contrasting "lineages" of either good or wicked forbears. Viewed this way, lineage divides at a genealogical "fork in the road," constructing distance and difference between the scions of these opposing groups. In this generation, their latter-day descendants exist in a state of lineal "quantum uncertainty" until their behavior allows the observer to determine their actual descent. It is only by the observation of their conduct (often in response to Jesus) that their "true" identity snaps into focus—at least, in Luke's eyes—so that they can be categorized as the "children of Abraham" (Luke 3:8b, 19:9) or the descendants of "those who killed the prophets" (6:26; 11:48). In Luke–Acts, Jesus' contemporaries either show themselves to be the scions of celebrated ancestors, or betray themselves as the issue of a long line of villains.

In this chapter, we will explore these two general patterns—the convergence on a shared human lineage in Adam, and the forking of lineages between illustrious or infamous lines of descent. These two strategies allow Luke to bind and to loose, to connect and to divide. Taken together, these patterns allow Luke to both assert ethnic solidarity between all human beings (at least, those in Christ) and to ethnically "other" those who persecute Christianity.

CONVERGING ON A SHARED ANCESTOR

We will first consider examples of how genealogy is depicted looking backward, converging on a single ancestor, with one example from Luke's gospel (the genealogy of Jesus) and one example from Acts.

170   *Chapter 5*

One Human Line: ". . . son of Adam, son of God" (Luke 3:23–38)

[23]Upon beginning [his ministry], Jesus was about thirty years old, being the son (as it was supposed) of Joseph, the son of Heli . . . [*64 generations omitted here*] . . . the son of Noah, the son of Lamech, [37]the son of Methuselah, the son of Enoch, the son of Jared, the son of Mahalaleel, the son of Cainan, [38]the son of Enos, the son of Adam, the son of God. —Luke 3:23–38

When reading Matthew, Jesus' lineage is almost the first thing the reader learns about him; by contrast, Luke's reader has already met Jesus' prototypically Judean family, overheard prophesies about his significance to Israel (hearkening back to promises to Abraham), and watched the exemplarily pious John baptize him. This means that Jesus' "Jewish credentials" have already been thoroughly established in Luke, *before* we ever learn his lineage. While Matthew's version is carefully structured to establish Jesus as a Judean of impeccable lineage,[10] Luke's Infancy Narrative has already done the heavy lifting in this department. Luke is therefore free to explore other genealogical themes with his genealogy, without compromising Jesus' "Jewishness."

The genealogy opens with the rather guarded declaration that Jesus was "reckoned" (ενομιζετο) the son of Joseph and through him descended from Joseph's own father, grandfather, and so on (3:23). Νομιζω hedges the connection with Joseph, at least biologically;[11] Jesus is "accounted," "considered," or "supposed" to be the son of Joseph, although the reader knows that his conception was accomplished by God through the Holy Spirit (Luke 1:31–35).[12] Ενομιζετο is an equivocation, conceding that this *specific* list of ancestors may not represent Jesus' exact lineage. Rather, this is an ideal genealogy: the sort of lineage the messiah would have.[13] In that Jesus is not technically Joseph's biological child, Jesus has the least "physical" kinship with those earliest in the list; but as the list counts the generations back in time, and those named are the ancestors of greater and greater numbers of Israelites, the "accuracy" of the lineage becomes likelier. By the time we get to David we are on solid ground, for Luke has already told us that Jesus descends from David (1:32; 1:69), *outside* of the context of genealogical lists.[14] Going on, things are even surer. Like all Judeans, Jesus descends not only "ideally" but also biologically from Jacob, Isaac, and Abraham (3:34). Thus, *Jesus' backward-looking genealogy becomes more confident the further back it goes.* By the time we reach the end of the list, we are absolutely certain: from a Judean perspective, *all* human beings descend from Adam (Gen. 5:1; Deut. 32:8; 1 Chron. 1:1).[15] The rhetorical effect of this structure is to place relatively little emphasis on Jesus' recent ancestors, relatively more

Genealogical Reconfiguration in Luke–Acts 171

on the middling generations, and a great deal of weight on those *last* named: the common ancestors of all humankind.[16]

As with many linear genealogies, the primary function of this list is to shore up status claims for its subject—Jesus.[17] But Luke's strategy is *not* to emphasize of Jesus' stake in Israel as a descendant of Abraham through the line of David. (Had this been Luke's primary intent, he could have highlighted this theme by structuring the genealogy to begin with Abraham, as Matthew does. Instead, Abraham is easy to overlook, almost "buried" in the midst of seventy-seven names stretching back to Adam.)[18] Rather, Luke's genealogy emphasizes that Jesus is the "son of God."

In ancient linear genealogies, the crucial names are typically the first and last.[19] At first blush, these seem to be Joseph and Adam, respectively. However, the genealogy actually opens and closes with the assertion that Jesus is the "Son of God" (Luke 3:22, 3:38). God is the alpha and omega of Jesus' lineage, its origin, and its telos. Luke has already previously revealed that Jesus is the "son of God" in a unique sense—in that God's Holy Spirit was directly involved in his conception (Luke 1:31–35; Acts 13:33). It is in this sense that God tells Jesus, "You are my beloved son; in you I am well-pleased" (3:22).[20] Jesus' genealogy follows hard on the heels of this declaration; it shores up this identification by laying out a *different* sense in which Jesus is God's "son"—that is, by an unbroken line of human descent stretching through the generations back to Adam, who was also "the son of God." By identifying Adam in this manner, Luke expresses another way in which any human being may be reckoned as God's son/child.[21]

Jesus, therefore, is God's son twice over. He is the "Son of God" in the *unique* sense that he is conceived by the Holy Spirit (1:35) and acknowledged by God's voice (3:22), and in the *generic* sense that he is a descendant of Adam, "the son of God" (3:38). Note that in this "generic" and genealogical sense, *the whole human* genos *can be understood as children of God.*[22] Between these two, we trace his descent across the intervening generations in Israel—Israel, which is itself described as the "son of God" in scripture (Exod. 4:22–23; Hosea 11:1; Jer. 3:19, 31:9).[23]

We begin to intuit that Jesus' genealogy has ethnic implications, which extend beyond its primary purpose of shoring up status claims for Jesus. Broadly speaking, these are twofold: (1) Firstl, not only Judeans but *gentiles* are invited to perceive that they have a genealogical stake in Jesus. (2) Second, all branches of the human family (gentile *and* Israelite) are invited to perceive themselves as children ("sons") of God, and in a sense related to each other. (Perhaps a third implication is discernible in the fact that gentiles must conform their religious/historiographic imagination to *Israel's* traditions, in order to understand Jesus' lineage and its significance; they must "learn to think like Judeans" before they can understand the genealogy's implications for *them*.)[24]

172   *Chapter 5*

Firstly, the lineage locates Jesus within the wider human family. Jesus is contextualized along a lineage within which all human beings may find themselves, arriving finally at shared ancestors like Noah (Gen. 9:19) and Adam (Deut. 32:8). Gentiles, too, then, have a genealogical "stake" in Jesus—at least, God-fearing gentiles do. God-fearers would know that Adam, "that first, earth-born (γηγενης) human, [was] the founder (αρχηγετης) of our whole [human] race (γενους)" (Philo, *On the Creation*, 136).[25] Because Adam was the originator and ancestor of all humanity, the Lukan genealogy asserts that Jesus is the culmination and savior of all humanity.[26] Descended from Adam, believing god-fearing gentiles need not see Jesus as "foreign" to them; nor, to the extent that their colonized imaginations may "center" Israel, need they any longer understand *themselves* as foreigners.[27] Indeed, gentiles share a genetic kinship (συγγένεια), however distant, with Jesus. Because religious affiliation could (re)shape ethnic identity in the ancient world, gentiles-in-Christ and Judeans-in-Christ began to sense that they were related to *each other*, as well.[28]

Second, the lineage suggests that *all human beings are children of God*, through Adam. Philo makes a similar point, explaining that "he [Adam] was the last whom the Maker and Father fashioned, God made man (ανθρωπος) partaker of kinship with Himself (της αὐτου συγγενειας μεταδους) in mind and reason, best of all gifts" (*On the Creation*, 77).[29] Jesus himself mentions that human beings are children of God:

> [34]If you lend to those from whom you hope to receive, what credit is that to you? Even sinners lend to sinners, to receive as much again. [35]But love your enemies, and do good, and lend without hope of return; and your reward will be great, and you will be sons of the Most High, because he is kindly to the ungrateful and the evil (πονηρους). [36]Be merciful (οικτιρμονες) just as your Father is merciful. (Luke 6:34–36)[30]

Jesus is not pronouncing the "Most High" their father in an immediate biological sense (as if overwriting human paternity).[31] But God's likeness is unmistakable, so that the ancient commonplace holds true: "the son resembles the father." So Jesus can instruct them not to be just "like," but *exactly* like" (καθως) their God. The character of the Father—who is loving to the undeserving, generous to the unrequiting, kind to the ungrateful, and merciful beyond reason—will be reflected in his children. Later, Jesus again asserts God's fatherhood—to both encourage God's children to trust in his goodness, and encourage them to follow in his footsteps.

> [11]What father among you, if his son asks him for a fish, will hand him a snake instead? [12]Or if he asks him for an egg, will hand him a scorpion? [13]If you then, despite being evil, know how to give good gifts to your children, how much

more will the heavenly Father give the Holy Spirit to those who ask it of him! (Luke 11:11–12 [cf. Matt. 7:11–13])

This assures his listeners that when they call upon their "Father, . . . give us each day our daily bread" (11:2), he will answer them. If they know how to feed their own sons, how much more will their Father feed them! Later, Jesus uses an implicit "how much more" argument (and reference to divine-child status) to exhort his audience to better and better works: If the dishonest "children of this age" are crafty in misallocating resources to profit themselves (and make allies along the way), *how much more* should the "children of light" properly employ "dishonest wealth" to make real friends, friends who can someday welcome them into their heavenly tents (Luke 16:8–9).[32]

In several passages, then, Luke reinforces an idea suggested by the genealogy: that every human (descended from Adam) is at least potentially a "child of God." This implication will be teased out more explicitly in Acts (17:26), as we shall see below.

One Human Line: "We are indeed God's *genos*" (Acts 17:24–31)

Hail to you, Zeus! For it is meet for any mortal to address you;
For we are your offspring (εκ σου γαρ γενος εσμεν), we alone allotted your likeness
Of all mortal creatures which live and tread the earth.
    — Cleanthes (3rd-century Stoic philosopher) "Hymn to Zeus," lines 3–5[33]

    . . . and in all ways, we all need Zeus:
For we are indeed his offspring (του γαρ και γενος ειμεν); and the Gentle One
Shows kindly signs to humans; he calls people to work,
    Recalling them to their way of life (βιοτοιο), and tells when the soil is best.
    (Aratus (3rd-century didactic poet), *Phaenomena* lines 4b–7a)[34]

Before we proceed to Acts 17, let us cast our attention back a few centuries to Greece's classical past. Some philosophical traditions described a god, most commonly Zeus, as the father of the human race.[35] Take, for example, the "Hymn to Zeus" by the third-century Stoic, Cleanthes. He rhapsodized, "we are your progeny," an assertion repeated in a poetic astronomical treatise, the *Phaeonomena*. Dio of Prusa calls Zeus our "forefather god" (προπατωρ θεος), and states that all human beings share his blood (*Or.* 12.29, 43). Closer to Luke's own day, the Stoic philosopher Epictetus explained that our common descent from Father Zeus means we should treat each other well. Masters should remember that their "slaves" are, in fact, their brothers:

174   *Chapter 5*

Slave, will you not bear with your own brother (αδελφου), who has Zeus as his progenitor (προγονον) and is, as it were, a son born of the same seed (εκ των αυτων σπερματων γεγονεν) as yourself and of the same sowing from above? . . . Do you not remember what you are, and over whom you rule—that they are kinsmen (συγγενων), that they are brothers by nature (αδελφων φυσει), that they are the offspring (απογονων) of Zeus? (Epictetus, *Disc.* 1.13.3–4)[36]

We can find analogous thinking among Hellenistic Judeans. Josephus calls God the παντων πατρι, "father of all" (*Ant.* 1.230) who "Himself is the father of the whole human race" (*Ant.* 1.262).[37] *3 Maccabees* calls God the "overseer and forefather (προπατωρ) of all things" (*3* Macc. 2:21).[38] Aristobolus, (2nd c. BCE) who holds that Greek philosophers stole their best material from the law, writes, "Aratus also speaks about the same things thus: . . . 'We are all in need of God everywhere. We are all his children; and he gently to humanity gives good omens . . .'" (qtd. in *Eus.* 13.13.6).[39] Notice that in this quote, Aristobolus carefully substitutes "Θεος" for "Διος," explaining, "We have given the true sense, as one must, by removing the (name) Zeus throughout the verses. For their intention refers to God, therefore it is so expressed by us" (*Eus.* 13.13.7).[40] Apparently, Hellenistic wisdom may *approximate* a Judean understanding of God, yet still require some translation or "correction."

The Letter of Aristeas similarly cites (but amends) pagan sources to demonstrate that Greek wisdom is compatible with Judean tradition.[41] Its Judean author assures King Ptolemy,

These ones worship God, creator and overseer of all, whom all worship including ourselves, O king, but naming him differently than "Zeus" (Ζηνα) or "Jove" (Δια). Not dissimilar to this, the ancients (πρωτοι) pointed out that the one "through whom all live and have our being" (δι' ὁν ζωοποιουνται τα παντα και γινεται), this one is the leader and lord of all. (*Aristeas* 16)[42]

Here it is claimed that although Judeans do not call upon Zeus by the same name, they worship the same god in whom all "live and move and have our being," just as "the [Greek] ancients" (πρωτοι) testified. This line may derive from the no-longer-fully-extant *Krētica*, a poem by the sixth-century BCE philosopher Epimenides:

But you [Zeus] are not dead, for you are established and live forever;
For in you we live and move and have our being.
(εν γαρ σοι ζωμεν και κινυμεθ' ηδε και εσμεν)[43]

Other scholars suggest that Posidinius should be credited with this line,[44] or that the line may be intended to vaguely allude to philosophical ideas

Genealogical Reconfiguration in Luke–Acts

generally.[45] What is important for our purposes is that a Judean author has enlisted a *Greek* thinker as an apologist for the *Judean Law*.

So, pagan authors, most notably Stoics, could and did assert humanity's universal descent from a shared father—God (Zeus). And Judeans could and did parrot such ideas, making their faith comprehensible in a Hellenistic milieu. This leads us precisely to Acts 17:22–31, a speech in which a highly Hellenized Judean—Paul of Tarsus—does just this.

The chapters leading up to Paul's visit to Athens have already primed the reader to consider the origins of all races in decidedly *Judean* terms.[46] Before we even meet Paul, the alert reader has already been reminded that the "nations" (gentiles) have a common origin and anticipate a common stake in Abraham.[47]

The Areopagus speech itself is part of his visit to Athens (Acts 17:15–34). Paul has been reasoning in the marketplace (αγορα) with "those who happened to be there"—a detail evoking Socrates, who engaged all sorts of men whom he met in Athen's agora in philosophical discussion.[48] Paul chances upon some Epicureans and Stoics, who ask Paul pointed questions and move the debate to the Areopagus.

Several details here suggest an ethnically charged confrontation between insiders and outsiders, with possible legal ramifications. The philosophers' various reactions to Paul may be read in this light (table 5.1).

Paul is disparaged as a "dabbler," a *spermologos*, a word which can refer to birds that peck the ground for seeds or scraps—and so: "scavenger," or figuratively "dilettante," "huckster," or "quack."[49] So far, so insulting. But it is the next two remarks which veil a possible threat (17:18b–19). Athenians were famed for their piety, and bad-mouthing their gods could be dangerous.[50] The introduction of new gods had been a capital offense in classical Athens; indeed, it was partially for this charge that Socrates himself was executed.[51] Athens could still be hostile toward foreign religions in the first century; Josephus reported that "the penalty decreed for any who introduced a foreign God (ξενον θεον) was death" (*Ag.Ap.* 2.267).[52] In light of this, the

Table 5.1 Paul's Dangerous "Foreign Ideas" in Athens

about Paul:	"What is this seed-picker (σπερμολογος) trying to say?" 17:18a
	"He seems to be a herald of foreign divinities (ξενων δαιμονιων)" 17:18b
to Paul:	"What is this new teaching (καινη διδαχη) which you are talking about?" 17:19
	"You are pouring some outlandish ideas (ξενιζοντα) into our ears!" 17:20a.

176   *Chapter 5*

Athenian philosophers' remarks seem less like idle inquiries, even barbed ones, and more like accusations.

The narrator remarks, "All the Athenians and the resident foreigners (ἐπιδημοῦντες ξένοι) would spend their time on nothing so much as talking about, or listening to, anything new (τι καινότερον)." This may sound as if the Athenians are potentially receptive to Paul's message. However, in light of Hellenistic moralists' attitudes toward prurient curiosity, Acts 17:21 is not necessarily a positive description of the Athenian crowds.[53] Nor should we assume that the city's intellectual elites—here represented by Epicureans and Stoics—would be sanguine about "all" the *demos* (including resident foreigners) flocking after every peripatetic-come-lately with a hot new thought to peddle. We have, rather, a charged atmosphere in which there might be a great deal of *interest* in a traveling teacher, but also a great deal of suspicious *scrutiny*—an atmosphere where the general residents of Athens might listen eagerly, but the intellectual elites might take exception to this attention. What if Paul riles up the "aliens" who live in Athens, including the Judeans, whose synagogues he has been frequenting (17:17a)? What if his "foreign superstitions" (ξέναι δαιμονια) anger the gods, causing them to punish the city? We have, in other words, a potent brew not unlike the mix of popular attention and elite scrutiny Jesus encountered in Jerusalem.[54] Add to this the marked contrast between cultural insiders and outsiders, and it seems likely that Paul could be in some real trouble.[55]

So, Luke characterizes Paul as a sort of "Socrates redivivus,"[56] dialoguing (διαλογιζομαι) with passersby in the agora, accused of the very charge which led to Socrates' death. Luke implicitly likens Paul's opponents to those who accused and killed Socrates—making Paul, in a sense, "more Athenian" than the philosophers! Or, to be more precise, aligning Paul with the *best* of Athens' past and aligning them with its worst. It is in this context, fraught with ethnic tension and heavy with classical allusion, that Paul delivers his defense of the gospel.

Paul's opening salvo targets Athenian idolatry, with its many so-called gods. He tells the Athenians, "I see you are exceptionally religious in all ways." This opener may serve either as a *captatio benevolentiae* meant to win them over, or as a chagrined criticism—indeed, it might function as both at once.[57] Paul seizes upon a chance detail, "an altar with this inscription: 'To an Uknown God'" (17:23a). There were, indeed, altars dedicated to unknown *gods* (plural) in ancient Athens;[58] Luke knowingly or unknowingly misquotes the inscription in the singular.[59] In such words, Paul sees an opening: "Therefore, what you worship as unknown, I will proclaim to you" (17:23b). As we saw above, this was a familiar tactic in Judean apologetics—claiming that a god whom gentiles worship under another name (or in this case, *no* name)

Genealogical Reconfiguration in Luke–Acts   177

is the same God whom the Jews worship.[60] Paul rejects the charge that he is preaching a "new" or even a "foreign" god—rather, he is revealing more about a god whom they already worship, albeit "unknowingly."[61] He explains,

> [25b]He himself gives life and breath to all. [26]And he made from one (εξ ἑνος)[62] every race (εθνος)[63] of human beings (ανθρωπων) to inhabit the face of the earth; having determined appointed periods and boundaries of their habitations, [27] that they might search for God, and perhaps grope for him and find him— although indeed, he is not far from each one of us. [28] For "in him we live and move and have our being," as even some of your own poets have said, "For we, too, are his offspring (γενος)."
> [29]Therefore being the offspring (γενος) of God, we should not consider gold or silver or stone, a thing shaped by human skill and imagination, to be like God.[30] God overlooked the times of ignorance; but now he instructs all people everywhere (ανθρωποις παντας πανταχου) to repent,[31] because he has fixed a day on which he will judge the inhabited world (*or* empire, οικυμενην) in righteousness, by a man whom he has appointed; in assurance of all [this] he has raised him from the dead. (Acts 17:26–31)

Laura Nasrallah calls this speech a rhetorical "a tour de force," weaving together materials from Judaism's and Hellenism's conceptual worlds: allusions to Greek poets, Jewish creation myths (Gen. 1–2), abstract geographical thinking, and the concrete built environment of Athens, with its stone gods.[64] Paul invokes both traditions (philosophical and Judean) to demonstrate that although the gospel is incompatible with Greek *religion*, it actually contains the best elements of Greek *philosophy*. Indeed, Paul attempts to co-opt philosophy so completely that it can only rightly be understood within the Christian movement![65]

Paul asserts that God created every race (εθνος) of human beings "from one" (Acts 17:26). This flatly contradicts one myth of the Athenians' origins, a theory called "autochthony," which held that they sprang from the very soil of Athens.[66] Humanity's creation "from one" echoes the Torah account (Gen. 2:7 // Isa. 42:50), recalling Adam, the first human being.[67] As Deuteronomy puts it,

> When the Most High distributed the races (εθνη),
> as he scattered the sons of Adam,
> he established boundaries of the nations (εθνων),
> according to the numbers of the angels of God (αγγελων θεου). (Deut. 32:8)

However, this creation "from one" also resonates with philosophies which postulated a common origin for the human species (e.g., Cicero, *Leg.* 22–39;

178   *Chapter 5*

Off. 3.28).[68] Paul enlists Greek thought to support the *Judean* account of human origins. Rather than coming from altogether distinct sources—some having sprung, self-generated, from their native soil—all human beings were made "from one."

But one *what*? The text itself is ambiguous. This "one" (ἑνός) may be grammatically masculine or neuter. If construed as masculine, it may take as its referent either "person" (ανθρωπος) or "race" (εθνος). Thus, Paul may be saying that all were made from one "person" (that is, Adam) or from one common "race." On the other hand, if ἑνός is neuter, it may refer to one "source"—a concept congenial to Stoic thought.[69] The manuscript tradition is also ambivalent. Several significant manuscript families, and many patristic witnesses, read that God created all "from one *blood* (αἵματος)."[70] In the mouth of a Judean, this would comprise an indirect reference to Adam, whose blood we all share. The word αἷμα could also refer to the semen, which contemporary reproductive theory regarded as a highly specialized form of compacted "blood."[71] Thus, all human races stem from the same "seed" (that of Adam). So, the ambiguous "one" from which all races came (Acts 17:26) could be a nod to either Judean or Stoic traditions about the origins of humanity. In any case, it conveys the sense that humanity shares a single origin and implies genealogical relatedness—however distant—between all people.

Paul adduces pagan sources to prove that all share a common origin in God. As we have discussed, "In him we live and move and have our being" (Luke 17:28a) is likely a line from Epimenides' *Krētica.*[72] The Judean *Letter of Aristeas* also cites this line as coming from a pagan source (*Arist.* 16). To Judeans, this citation would also subtly disparage the idols dotting the Athenian cityscape. In the Septuagint, the three verbs "live" (ζωμεν), "move" (κινητησονται), and "be" (εσμεν) often occur in the context of *anti-idolatry polemic.* According to Israel's sacred writings, the so-called gods of idolators do not live, cannot move, and have no being.[73]

Paul adds, "even some of your own poets said, 'We, too, are his offspring (γενος).'" This line is found in Cleanthes' "Hymn to Zeus"[74] and repeated in Aratus' *Phaenomena,*[75] both from the third century BCE Because all people are his children, all "grope" for him (Acts 17:27). As one Stoic put it:

> All human beings are oriented towards the divine, so that they are driven by a powerful yearning to venerate the gods from close at hand, serving him, drawing close to him, touching him with full conviction, sacrificing to him and decking him with garlands. For human beings behave towards the gods in exactly the same way as little children who are separated from their father or mother; these experience an irresistible longing for their parents and stretch out their hands yearningly to them in dreams, although their parents are not in fact present. (Dio, *Or.* 12.60–62)[76]

Genealogical Reconfiguration in Luke–Acts 179

Paul's allusion—whether to Cleanthes, Aratus, or Stoic thought more generally—affirms that God is the parent of all human beings.[77] A common origin for all humanity means that there is no impassable genetic gulf between Judeans and other peoples; all are ultimately the *genos* of God.[78] All human beings can trace their lineage back to the "one" from which they have all been made (i.e., Adam) and beyond him, to God, whose race/progeny they are.[79]

Sadly, this shared origin does not mean that all "know" God. It prompts them, as it were naturally, to reach for God—but blindly. Grammatically, the phrase "If they might perhaps grope for him and find him" (Acts 17:27) is a counter-to-fact conditional; it actually expresses *doubt* that pagans can "reason their way to God" by their own cleverness.[80] Human logic and inborn yearning have led Greek philosophers to intuit certain things about God, but these inklings cannot compare to what has been unveiled by revelation. This is why it is necessary for Paul to "reveal" the full truth of their unknown God to them: without God's self-revelation entrusted to Israel, they cannot arrive at it on their own. Forms of the word "ignorance/unknowing" appear three times in the speech (twice in verse 23, once in 30), stressing the limits of what can be known "by men's imaginations" (ενθυμησεως ανθρωπου, 17:29). This complex of ideas—kinship with God, failure to know him, and clumsy attempts to worship him through material objects—appears in an appeal made by the Stoic, Epictetus:

> You are a fragment of God; you have within you a part of him. Why, then, are you ignorant (αγνοεις) of your own kinship? Why do you not know the source from which you have sprung? . . . You are bearing God about within you, you poor wretch, and you know it not! Do you suppose I am speaking of some external God, made of silver and gold (αργυρουν τινα η χρυσουν)? It is within yourself that you bear him. (Epictetus, *Diatr.* 2.8)[81]

The philosopher shares Paul's exasperation that those who are intimately related to God turn away from him in their ignorance, to manufactured gods of silver or gold (17:29).

Paul's speech, then, *rejects* standard Greek religious piety with its sacrifices to the gods, but *appropriates* certain philosophical ideas. Paul points out commonalities between their thinking and his own theology and attempts to demonstrate that the Way is compatible with, or even represents, the best of Greek *paideia*.[82] Indeed, the Christian message perfects what the philosophers only groped toward, so that "The Christian movement embodies the philosophically elite's ideals better *and more consistently* than do the Athenians."[83] Paul implies that earlier Stoics had hailed his gospel at a distance; if the latter-day philosophers of Athens reject him, it only proves that they are poor descendants of their supposed teachers. In terms of intellectual lineage,

180   *Chapter 5*

Paul has denigrated the "pedigree" of Athens's intelligentsia and claimed it as
his own. This resembles Luke's consistent polemic against *Judean* intellectuals, as well: Israel's celebrated heroes anticipated the gospel, but its latter-day
scribes do not accept it. Christians are cast as both better Judeans than (most)
Judeans and better Greeks than (most) Greeks.

For those gentiles who *do* recognize what their pagan forbears vaguely
intuited, there is solidarity, commonality, and kinship—with each other and
even with Israelites. They "descend" from those wise pagans who intimated
there is one God, from whom all derive. Cornelius, for example, meets both
of the requirements outlined in Acts 17:29. Oliver explains, "He stems from
God's "genus' and has fully abandoned idolatry, and archetypically embodies
the ideal Gentile followers of Jesus who can now rightfully and freely associate themselves with the rest of the commonwealth of Israel."[84] The altar dedicated to the "Unknown God" calls gentiles to follow Abraham's existential
decision to turn away from idols, toward the Most High. From this block of
Athenian stone, God can provide children for Abraham.

The racial implications of this speech, then, are several. (1) *Common
ancestry*: all humans descend from "one" (one blood, or source, or ancestor;
i.e., Adam). All εθνη, then, are related, however distantly; racial theories
which posit unique origins for certain races, such as autochthony, are ruled
out. This emphasis on commonality might foster a sense of ethnic kinship
between those of different races. (2) *Children of God:* Furthermore, all
human beings descend from God; that is, the whole human *genus* is God's
genos. All humans therefore share kinship, not only with each other, but with
God (and, as Luke 3 asserts, with Jesus). (3) *Cultural Imperialism:* Knowledge of this divine origin was *inferred* by the wisest pagan philosophers, but
is only fully realized in God's revelation—a revelation historically entrusted
to Israel, and recently perfected in a Judean, Jesus. Realizing one's birthright
therefore requires aligning one's own perspective with Israel's (as the Way
interpreted it). So, for gentiles to fully claim their identity as God's children,
they must turn their backs on much that marks them as culturally (and ethnically) distinct.

DIVERGING FROM SHARED ANCESTORS

This last point anticipates our next turn. Luke divides both gentiles, and
Israel, into two broad groupings: those who oppose the message about Jesus
and those who welcome it. He rhetorically associates each division with
either villainous or valorized ancestors, assigning each to a different "lineage," depending on where their loyalties lie.

Diverging Lines: *Whose* Fathers Killed the Prophets?

> And *our ancestors* killed your prophets who testified (μαρτυραντο) against them, to turn back to you. . . . —Nehemiah 9:26[85]

> So you testify (μαρτυρειτε) that you approve the deeds of *your ancestors*—because *they* killed them, and *you* build up their tombs! —Luke 11:48[86]

Judean literature had a longstanding pattern of recounting *past* iniquities alongside *contemporary* confession.[87] The people must "confess the sin of their ancestors" so that God will remember his covenant with Abraham (Lev. 26:40–42); frequently, these ancestors are denoted with the pronoun "our." Daniel, begging God's mercy for the nation, rehearses the history of their misdeeds, including the failure of "our ancestors" to heed the prophets (Dan. 9:6–16).[88] A particularly elaborate instance of this trope occurs in Nehemiah 9, when all the "descendants of Israel" separate themselves from the "descendants of strangers" (υιου αλλοτριου) and confess the sins of their πατερων (Neh. 9:2). This nationalistic confession looks as far back as Abraham, proceeding through the exodus and settlement of Canaan, to the exile, and down to the Persian period, twice lamenting that these ancestors ignored the prophets whom God had sent them (Neh. 9:7–37).

In this recurring motif, the wickedness of Israel *in the past* informs national repentance *in the present*. It is as if the current generation is answerable for the failures of their ancestors, down through the years. Paradoxically, this admission steels their resolve to follow God today. The memory of how "our ancestors" sinned before God contributes to a current state of penitence. It also places the descendants' sin into historical perspective: Israel has *always* struggled with faithfulness.[89]

Luke employs this motif, with a very significant change in phraseology. Jesus does not remind his fellow Judeans that "*our* ancestors" have long tried God's patience; instead, he describes ancient evildoers as "*their* ancestors" (thereby excusing his disciples from their descent) or as "*your* ancestors" when speaking to his opponents (thereby attributing a line of descent to his opponents, from which Jesus excuses himself). Jesus does the former in the Lukan beatitudes (6:22–23, 26), and he does the latter when he denigrates the lawyers (νομικοι) as the latest generation of a long line of prophet-killers (11:47–51). This way of thinking is implicit in other passages, in which Luke alludes to Israel's history, either briefly or at length, in such a way as to suggest that some latter-day Judeans resemble a particular strand of Israelite precursors—whether wicked or righteous.[90]

In the last of the Beatitudes, Jesus tells his audience:

²²Blessed are you whenever people hate you and whenever they ostracize you and revile you and speak ill of you, for the sake of the Son of Man. ²³Rejoice on that day and leap, for behold, your reward in great in heaven; for their ancestors (πατερες) did the same things to the prophets.

²⁶Woe to you whenever people speak well of you, for their ancestors did the same thing to the false prophets. (Luke 6:22–23, 26)

Luke's version differs from Matthew's Beatitudes. Matthew mentions no "ancestors," simply concluding: "so *they* persecuted the prophets" (Matt. 5:11–12). Only Luke specifies *who* did the persecuting—"their ancestors"—bringing issues of descent into play. In Luke, the saying is addressed, not to general crowds, but to disciples (Luke 6:20). In accusing *their* (not "our") ancestors of these heinous crimes, Jesus draws a line from those who *had* persecuted the prophets, and those who *will* persecute his own disciples. And, Jesus suggests a connection between the prophets who were persecuted in their day, and his disciples who are persecuted today. We have, at least rhetorically, a redrawing of genealogical lines based on response to Jesus; a sort of lineage-in-miniature (see figure 5.1).

This simplified sketch of redrawn lines does not really discuss *all* Israelites. Most ancient Israelites were neither prophets nor those who mistreated them. And among first-century Judeans, most were neither disciples, nor persecutors of disciples. Perhaps we might imagine a general mass of relatively "neutral" Israelites between these two poles, but effective rhetoric thrives on contrasts, not subtlety. Here, Jesus' saying suggests that some latter-day Judeans are the heirs (or indeed, children) of two very different strands within Israel, these imagined lines of descent. Of course, they are just that, *imagined*: Jesus is not making assertions about who descends from whom, *biologically*. Notice that Jesus has departed from Israel's longstanding tradition of

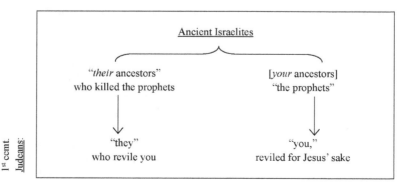

Figure 5.1 Realigned Ancestry in Luke 6:22–23. *Source*: Created by Andrew Benko.

Genealogical Reconfiguration in Luke–Acts 183

claiming *all* ancestors, for good or for ill, for *all* their latter-day descendants. Formerly, Israel would confess what "their" (collective) ancestors had done. Jesus has sliced Israel's past in twain: he has divided out the good ancestors from the bad, and assigned descent from these to his contemporaries—some to his disciples and some to his enemies.

Similar thinking is found in the woes Jesus pronounces upon the experts in the law (νομικοι):

> [47]Woe to you, because you build up the tombs of the prophets, whom your ancestors killed.[48] So you are witnesses that you approve of the deeds of your ancestors; because they killed the prophets, and you build them [tombs].
>
> [49]On account of this the Wisdom of God said, "I will send you prophets and apostles, and they will kill and persecute some of them," [50]so that this generation may be charged with the blood of all the prophets spilled since the founding of the world,[51] from the blood of Abel up until the blood of Zechariah who perished between the altar and the sanctuary. Yes, I tell you, it will be charged to this generation. (Luke 11:47–51)

"Your ancestors" who killed the prophets are mentioned twice in quick succession (cf. 6:23, 26), emphasizing the accusation: the lawyers are the offspring of the worst offenders of Israel's past. Places of burial (and tombs) were a point of ethnic pride, which provided a sense of connection both to one's land and one's ancestors. Here, however, Jesus flips the logic, reinterpreting the prophets' tombs as monuments to those who killed them. These are the "ancestors" whom the lawyers honor.

Verses 49–51 trace a "lineage" of rejected prophets, stretching back to the first days of humankind—begun with Abel, including Zechariah, and stretching forward to rejected prophets in the last days.[91] The corresponding "lineage" of prophet-killers, then, also stretches back to the days when Adam walked the earth: Cain, as his killer, would be the progenitor of this line. The lawyers' approval of their ancestors' crimes has a "juridical" outcome—they "inherit" the blood guilt accrued over generations of murder.

The death of Zechariah was recounted in 2 Chronicles (24:20–22). He was stoned to death in the court of the Temple, and his last words ("May the LORD see and obey!") anticipate some future response on God's part. The story was a source of continued reflection in Judean literature (*b. Git.* 58b; *Lam. Rab.* proem 23; *Eccl. Rab.* 3.19; *Lives.Proph.* 23:1). Zechariah, John's father, shares the prophet's name, and he also works in the temple and prophesies—although happily, he does not share his fate (Luke 1:64). In "this generation," the prophetic Stephen is killed by stoning,[92] and his final cry mirrors but reverses Zechariah's last words: "Lord, do not hold this sin against them!" (Acts 7:60).[93] We have, then, at least two latter-day figures who echo their

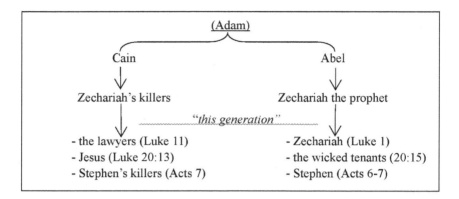

Figure 5.2 Realigned Ancestry in Luke 11:47–51. *Source*: Created by Andrew Benko.

"ancestor," Zechariah. They belong to a long line of prophets stretching back dawn of humanity, originating with Abel (see figure 5.2).

In the speech in Solomon's Portico, Peter calls his audience, whom he hopes to persuade, "sons of the prophets" (Acts 3:25). In Acts, kinship language ("brothers," 3:17) and language of "our ancestors" (3:13) is often featured in speeches directed to fellow Judeans—affirming their shared ancestry to connect with the audience (cf. 13:32, 26:6).[94] However, Peter's also contains a warning:

> [22]Moses said, 'The Lord your God will raise up for you from among your kinsfolk (αδελφων) a prophet like me. You must listen to whatever he tells you [Deut 18:15]. [23]And it will be that everyone who does not listen to that prophet will be utterly rooted out of the people' [cf. Lev 17:4]. [24]And all the prophets, as many as have spoken, from Samuel and those after him, also predicted these days. [25]You are the descendants of the prophets (υιοι των προφητων) and of the covenant that God gave to your ancestors, saying to Abraham, 'And in your descendants all the families of the earth shall be blessed' [Gen 12:3]. (Acts 3:22–25)[95]

Peter has quoted the "descendant-mediated" version of God's blessing of the nations in Abraham (Gen. 12:3, 18:18), stressing that the nations will be blessed in Abraham's descendants rather than directly "in" him (Gen. 22:18).[96] Peter has also enlisted all the prophets of Israel's long history—Moses, Samuel, and "those after him"—in support of *his* interpretation of "these days." Jesus himself is the "prophet like Moses" foretold in Deuteronomy 18:15, 18–19. Peter has lengthened Moses' prediction with material from elsewhere in the Torah, adding a dreadful consequence: If the "children

Genealogical Reconfiguration in Luke–Acts 185

of the prophets" do not recognize the one whom the prophets foretold, they will be "rooted out." Jocelyn McWhirter summarizes:

> The choice is clear. Repentance will lead to forgiveness, times of refreshing, the sending of God's Messiah, and the blessing promised to Abraham in Gen. 22:18. If Jerusalem's Jews do not listen, however, they will suffer the curse pronounced on Abraham's uncircumcised descendants (Gen. 17:14) and Israelites who eat leaven during Passover (Exod. 12:15, 19). They 'will be utterly rooted out of the people' (Acts 3:23).[97]

Peter's threat of excision from the people is similar to texts from Qumran, which imagine a purified Israel purged of unworthy members (*1QS* 5.8–13; *CD* 3.12–17).[98] Here, Israel is similarly reconfigured by the *subtraction* of certain Judeans: in this case, those who do not listen to the "prophet like Moses," Jesus.

There is a certain fluidity to lineage in these passages; individuals are aligned with certain ancestral figures *based on their behavior today*.[99] Those whom Peter hopes to persuade are hailed as "sons of the prophets," but they can still be "cut off" if they fail to heed the prophet like Moses, Jesus (Acts 3:23).[100] Peter attributes honorable descent to this audience "optimistically" because he hopes to convince them. Indeed, as it so happens, "many of those who listened to the message believed, about five thousand men" (4:4). These listeners, at least, have been confirmed in their constructed genealogical identity as sons of the prophets.

In Acts 7, Stephen is less optimistic about his chances. He has good reason to be: his situation and audience are entirely different.[101] Stephen's survey of Israel's past is delivered to the same religious elites who secretly arranged for his arrest. Because his false accusers claimed that they "heard him speaking blasphemous words against Moses and God" (Acts 6:11), his defense sets out to demonstrate the *opposite*—that the gospel is consistent with the hopes of Israel's ancestors. His speech is packed full of the "stuff" of race—kinship, ancestry, way of life, and homeland.[102]

Stephen relates that God kept faith with Abraham, giving him descendants. However, many of these descendants did not keep faith with God. The tribal patriarchs rejected their very first prophet, their brother Joseph (Acts 7:9–16), and their descendants were less than receptive to the prophet Moses—both in his own day, and down through the generations (Acts 7:17–50).[103] Like Peter, Stephen also cites Moses' prediction of a "prophet like me" (7:37) to come. He recounts that many of Israel's ancestors "rejected" Moses (7:35), "thrust him aside" (7:27), and "refused to obey" him (7:39). For Stephen, a clear line is being drawn from Moses to Jesus—and from those who threatened Moses to Stephen's own audience. Jesus bears a

186   *Chapter 5*

family resemblance to Moses, but *they* resemble those who rejected him.[104] What Stephen says about Moses and his generation, could aptly be said of Jesus and *his*: "he supposed that his kindred (αδελφοι) would understand that God was saving them by his hand—but they did not understand" (Acts 7:25).[105]

Concluding his speech, Stephen *explicitly* compares his audience to the worst villains of Israel's past:

> [51]You stiff-necked ones, uncircumcised in hearts and ears: you are always resisting the Holy Spirit—as your ancestors [did], so do you. [52]Which of the prophets did your ancestors not persecute? And they killed those who foretold the coming of the righteous one, whom you now betrayed and murdered, [53]you who received the law delivered by angels but did not keep it. (Acts 7:51–53)

Stephen has turned the tables, accusing his accusers of the very charge they leveled at him: abandoning the law of Moses and the ancestral customs.[106] Because the law demands they heed the prophet like Moses (Deut. 18:15–20), *not* listening to Jesus is a violation of that law. Dulcinea Boesenberg points out,

> Stephen claims that the Israelites rejected the law from the beginning, and just like the Israelites who turned immediately from the law with their worship of the golden calf (7:41), their descendants (Stephen's audience) have not kept the law. These are the same Jews whom Stephen accuses of following in the path of *their* ancestors by opposing the Holy Spirit (7:51) and persecuting the prophets (7:52). It is these Jews who do not follow Jesus, but who follow the ways of *their* ancestors, who are accused of rejecting their ethnic customs. Stephen refuses to share ancestry with Jews who do not observe the law.[107]

Stephen's switch to "*your* ancestors" as those who killed the prophets is telling. The wording departs from typical Judean rhetoric that "our" ancestors sinned (Acts 7:51–52).[108] Instead, Stephen suggests that some Judeans are the heirs of one set of ancestors (e.g., Abraham, Joseph, Moses, the prophets), whereas others are the heirs of a very different set. Stephen himself belongs to the long line of the prophets, *not* to their killers.

To Stephen, the council's misdeeds reveal (or construct?) their true ancestry. Acts 7:51–53 echoes the cultural truism that "the son is like the father" (cf. Luke 6:35–36, Sir. 40:1–4; John 5:19); thus, the "sons and brothers" whom Stephen addresses are in fact following in the footsteps of *their* forefathers, who killed the prophets.[109] In Stephen's retelling of history, his audience's forebears have "always" rejected God's prophets and turned toward idols,[110] but Stephen's own forebears comprise a laundry list of Israel's greatest heroes (see figure 5.3).

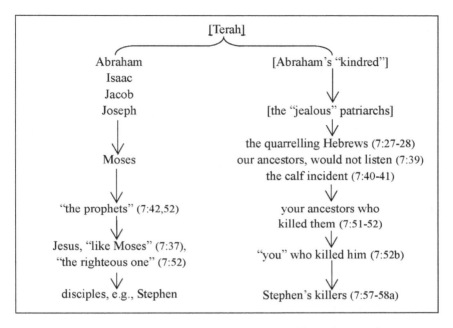

Figure 5.3 **Realigned Ancestry in Acts 7.** *Source:* Created by Andrew Benko.

In summary, the way that Luke–Acts retells Israel's history broadly suggests two streams of ancestors: the prophets along with those who heeded them, and those who rejected (or even killed) them. Speaking to opponents, Luke's protagonists sometimes describe the latter as "your" ancestors, thus polemically assigning villainous ancestry to Judeans who resist the gospel. Although they are still acknowledged as Judeans, this rhetorical pattern does have ethnic implications. The construction of a valorized lineage with scions of Israel's best and brightest, and of a villainized lineage whose offspring repeat the sins of the past, creates a sort of division *within Israel*. Both sides of this divide understand themselves to be the proper expression of their ethnic heritage, and understand the opposing side to be ethnic deviants. Christian Judeans understand those who persecute them to have turned their backs on the promises made to their fathers, and the hope conveyed to Israel by the prophets. Non-Christian Judeans understand the disciples as apostates from the Law of Moses, who have abandoned the proper observance of their ancestral ways (6:13–14). Both groups define themselves as prototypical, and the other side as degenerate, *using explicitly racial reasoning.*

Luke spends a huge amount of energy demonstrating that Judeans who follow the Way are *more*, not less, Judean for it. The news about the messiah Jesus is firmly embedded in a matrix of promises made to Israel's ancestors

188 Chapter 5

(e.g., Luke chapters 1–2, Acts 13:26, 32–37, 26:6). Prototypical Judeans anticipate, endorse, or join the Way, thus giving the movement a stamp of ethnic authenticity.[111] Jesus and his disciples resemble the famed prophets of old in various ways, demonstrating continuity with Israel's most celebrated forebears.[112] Indeed, many are explicitly *called* prophets or engage in clearly prophetic activity.[113]

But Luke must especially defend the Judeanness of the Way on one particular front: Torah observance. In the face of accusations to the contrary,[114] characters like Paul continually insist they have "done nothing against our people (λαῳ) or the customs of our fathers (τοις εθεσιν τοις πατρῳοις)" (Acts 28:17), that they have taught "nothing except what the prophets and Moses said would come to pass" (Acts 26:22).[115] They counter: it is actually those who reject the gospel who reject the prophets.[116] As Paul tells some Roman Judeans who did not believe him: "The Holy Spirit was right in saying to *your* ancestors through the prophet Isaiah: 'Go to this people and tell them you will indeed listen, but never hear, and you will indeed look, but never see'" (Acts 28:25b–26). In Paul's understanding, Isaiah did not criticize *our*, but "your" ancestors: those who cannot "hear" Paul's message are the latter-day children of those who were deaf to the prophets.

Paul's case illustrates that one's classification along these imagined lineages is changeable. As a younger man, then known as Saul, he once stood among those to whom Stephen said, "*your* ancestors killed the prophets," as a solemn witness while he was stoned (Acts 7:58, 8:1). Paul once aligned himself with one series of ancestors but has now repented and aligned himself with another.

Diverging Lines: Godly Gentiles vs. Godless Idolators

Luke's implied audience is largely gentile, or at least contains significant gentile elements. Francis Bovon proposes three main target segments among Luke's audience: Hellenistic Judeans, educated gentiles, and Christians unsettled by anti-Christian polemic (Luke 1:4, Acts 22:30).[117] Some scholars narrow the implied reader of Luke–Acts to the "God-fearer," specifically;[118] indeed, it is not unlikely that our author is himself a God-fearer.[119] In the narrative world of Luke–Acts, God-fearers (1) fear and worship Israel's God with authentic devotion, but (2) have not fully converted (including circumcision), and thus (3) find themselves both attracted to Judaism and blocked, simultaneously invited and disinvited; until they can be (4) "joined to" the community of Judeans (rather than replacing it) by commitment to the risen messiah. For such folk, figures such as the Centurion of Capernaum (Luke 7), the Ethiopian Eunuch (Acts 8), and Cornelius (Acts 10) serve as prototypes of both exemplary piety and coming to faith in Jesus.[120]

Genealogical Reconfiguration in Luke–Acts   189

Some God-fearers may have been content to simply honor Israel's god alongside their own pantheon and to adopt some Judean practices. The existence of interested gentiles at the fringes of synagogue life, well-attested not only in Luke but other literary and epigraphic evidence, suggests that diaspora synagogues were happy to accommodate gentiles who desired this sort of partial engagement. But other God-fearers who desired a fuller engagement with Judaism may have experienced their own racial identity as a barrier to being joined to Israel. To the extent that they have heard Israel's sacred story, they have learned that the Most High has a relationship with a very particular people, descended from specific ancestors. This need not have stemmed from any particular ethnocentricity on the part of the Judean community itself, but simply the reception and contemplation of Israel's sacred scriptures. To the extent that interested gentiles have *internalized* the worldview of these stories, they may have come to understand themselves as having the "wrong" ancestors. Sincere God-fearers may have learned to value Israel's lineage (and ethnic identity) as conveying a special standing with God, and learned to *devalue* their own lineage (and ethnic identity) as neutral at best—at worst, as an outright barrier to their relationship with Israel's god. Perhaps they have begun to conceptualize themselves not (only) as members of specific races (Greeks, Macedonians, Parthians, Syrians, etc.) but as "gentiles" (עמים/εθνη, in the sense of "non-Judeans"), with the negative valence this label sometimes carries in the Bible.

It is largely a *genealogical* dilemma facing God-fearers. Luke has firmly situated Jesus within the context of promises made to Israel's ancestors, about the blessings promised to their descendants, the people of Israel. Gentiles among Luke's readers might want to know: What do these promises have to do with *me*, a gentile? Can I inherit the blessings of Abraham, the covenant promises God made to his people? Can I, indeed, be joined with God's people?

Luke offers a twofold solution. First, Luke invokes a "lineage" of virtuous or included gentiles from Israel's own historical memory, allowing gentiles to see themselves *as gentiles* reflected in Israel's sacred story and to understand themselves as the successors of these virtuous forbears. We have already seen that the genealogies of Luke 3 and Acts 17 contain references to Adam, the first human (father of Israelites and gentiles alike); we shall see other examples below. Second, Luke suggests that God-fearers are "added to" the line and family of Abraham (Luke 3:8; 13:24–30) and joined to Israel by following the four prohibitions handed down by the Jerusalem Council (Acts 15:19–21, 28–29), which are consistent with regulations for gentiles (עמים) who wish to reside in Israel (cf. Lev. 17–18).[121]

Therefore, gentile Christians can imagine their family trees rooted in two soils: one gentile, one Israelite. On the one side, they figuratively descend from the virtuous gentiles dotting Israel's history (and from their own poets

190   *Chapter 5*

who have "groped" toward God, Acts 17:28). On the other side, they also
descend from Abraham, by repeating his radical resolution to leave relatives
(συγγενειας) and "father's household" (οικου του πατρος) to be made into
a great nation (Gen 12:1–2; Acts 7:3).[122] This last point also implies a fork
in the gentile family tree: some who repeat Abraham's exodus from Haran,
and others who are "left behind" in their idolatry. Although God can raise
up "children for Abraham" from stones (Luke 3:8), it seems others prefer
"stones" shaped by human hands (Acts 17:29).

Our Father, Naaman (Luke 4:25–27)

Jesus begins his public ministry in Nazareth, "where he had been raised,"
(4:16), and he proclaims the "Year of the Lord's Favor" fulfilled in the synagogue (Acts 4:17–21 // Isa. 61:1–2). Luke alone supplies us with the passage
read on this occasion: an oracle from Isaiah. The rest of that passage foretells
the involvement of "foreigners" (αλλογενεις and αλλοφυλοι) in the tending
of Israel's vines, with the wealth of the "nations" (εθνη) streaming there, at
the same time his audience's "descendants" (σπερμα and εκγονα) are held in
high repute "among the *ethnē*" in diaspora (Isa. 61:1–11). Israel's restoration
will involve other races and will take place "in the sight of the nations," both
in their land and abroad. Thus, the reading for the day anticipates not only
Jesus' healing miracles among fellow Israelites, but also the *involvement of
the gentiles* in the reception and distribution of God's blessings—a theme that
will be taken up in the next few verses (Luke 4:24–27).

The villagers may have been initially excited about such a message. Locals
who had achieved high status were expected to leverage their position to benefit their home πατρις (e.g., *Ant.* 14.143–44; *War* 2.590).[123] But Jesus dashes
such hopes: he will not perform any healings in Nazareth. He explains:

> [25]In truth I tell you that there were many widows in Israel in the days of Elijah,
> when the sky was closed for three years and six months, as there was a great
> famine in all the land; [26]yet Elijah was sent to none of them, but only to a wid-
> owed woman in Zarephath of Sidon. [27]And there were many lepers in Israel in
> the time of Elisha the prophet, yet he cleaned none of them, but only Naaman
> the Syrian. (Luke 4:25–27)

Initially receptive, the crowd sours when Jesus makes it clear that his work
will also benefit gentiles, despite the presence of many needy "in Israel"
(4:25, 27) in his own day—perhaps some in his own village. David Smith
suggests Luke 4:16–30 reflects the later tensions between the Way and Judaism, or even with certain forms of Judean Christianity—and Jesus' remarks
about Elijah and Elisha echo this polemical context. The crowd's objection—
"physician, heal thyself"—could in fact reflect the attitude of increasingly

Genealogical Reconfiguration in Luke–Acts 191

marginalized Judean Christians, who resent the influx of gentiles into the church.[124]

Anecdotes about Elijah and Elisha illustrate the proverb "no prophet is acceptable in his hometown" with examples from Israel's classical past.[125] Jesus reminds the villagers of two times when a wonder-working prophet withheld benefits from their own countrymen "in Israel," yet assisted foreigners. The widow of Zarephath fed Elijah, and he made her flour and oil last for many days (1 Kings 17:8–16), later restoring her dead son to life (17:17–23). The Syrian general Naaman, hearing rumors of Elisha's power, sought him out and was cleansed of his leprosy (2 Kings 5:1–14). In both cases, Israel was under a period of national judgment on account of idolatry (1 Kings 16:29–17:1; 2 Kings 3:1–3). In both tales, a foreigner is spurred to a confession of Israel's God (1 Kings 17:24; 2 Kings 5:15). Naaman even vows to serve the LORD, although he is unable to extricate himself from national and personal responsibilities that make this difficult:

> Please let two mule loads of earth be given to your servant, for your servant will no longer offer burnt offering or sacrifice to any god except the LORD.[18] But may the LORD pardon your servant on one count: when my master goes into the house of Rimmon to worship there, leaning on my arm, and I bow down in the house of Rimmon, when I do bow down in the house of Rimmon, may the LORD pardon your servant on this one count. (1 Kings 5:17–18)[126]

Naaman is bound by geography and culture. Having realized "there is no God in all the earth except in Israel" (2 Kings 5:15) but required to go home, Naaman brings as much of Israel's earth back to Aram as he can carry. Having realized that idols are false, but required by his social obligations to accompany his master to the temple of Rimmon, he asks God to excuse him when he bows. The demands of homeland and custom stand in his way. In the conflict between his desire to devote himself to the God of Israel and his inability to fully execute that resolve, Naaman foreshadows the dilemma of the first-century God-fearer—who feels attracted to Israel, but perhaps hesitating at the edge of full inclusion (including circumcision).

These two gentile figures might be thought of as the "ancestors" of latter-day gentiles who receive similar benefits and who make similar confessions of faith. In Luke, these two are echoed in adjacent stories: the healing of a centurion's servant (7:1–16) and the raising of a widow's son (7:11–17). Although the widow of Nain is a Galilean,[127] the unnamed centurion is a foreign soldier, like Naaman. As in the story of Naaman, the healing takes place at a distance. Like Naaman, he sends an emissary instead of coming personally, in this case, the "Judean elders" who explain he is worthy of this favor, "for he loves our nation (εθνος) and he himself built our synagogue" (7:4).

192   *Chapter 5*

But the centurion himself does not believe that he is "worthy" to receive Jesus in his house (7:5)—perhaps aware of purity concerns that complicate such a visit (Acts 10:28). Robert Beck explains,

> His contradictory invitation represents his own sense of being called—the gentile centurion finds himself in a paradoxical position in which he is both invited and excluded. His blocking of Jesus reflects his own qualms about overcoming the blocks that he himself, as a gentile, faces. The sympathetic gentile reader would recognize not only the centurion's attachment to the synagogue, but also the frustration of being attracted and blocked at the same time.[128]

We can also see a family resemblance between the general Naaman and Cornelius, "a centurion of the Italian Cohort" stationed in Caesarea (Acts 10:1). In this case, there is no illness, but Cornelius is also a foreign soldier in the holy land, who also sends a messenger to a religious figure. Like the centurion of Capernaum, he is described as pious (10:2, 4). He is vouched for by Judean elites—indeed, "the whole Judean *ethnos*" speaks well of him (10:22). Whereas Elisha "cleansed" (εκαθαρισθη) Naaman of leprosy, Peter's recent vision teaches him "I should call no person unclean (εκαθαρτον)."[129] Gentiles are not inherently impure: "I truly understand that God is not partial, but that in every race whoever fears him and does what is right is acceptable (δεκτος) to him" (Acts 10:34b–35).

Gentile Queens and Gentile Cities (Luke 11:29–32)

> [29]This generation is a wicked generation; it seeks a sign, and no sign will be given to it, except the sign of the prophet Jonah. [30] For as Jonah became a sign to the people of Nineveh, just so will the Son of Man be [a sign] to this generation. [31] The queen of the south will rise up in judgement against the men of this generation and condemn them, because she came from the ends of the earth (περατων της γης) to hear the wisdom of Solomon, and behold, one greater than Solomon is right here![32] The men of Nineveh will rise up (αναστησονται) in judgment against this generation and condemn it; because they repented at the preaching of Jonah, and behold, one great than Jonah is right here! (Luke 11:29b–32)

Drawing from Israel's historical memory, Jesus reminds a crowd about bygone gentiles who heeded the words of God's messengers. Jesus warns them that his contemporaries who ignore the Son of Man will stand judged by these ancients. It is striking to see gentiles elevated over Israel in this eschatological judgment scene.[130] They include two parties of faithful foreigners

Genealogical Reconfiguration in Luke–Acts 193

from the past: the "Queen of the South" and the men of Nineveh. We will consider each in turn, and echoes of these figures throughout Luke–Acts.

The "Queen of the South" (βασιλισσα νοτου) refers to the Queen of Sheba (βασιλισσα Σαβα) who came to hear Solomon's wisdom (1 Kings 10:1–13 // 2 Chron. 9:1–12). The exact referent of "Sheba" is elusive. In the Table of the Nations in Genesis 10, "Sheba" appears as a descendant of Cush (associated with Africa), but *also* as a descendant of Shem (10:6,28). "Sheba" might be associated with Saba in the Arabian Peninsula, the home of the Sabeans (Jer. 6:20; Ps. 72:15); but it might look further south to a region near Cush / Ethiopia (Isa. 43:3, 45:14). In this latter vein, Josephus reports that the "Queen of Egypt and Ethiopia" visited Solomon (*Ant.* 8.168–75).[131] Origen follows this tradition, identifying her as "the Sheban Queen of the Ethiopians," and as the "black and beautiful" woman whom Solomon praises in the Song of Songs (Orig., *Comm. Songs* 2.2).[132]

In the biblical tradition, the Queen of Sheba recognized Solomon's great wisdom and gave him a huge quantity of gold and spices. She exclaimed, "Blessed be the LORD your God, who has delighted in you!" (1 Kings 10:9–10). The queen might serve as an archetype for latter-day gentile pilgrims, who bring their wealth to enrich Jerusalem and its temple, and who confess the greatness of its God. Indeed, Third Isaiah lists Sheba among the nations who will bring their gold and sacrificial animals to Jerusalem, where "they shall be acceptable (δεκτα) on my altar" (Isa. 60:6–7).[133] In Acts, the Ethiopian Eunuch proves to be a "spiritual grandson" of the Queen of Sheba, in his own generation (Acts 8:26–27).[134]

This visiting Ethiopian is a court official, the treasurer of "the Candace, the Queen of the Ethiopians" (Acts 8:27)—a phrase evocative of the Queen of Sheba for those familiar with scripture.[135] Like the Queen of Sheba who came from "the ends of the earth" (Luke 11:31), he has come from far-off Ethiopia. This man of considerable status and wealth went to Jerusalem to worship (8:28), but his status as foreigner[136] and eunuch would likely have ruled out entering the Temple past the outer balustrade, where an inscription sternly warned,

Μηθενα αλλογενη εισπο- ρευεσθαι εντος του πε- ρε το ιερον τρυφακτου και περιβολου. Ός δ' αν λη- φθη, έαυτωι αιτιος εσ- ται δια το εξακολου- θειν θανατον.[137]	No foreigner is to ent- er within the balu- strade of the temple and the enclosure. And whoever is caught is himself responsible for his result- ing death.

194   *Chapter 5*

Philo and Josephus both discuss this prohibition and its consequences, and a scene in Acts imagines a crowd's response to its (supposed) violation (Acts 21:28).[138] Although being a foreigner would have sufficed to exclude one, status as eunuch was a further hindrance (Lev. 21:17–21, Deut. 23:2 LXX; cf. *Ant.* 4.290–91).[139] The eunuch is simultaneously attracted to Judaism, and blocked—drawn to Israel's center and its scriptures, but barred from its Temple.

When Philip reaches the Ethiopian, he is reading a passage from Isaiah:

> Like a sheep he was led to the slaughter,
>   and like a lamb silent before its shearer,
> so he does not open his mouth.
>   In his humiliation, justice was denied him.
> Who can describe his generation?
>   For his life is taken away from the earth. (Acts 8:32–33 [Isa. 53:7–8])

The official asks whether the prophet is talking about himself or about another (Acts 8:34). Perhaps the eunuch sees his *own* experience mirrored in the prophet's words. After all, who can describe *his* "generation" (γενεαν)? He will have none—no children, no lineage, no further shoots on the family tree after him. Like the dishonored Servant of Isaiah 53, whose life was "taken from the earth," perhaps he too "will see seed (σπερμα) and long life" (Isa. 53:2–8). Beck comments, "The problem for the eunuch is that he has no place in the historical narrative of God's people, since he has no offspring to continue his story."[140]

Numerous interpreters note that *another* passage from Isaiah, near the one the eunuch is reading, speaks even more directly to the Ethiopian's situation:[141]

> [3] Let not the foreigner (αλλογενης) who joins himself to the Lord say,
> "The Lord will surely separate me from his people (λαου),"
>   and let not the eunuch say, "I am a withered tree."
> [4] For thus says the Lord:
> "To the eunuchs who keep my sabbaths
>   and choose what I desire and hold fast to my covenant,
> [5] I will give them, within my house (οικω) and within my walls,
>   a monument (τοπον ονομαστον) better than sons and daughters;
>   I will give them an eternal name (ονομα) and it shall not die off (εκλειψει).
> [6] And to the foreigners (αλλογενεσι) who join themselves to the Lord,
>   who love my name, to be my male and female slaves,
> who keep my sabbaths and do not profane them,
>   who hold fast to my covenant,
> [7] I will bring lead them to my holy mountain,

Their burnt offerings and sacrifices will be acceptable (δεκτος) on my altar,
for my house will be called 'A House of Prayer for All Races (εθνησιν).'"
(Isaiah 56:3–7 [LXX])[142]

If Isaiah 56 also comprises the conceptual background for the Ethiopian's question, then its promises should apply to him as well.[143] After all, this visiting Ethiopian is *both* a foreigner *and* a eunuch. But this oracle asserts that a Godly foreigner, even a childless one, is not a "dead tree." Instead, they are promised a family rooted in Israel, planted in the very Temple, and fertile: producing "many seeds (σπερμα) and long life." Recall that trees and vegetative imagery could be used to describe descent and lineage, among both Judeans *and* non-Judeans.[144]

Whatever the accidents of his genetic descent may be, the Ethiopian Eunuch is a child of Naaman, the Queen of Sheba, and other worthy gentiles who have come to praise the name of God. He is a living instance of God's promises regarding eunuchs and foreigners, spoken through Isaiah so long ago (Isa. 56:3–7). Together, the citation of Isa. 53:7–8 and the allusion to Isaiah 56 demonstrate that God-fearing gentiles such as this man can be joined with God's people, added to their family tree, given a name (ονομα) and a monument (τοπος ονομαστον) better than descendants, and that they are "acceptable" (δεκτος) to God.[145]

At least metaphorically, something *genealogical* is happening to this man. This latter-day offshoot of the "Queen of Ethiopia" who visited Solomon (*Ant.* 8.168–75) can be grafted into God's people. Aaron Kuecker remarks, "Just as Jesus' lack of 'descendants' did not prevent God from giving him a new and large 'family' (cf. Luke 8:21), the eunuch's lack of 'descendants' will not prohibit him from being incorporated into a new and large 'family.'"[146]

Let us return to Luke 11. Along with the "Queen of the South," Jesus also mentioned Jonah. Jonah, a native of the Northern Kingdom (2 Kings 14:23–27), was appointed by God to prophesy to the people of Nineveh, a major city of the Assyrians (Jonah 1:1–2), Israel's enemies. He initially fled to avoid this duty, not wanting the hated Assyrians to receive God's mercy (4:1–3). Eventually, his warnings led all in Nineveh—humans *and* animals—to repent in sackcloth and ashes (3:1–10), and God's wrath was averted. With this allusion, Jesus reminds his audience of an ancient Israelite who had wished to limit God's grace to his own nation, and of a foreign people who responded faithfully to God and received that grace.

Luke has inherited this saying from the Q source, but he has reworked it to emphasize certain themes [see table 5.2]. In Matthew's version, the meaning of the "sign of Jonah" is elaborated in terms of Jesus' death and resurrection (Matt. 12:40). Luke lacks any mention of the whale, instead explaining that

196   *Chapter 5*

Jonah was given *"as a sign to the gentiles"* (Luke 11:30). With no reference to Jesus' death and resurrection, there is relatively more weight placed on the Ninevites' response to Jonah's message, and on their *own* resurrection (αναστησονται, verse 32). In other words, Luke's "sign of Jonah" does not prove that Jesus rose, but that *repentant gentiles will rise*, vindicated—even to a position of judgment over (unrepentant) Israelites. Remember, John the Baptist already described repentance as *the* defining characteristic of Abraham's children (Luke 3:8). The book of Jonah describes the exaggerated, even comical repentance of Nineveh (Jonah 3:6–9): the city's king, human population, and even its livestock dress in sackcloth, fast, and wail, as they "repent of their evil ways and the violence that is in their hands" (or on their hooves?). If it is repentance that marks the children of Abraham, the Ninevites have it in spades, exactly the sort of "stones" God would raise up as children of Abraham (Luke 3:8) (table 5.2).

This saying about resurrected gentiles (11:29–32) anticipates *another* scene of eschatological judgment. Jesus tells a crowd that some of them will "wail and gnash your teeth when you see Abraham and Isaac and Jacob" reclining to feast with those "from east and west and north and south," while they themselves will be excluded (13:28–29). The warning resembles a scene imagined by Rabbi Yonatan: in the future, Abraham would be told by God, "[Some of] your children have sinned against me." Abraham would reply "If so, let them be eradicated to sanctify your name" (*t.Shabbat* 89b 4). Similarly,

> Anyone who has compassion for God's creatures, it is known that he is of the descendants of Abraham, our father, and anyone who does not have compassion

Table 5.2   The "Sign of Jonah" in Matthew vs. Luke

Matthew 12:39-41	Luke 11:29-30,32
[39]An evil and adulterous generation seeks out a sign, but no sign will be given to it, except the sign of the prophet Jonah.	[29]This generation is an evil one; it seeks a sign, and no sign will be given to it, except the sign of the prophet Jonah.
[40]For as Jonah was in the belly of the fish three days and three nights, so the Son of Man will be in the heart of the earth for three days and three nights.	[30]For as Jonah became a sign to the people of Nineveh, just so the Son of Man will be [a sign] to this generation...

both conclude versions conclude:

The men of Nineveh will rise up in judgment against this generation and condemn it; because they repented at the preaching of Jonah, and look, one great than Jonah is here.

Genealogical Reconfiguration in Luke–Acts

for God's creatures, it is known that he is not of the descendants of Abraham, our father. (*t. Beitzah* 32b)[147]

Some early Jewish sages imagined Abrahamic descent to be tangled up with following in his footsteps.[148] These sayings may be preserving *earlier* traditions, similar to some articulated by early Christians (Q 3:8; Gal. 3:7; John 8:39–40), suggesting that descent from Abraham could be weakened by bad behavior, or forged by good.

Several gentile cities are mentioned in Luke 10:12–15. Galilean cities which reject Jesus' message are worse than Sodom, Tire, and Sidon, "For if the mighty works done in you had been done in Tyre and Sidon, they would have repented long ago, sitting in sackcloth and ashes" (Luke 10:13). Here, the rhetorical function of the gentile cities is largely negative, emphasizing that some Judean towns are "even worse than" gentiles, and will fare "even worse" in the time of judgment (10:12, 14–15). But the mention of "sackcloth and ashes" also reminds us how *well* the men of Nineveh will fare when they rise (11:32). Unlike the residents of Tyre and Sidon who "would have" repented at such signs, Nineveh actually *did* repent at the "sign of Jonah."[149]

In conclusion, Luke 11:29–32 holds up the Queen of Sheba and the people of Nineveh as forerunners of gentile converts. The gentile Christians of Luke's own day, drawn into what is conceptually an *Israelite* identity (and aware of their *non*-Judean origins), can look to these figures as their pious forbears, their "ancestors" in coming to know the God of Israel. The genealogical reconfiguration of Christian gentiles hearkens back to these wise gentile ancestors, but they also walk directly in the footsteps of Abraham himself[150] (see figure 5.4).

KINSHIP GAINED; KINSHIP STRAINED

As for these kinships (συγγενειαι), as we call them, which have come down from our ancestors (εκ προγονων) and are based on blood-relationship (αφ' αἱματος), or those derived from intermarriage (επιγαμιας) or from similar causes, let them be cast aside if they do not seek earnestly the same goal, namely, the honour of God, which is the indissoluble bond of all the affection which makes us one. For those who are so minded will receive in exchange kinships (συγγενειας) of greater dignity and sanctity. —Philo, *Special Laws* 1.317[151]

As we saw in chapter 1, ancient pagans, Judeans, and later, Christians could all discuss religious adherence in ethnic terms. A shift in religious practice could change one's sense of *relatedness* to others. This could have both

Chapter 5

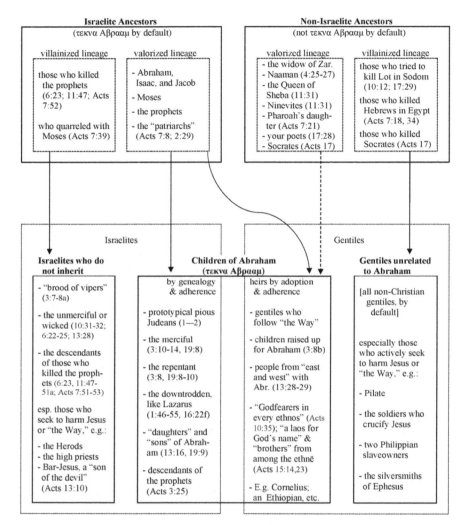

Figure 5.4 **Ancestral Lines, Redrawn in Luke–Acts.** *Source*: Created by Andrew Benko.

constructive and deconstructive effects: kinship was forged with the new group, but old relationships were destabilized. In the passage above, Philo discusses both aspects. Those "so-called kin" who turn their backs on God are to be "cast aside," whereas those who come to Israel's God find "kinships of greater dignity." A convert to Judaism could be considered not only a "Judean," but also a "brother"; an apostate from Judaism could be thought of as not only a traitor to their race, but as "no longer related to us."

As we will see, we can find similar thinking in Luke–Acts. One's religious conduct has the power to forge kinship but also the power to trouble it. Those

Genealogical Reconfiguration in Luke–Acts

who come to know Jesus are understood as "brothers" (and sisters) with each other—even those who came from different ethnic groups. However, those who come to faith in Jesus are *also* understood as ethnic deviants by most members of their group of origins.

Faith in Jesus had the potential to reconfigure family relationships, to de- (or re-) construct kinship (*sungeneia*). Consider Jesus' shocking announcement:

> [51]Do you think I have to give peace in the earth? No, I tell you, but rather division (διαμερισμον)! [52]For now five in one household (οικω) will be divided (διαμερισμενοι), three against two and two against three. [53]They will be divided (διαμερισθησονται), "father against son and son against father, mother against daughter and daughter against mother, mother-in-law against her daughter-in-law and daughter-in-law against mother-in-law." (Luke 12:51–53)[152]

Jesus (and one's response to him) has the power to reweave kinship ties. Luke's version features the word "division" (διαμεριζειν) three times in quick succession, although it is lacking in Matthew's (Matt. 10:34–36). Philo corroborates that apostates might face total rejection from their estranged kin (*Spec.Leg.* 1.316).[153] If Jesus' warnings are any indication, some Christ-followers faced similar estrangement from their families (Luke 12:51–53). Indeed, the potential disciple must proactively steel himself for such rejection, "counting the cost" of following Jesus—prepared to "hate his own father and mother and wife and children and brothers and sisters" (Luke 14:26, 28–33; cf. 18:28–30).[154]

Jesus downplays the significance of *biological* relatedness in comparison with spiritual kinship—both in his teachings and in his own family relationships. Once, as a young man, he failed to rejoin his parents on a trip back from Jerusalem, remaining in the Temple. His mother scolded him, "your father and I have been worried sick looking for you," to which Jesus replied, "Didn't you know I had to be in my father's house?" (Luke 2:48–49). Jesus' rejoinder undermines the status of his parents: "Oh, my '*father*' was looking for me, was he?" Consider another time his family came looking for him:

> [19]And his mother and his brothers came to him, but they were unable to reach him because of the crowd. [20]And they told him, "Your mother and your brothers are standing outside, hoping to see you." [21]But he answered them, "My mother and my brothers are those who hear the word of God, and do it." (Luke 8:19–21)[155]

Both times, when his natural kin come looking for him, Jesus *redefines kinship.* Later in the gospel, a woman loudly blesses the womb that bore him and the breasts that nursed him—strikingly intimate and biological images of motherhood. Jesus refocuses her blessing on "those who hear the word of God and keep it" (Luke 11:27–28), echoing the saying about who his "true" mother and brothers are (8:21).

200   *Chapter 5*

Jesus predicts (or even demands) that some kinship ties be broken, but he also promises that new ones will be gained. The disciples will not be a conglomeration of orphans, but a new family. Although Jesus does affirm the general obligation to honor one's parents (Luke 18:20), he nevertheless assures those who have "left house (οικιαν) or wife or brothers or parents or children for the sake of the kingdom of God," that they will receive many more "in this age" (Luke 18:29–30)—new relations to replace those they have lost. All believers will be their family—new brothers, sisters, mothers, and children in the faith. As it turns out, many of Jesus' blood family *will* eventually be incorporated into this wider kinship network, but presumably not all of them. His mother Mary and brother James are incorporated into this family, not because of their biological connection to Jesus (cf. Acts 1:14), but because they were willing to follow him like any other disciple—willing to hear the word of God, and do it.

Designating "Brothers"

The term *brother* could express a sense of ethnic kinship, either between members of the same race, or between members of different (but presumed related) races. To put it another way: who could, or could not, be identified as a "brother" was often an *ethnic* issue.[156] So, for example, Judeans could address each other as "brother," as seen throughout Acts.[157] As an example of the term being used *between* races, we might consider Israel and Edom. The biblical account constructs the Edomites and Israelites as "brothers," as the descendants of the brothers Esau and Jacob, respectively (Gen 36:9; Dt 23:7; Mal 1:2; Obad 1:12). Later, "Edomites" (אדומים) become "Idumeans" (Ιδουμαιοι) in the Greek of the Septuagint. During the Jewish War, Judeans addressed a company of Idumeans outside Jerusalem as their "kinsmen" (συγγενεῖς, J.W. 4.265). By this time, Idumeans were "brothers" twice over, both by shared ancestry, and as Judeans themselves, having adopted *Ioudaismos*.[158] When Hasmonean diplomacy proposed a genealogical connection between Judeans and Spartans, they addressed the latter as "brothers" (1 Macc. 12:6,11,21), connected by "brotherhood" (αδελφοτητος, 1 Macc. 12:17).

In Acts, Judeans who believe in Jesus *remain* Judeans; they never surrender this identification.[159] They also continue to address *other* Judeans as "brother" (αδελφος), and vice-versa.[160] In Pisidian Antioch, synagogue officials call Paul and his fellow missionaries "αδελφοι" (Acts 13:15), and Paul addresses those in the synagogue, both "sons of Abraham's stock" and gentile "god-fearers" (13:16), as "my brothers" (13:26).[161] (He even reminds this entire audience that God chose "*our* ancestors" [13:17, 32], which seems to attribute Abrahamic ancestry to God-fearing gentiles!).

Genealogical Reconfiguration in Luke–Acts   201

Throughout Acts, Judean Christians continue to understand other Judeans in terms of kinship, regardless of whether the speaker feels optimistic that his audience might come to believe in Jesus (Acts 2:29, 3:17), or not (7:2–53; 23:1–5).[162]

A novel usage of "brother" emerges after the Jerusalem Council. Prior to Acts 15:23, no non-Israelite is addressed as a "brother" of a Judean.[163] (Believing Samaritans had been addressed as "brothers" immediately before, in Acts 15:3, when they rejoiced alongside Judeans to learn that the "gentiles" were converting).[164] After Acts 15, Luke uses "brother" in two ways: (1) to express common ethnic solidarity between naturally born Judeans, and (2) to describe the kinship between members of the Jesus group, regardless of their origins.[165] The letter opens:

> The brothers, both apostles and elders (*i.e., Judeans*),
>   to the brothers from the nations (αδελφοις εξ εθνων, *i.e., gentiles*),
>   greetings! (Acts 15:23)[166]

This is a shift in usage—for gentiles to be designated "brothers" of Judeans. Nothing requires us to understand 'brother' in a different sense when used among disciples, to distinguish it from its use between Judeans.[167] Dulcinea Boesenberg writes,

> Αδελφοι serves as an in-group term shared by Jews in the Way and other Jews, suggesting that when this term is applied to gentiles in the Way, it locates them within the bounds of kinship shared by all Jews. The term αδελφοι is not in-group language unique to the Way; Luke does not construct the Way as a new and different kinship group. Rather, certain gentiles are brought into the kinship shared by Jews.[168]

I would amend Boesenberg's position very slightly: Since the Samaritan believers were already identified as "brothers" *before* this (Acts 15:3), these gentiles' "brothers" are being welcomed into a pre-existing *pan-Israelite "brotherhood,"* not just a Judean one.[169] The "brothers" in Antioch, receiving the letter, rejoice and send Paul and Barnabas back to their "brothers" in Jerusalem (15:32). The two missionaries furthermore resolve to visit the "brothers in every city where we proclaimed the word of the Lord" (15:35). Israelites (Judeans and Samaritans) and non-Israelites can now be "brethren;" the term now clearly includes gentiles.[170]

As I suggested in chapter 1, it may be less misleading to call such language *constructed kinship*, rather than the more widely used *fictive kinship*. "Fictive" connotes false, or unreal; but such socially conditioned kinship

202   *Chapter 5*

can be experienced as very "real" to the actual social actors. Philo described
the kinship binding proselytes to Israel as *more* real, not less, than that of
mere blood (*Virtues* 79; *Spec.Leg.* 1.317; *Rewards* 152).[171] Several sources
describe the "fictive" kinship among the Essenes as creating strong bonds with
concrete outworkings—including filial piety, shared patrimony, implications
for marriage arrangements, and the duty to support one's elders.[172] The
Hippocratic Oath creates a "fictive" father–son relationship between teacher
and student, with very real "familial" obligations.[173] When we hear early
Christians address each other as "brother" or "sister," or speak of their
"fathers" or "mothers" in the faith, we should not unexaminedly assume this
language is merely metaphorical (e.g., John 19:26–27). Constructed kinship
had real-world outworkings in early congregations: it could be used to invoke
filial obedience (1 Thess. 2:11–12; 1 Cor. 4:14–15, 21; 1 John 2:1), designate
"heirs" of one's authority (Phil. 2:22; 1 Cor. 4:17; 1 Tim. 1:2), foster familial
affection (1 Thess. 2:17–20; 2 Cor. 6:11–12), obligate financial support (1
Cor. 16:15–16; 2 Cor. 8–9; 12:14–15; 1 John 3:11–18, James 2:15–16), or
radically reframe the relationship between a master and a slave (Philem. 1:10,
16).

John the Baptist once said that God could raise up "children for Abraham"
from the stones near the Jordan River (Luke 3:8). Now, believing Judeans,
Samaritans, and *ethnē* are all "siblings" with each other (Acts 15:23, etc.),
part of a pan-Israelite brotherhood, and joint-heirs of the blessings promised
to Abraham (Acts 3:25 // Gen. 12:3). Confessing the same Christ and filled
with the same Spirit, all members of "the Way" descend from the same
ancestors (whether directly or indirectly), and all share a sense of kinship
with each other.

Ethnic Deviance, and Estrangement between "Brothers"

> The incomer has turned his kinfolk (συγγενεῖς), who in the ordinary
> course of things would be his sole confederates, into mortal enemies,
> by coming as a pilgrim to truth and the honouring of One who alone is
> worthy of honour, and by leaving the mythical fables and multiplicity
> of sovereigns, so highly honoured by the parents and grandparents and
> ancestors (γονεῖς καὶ πάπποι καὶ πρόγονοι) and all the blood relations
> (οἱ ἀφ᾽ αἵματος) of this immigrant to a better home. —*Spec.Leg.* 4.178[174]

Philo describes the convert to Judaism as a sort of pilgrim, striking out from
his parent's house and homeland in search of God. The proselyte undergoes
a sort of ethnic deracination, uprooted from ancestry, culture, homeland—but
there is also a more personal bereavement from family relations (συγγενεῖς),
who are now their enemies.[175] Because proselytes "have left their country

Genealogical Reconfiguration in Luke–Acts   203

(πατριδα), their kinsfolk (συγγενεις) and their friends (φιλους) for the sake of virtue and religion," Philo demands, "Let them not be denied another citizenship (πολεων) or other ties of family (οικειων) and friendship (φιλων), and let them find places of shelter standing ready for refugees to the camp of piety" (*Special Laws* 1.52).[176] Philo's description of the life-changing journey of the convert is reminiscent of Abraham's story. Like Abraham, the convert has left "country and kindred and father's house" (Gen. 12:1) to seek God. Like Abraham, the convert may make enemies of their own kindred as they reject their religious practices as "idolatry" (cf. *Asen.* 11:4–5; *Jub.* 12:1–8, 12–14; *L.A.B.* 6:1–18).[177]

Some gentile sources corroborate this impression. Tacitus criticizes "those who are converted to [the Judeans'] way of life," complaining that "the earliest habit they adopt is to despise the gods, to renounce their country (*patriam*), and to regard their parents (*parentes*), children (*liberos*), and brothers (*fratres*) as of little consequence" (Hist. 5.5.1).[178] Perhaps Philo demands such an effusive welcome for proselytes (*Virt.* 103; *Spec.Leg.* 1.51–53; *Legat.* 210–11) because of their alienation from their families of origin—so that their "adoptive" kin must embrace them all the more.[179]

On the other hand, Philo says that Judeans sever all "bonds of affection" (*oikeiotētos*) with apostates from Judaism, be they "brother or son or daughter or housemate or true *philos*," and eject them from their families (*Spec.Leg.* 1.316). A similar phenomenon can be discerned in the early Corinthian church; Paul notes that some marriages were breaking up over the new Christian faith (1 Cor. 7:12–16).[180] Jesus himself describes estrangement, powerful enough to tear families apart, as one possible consequence of discipleship (Luke 12:51–53).

In Acts, although Christian Judeans continue addressing non-Christian Judeans in terms of kinship, there is sometimes hostility between these "kin." So, although Stephen addresses members of the Sanhedrin as "brothers and fathers" (Acts 7:2) and speaks to them of "our [shared] ancestors" (7:19), he also associates them with a particularly ignoble line of Israelites: those who first rejected Moses (7:25–28) and later killed the prophets (7:51–52). Moses' attempted intervention between two fighting Hebrews mirrors the tragedy of Stephen's own situation:

> [25]He supposed that his own kindred (αδελφους) would understand that God was rescuing them through his hand, but they did not understand. [26]And the next day Moses saw two men fighting, and he tried to make peace between them, saying, "Men, you are brothers (αδελφοι); why are you hurting each other?" (Acts 7:25–26)

204   *Chapter 5*

Alas for Stephen, his "brothers" repeat the crime of those two infighting "brothers." Having judged Stephen as a deviant, his own "kindred" reject him, disavow him, and even kill him. Essentially, they follow the script laid out by Philo: "If a brother [commits apostasy]—then we must punish them as a public and common enemy . . . hurry without delay to assault the profane man, judging his death lawful" (*Spec.Leg.* 1.316). Appropriately to their way of thinking, they subject their "brother" to the punishment Moses ordained for blasphemy—they put him "out of the camp," and to death by stoning (Acts 7:57–58; cf. Lev. 24:10–23).

Throughout Acts, Judeans who follow Jesus must continually defend themselves from the charge that they are deficient, apostate, or disloyal to their people and the traditions of their ancestors—that is, their Israelite "brothers" frequently label them as ethnic deviants (see table 5.3). Examples abound. Many scoffed at the Spirit-filled antics of the apostles on Pentecost, prompting Peter to insist that the believers were not drunk, but are "your sons

Table 5.3   Charge that the Way Fosters Ethnic Deviance Among Judeans

Situation	Charges
In Jerusalem, some diaspora Judeans and false witnesses charge Stephen before the Sanhedrin:	"We have heard him saying blasphemous words against Moses and against God... and against the Law; for we heard him saying that Jesus of Nazareth will destroy this place and <u>overturn the traditions</u> (εθη) that Moses handed down to us." –Acts 6:11, 13-14
In Corinth, Paul is accused by "the Judeans" before Gallio the proconsul:	"This man is persuading people to worship God (σεβεσθαι τον Θεον) <u>contrary to the law</u> (νομον)." He rules, "Since it is a matter of words and names in <u>your own law</u> (του νομου του καθ' υμας), see to it yourselves; I don't want to be a judge of those things." – 18:13, 15
In Jerusalem, James and the elders warn Paul of false reports circulating about him in Jerusalem:	"They have been told about you that you teach all the Judeans living among the gentiles <u>to abandon Moses</u> (αποστασιαν απο Μωυσεως), telling them not to <u>circumcise their children</u>, nor to walk according to the <u>customs</u> (εθεσι)." –Acts 21:21
In the Jerusalem Temple, Paul is falsely accused by some Judeans from Asia, who stir up a crowd:	"Men, Israelites, help! This is the man who is teaching everyone, everywhere<u>, against the people, and the law, and this place</u> [the Temple]. More than that, he has brought Greeks into the Temple and profaned this holy place." –Acts 21:28
High priests and elders accuse Paul before the governor Felix:	"We have found this man to be a plague; he causes <u>riots</u> (κινουντα στασιν) among all Judeans throughout the world. ...He even tried to <u>profane the Temple</u>..." –Acts 24:5-6,8
Festus summarizes the charges to Agrippa:	"certain points of disagreement about <u>their own religion</u> (ιδια δεισιδαιμονιας)" –Acts 25:19
Paul explains what he is charged with, to King Agrippa:	Paul understands himself to be on trial on account of the "<u>customs</u> and controversies of the Judeans (Ιουδαιους εθων τε και ζητηματων)" –Acts 26:3

Genealogical Reconfiguration in Luke–Acts   205

and daughters" whom Joel foretold would one day prophesy (Acts 2:17 // Joel 2:28). Stephen faced hostility from both diaspora Judeans and local elites (6:9–7:1), who report, "We heard him speak blasphemous words against Moses and God"—an accusation with both religious and ethnic connotations. Stephen denies the charge that he spoke blasphemously against Moses or the Law; he demonstrates a deep respect *for* Torah, and argues that his faith is grounded *in* Torah (table 5.3).[181]

In Judean eyes, abandonment of Judaism's ancestral customs was a dire charge (1 Macc. 2:19–29, 49–70; 4 Macc. 4:26; *War* 7.47–53; Philo *Jos.* 254; *Moses* 1.31).[182] Under the law of Moses, such behavior might be understood to merit the death penalty (Lev. 24:10–23; *Spec.Leg.* 1.316). But if allowed by their Roman rulers to "see to the matter yourselves" (Acts 18:15), it would still be the case that *Roman* law would not allow them to exercise the death penalty—not, at least, for racial nonconformity, such as failure to conform "their law" and to religious "customs." In practice, this limitation might be circumvented by mob action (Acts 7:7:58),[183] conspiracy to ambush a prisoner in transit (23:12–22), or falsely adding *political* charges that might merit capital punishment (17:6–7, 24:5a). Before his vision of Christ, Saul himself was "breathing threats and murder" against the early disciples (9:1). Although he was only vested with the authority to *arrest* Christians (8:3; 9:14, 21), those swept up in such a dragnet might face illegal or quasi-legal execution (14:19, 26:10)[184] or be killed by a client-king like Herod Agrippa I (as James was, 12:1–2).

Countering the charge that the first disciples were traitors to their *ethnos*, the Acts church asserted a firmly Judean identity. Luke notes that the Jerusalem *ekklēsia* continued to frequent the Temple (Acts 2:46, 3:1, 5:11, 5:25, 24:18) and enjoyed the favor of "all" of the people (2:47, 5:16). Much in the same way that prototypical Israelites had heralded Jesus' coming,[185] exemplars of Judean religiosity continue to be attracted to The Way, including priests (Acts 6:7) and Pharisees (Acts 15:5, 26:5).[186] Throughout Acts, Judean Christians not only continue to follow the Law[187]—they even police their fellow Judeans (including Paul himself) to ensure that *they* are doing the same (Acts 11:3; 16:1–2; 21:20–21).[188] Dulcinea Boesenberg observes, "Luke is careful to present the Jewish members of the Way as law observant, and the gentile members of the Way as joining them in accordance with the law."[189] Within Acts' narrative world, all of this fosters the impression that it is the movement's *opponents* who are the true outliers/deviants, rather than Judean Christians.[190]

Luke's protagonists defend themselves vigorously against the charge that they have abandoned the Law of Moses, Paul especially.[191] When brought before King Agrippa, Paul understands himself to be on trial on account of the "customs and controversies of the Judeans (Ιουδαιους εθων τε και

206   *Chapter 5*

ζητηματων)" (Acts 26:3). He therefore rehearses his Judean *bona fides*: his way of life (βιωσιν) since youth, his upbringing among the people, his training as a Pharisee, his "hope in the promise God made to our ancestors" (26:4–7a). Paul highly values this identity. Joshua Jipp summarizes, "If ancient notions of ethnicity center upon shared ancestral customs, family, paideia, land, language, the gods and their cults then Luke's Paul can be seen as making a powerful and repetitive argument regarding the importance of his Jewish ethnic identity."[192] Paul later tells the Roman Judeans, "Men, brothers, . . . I have done nothing against our people (λαῳ) or the customs of our ancestors (εθεσι τοις πατρῳοις)" (Acts 28:17).

And what of the gentile? What effects might faith in Christ have upon the gentile believer's identity? Would their families be able to accept a relative's rejection of their ancestral traditions, their piety, their customs? Would they understand the convert's adoption of an alternate lifestyle in "The Way" (ἡ ὁδος) as the betrayal of their *own* "way," their own relatives, their own people?[193] (Remember, this *is* how converts to Judaism were often viewed).[194]

In his first letter to the Thessalonians, Paul commends his gentile audience for how they "turned (επιστρεψατε) to God from idols" (1 Thess. 1:9), using a verb which is practically a technical term for conversion in Acts.[195] Given the extent to which religious piety permeated all aspects of public, private, and family life, such a "turn" would trouble relationships at a variety of levels. Horrell argues,

> That this was the case is indicated in the letter by the report that the Thessalonians have suffered hostility from their people (των ιδιων συμφηλετων, 2:14). In other words, this transfer of allegiance has involved some kind of rupture with "their people" comparable to what we find in the accounts of Jewish proselytism presented in Philo and Josephus.[196]

In some Pauline churches, the social consequences of conversion included the destabilization of marriages (1 Cor. 7: 12–13) and wondering whether the children from half-Christian marriages are "holy" (7:14). Paul's "preference" for celibacy, despite the acceptance of marriage "by way of concession" (7:6–8, 27), might cause early Christians to conclude that they should dissolve existing betrothals (7:28, 32–38) or even marriages (7:10–11, 15); or that they should stop having sexual relations with their existing spouses (7:1–5).[197] One can imagine that any of these would cause major conflicts with gentile partners, who do not share their convictions! We see later Christians trying to walk back some of Paul's positions and reinforce the traditional household (e.g., 1 Timothy 5).

Genealogical Reconfiguration in Luke–Acts 207

Other streams of Christian literature continued to explore the family-destabilizing implications of conversion. David Konstan notes:

> Taken generally, the Apocryphal Acts of the Apostles share an ascetic orientation in regard to sexuality that finds expression in a repeated narrative formula: the apostle converts a married man or woman to the worship of Christ, which entails in turn the renunciation of carnal relations. If one of the partners to the marriage remains unconverted, she or he may seek to retaliate for this disruption in conjugal life. When the offended spouse is powerful enough to encompass the apostle's death, the narrative is brought to a conclusion in the form of a martyrdom or passion. Three out of the five Acts that survive in substantial portions terminate in this way.[198]

For example, in *The Acts of Paul and Thecla,* Paul's enemies complain that "He [Paul] deprives young men of wives, and maidens of husbands" (*Acts of Paul* 2:16). The specter of marital dissolution whips the elite men of Iconium into a panic, so that they cry out: "Away with the magician, for he has corrupted all our wives!" (3:9). When Thecla refuses to explain why she will not marry her fiancé Thamyris, her own mother cries out, "Burn the wicked wretch! Burn in the midst of the theater her that will not marry, in order that all the women that have been taught by this man may be afraid." (5:8). Within the narrative world of *Paul and Thecla*, Christianity is profoundly disruptive of family life. But it can foster *new* kinships, too: In Antioch, Queen Tryphaena receives Thecla as a "second daughter" in place of a daughter who died. Happily, Thecla is eventually reconciled to her birth mother, as well.

So, we have one trajectory of the later Pauline tradition, reassuring husbands that Christianity would not disrupt their families (or their *patria potestas*); and another trajectory of Pauline literature celebrating such disruption! Both testify to the potential of early Christianity to destabilize families—although they take a different view of this possibility.

But what of the narrative world of Luke–Acts? Jesus said that he came to bring "division" to households and families (Luke 12:51–53). Although he delivered this warning to an Israelite audience, he did not limit the reach of such disruption to ethnic Israel. There are very few chances in the gospel itself to assess the effect of discipleship on gentile family relations. The Centurion of Capernaum is seemingly a patron of the local synagogue, but not a full proselyte to Judaism (Luke 7:3–7). As a man accustomed to authority within his own household (7:8), his social position likely allows him to maintain both friendship with the synagogue and contact with his familiars. Luke's gospel *foreshadows* the full incorporation of gentiles, but we have to wait until Acts to see what will happen to them.

208   *Chapter 5*

In Acts, however, it is a different story. We find that "the Way" threatens to transform "decent, upstanding gentiles" into cultural misfits, who no longer honor the gods, the laws of Rome, or their ancestral customs. As discussed above, such changes had *racial* ramifications, with the power to create conflict between relatives, or even tear families apart. The Way undermines traditional pagan worship (Acts 14:11–18; 17:29; 19:27), subverts or twists Greek thought (as the philosophers of Athens recognize, 17:19–28), and condemns accepted magical practices (16:16–18, 19:18–19). The Ephesians' alarm that Christianity may totally overthrow the worship of Artemis (19:26–27) strongly resembles a real-life governor's alarm in Bithynia, over a generation later: "The temples . . . had been almost deserted" and "very few purchasers [for sacrificial animals] could be found" (Pliny, *Letters,* 10.97). Pagans (i.e., gentiles) who joined the Way might well be viewed as ethnic deviants by residents of their towns, even by their own relatives (see table 5.4).

A wedge is also driven between various Judeans. This distance is *racial* in character, grounded in both parties' perception that their opponents have abandoned their ancestral practices, the "distinct way of life" so definitive of each *ethnos*. Each side defines Israelite prototypicality differently and therefore holds that *it* best represents the people.

In Acts, Christian Judeans hold that to embrace Israel's Messiah (Jesus) is an act of faithfulness to Israel's God and to their ancestral customs. For those who accept Jesus, this conviction may lead to the re-evaluation of some of Israel's primary identity markers. Therefore, "those Jews who are

Table 5.4   Charge that the Way Fosters Ethnic Deviance Among Gentiles

Situation	Charges
In Philippi (a Roman colony), Paul and Silas are accused by slaveowners in the marketplace:	"These men are disturbing our city; they are Judeans, and are advocating <u>customs</u> (εθη) it is not acceptable for us, <u>as Romans</u>, to accept or to practice." –Acts 16:21
In Thessalonica, "Jason and some brothers" are accused by "jealous" Judeans, before city officials:	"These people have been <u>turning the world upside-down</u>... They are all acting contrary to the decrees of Caesar (δογματων Καισαρος), saying there is another emperor (βασιλεα) named Jesus," –Acts 17:6-7
In Athens, Paul brought before the Areopagus by some philosophers:	"He seems to be an advocate of <u>foreign divinities</u> (ξενων δαιμονιων)," proclaiming a "<u>new teaching</u>" (καινη διδαχη) and "<u>outlandish</u> (ξενιζοντα) ideas" –Acts 17:18-20
In Ephesus, Paul accused by Demetrius the silversmith, first before other artisans, and eventually in the theater, rallying a mob:	"In almost all Asia, this Paul has persuaded and drawn away huge crowds, saying that hand-made gods are not really gods... <u>The temple of Artemis will be scorned as worthless</u>, and also she whom all Asia and the world revere will be stripped of her majesty." –Acts 19:26-27; they chant, "Great is Artemis of Ephesus!" (19:28,34)

Genealogical Reconfiguration in Luke–Acts

not sympathetic to Paul's proclamation that Jesus is Israel's Messiah receive harsh words of prophetic judgment, as Paul plays the role of the prophet Isaiah while his fellow Jews who reject his message take on the guise of those ancient Israelites who rejected the prophet (Acts 28:25–27; Isa. 6:9–10)."[199] But for those who do *not* accept the claim that Jesus is the resurrected ruler of Israel and the nations, the charges against Paul (Acts 21:27–28) are perfectly valid.[200] Many Judean elites understand Paul to be teaching others to ignore the Law of Moses, largely based on the movement's relaxed expectations for gentiles (Acts 15:19–20). When Paul insists, "I have done nothing against the people (τῳ λαῳ) or the customs of our fathers (εθησιν τοις πατρῳοις)," his testimony rings true—*but only if one accepts the root premise that Christ is the messiah* (Acts 28:17).

Paul is accused by diaspora synagogues of tampering with their customs (17:5–8; 18:5–13).[201] Some of these "customs" may include a relaxed attitude about sympathetic gentiles, who wished to be friends of the synagogue without abandoning the gods (and without alienating their kin). Paul's insistence that gentile God-fearers must decisively abandon their gods could create serious difficulties for diaspora synagogues.[202] Paula Fredricksen explains:

> Such a destabilizing and inflammatory message [i.e., to turn away from their native cults and gods to the God of Israel], radiating from the synagogue, could make the Jewish urban community itself the target of local anxieties and resentments. Alienating the gods put the city at risk; alienating the pagan majority put the diaspora synagogue at risk—especially when the behavior occasioning the risk, an exclusive commitment to the god of Israel, was so universally and uniquely associated with the Jews themselves.[203]

In one way then, the socio-ethnic issues at play mirror the tale of King Izates' conversion; one Judean told him he must be circumcised, but another Judean assured him that he could remain a good God-fearer without doing so—largely out of fear of reprisals from his majority-gentile society.[204]

Paul told Agrippa, "I now standing trial on account of the hope in the promises God made to our ancestors." To Luke, these "promises" include God's word to Abraham that "In your offspring, all the families of the earth shall be blessed" (Acts 3:25; Gen. 12:3; 18:18; 22:18).[205] In Luke–Acts, we see the world through Luke's "diasporic gaze," himself a subcultural adherent of the (nondominant) Judaic worldview. In this worldview, "All Jews—Judeans, Samaritans, proselytes and diasporans—are reclaimed by Luke as Jews."[206] (I would amend this to read "as Israelites," rather than "as Jews," but Rhamie's point is well made). This shift in identification has the potential to foster a sense of relatedness between Jesus-believing Judeans and their gentile

210 *Chapter 5*

"brethren," but it could drive a wedge between these same Judeans and other Judeans, based on differences in how/whether gentiles could be incorporated. Each viewed the other side's answer as deficient in its Jewishness—or "Judeanness," to capture the racial character of what was at stake.

Gentiles, meanwhile, have had their sense of ethnic identity unsettled by conversion. We saw that gentile proselytes who *fully* converted to Judaism (by circumcision, if male) were commonly acknowledged as "Judeans," and shared a real sense of kinship with other Judeans, beyond what mere god-fearers experienced. At the same time, they might be understood by their fellow gentiles as traitors to their people, their customs, and even their families (see figure 5.5). In like manner, gentiles who follow the Way in Acts join what is essentially an *Israelite* identity,[207] and they have become the "brothers" of Israelites in the *ekklēsia*. Having abandoned the worship of idols, they have made a radical break with the ancestral traditions of their own respective peoples—and closer to home, they have turned their back on the customs of their own families (except in those cases where entire households convert at once).[208] The Judeans who welcome them are themselves effected; many of their own kinsfolk see them as disobeying Moses for including the gentiles in this way (figure 5.6).

To be clear, we *are* not proposing a contrast between "Christian universality" and a supposed "Jewish exclusivity." In general, the Judaism of Luke's day was neither xenophobic nor exclusivistic. There were well-worn paths by which gentiles could join themselves to Israel, whether fully (proselytes) or partially (god-fearers and sympathizers). No, the major misalignment between Christian and non-Christian Judeans was not *whether* gentiles could be welcomed into Israel, but *how* this could be accomplished. The stakes of the question are high—so high that those who arrive at a different answer are seen as deviants. Judeans of "the Way" and mainstream Judeans *both* feel that their own party is prototypically Israelite, while the others are deficiently so (see figure 5.6).

CHAPTER CONCLUSIONS

Luke's retelling of Israel's history presents two strands of ancestors and assigns descent from these to his contemporaries based on whose footsteps they follow. From Luke's perspective, Judeans who prove to be "God-fighters" (θεομαχοι; Acts 5:39) will be trunks cut off at the root (Luke 3:9), figs uprooted from the vineyard (Luke 13:6–9; cf. Isa. 5:1–7; Jer. 2:21; 24:1–5), tenants ejected from the vineyard (20:13–16), the "spawn of vipers" (3:8a).[209] On the other hand, gentiles who prove to be "God-fearers" (θεοφοβοι) and who accept baptism are joined to Israel, raised up as children for Abraham (Luke 3:8b), who will join their "ancestor" Abraham at the eschatological

Genealogical Reconfiguration in Luke–Acts 211

Figure 5.5 Ethnic Reconfiguration of Proselytes to Judaism. *Source*: Created by Andrew Benko.

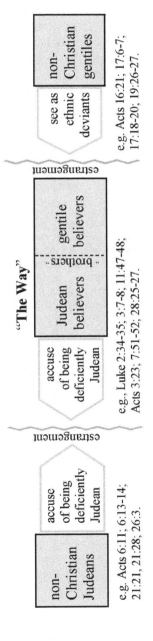

Figure 5.6 Ethnic Reconfiguration of Those Joining the Way. *Source*: Created by Andrew Benko.

212 *Chapter 5*

feast (Luke 13:28–29; 16:23; Acts 3:25). This reconfiguration of genealogical descent has present-tense implications for those whose identities have been thus reconfigured: the kinship between Judeans may be strained as they hold each other to be defectors from their nation, and gentile converts alienate their own kith and kin by abandoning their gods and cleaving to an "alien" people.

In our concluding chapter, we will review our argument thus far and briefly consider how Luke's racial reasoning worked upon the imagination of its original audience, as subjects of the Roman Empire—and how it works upon its reader's imagination, today.

NOTES

1. Colson: LCL. cf. *Rewards* 172:

> For just as when the stalks of plants are cut away, if the roots are left undestroyed, new growths shoot up which supersede the old, so too if in the soul a tiny seed be left of the qualities which promote virtue, through other things which have been stripped away, still from that little seed spring forth the fairest and most precious things in human life, by which states are constituted manned with good citizens, and nations (εθνη) grow into a great population (πολυανθρωπιαν). ((Colson: LCL). cf. Staples (*The Idea of Israel*, 256), who reads the "root" as a reference to Abraham (see also *Rewards* 166, where Abraham is mentioned); cf. also Brogen, "There Shall Come Forth a Man," 348)

2. On religion being especially salient in the construction of Jewishness, see the work Love Sechrest has done on the semantic fields of εθνος and γενος in Judean literature (*A Former Jew*, 54–109); for the slipperiness of ancient race in general, see chapter 1, "Race / Ethnicity in Mediterranean Antiquity."

3. On Judeans being children of Abraham, see especially chapter 4. On *Samaritans* being children of Abraham by default, see Benko and Penwell, *Good Samaritans: Samaritan Ethnicity and Evangelism in Luke–Acts* (forthcoming).

4. Again, I assume the general contours of the "Q" hypothesis. But even if we assume the Farrer hypothesis (with Luke working directly with Mark and Matthew, eliminating the need for "Q"), the point stands: Luke's account of the ministry of John the Baptist contains ethical instructions not found in Matthew's, giving a clearer picture of the character of Abraham's "children."

5. Q's troubling of Abrahamic identity (Q 3:8) comes into greater focus in Luke's telling of the ministry of John the Baptist (Luke 3:9–18), where it is explicitly associated with *ethical conduct*, or lack thereof. See chapters 3 and 4.

6. E.g., *IKyme* 39 = PH268310; Aristotle, *Eudemian Ethics* 7.1241b.24–26; *TAM* V.2 1148; *PLond* VII 2193 = *NewDocs* I 5; Artemidoros *Oneirocritica* 4.44, 5.82; *TAM* V.2 1148 *CIL* XIV 4315, *CIL* VI 727, *CIL* VI 377, *CIRB* 104 = *PH* 182821, *CIJ* 694.

7. E.g., *Hipp.Oath* 7–15; Plut. *Adv.Col.* 1117B; Lucr. *De rerum natura* 5.8. See David Sedley, "Philosophical Allegiance in the Greco-Roman World," 97–119 in

Genealogical Reconfiguration in Luke–Acts 213

Philosophia Togata, Miriam Griffin and Jonathan Barnes, eds. (Oxford: Clarendon, 1989), 97; Loveday Alexander, "IPSE DIXIT: Citation of Authority in Paul and in the Jewish and Hellenistic Schools," 71–71, 108–115; Denise Kimber Buell, *Making Christians* (Princeton, NJ: Princeton University Press, 1999), 5–6; Keith Hopkins, "Seven Missing Papers," in *Parenté et Stratégies Familiales dans l'Antiquité Romaine. Actes de la table ronde des 2–4 octobre 1986* (Paris, Maison des sciences de l'homme), Jean Andreau and Hinnerk Bruhns, eds. (Collection de l'École Française de Rome 129; Palais Farnèse: l'École Française de Rome, 1990), 624.

8. E.g., Philo *On Moses* 2.4.18–20, *On the Virtues* 20.102–103, Jos. *Ant.* 20.38–41; Tacitus, *Histories* 5.5; cf. Stephen G. Wilson, *Leaving the Fold: Apostates and Defectors in Antiquity* (Minneapolis, MN: Fortress, 2004), 24–25; Barclay, "Deviance and Apostasy," 133.

9. E.g., Acts 13:26; see the discussion below.

10. Saldarini, *Matthew's Christian-Jewish Community,* 171; Harrington, *Matthew* (Sacra Pagina), 30–32; Neyrey, *Honor and Shame in the Gospel of Matthew,* 97–98; Malina and Rohrbaugh, *Social-Scientific Commentary on the Synoptic Gospels,* 24; Carter, *Matthew and the Margins,* 57–66.

11. Punt, "The Politics of Genealogies in the New Testament," 383; Culpepper, *Luke,* 94.

12. cf. "Νομιζω" in *BDAG* and *LSJ.*

13. Fuller, *The Restoration of Israel,* 201 N 17. Alternatively (or perhaps simultaneously), ενομιζετο could speak to *legal* status: Jesus is "accounted" Joseph's son legally—i.e., through adoption, which in the ancient world conferred all the same rights and honor as biological sonship. cf. Bovon, *Luke,* 1.136–137, and Malina/Rohrbaugh, *Social-Science Commentary on the Synoptic Gospels,* 305–306.

14. Jesus' Davidic ancestry was also asserted in other early Christian sources, *outside* of the context of a formal genealogy (Rom. 1:3; 2 Tim. 2:8; Rev. 5:5; Heb 7:14). Paul specifically claims that Jesus is the son of David κατα σαρκα, "according to the flesh" (Rom. 1:3). Bovon, *Luke,* 1.134–135.

Both "divine" (ideal) and "human" (biological) sorts of descent may be in play here. Regarding Jesus' Davidic descent, Levine cites 2 Sam 7:12–14, where God essentially promises to *become* the "father" of David's own son! (Levine, "Jesus 'Son of God' and 'Son of David,'" 419).

15. cf. *L.A.B.* 1:1; *Life of Adam and Eve* [Latin, 24:3–4; Greek 5:1, 42:3].

16. Luke's unusual "reverse order" genealogy—"counting down" to humanity's common originator Adam—has this effect, so that unlike "Matthew's perspective [which] is dominated by the privileged status of Abraham's descendants; Luke's shows a universalizing tendency." Bovon, *Lukas,* 121–127; *Luke,* 1.134–135. Josephus' genealogy of Noah is also laid out in reverse order, terminating with Adam (*Ant.* 1.79).

17. Ancient genealogies regulated social status and establish the honor/shame due to an individual by virtue of their birth. J. A. Loubser, "Invoking the Ancestors: Some Socio-Rhetorical Aspects of the Genealogies in the Gospels of Matthew and Luke," *Neotestamentica* 39.1 (2005): 127.

18. Siker, *Disinheriting,* 109.

214   Chapter 5

19. Punt, "Politics of Genealogies in the New Testament," *Neotestamentica* 47.2 (2013): 373–398, 378.

20. Later, Luke lifts a similar declaration of sonship from the Psalms. God's words to David are now applied to *Jesus*: "You are my son; today have I begotten (γεγεννηκα) you." cf. Ps 2:7 // Acts 13:33.

21. Punt, "The Politics of Genealogies in the New Testament," 382–383; Bovon, *Luke,* 1.134; Culpepper, *Luke*, 95.

22. While this implication is not further elaborated upon in Luke 3:23–38, it will resurface (6:34–36; 11:11–13; 16:8), and will be explicitly discussed in Acts 17.

23. One of Jesus' ancestors, David, is also God's "son" (2 Sam 7:14).

24. Jeffrey Punt reminds us that Luke is writing from within Rome's imperial system—with its own matrix of rulers, peoples, and historical memories (all of which Luke is well aware of; consider "Aeneas" in Acts 9:3). Yet, Luke firmly stakes Jesus' identity within *Israel's* historical memory. This is a political choice, as well as an ethnic one—eschewing Rome's ideological narrative for Israel's. cf. Punt, "The Politics of Genealogies in the New Testament," 379. We will explore some imperial/ethnic intersections in Luke–Acts more broadly (beyond the genealogy) in the conclusion.

25. Colson/Whitaker: LCL.

26. Siker, *Disinheriting,* 109.

27. A god-fearing gentile would have heard the scriptural trope of the "gentile" (גוי/עם/εθνη) as "foreigner" many times, and many who stopped short of full conversion likely internalized this identification. For another example of such a "colonized" vision of gentile identity (now overcome in Christ), see Eph. 2:19.

28. cf. Philo: "It could not but be that his [Adam's] descendants, partaking as they did in the original form in which he was formed, should preserve marks, though faint ones, of their kinship (συγγενειας) with their first father (προπατορα)."—*On the Creation*, 145 [Colson/Whitaker: LCL].

29. Trans. Colson/Whitaker: LCL (but correcting their reversal of ποιητης και πατηρ).

Unsurprisingly for a Platonist, Philo limits this relatedness to our *rational* faculties:

> And what is this kinship? On the one hand, as regards the mind, every human being (ανθρωπος) is related (ῳκειωται) to divine reason (λογῳ θειῳ) having been made the imprint or fragment or ray of that blessed nature (μακαριας φυσεως); on the other hand, as regards the body, conformed to all the world. (*On the Creation*, 146, my trans.)

Philo laments that these gifts, originally so pronounced in Adam, are successively weaker in each generation, until they are quite feeble by his own day (ibid., 140–141).

30. My trans. Contrast Matt. 5:43–48; instead of racializing the group who might not be expected to do good works (as "gentiles"), Luke describes them as "sinners." Aligning with Lukan themes, the characteristic of the father which his children should exhibit is "mercy," not Matthew's "perfection."

31. Levin, "Jesus 'Son of God' and 'Son of David,'" 418–419.

Genealogical Reconfiguration in Luke–Acts 215

32. "Sons of light" does not appear elsewhere in the synoptic gospels, but the phrase *is* found in the Qumran literature (1QM 1:1–14; 1QS 1:9) and other NT sources (1 Th. 5:5; John 12:36; Eph. 5:6–8).

33. My trans.

34. My trans.

35. E.g. Hom. *Iliad* 1.544; Dio of Prusa *Or.* 12.29, 42; 36.56; cf. Epict. *Discourses* 13.13.3. Pervo, *Acts*, 436.

36. trans. Oldfather: LCL.

37. cf. Ant. 1.20, 2.152; 4.262. Popović, "God the Father in Flavius Josephus," 182–189. Note that Popović cautions that we cannot be certain that Josephus' influences are Stoic (or even Greek), and we might be better served comparing these passages to *Roman* ideas about divine fatherhood (191–196).

38. προπατωρ is otherwise unattested in the LXX, but echoes Sophocles' phrase "Zeus, forefather of my forebears" (Soph. *Aj.* 389) or the aforementioned Dio of Prusa. Popović, "God the Father in Flavius Josephus," 192.

39. trans. Collins: TOTP.

40. trans. Collins: TOTP.

41. ca. 3rd c. BCE–1st c. CE. For this fairly wide range, see Shutt, *TOTP*, 2.8–9.

42. my trans.

43. My translation is from J. Rendel Harris' speculative reconstruction of the Greek, based on fragmentary mentions in a Syriac commentary by Isho'dad of Merv (9th c. CE) and Callimachus' partial quoting of Epictetus in his "Hymn of Zeus." Craig Keener has noted that this quote appears in "Jewish anthologies of proof-texts useful for showing pagans the truth about God" (*IVP BBC:NT*, 374).

44. Matthew, NOAB n. Acts 17:28; and Balch, "The Areopagus Speech: An Appeal to the Stoic Historian Posidonius against Later Stoics and the Epicureans," in *Greeks, Romans, and Christians: Essays in Honor of Abraham J. Malherbe*, David L. Balch, Everett Ferguson, and Wayne A. Meeks, eds. (Minneapolis, MN: Fortress Press, 1990), 52–79.

45. Rowe, *World Upside Down*, 37.

46. Acts 1–3 subtly echoes several Genesis passages explaining the origins of the earth's peoples: these include the "Table of Nations" enumerating the descendants of Noah (Gen. 10 // Acts 2:5–11). Baker points out that Acts 2:4–11 can *also* be read fruitfully in comparison to lists of peoples subjugated under the Roman empire; cf. Baker "From Every Nation."

47. Luke echoes but subverts the "Tower of Babel" etiology for the races' geographic distribution and linguistic diversity (Gen. 11:1–9 // Acts 2:1–4, 8) and echoes God's promise to Abraham that "all lineages (πατριαι) of the earth will be blessed in your descendants" (Acts 3:25 // Gen. 22:18). cf. Hays, *From Every People*, 164–165.

48. Wall, *Acts* (NIB), 244.

49. Jipp, "Paul's Areopagus Speech," 571; cf. LSJ, "σπερμολογος."

216   *Chapter 5*

50. Livy 14.27; Pausanias 1.17.1; Strabo 9.1.16; Jos. *Ap.* 2.130. Gill, "Achaia," in *The Book of Acts in its First-Century Setting,* vol. 2, David Gill and Corad Gempf, eds. (Grand Rapids, MI: Eerdmans, 1994), 443–445; cf. Pervo, *Acts,* 426 FN 17.

51. Socrates accused of introducing "new gods" (καινους θεους) Plato, *Euthyphr* 3B; "other, novel spiritual beings" (ἑτερα δαιμονια καινα) *Apol.* 24B; cf. Xenophon *Mem.* 1.1.1. Jipp, "Paul's Areopagus Speech," 571; Horst, "From One Person?," 79; Wall, *Acts* (NIB), 244.

52. cf *Ag. Ap.* 2.262–268. Jipp, "Paul's Areopagus Speech," 572; Pervo, *Acts,* 427.

53. e.g., Seneca *Ep.* 88.36–38; Plut. *Superst.* 171F; Apul. *Metam.* 5.6.3; 6.20.5. See Patrick Gray, "Athenian Curiosity (Acts 17:21), *NovT* 47 (2005): 109–116.

54. e.g., Luke 19:28–21:4.

55. Thus, in verse 19, Paul is not merely "taken" but "apprehended," implying formal or informal arrest (cf. επιλαμβανο, LSJ). Similarly, "We would hear more from you" is more than just a polite request to better understand Paul's thinking—it takes on the connotation, "Explain yourself." (Jipp, "Paul's Areopagus Speech," 573; Pervo, *Acts,* 428). The *LSJ* gives meanings for επιλαμβανω like "lay hold of, seize, arrest."

Malina and Pilch resist reading the verb as "arrest," based on the aforementioned curiosity of the Athenians (Acts 17:21; Malina and Pilch, *Social-Science Commentary on the Book of Acts*, 126). However, Acts (and even Luke, cf. 19–21) contains a recurring pattern of *popular interest coupled with elite suspicion*, generally culminating in a speech that is half legal-defense, half sermon. The prevalence of this pattern suggests we read the Areopagus speech in this light as well.

56. Jipp, "Paul's Areopagus Speech," 570.

57. Mărculet, "Elements of Inculturation in Saint Paul's Speech from Areopagus," 30–32; Malina and Pilch, *Social-Science Commentary on the Book of Acts*, 126. The word he uses to describe them, δεισιδαιμονεστερους, can just as readily mean "extremely superstitious" as "religious" (Jipp, "Paul's Areopagus Speech," 576).

58. For example, Pausanius' report that there were "even altars of gods named "Unknown' (Αγωνστων)" in Athens (Paus. 1.1.4). cf. Paus. 5.14.8; Diog. Laertes *Lives* 1.110. Malina and Pilch, *Social-Science Commentary on the Book of Acts*, 127; Mărculet, "Elements of Inculturation in Saint Paul's Speech from Areopagus," 29; Jipp, "Paul's Areopagus Speech," 578.

59. Jerome succinctly corrects "Paul": "In actuality, the altar inscription read 'to the gods of Asia, Europe, and Africa, and to the unknown and foreign gods'—and not, as Paul would have it—"to an unknown god" (Jerome *Comm. in Titum* 1:12) Mărculet, "Elements of Inculturation in Saint Paul's Speech from Areopagus," 29–30.

60. Aristobolus qtd. in Eusebius, *Church History,* 13.13.7; *Aristeas* 16.

61. Haenchen, *Acts of the Apostles,* 246; Wall, *Acts* (NIB), 246; Schnabel, "Contextualising Paul in Athens," 178; Horst, "From One Person?," 79; Stroup, *Jews Who Became Christians,* 38.

62. αἵματος is added after "from one" in D E L 614, 945, 1241, 1505 𝔐 gig sy; Irlat; Nestle-Aland, 28th. If missing, "One *person*" may be implied, *if* we understand "one" to anticipate "people" (ανθρωποι).

63. γενος in D.

64. "Paul offers a religious option that draws on the rhetoric, traditions, and literature of ancient Greece. He recalls the glories of ancient Greece but also announces God's command and impending judgment on the *oikumene*. Clearly, Roman imperial command, judgment, and reign over the world, as well as Roman imperial claims to be and to represent the divine, are paltry in the face of Paul's God." (Nasrallah, "Acts, Greek Cities, and Hadrian's Panhellenion," 564). For a thick description of Athen's urban environment of gods and altars, see Schnabel, "Contextualising Paul in Athens," 172–174.

65. Jipp, "Paul's Areopagus Speech," 568.

66. e.g. Eurip. *Ion* 260–272; Plato *Men.* 237b–38b. cf. Isaac, *Invention of Racism,* 114–124; Hall, *Ethnic Identity in Greek Antiquity,* 53–56; Roy, "Autocthony in Ancient Greece," 242, 244–246.

67. Accomplished by breathing into them (Gen. 2:7); see Acts 17:25 "he gives all life and breath (πνοην) to everyone."

68. Jipp, "Paul's Areopagus Speech," 581–582.

69. Horst, "From One Person?," 80–84.

70. cf. Cannon, 31–33.

71. Pervo, *Acts,* 435–436, cf. N 104.

72. Mărculet, "Elements of Inculturation in Saint Paul's Speech from Areopagus," 41. Malina and Pilch suggest that this "quote" may actually be a Lukan composition which *sounded* like it could have a pagan source; *Social-Science Commentary on the Book of Acts*, 128.

73. e.g., Isa. 37:19; 41:7, 40:18–20; 46:7; Jer 10:19; 16:19; Wis 13:6–19; 15:16–17; Bel and the Dragon 5; *Jub* 12:5; 20:7–8. cf. Gärtner, *Areopagus Speech and Natural Revelation,* 219–223; Jipp, "Paul's Areopagus Speech," 584.

74. Many authors have proposed an allusion to Cleanthes here: cf. Long and Sedley, "The Hellenistic Philosophers," 326–327; Mărculet, "Elements of Inculturation in Saint Paul's Speech from Areopagus," 42–43; Schnabel, "Contextualising Paul in Athens," 179; Nasrallah, "Acts, Greek Cities, and Hadrian's Panhellenion," *JBL* 127.3 (2008): 563.

75. Cadbury, *The Making of Luke–Acts,* 122 n. 10; Nasrallah, "Acts, Greek Cities, and Hadrian's Panhellenion," 563 n. 120; Pervo, *Acts,* 439. Both Acts and Aristobolus replaced Genesis' description of humanity being created in the "image of God" with rather the "*genos*" of God, from Aratus' *Phaen* (Pervo, *Acts*, 432).

76. qtd. in Jipp, "Paul's Areopagus Speech," 583.

77. Rowe, *World Upside Down,* 37–38. Consider also Ovid's assertion that humanity bears the "seed of the kindred of heaven" (*Met.* 1.78–88).

78. Pervo, *Acts,* 438.

79. cf. also Gruen, *Rethinking the Other,* chapters 9–10.

80. Jipp, "Paul's Areopagus Speech," 582; Hubbard, "Paul the Middle Platonist?," 482.

218   *Chapter 5*

81. qtd. in Jipp, "Paul's Areopagus Speech," 577.

82. Pervo, *Acts,* 428, 435.

83. Jipp, "Paul's Areopagus Speech," 576; emphasis in original.

84. "Therefore, being God's offspring (γενος), we should not to think of gold or silver or stone—an image formed by skill and the imagination mortals—to be like the God" (Acts 17:26). Oliver, *Torah Praxis*, 354.

85. cf. Neh 9:30. My translation; for the subject "they," picking up its referent ("our ancestors") from Neh 9:6, 16, and so on.

86. Italics representing emphatic nominative pronouns. Μαρτυρειτε in 𝔓75 A C D K W Γ Δ Θ Ψ *f*1.13 and others; א B L 700 read "μαρτυρες εστε".

87. 2 Kings 22:13; 2 Chronicles 29:3–11, 30:6–9, 34:21; Ezra 5:12, 9:7, 10:11; This pattern is especially prominent in the Psalms: see (Ps 79:8, 95:9, 106; Jer 3:22b–25, 14:20; Lam 5:7; Judith 7:28, 8:18–27; Baruch 1:15–2:24, 3:2–8; Azariah 1:3–13; 1 Esdr 8:73–77; 2 Esdr 9:29–32).

The variant form *"your* ancestors" occurs when God is speaking, as in Jer 35:15, where God reminds his people of their longstanding failure to heed the prophets. cf. Jer. 7:25–28, 25:4–6; 2 Chr. 24:19, 2 Chr. 36:15–16.

88. More broadly, Daniel 9:1–19.

89. Bovon, *Luke,* I.5.

90. Acts 3:12–26; 7:2–53.

91. cf. also Luke 20:9–19, where a long line of prophets have been killed by a long line of prophet-killers. Note that in this parable, the "wicked tenants" who kill the prophets are ejected from the vineyard—an age-old ethnic metaphor for Israel. Those who kill(ed) the prophets, then, are "put out of Israel," in a sense.

92. Stephen is prophetic in that he receives visions (Acts 7:56), speaks prophetically, and his face shines "like an angel" (6:15), recalling Moses.

93. McWhirter, *Rejected Prophets*, 109.

94. Boesenberg, "Negotiating Identity: The Jewishness of the Way in Acts," 61.

95. NRSVue, with biblical citations added.

96. van der Lans, "Belonging to Abraham's Kin," 315–316.

97. McWhirter, *Rejected Prophets*, 101.

98. Boesenberg, "Negotiating Identity: the Jewishness of the Way in Acts," 66. Boesenberg holds that this redefinition of Israel is a matter of *subtraction* only, not *addition*: gentiles are not invited to join Israel.

99. See chapter 1, under *"subscriptive descent."*

100. cf. Jervell, "Sons of the Prophets," 96–121 in *The Unknown Paul: Essays on Luke–Acts and Early Christian History* (Minneapolis, MN: Augsburg, 1984), esp. pp. 107–108, 101–102.

101. Peter's speech was made in public, in the aftermath of a healing that left "all the people" amazed (3:9–11). Stephen, on the other hand, has been "set up" after making enemies of Hellenized Judeans from the diaspora (6:9–10); he is accused by false witnesses and brought before the Council (6:11–7:1).

102. e.g., the racially loaded words "kindred," "ancestors," "descendants," "patriarchs," and "race" (*ethnos, genos,* and *laos*) make several appearances throughout the speech.

Genealogical Reconfiguration in Luke–Acts

103. McWhirter, *Rejected Prophets*, 105–106.

104. Malina and Pilch remark, "Jesus fits into this story in multiple ways: he is of the lineage of Abraham, a prophet like those foretold by Moses, and killed as a prophet." *Social Scientific Commentary on the Book of Acts*, 60.

105. McWhirter further notes that "Just as the Israelites rejected Moses twice— first in Egypt, then in the wilderness—so the Jerusalem authorities will reject first Jesus, then Peter and the apostles" (*Rejected Prophets*, 96).

106. Kinzer, *Jerusalem Crucified*, 114.

107. Boesenberg, "Negotiating Identity: The Jewishness of the Way in Acts," 72; cf. McWhirter, *Rejected Prophets*, 104–105.

108. Matthews, *Perfect Martyr*, 71–73.

109. Malina and Pilch, *Social Scientific Commentary on the Book of Acts*, 59.

110. Idolatry is a significant subtheme of the speech: part of ancient Israel's rejection of Moses was a turn toward idols like the golden calf (Acts 7:39–42). Recall that, according to widespread tradition, Abraham had made an existential break with his family of origin by rejecting their idolatry (e.g., *LAB* 6.1–18, 23.5; Philo *Abr.* 63–70; 4 Macc. 6:17–22; see chapter 2 for examples). Although all Israelites descend from Abraham biologically, it seems that some "take after" the family he left behind in Haran. If some Judeans *attenuated* their ancestral ties to Abraham by returning to idols, one wonders: could some gentiles *retrace* his decisive turn from idols, going out "from their land and their kindred" (7:3) thus forging their *own* connection with the founder?

111. Prototypical Judeans anticipate Jesus: (Luke 1:5–80; 3:16–17). Prototypical Judeans endorse Jesus or the Way: (Luke 2:25–38; 8:41), including Gamaliel who wonders whether the Way might be "from God" (Acts 5:34–39; 22:3). Prototypical Judeans even *join* the Way (Acts 6:7; 9:13–16; 15:5; 22:12–14). Jervell aptly notes that in Acts, "it is those Jews who are faithful to the law, the real Jews, the most Jewish Jews, that become believers." *Luke and the People of God*, 46; cf. 50.

112. Jesus is compared with Moses explicitly several times, and many of his activities mirror the deeds of Elijah or Elisha. The raising of the widow of Nain's son (Luke 7:11–17) echoes the raising of the widow of Zarephath's son (1 Kings 17:17–24) in geographical location, in narrative form, and in that both "gave him to his mother" (και εδοκεν αυτον τη μητρι αυτου) afterward (Luke 7:15 // 1 Kings 17:23 [LXX]). Beck, *A Light to the Centurions*, 54.

John the Baptist resembles Elijah as well (Luke 1:17), although less strongly than in Mark (Mark 1:6 // 2 Kings 1:8; Mark 9:13). Philip also resembles Elijah, moving at the Spirit's command): he gets up and goes at Spirit's command (Acts 8:26–27 // 1 Kgs 17:9–10; Acts 8:39 // 1 Kgs 18:12). Peter's deeds resemble Elijah/ Elisha resuscitation stories featuring a corpse in an upper room (Acts 9:32–35 // 1 Kings 17:19, 2 Kings 4:10, 32–35), whose eyes open when he prays (Acts 9:37–40 // 1 Kings 17:19, 2 Kings 4:10, 32–35). McWhirter, *Rejected Prophets*, 113.

113. Those explicitly called prophets include Anna (Luke 2:36), the five prophets in Antioch (Acts 13:1), Judas and Silas (15:32), and Agabus (21:10–11). Those engaging in prophetic activity include Zechariah, Mary, and Elizabeth (Luke 1–2), Simeon (2:29–32), and the prophesying daughters of Philip (Acts 21:9).

220   *Chapter 5*

114. e.g., Acts 6:11–14; 18:13–15; 21:21, 28; 24:5–8.

115. cf. Acts 26:6.

116. "He defends the church against Jewish polemic by claiming that the Christian communities are the legitimate heirs of the prophecies of Scripture."— Bovon, 1.9.

117. Bovon, 1.9.

118. Beck, *A Light to the Centurions,* 1–23; Fox, *Hermeneutics of Social-Identity in Luke–Acts*, 53–63.

119. Francis Bovon suggests that Luke is an educated God-fearer—perhaps from Macedonia, given his precise knowledge of Macedonia and its Roman institutions (Bovon, Luke, 1.9). Fuller holds that Luke may have been either a Diaspora Judean OR a God-fearer (*The Restoration of Israel*, 198 N 5); Paul Smith suggests Judean (*Luke was not a Christian*).

To be clear, if Luke *is* a gentile (whether convert or God-fearer), he is certainly one whose imagination has been profoundly reshaped by Israel's scriptures, and who understands Jesus' significance within this framework.

120. Beck, *A Light to the Centurions,* 1–23; cf. Fox, *Hermeneutics of Social-Identity in Luke–Acts*, 63–78.

121. Pervo, *Acts*, 376–377; Boesenberg, "Negotiating Identity," 68–72.

122. For more on gentiles' descent from Abraham, see chapter 2.

123. Kuecker, 86–89.

124. Smith, "Luke, the Jews, and the Politics," 111–121.

125. Beck, *A Light to the Centurions*, 54.

126. NRSVue.

127. Although in her story, we may detect a narrative echo of the *non*-Israelite widow of Zarephath.

128. Beck, *A Light to the Centurions*, 10.

129. 2 Kgs 5:14 / Acts 10:28b.

130. The men of Nineveh will "rise" to judge Jesus' listeners—a word used for resurrection—implying this is an eschatological scene.

131. cf. *Ant.* 2.5–10.

132. Origen also explicitly cites Josephus as evidence that she is from Ethiopia (Origen *Comm.Songs* 2.1).

133. cf. "in every race whoever fears God and does what is right is acceptable (δεκτος) to him" (Acts 10:34).

134. The Ethiopian also echoes Naaman, as another high-ranking foreign official who comes to Israel, but the allusion to the Queen of Sheba is stronger.

135. Again, Cush was sometimes identified with Ethiopia; e.g., Isa. 43:3, 45:14; Jos. *Ant.* 8.168–175; Origen, *Comm.Songs* 2.1–2; Josephus, *Ant.* 8.168–175. See also Hays, *From Every People and Nation,* 172–176.

136. I hold that the Ethiopian Eunuch "scans" as a foreigner who is favorably inclined toward Judaism, not a genealogical Israelite nor a full convert—especially in light of his seeming infacility with the interpretation of Jewish scriptures (Acts 8:30–31), and the "othering" detail that he is a eunuch, who "may not enter the assembly of the Lord" (Deut. 23:1).

Recently, this prevalent interpretation of the Eunuch's ethnic identity has been called into question. Both Margaret Aymer and Gifford Rhamie hold that the Ethiopian may be understood as a Jew (Aymer, "Exotica and the Ethiopian of Acts 8:26–40: Toward a Different Fabula," *JBL* 142.3 [2023]: 533–546; Rhamie, "Whiteness, Conviviality, and Agency" [1999], chapter 4). Rhamie argues that in the expansive sensibilities of Luke, "all Jews—"Judaeans, Samaritans, proselytes and diasporans—are reclaimed by Luke as Jews; and all Graeco-Roman gentiles— including Godfearers—are extended the same hand of fellowship" (201–202). Aymer notes that the passage he is reading (from Second Isaiah) suggests *exile* as a significant intertextual background; perhaps we should read the Ethiopian Eunuch as an Exilic Jew, born and raised by Jews, enslaved and forced to undergo the violence of castration (543–545).

There is much to recommend such a reading. In favor of this proposal is the fact that the story comes *before* Acts 10, with Peter's mission to Cornelius' (gentile) household. However, several factors may suggest a gentile identity for the eunuch: the double emphasis that he is an *Ethiopian* working for the *Queen of the Ethiopians* (Acts 8:27), his inability to understand Jewish scripture without assistance (8:30–31), and his somewhat defiant question, "What can *prevent* (κωλυσαι) me from being baptized?"—mirroring Peter's later insistence that nothing should *prevent* (κωλυσαι) Cornelius' household from being baptized (Acts 8:36; 10:47). Both of the latter encounters are directly arranged by angels (Acts 8:26; 10:3–4, 10–16).

137. My translation. For the Greek text, see *Corpus Inscriptionum Iudaeae/ Palaestinae,* vol. 1, edited Hannah Cotton et al., 42–43.

138. Philo explains that "all those not of the same race (ουχ ὁμοεθνων)" would be sentenced to death without appeal, for violating the Temple's inner confines (Embassy 212).

139. Kuecker, *The Spirit and the Other*, 164; Beck, *A Light to the Centurions*, 11–13.

140. Beck, *A Light to the Centurions*, 12; cf. Kuecker, *The Spirit and the Other*, 167.

141. This connection pointed, for instance, by Kuecker, *The Spirit and the Other*, 161–168; Beck, *A Light to the Centurions*, 12; Sechrest, *Race and Rhyme*, 184–185, 182 FN 57 & 58; Keener, *Bible Background Commentary: New Testament*, 346; *NISB,* Acts 8:36 N.; Wall, *Acts* (NIB), 143.

142. My translation; cf. also *Wisdom of Solomon* 3:14.

143. Kuecker, *The Spirit and the Other*, 167.

144. cf. chapter 4, and Benko, *Race in John's Gospel*, 201–202.

145. cf. Acts 10:34–35.

146. Kuecker, *The Spirit and the Other*, 167.

147. *trans.* The William-Davidson Talmud, accessed at www.sefaria.org/Beitzah .32b on August 28, 2023.

148. Maimonides expressed similar ideas much later. He held that "The children of our father Abraham are merciful people who have mercy upon all" (*Hilkot Avadim* 9:8), and even that "if someone is cruel and does not show mercy, there are sufficient grounds to doubt his lineage" (*Matanot Aniyim* 10:2).

222   *Chapter 5*

149. Even their king "removed his robe, covered himself in sackcloth, and sat in ashes" (Jonah 3:6).

150. For simplicity's sake, this chart omits Samaritans, who, as I will argue in my next book, Luke *does* treat at ethnic Israelites.

151. Colson: LCL; cf. *Rewards* 152.

152. My trans.; cf. Micah 7:6.

153. "If a brother or son or daughter, or housemate (οικουρος) or true friend (γνησιος φιλος), or anyone else who seems to wish us well, entices us to do the same—to rejoice with the multitude and participate in their temples and libations, and even sacrifices—then we must punish them as a public and common enemy, holding as trifles the ties that bind us (οικειοτητος); and we must publish reports about him to all lovers of piety, who will hurry without delay to assault the profane man, judging his death lawful." (Philo, *The Special Laws* 1.316; my trans).

154. Compared to the parallel version (Matt. 10:37–38), Luke has amplified the theme of familial rejection with the word "hate," adding "brothers and sisters" to the list of estranged kin.

155. my trans; cf. Mark 3:31–35 // Matt. 12:46–50.

156. Kuecker, *The Spirit and the Other*, 182.

157. Acts 2:29; 3:17; 7:2; 13:26, 38; 22:1; 23:1, 5–6; 28:17.

158. That Idumeans are Judeans, see Josephus, *Ant.* 13.257–258.

159. Boesenberg, "Negotiating Identity: The Jewishness of the Way in Acts," 60–61; Kinzer, *Jerusalem Crucified, Jerusalem Risen*, 131.

Mitzi Smith argues the contrary: that in Acts, Luke constructs the *Ioudaioi* as the "external other," a literary foil to those who follow "The Way." Smith notes that in Acts, the early church is in both "continuity and discontinuity" with other Judeans of their era; "It [Acts] constitutes a dialectic between the language of abandonment and the practice of remaining in dialogue with the synagogue and the Jewish people" (Smith, *The Literary Construction of the Other in the Acts of the Apostles* (Eugene, OR: Pickwick, 2011), 58–59). Jason Moraff wonders how exactly Smith is using "continuity" and "discontinuity," apart from spatial proximity and dialogue. Some level of social distance from the synagogue need not construct the Judeans as the absolute "external other" of the *ekklesia*; after all, the Qumran community had withdrawn from both Temple worship and synagogue involvement, and moreover relocated to their own enclaves, and yet *they* remained within the boundaries of first-century Judaism (Moraff, "Recent Trends in the Study of Jews and Judaism in Luke–Acts," *CBR* 19.1 (2020): 66–67).

I am skeptical of Smith's proposal because of the many signs of sustained contact between the early church and Judeans, both in Acts. The professed identity of both Paul and the Jerusalem church remains thoroughly Judean, even at the end of the book (c.f. Acts 21:20–24; 22:1–3, 28:17–21). Indeed, it might be truer to the text to speak of *gentiles* as the work's "external other," rather than the Jews! It is the introduction of gentiles into the Way that causes such hand-wringing among its leaders; by contrast, fellow Judeans (and Samaritans) can be added with little difficulty—as they are, in many ways (culturally, linguistically, religiously), "the same as us."

Genealogical Reconfiguration in Luke–Acts 223

160. e.g., Acts 2:29; 3:17; 7:2; 13:26, 38; 22:1; 23:1, 5–6; 28:17.

161. Ανδρες, αδελφοι, υιοι γενους Αβρααμ και οι εν υμιν φοβουμενοι τον θεον. Much depends on whether the first word of the speech, ανδρες, αδελφοι refers to *both* parts of the compound address, or only to the first part (Judeans). An inclusive interpretation is that Paul is addressing "Brothers, (*who include both* sons of the race of Abraham, and those God-fearers among you)," while a narrower interpretation would read, "Brothers (*that is*, sons of the race of Abraham), *and* those God-fearers among you. . . ." I am inclined to read the address in the former sense, anticipating its more expansive usage between Judeans and gentiles beginning in Acts 15.

Even if we understand "brothers" to refer *only* to the natural-born Judeans in the synagogue, it is still the case that all present (including God-fearers) are reminded of the promises God gave to "*our* ancestors" (13:32). That is, sympathetic gentiles have Israelite "ancestors," in a sense.

162. Boesenberg, "Negotiating Identity," 62.

163. Indeed, no gentile is called the "brother" of an Israelite across all four gospels; this holds true across relevant ancient literature with the exception of texts describing the supposed "relatedness" of Judeans and Spartans (1 Macc. 12:1–23, 14:16–23; 2 Macc. 5:8–9; *Ant.* 12.225–228; 13.43–45, 163–170). Kuecker, *The Spirit and the Other*, 187.

164. cf. Acts 9:31; the Samaritan church is well-established before "these gentiles" join the movement (Acts 10). Luke–Acts categorizes the Samaritans as estranged Israelites and treats their reconciliation to Judeans within "the Way" as part of the restoration of Israel, which precedes gentile inclusion. See the forthcoming *Good Samaritans: Samaritan Ethnicity and Evangelism in Luke–Acts*, Penwell and Benko.

165. "brother" as intra-Israelite address: Acts 22:1, 5, 13; 23:1, 5, 6; 28:17, 21. "brother" for undifferentiated followers of the Way: Acts 15:23, 32, 33, 36, 40; 16:2, 40; 17:6, 10, 14; 18:27; 21:7, 17, 20; 28:14, 15. List from Kuecker, *The Spirit and the Other*, 214; cf. FN 153. cf. Boesenberg, "Negotiating Identity: the Jewishness of the Way in Acts," 60–61.

166. Diasporic Judeans would also be among the audiences of the letters, but that it is primarily addressed to gentiles is made clear from the instructions at the end: no greater burden is placed upon "you" than a few simple commands (Acts 15:28–29). The "you" of the letter are not only brothers—they are *gentiles*.

167. Kinzer, *Jerusalem Crucified*, 131.

168. Boesenberg, "Negotiating Identity: the Jewishness of the Way in Acts," 61.

169. Note that *laos* ("the people") undergoes a similar shift after Acts 15:14; formerly used in the singular to denote Israel, the term can now include gentiles, suggesting that gentiles are in some way added to an *Israelite* identity. (Kuecker, *The Spirit and the Other*, 204–205).

170. "Greeks and no small number of the elite [Thessalonican] women" are among the "brethren" in Thessalonica (Acts 17:4–10). Later, "not a few Greek women and well-mannered men" are added to the "brothers" of Beroea (17:11–14).

171. See also *De Agricultura* 6; cf. Gruen, "Philo and Jewish Ethnicity," 186–194 for discussion of the passage above.

172. Philo: *Every Good Man,* 79, 87; *Hypothetica* 11.13; Jos. *War* 2.122; CD 13.12–16; 4QDa 9.3.1–6; 1QHa 15.20–22; cf. Palmer, *Converts in the Dead Sea Scrolls,* 130–136; Jodiranta and Wassen, "A Brotherhood at Qumran," 182–184, 192–193, 202.

173. See chapter 1.

174. Colson: LCL. *See* Barclay, "Deviance and Apostasy," 133 for discussion.

175. For a discussion of this passage and the issues it raises, see Nicholas Taylor, "The Social Nature of Conversion," in *Modelling Early Christianity: Social-Scientific Studies of the New Testament and its Context,* Philip Esler, ed. (New York: Routledge, 1995), 133–136.

176. "Thus, while giving equal rank to all in-comers (επηλυταις) with all the privileges which he [Moses] gives the native-born (ευπατριδαις), he exhorts the old nobility to honour them not only with marks of respect but with special friendship and more than ordinary goodwill. And surely there is good reason for this; they have left, he says, their country (πατριδα), their kinsfolk (συγγενεις) and their friends (φιλους) for the sake of virtue and religion. Let them not be denied another citizenship (πολεων) or other ties of family (οικειων) and friendship (φιλων), and let them find places of shelter standing ready for refugees to the camp of piety." (Special Laws 1.52 [Colson: LCL])

177. cf. further *Joseph and Asenath* 12:12–14.

178. qtd. in Isaac, *Invention of Racism,* 453. Romans could also speak of adopting a foreign way of life as "pollution," "contamination," or "infection;" cf. Isaac 479–480.

179. Erich S. Gruen, "Philo and Jewish Ethnicity," in *Strength to Strength: Essays in Honor of Shaye J. D. Cohen,* Michael L. Satlow, ed. (Atlanta, GA: SBL: Brown Judaic Studies, 2018), 183–186; Barclay, "Deviance and Apostasy," 133; Horrell, "Religion, Ethnicity, and Way of Life," 50.

The intense familiar love Paul describes within early *ekkēsia* might hint at similar estrangement between believers and their former relatives: see 1 Thess. 4:9–10; Phil. 1:8–9a, 2:2, 4:1; 1 Cor. 5:13b–15, 13:1–13, 16:14; 2 Cor. 2:1–10; Philem. 8–20; Gal. 5:13; Rom. 12:10, 13:8–10.

180. Barclay, "Deviance and Apostasy," 133. Note that Paul must advise his audience *not to initiate such divorces themselves* (1 Cor. 7:12–13), so such separation was not always forced upon the Christian spouse. Then again, not all non-Christian spouses would "consent to live" with their Christian spouse.

181. Indeed, he accuses his accusers of the very deviancy they charge against him. Kinzer, *Jerusalem Crucified, Jerusalem Risen,* 114.

182. Jipp, "The Paul of Acts," 65.

183. cf. Matthews (*Taming the Tongues of Fire,* 70), who notes:

Elite Romans prided themselves in their legal system, the judiciousness of their trial procedures, their fair, orderly and benevolent treatment of residents in provinces they occupied. What they disdained, in contrast, was mob behavior—extralegal, impulsive, and uncontrolled violence emanating from crowds that threatened to degenerate into *stasis* or rebellion.

Genealogical Reconfiguration in Luke–Acts   225

184. cf. 5:26, where it is the Temple authorities who fear such extrajudicial violence.

185. Like the Abrahamic Zechariah and Elizabeth, of priestly lineage (Luke 1:5–7), David-descended Joseph (1:27), prophesying Anna (2:36–38), devout Simeon (2:25–27), and Elijah's body-double, John the Baptist (1:17, 3:2b–3). See chapter 3.

186. Moreover, the famed Pharisee Gamaliel is identified as Paul's own teacher (22:3) and is willing to give the nascent movement at least the benefit of the doubt, suggesting it might be "of God" (5:34–39).

187. Jipp, "The Paul of Acts," 64.

188. Boesenberg, "Negotiating Identity," 71.

189. Boesenberg, "Negotiating Identity," 72.

190. Jervell, *Luke–Acts and the People of God,* 54.

191. (e.g. Acts 16:1–5; 21:20–26; 22:1–5; 24:11–18; 26:4–5,22–23).

192. Jipp, "The Paul of Acts," 62–63; cf. Oliver, *Torah Praxis after 70 CE,*" 320–398; Miller, "Reading Law as Prophesy: Torah Ethics in Acts," in *Torah Ethics and Early Christian Identity,* Susan Wendel and David Miller, eds. (Grand Rapids, MI: Eerdmans, 2016), 82–83.

193. Horrell notes that although the earliest Christians do not describe Christianity as a *patrios* or *ethos* (as Judeans did with Judaism), they did describe it as "the Way" (Acts 9:2, 22:4, 24:14). Horrell, *Ethnicity and Inclusion,* 142–143.

194. For example, see chapter 1.

195. cf. Acts 9:35; 11:21; 14:15; 15:19. Horrell, *Ethnicity and Inclusion,* 143.

196. Horrell, *Ethnicity and Inclusion,* 144.

197. cf. *The Acts of Paul and Thecla.*

198. Konstan, "Acts of Life: A Narrative Pattern in the Apocryphal Acts," *Journal of Early Christian Studies* 6 (1998): 15.

199. Jipp, "The Paul of Acts," 74.

200. Jipp, "The Paul of Acts," 61–62, cf. 71–72.

201. cf. similar accusations made by his enemies "from Asia" 21:27, 24; 19.

202. Jipp, "The Paul of Acts," 74–75; cf. Goodman, "The Persecution of Paul by Diaspora Jews," in *The Beginnings of Christianity,* Jack Pastor and Menachem Mor, eds. (Jerusalem: Yad Ben-Zvi Press, 2005), 385.

203. Paula Fredriksen, *Paul: The Pagans' Apostle* (New Haven, CT: Yale University Press, 2017), 92.

204. See chapter 1.

205. Beck, *Light,* 31.

206. Rhamie, "Whiteness, Conviviality, and Agency," 202–203; cf. Stroup's assertion that Luke presents both born Jews and converts as Jewish, *Christians Who Became Jews,* 37, 67, 161 N 89.

207. Rhamie, "Whiteness, Conviviality, and Agency," 202–203; Stroup, *Christians Who Became Jews,* 67–68.

208. Households convert en masse in Acts 10:1–11:18, 16:11–15, 16:25–34, 18:1–11.

209. "Luke is aware of Jewish opposition to the missionaries and their message. But for him this opposition is not a representative expression of the attitude of Israel

226   Chapter 5

toward the gospel. Those circles out of which opposition arises are not he legitimate representatives of the people of God." (Jacob Jervell, *Luke–Acts and the People of God,* 54)

Jason Moraff argues that Luke does not represent a "supersessionist" theology, but rather that "genealogical Israel (the Jewish people) remains God's people because of election." He notes that the trope that some in Israel will be *cut off* from the people is a "common prophetic warning to the descendants of Abraham, Isaac, and Jacob" (Acts 3:23; cf. Lev. 23:29, Deut. 18:15–20) and that Israel has always struggled to respond faithfully to God. He argues that Israel as a corporate genealogical entity, in its entirety, is the focus of God's salvation, on account of its election and receipt of the covenant.

However, Moraff several times admits that *some* genealogical Israelites may be somehow excluded from Israel. Consider: "Despite Israel's frequent infidelity, God remains faithful to them. . . . *Some may be pruned from Israel.* But the covenant cannot be annulled." Again: "The 'many in Israel'—the corporate entity *with the potential exclusion of some of its members*—fall then rise." Or again: "those who do not listen to Jesus, the prophet like Moses, *will be cut off from the people.*" [Italics added]. Such statements would seem to undermine Moraff's position that corporate Israel is in no way reframed or redefined by Luke's rhetoric. Although the tropes may be found in Israel's scriptures, Luke has redeployed them in a new historical moment, now reframed with a new focal referent (messiah Jesus), to make novel assertions about who will be "cut off" from the people—patently a form of (theologically based) racial reasoning.

I await the upcoming book this article encapsulates with great eagerness, and especially look forward to seeing how Moraff resolves the tension between "all" or "corporate" Israel being the recipient of the promised covenantal salvation, despite "some" in Israel being cut off. (Moraff, "Children of the Prophets and the Covenant: A Post-Supersessionist Reading of Luke–Acts," *Religion* 14.120 [2023]: 1–17).

Conclusion

Carving a New People from an Old Block

In Luke's two-volume work, the evangelist has made his case: all who follow Christ, Judean and gentile alike, have a stake in Abraham. Luke's thumbnail sketches of Israel's past suggest that there have long been two disparate "lines" among them: those who resist God's purposes, and those who promote them. According to Luke, those who follow Jesus have a more genuine claim upon Israel's founder than do those who persecute them. Between these two extremes, of course, falls the vast majority of late first-century Judeans, who neither confessed Jesus as the messiah *nor* actively persecuted his followers. *Their* descent from the patriarch is assumed, so long as they are not egregiously un-Abrahamic; and even then, they can repair this association by repenting. Luke lays the foundation for this position in his gospel and builds upon it in his sequel (Acts), where he sweeps gentiles up in this realignment of lineage. In the synagogue in Pisidian Antioch, Paul calls both god-fearers and natural-born Judeans "brothers" (Acts 13:26) and reminds the whole group of what "God promised *our* ancestors" (13:32). As the book progresses, the reader is left with the distinct impression that "The Way," the followers of Jesus, are Abraham's genuine (although in some cases, adopted) family.

In order to carve out a niche for these so-called "Christians" (Acts 11:26; 26:28) in the Roman world, Luke portrays them very carefully. One strategy is the consistent message that Christians are heirs to an *ancient* faith—that they are indeed the most authentic representatives of a very ancient *ethnos,* the Judeans. New religious expressions were subject to suspicion and scrutiny, but *ancient* religions were generally tolerated even when disliked—particularly when observed by their original practitioners (and better still, in their countries of origin). Conversely, the spread of foreign practices to new

228   *Conclusion*

locales, or especially to new peoples, could incite hostility. Around 170 CE, Celsus criticizes Christianity for this very issue:

> The Jews became a distinct race (εθνος ιδιον), and enacted laws in keeping with the customs of their country (επιχωριον) and keep them to this day; and they observe a mode of worship which, whatever it is, at least comes from their ancestors (πατριον). They act in these respects like other people, because each nation retains its ancestral customs (πατρια), whatever they are. . . .
>
> Let the second party come forward; and I shall ask them whence they come, and whom they regard as the originator (αρχηγετην) of their ancestral customs (πατριων νομων). They will say, No one, because they spring from the same source as the Jews themselves, and derive their instruction and theme from nowhere else, notwithstanding they have deserted the Jews. (Celsus (qtd. in Origen *Contra Celsum*, 5.25, 33)[1]

If Celsus is no particular fan of Judeans, at least they are very old, and they follow their own beliefs. The same cannot be said of "the second party"— Christians. He is unimpressed with their pretensions to derive from Israel; after all, "they have defected/rebelled (αφηκα) from the Judeans." According to Celsus, Christians are a rootless, baseless group, playing at a Jewishness that is not really theirs. These sorts of prejudices were likely already coalescing a century earlier, when Luke had tried to characterize the Way as an *ancient* movement—the organic continuation of Israel's past.

Another strategy Luke employs to promote the legitimacy of this "people" is to *contrast* it with mainstream Judeans. It is no surprise that Christians come across favorably in these comparisons. Much like the elites who commissioned the sculptures in the *sebasteieon* of Aphrodisias, Luke uses Judeans to "think with," as he promotes the honor of his own "people" (followers of the Way). Especially in Acts, we find Luke maligning (non-Christian) Judeans and valorizing the early church. The former are a source of unrest and disorder (Luke 4:29; Acts 13:50),[2] as they were frequently viewed by gentile critics (Tacitus, *Hist.* 5.3.1; Philostratus *Vita. Apoll.* 5.3).[3] The latter, by contrast, are non-threatening to the Roman order; they are described as law-abiding and peaceful (Luke 22:53; Acts 18:14–16).[4] By the time Luke was writing, the Judean Revolt had only reinforced prejudices against Judeans as dangerous, antisocial, or subversive. Luke finds it expedient to depict his *Christian* Judeans as embodying the best of this ancient people's past and to depict their Judean *opponents* as embodying the worst of gentile prejudices—practically caricatures-made-flesh of the suspicious, riotous underminer of the public peace. Everything negative about how pagans perceive Judeans has been projected outward, at the church's enemies. Luke portrays his protagonists, in other words, as "good Judeans," model subjects of the empire, and portrays their antagonists as "bad Judeans."[5]

Conclusion 229

Luke, then, is both champion and character-assassin of the *Ioudaioi*. He is radically assertive of the value of Israelite identity, and radically derogatory toward particular Judeans—specifically, those who persecute the Way.[6] To defend the legitimacy of the *ekklesia's* Jewishness, he attacks the legitimacy of those who would denigrate them.[7] Such identity politics are not a neutral exercise, especially in writings later to be enshrined as "gospel": they had real-world consequences in the way Christians treated real-world Jews, both in Luke's day and in generations to come. We might well ask: What are the ethical outworkings of such racial reasoning? What sort of effect did this gospel have on the ethnic imagination of its original audience? And what sort of effect might it have on its listener today—a listener who is, statistically speaking, likely to be a non-Jew?

On the positive side, Luke's narrative likely allowed his audience to imagine themselves, as he intended, as a "natural" part of the family of Abraham—foretold to Israel's earliest ancestors and adopted into an Israelite identity. This fostered the forging of a positive (ethnic) group identity within the early churches. Members were now "brothers" and "sisters," related (συγγενεῖς) as members of the same people and "descendants" (in a manner of speaking) from the same ancestors. Also positive is the conviction that all human beings, regardless of their racial origins, were eligible for membership in this expanded Israelite identity; this might well have disposed the "brothers" favorably toward all outsiders, disregarding ethnic boundaries.[8]

But there would have been negative implications to Luke's ideas, as well. Gentile believers were offered a share in a new set of ancestors, but accepting this offer minimized the importance of their flesh-and-blood ancestors. As we saw, Philo observed a similar de-racination in gentile converts to Judaism—many experienced it as a sort of "social death" to their former families. Luke–Acts assumes its audience is now familiar with (and values) Judean teaching. Gentile converts are expected to conform their worldview to an idiosyncratic, colonizing version of diasporic Judaism, in order to adopt their new identity—learning (and valuing) Judean myths above Greek or Roman ones (or whatever race they came from).[9] In a way that Judean or Samaritan converts to the movement might not have had to, gentile adherents of the Way would have to put (aspects of) their former selves to death in order to embrace their new identity.

In terms of their attitude toward Judeans, how might Luke's audience have been influenced by his gospel? If they accepted Luke's presentation of the Way as the long-foretold culmination of Israel's hopes, they would likely see contemporary Judeans who opposed the Way as misguided, at best. Those who were Judeans themselves likely understood themselves to embody a more authentic expression of this identity. Those from gentile stock would likely feel hostile toward Judeans who informed them they had no stake in

230   *Conclusion*

Abraham, no standing in Israel. Of course, because they have not actually
converted to Judaism (including circumcision), this would be their standing,
in Judean eyes. With Luke's bifurcated retelling of Israel's history and with
his description of the disciples' enemies, his audience might further understand most Judeans (i.e., non-Christian ones) to stand in "genealogical continuity" with the worst of Israel's past—as latter-day sprigs on the same branch
of the family tree that once rebelled against Moses, resisted the prophets, and
(much later) killed Stephen. By contrast, Christians, whatever their origins,
might see themselves as belonging to the "good" side of Israel's family tree.
This sort of polar view could obviously lead to some very dangerous "us vs.
them" thinking.

Sadly, this potential for harm was not limited to the early church. The anti-
Jewish sentiment of *first*-century Christians, echoed and amplified through
the years, becomes the Anti-Semitism of *twenty-first* century Christians.[10]
Therefore, the study of Luke's racial reasoning is by no means "academic," in
the pejorative sense. It isn't enough to point out that an ancient text builds the
positive ethnic identity of its audience by negatively characterizing another
group. Rather, Christians, for whom Luke is scripture, must grapple with *how*
exactly this text is authoritative for us—*how* to use and venerate it. What life-
giving, "Christlike" possibilities are to be celebrated and put into action? And
what harmful, problematic aspects of Luke's ideology are to be recognized,
acknowledged, but ultimately rejected?

TWO BROTHERS

Perhaps a helpful metaphor can be found in a tale of two brothers: one who
demands his inheritance early and squanders it on revelry, and one who
remains faithfully devoted to his father all the while (Luke 15:11–19). In the
end, the prodigal son is reunited with his father; but one burr in this supposed
"happy" ending is the elder son's objection to his brother's return (15:20–30).
The dutiful son cannot even bring himself to acknowledge the prodigal as his
brother, instead calling him "this son of yours" (15:30). Despite his father's
"plea" (παρακαλει) that he welcome him back, the story leaves it ambiguous
as to whether the two children were ever reconciled (15:28a, 31–32).

In its narrative setting, the story obliquely contrasts the crowds of disciples
traveling with Jesus (Luke 14:25) and the "Pharisees and scribes" who com-
plained that the former were a rabble of sinners (15:1–2). The parable of the
Lost Son is one of three parables addressing this assessment.[11] But by Luke's
own day, these "disciples" and "Pharisees" have left behind two groups
of "descendants"—early Christians, successors to the disciples, and early
Rabbinical Jews, successors to the Pharisees—both rapidly reorganizing in

Conclusion 231

the wake of the Temple's destruction. Recall that Luke portrays the Way (included gentiles welcomed into its ranks) as heirs to an essentially *Israelite* identity. Understood this way, the rabbinic Jews and Christians of Luke's own day are themselves "brothers." Despite the father's plea (Luke 15:28–32), these two brothers are estranged by the time the gospel is written, with no reconciliation in sight.

As we saw in chapter 2, Judean tradition had long used the image of "brothers" for related peoples, going all the way back to the ancestral narratives in Genesis. The sons of Abraham represent not only themselves, but the nations who will one day spring from them (Gen. 17:19–20, 21:12–13, 18),[12] as could also be said of Jacob and Esau in their generation (Gen. 27:29, 40, 36:1–43).[13] One of the most haunting aspects of these tales is the bitter estrangement of the various brothers—with only ambiguous or partial reconciliation, at best (Gen. 25:9; Gen. 32–33).[14] The races descended from them could likewise be described as "brothers."[15] War between such races, for example between Israel and Edom, was described as betrayal by a "brother" (Num. 20:15–21; Amos 1:11; Ps. 137:7; Obad. 1:10). In the first century, the Idumeans, as descendants of the ancient Edomites, could still be thought of as "brothers" of Judeans.[16] Tragically, violence continued to break out between these brothers,[17] and Judeans could look down on the Idumeans as "not really" us.[18]

The kingdoms of Judah and Israel could be described as "brothers" (1 Kings 12:24; 2 Chr. 28:8), or in some instances, sisters.[19] Latter-day Samaritans, claiming descent from the Northern tribes, understood themselves as fellow Israelites, but they were often not acknowledged by their claimed kin.[20] Although Luke does see them as two distinct races (Luke 17:18, Acts 8:9), he understands them both as *Israelite* races.[21] The Samaritan and Judean believers are "brothers," and they marvel *together* at the inclusion of "the gentiles" (Acts 15:3).

Both of these fraternal pairs (Jacob / Edom, and Israel / Judah) act out the same tragedy: "related" races do not always treat one another in a brotherly way. In both cases, the sources continue to hold up brotherly conduct as the *ideal*, which ought to determine how they treat one another. The fact that relations broke down was a tragedy—but it did not undermine the expectation itself. Like the forgiving father in Jesus' parable, Israelite traditions "plead" for justice, fair dealing, and reconciliation between such "brothers" (Deut. 2:4–5; 2 Chr. 28; Luke 15:28–32).

We might apply the same plea to Christians and to (non-Christian) Judeans. These "brothers" (to Luke's way of thinking) find themselves at loggerheads across the pages of Acts. The nascent church is consistently condemned as deviant, blasphemous, and less-than-fully-Judean. Luke returns the favor in his characterization of the movement's enemies. In other words, Luke answers rejection ("You're not really Judean") with rejection ("No, *you're* deficiently

232 *Conclusion*

Judean"). We might well ask the evangelist: is this churlish response consistent with the teaching of your gospel's protagonist? Jesus himself would not let his disciples answer violence with violence (Luke 6:29, 22:50–51), nor hatred with hatred (6:28), nor even rejection with rejection (9:54–55). If some, even their "brothers," wish to treat them as enemies—well, Jesus would only demand they love them all the more (Luke 6:27, 35–36).

We noted a widespread pattern of *ranking* the branches of Abraham's family tree, in Judaism. Starting with his own sons, and down through the *ethnē* descended from them, certain parties were deemed closer to the ancestor, their stake surer, and their inheritance greater.[22]

Philo explains:

> Among the founders of our race (γενους αρχηγετων) . . . the first [Abraham] was the father of many children, begotten on three wives . . . in hope of multiplying the race (γενος). But of his many sons, only one was appointed to inherit the patrimony (πατρωων αγαθων). All the rest failed to show sound judgment and as they reproduced nothing of their father's qualities, were excluded from the home and denied any part in the grandeur of their noble birth. (Philo, *On the Virtues*, 206–207)

Other sons/brothers/peoples might be "related" to him after a fashion, but are subordinate, second-class. This thinking permeates not only the Hebrew Bible but also subsequent Judean literature about the patriarch. In some ways, Luke has reinscribed this pattern by presenting *his* favored "Abrahamic people" (the Christians of "the Way") as a more legitimate one than the Developing Judaism of his day.

But an intergroup ethic actually based on Jesus' exhortation of radical other-love would demand a loving stance toward the "other"—even if that "other" denies one's own legitimacy. In ethnic terms, the Israelite "people" Luke claims are called into being in Christ need not belittle any other people in order to be who they are. Indeed, as Jesus would have it, they *must* not. Any anti-Jewish outworkings of Luke's thought, and antisemitic interpretations of his gospel, must be rejected as counter to Jesus' own teaching. May his latter-day readers—those would-be "children of Abraham," raised from the unlikeliest of stones—not be such "blockheads" that they seek to demolish the very rock from which they were hewn.

NOTES

1. Crombie: ANF, with minor changes in consultation with the Greek; cf. Marcovich, *Origenes Contra Celsum libri VIII* (Leiden: Brill, 2001).

Conclusion 233

2. See also Luke 4:29; 11:46–51; 23:18–25; Acts 7:54–58; 9:1; 9:23; 12:1–3; 13:50, 14:19; 17:5–8; cf. Matthews, *Taming the Tongues of Fire*, 70.

3. See also Josephus *Ant.* 13.245; Diodorus, *Bib.Hist.* 34–35.1.1.

4. See also Luke 23:4,14,22; Acts 16:28,37–39; 19:37; 26:30–32.

5. See also Matthew's discussion, *Taming the Tongues of Fire*, 55.

6. See Matthews' brief musing on the simultaneous *pro-* and *anti*-Jewishness of Luke–Acts, and its real-world outworkings in history (*Taming the Tongues of Fire*, 70–72).

7. Jacob Jervell, *Luke–Acts and the People of God*, 54.

8. As David Horrell insists we keep in mind, *the same was true of first-century Judaism*. That is, the form of expanded Israelite identity offered by the Christians was no more "universal" than that offered by Jews; both had mechanisms for integrating gentiles. The only difference was the *terms* under which the outsider could be included. Judaism insisted upon full observance of the Law of Moses, including circumcision; Christians insisted upon baptism, confession of Jesus as the Christ, and belief in his resurrection (cf. Horrell, *Ethnicity and Inclusion*).

9. Rhamie notes that Luke writes from a Judean perspective, "couching his Hebrew epistemology within the Graeco-Roman rhetorical tools of his Hellenistic day" ("Whiteness, Conviviality, and Agency," 205–206).

10. Matthews rightly observes that "Luke himself, writing from his precarious position under empire, could not have envisioned the full effects that his rhetorical violence would, ultimately, have. Luke's only violent weapons are his words" (Matthews, *Taming the Tongues of Fire*, 71).

11. The Parable of the Lost Sheep (15:3–7), the Parable of the Lost Coin (15:8–10), and the Parable of the Lost Son and his Brother (15:11–32).

12. cf. Gen. 25:1–6, 12–18.

13. Later still, the brothers of Joseph also represent not only themselves but the tribes descended from them (Gen. 49:1–27; comp. Deut. 33:6–25).

14. After Jacob's intense fear that Esau's folk will attack his own people (Gen. 32:1–21), the two are able to embrace and weep (33:3–4). However, Jacob seems anxious that they travel separately after this brief reunion and settle in different places (33:12–17). cf. *Jubilees* 37:21–22.

15. For example, Israelites and Edomites were "brothers." *See* Num. 20:14; Deut. 2:4–5, 23:7; Amos 1:11; Obad. 1:10.

16. See the Greek of Deut 23:89 [LXX]. Furthermore, they are relatives (συγγενεις, Jos. *War* 4.245, 265, 274) "fellow-tribesmen" (ὁμοφυλοι, *War* 4.276), "nearest-relatives" (συγγενεστατοις εθνεσιν, *War* 4.278).

17. "and many while reminding them of their kinship and imploring them to respect their common Temple were transfixed by their swords." Josephus, *War* 4.311 [Thackeray, LCL]; cf. *Ant.* 13:257.

18. as in Jos. *Ant.* 14:403; cf. Thiessen, *Contesting Conversion*, 88–110.

19. Jer 3:6–4:4; Ezek. 23:1–4.

20. With some notable exceptions! The Chronicler acknowledges those who remained in the North after 722 as authentic Israelites (1 Chr. 30:1–2; 34:9), and

234   *Conclusion*

some of the returning exiles, even some of the priestly class, felt close enough with the Samaritans that they intermarried (Neh. 13:28–29).

21. For more on Luke's assessment of Samaritans as Israelites, and this assessment's place in his overall ethnic ideology, see our forthcoming *Good Samaritans: Samaritan Ethnicity and Evangelization in Luke–Acts,* Stewart Penwell and Andrew Benko.

22. See chapter 2.

Bibliography

Abegg, Martin Jr., Peter Flint, and Eugene Ulrich. *The Dead Sea Scrolls Bible: The Oldest Known Bible Translated for the First Time into English*. New York: HarperSanFrancisco, 1999.

Abegg, Martin Jr., Michael Wise, and Edward Cook. *The Dead Sea Scrolls: A New Translation*. New York: HarperSanFrancisco, 1996, 2005.

Alexander, Loveday. "IPSE DIXIT: Citation of Authority in Paul and in the Jewish and Hellenistic Schools." Pages 103–128 in *Paul Beyond the Judaism/Hellenism Divide*. Edited by Troels Engberg-Pedersen. Louisville, KY: Westminster John Knox, 2001.

Alexander, Loveday. "Paul and the Hellenistic Schools: The Evidence of Galen." Pages 60–83 in *Paul in his Hellenistic Context*. Edited by Troels Engberg-Pedersen. London: T&T Clark, 2004

Argyle, A. W. *The Gospel according to Matthew*. New York: Cambridge University Press, 1963.

Ascough, Richard S., Philip A. Harland, and John S. Kloppenborg. *Associations in the Greco-Roman World: A Sourcebook*. Waco, TX: Baylor University Press, 2012.

Avioz, Michael. "Abraham in Josephus' Writings." Pages 93–108 in *Abraham in Jewish and Early Christian Literature*. Edited by Sean A. Adams and Zanne Domoney-Lyttle. London: T&T Clark, 2019.

Balch, David L. "The Areopagus Speech: An Appeal to the Stoic Historian Posidonius against Later Stoics and the Epicureans." Pages 52–79 in *Greeks, Romans, and Christians: Essays in Honor of Abraham J. Malherbe*. Edited by David L. Balch, Everett Ferguson, and Wayne A. Meeks. Minneapolis: Fortress Press, 1990.

Baker, Cynthia. "From Every Nation Under Heaven." Pages 79–100 in *Prejudice and Christian Beginnings*, edited by Laura Nasrallah and Elisabeth Schüssler Fiorenza. Minneapolis: Fortress, 2009.

Barclay, John M. "Deviance and Apostasy: Some Applications of Deviance Theory to First-Century Judaism and Christianity." Pages 104–127 in *Modelling Early*

236 *Bibliography*

Christianity: Social-Scientific Studies of the New Testament in its Context. Edited by Philip F. Esler. New York: Routledge, 1995.

Barclay, John M. "Ἰουδαιος: Ethnicity and Translation." Page 46–58 in *Ethnicity, Race, Religion: Identities and Ideologies in Early Jewish and Christian Texts, and in Modern Biblical Interpretation.* Edited by Katherine M. Hockey and David G. Horrell. New York: T&T Clark, 2018.

Barreto, Eric. *Ethnic Negotiations: The Function of Race and Ethnicity in Acts 16.* Tübingen: Mohr Siebeck, 2010.

Baumann, Gerd. *The Multicultural Riddle: Rethinking National, Ethnic and Religious Identities.* New York: Routledge, 1999.

Baumgarten, Joseph M. "Purification after Childbirth and the Sacred Garden in 4Q265 and *Jubilees.*" Pages 417–427 in *New Qumran Texts and Studies.* Edited by George Brooke and Florentino García Martínez. Boston, MA: Brill, 1994.

Beck, Robert. *A Light to the Centurions: Reading Luke–Acts in the Empire.* Eugene, OR: Wipf & Stock, 2019.

Bell, Richard. *Provoked to Jealousy: The Origin and Purpose of the Jealousy Motif in Romans 9–11.* Tübingen: Mohr Siebeck, 1994.

Benko, Andrew. *Race in John's Gospel: Toward an Ethnos-Conscious Approach.* New York: Fortress Academic, 2019.

Boatwright, Mary T. *Peoples of the Roman World.* Cambridge: Cambridge University Press, 2012.

Bock, Darrell. *Luke* (Baker Exegetical Commentary on the New Testament), 2 volumes. Grand Rapids, MI: Baker, 1996.

Boesenberg, Dulcinea. "Negotiating Identity: The Jewishness of the Way in Acts." *Journal of Religion and Society Supplemental Series* 13 (2016): 58–75.

Borgen, Peder. "'There Shall Come Forth a Man': Reflections on Messianic Ideas in Philo." Pages 105–127 in *Illuminations by Philo of Alexandria: Selected Studies on Interpretation in Philo, Paul, and the Revelation of John.* Studies in Philo of Alexandria series. By Peder Borgan; volume editor Torrey Seland. Leiden: Brill, 2021.

Bovon, François. *A Commentary on the Gospel of Luke.* Three vols. Hermeneia. Minneapolis, MN: Fortress, 2002–2012.

Brooks, James A. and Carlton L. Winbery. *Syntax of New Testament Greek.* Lanham, MD: University Press of America, 1979.

Brown, Raymond. *Birth of the Messiah: A Commentary on the Infancy Narratives in the Gospels of Matthew and Luke.* New York: Doubleday, 1999.

Brown, Raymond. "Gospel Infancy Narrative Research from 1976 to 1986: Part II (Luke)." *CBQ* 48.4 (1986): 660–680.

Buell, Denise Kimber. *Making Christians.* Princeton, NJ: Princeton University Press, 1999.

Buell, Denise Kimber. *Why This New Race: Ethnic Reasoning in Early Christianity.* New York: Columbia University Press, 2005.

Byron, Gay. *Symbolic Blackness and Ethnic Identity in Early Christian Literature.* New York: Routledge, 2002.

Byron, John. *Cain in Text and Tradition: Jewish and Christian Interpretations of the First Sibling Rivalry.* Leiden: Brill, 2011.

Bibliography

Cadbury, Henry J. *The Making of Luke–Acts.* Ada, MI: Baker, 1999.

Carter, Warren. *Matthew and the Margins: A Sociopolitical and Religious Reading.* New York: Orbis, 2001.

Charles, R. H., translator. *The Apocrypha and Pseudepigrapha of the Old Testament.* Oxford: Clarendon Press, 1913.

Charlesworth, James H. *The Odes of Solomon.* Oxford: Clarendon, 1973.

Charlesworth, James H., editor. *The Old Testament Pseudepigrapha.* Two volumes. Doubleday, NY: Garden City, 1983–1985.

Christian, Ed. "The Rich Man and Lazarus: Abraham's Bosom, and the Biblical Penalty *Karet* ('Cut Off')." *JETS* 61.3 (2018): 513–523.

Cicero. Translated by Winstedt, et al., 28 volumes. Loeb Classical Library. Cambridge, MA: Harvard University Press, 1966–1992.

Cohen, Shaye. *The Beginnings of Jewishness: Boundaries, Varieties, Uncertainties.* Berkeley, CA: University of California Press, 1999.

Collins, Raymond. *The Power of Images in Paul.* Collegeville, PA: Liturgical Press, 1989.

Concannon, Cavan. *"When You Were Gentiles": Specters of Race and Ethnicity in Roman Corinth and Paul's Corinthian Correspondence.* New Haven, CT: Yale University Press, 2014.

Cotton, Hannah M. Leah Di Segni, and Werner Eck, editors. *Corpus Inscriptionem Iudaeae/Palaestinae* vol. 1. Boston, MA: DeGruyter, 2010.

Coxe, A. Cleveland. "Introductory Note to Gregory Thaumaturgus." Pages 3–6 in *Ante-Nicene Fathers,* vol. 6. Edited by Alexander Roberts and James Donaldson. Peabody, MA: Hendrickson, 1994 [1886].

Cromhout, Markus. *Jesus and Ethnicity: Reconstructing Judeans Ethnicity in Q.* Eugene, OR: Wipf & Stock, 2007.

Culpepper, Alan. *Luke,* New Interpreter's Bible. Nashville, TN: Abingdon, 1995.

Dahl, Nils. "The Story of Abraham in Luke–Acts." Pages 138–158 in *Studies in Luke–Acts.* Edited by L. E. Keck and J. L. Martyn. Nashville, TN: Abingdon, 1966.

Docherty, Susan. "Abraham in Rewritten Scripture." Pages 59–74 in *Abraham in Jewish and Early Christian Literature.* Edited by Sean A. Adams and Zanne Domoney-Lyttle. London: T&T Clark, 2019.

Domoney-Lyttle, Zanne. "Abraham in the Hebrew Bible" Pages 9–28 in *Abraham in Jewish and Early Christian Literature.* Edited by Sean A. Adams and Zanne Domoney-Lyttle. London: T&T Clark, 2019.

Esler, Philip F. "Ancient Oleiculture and Ethnic Differentiation: The Meaning of the Olive-Tree Image in Romans 11." *JSNT* 26.1 (2003): 103–124.

Esler, Philip F. *Conflict and Identity in Romans, The Social Setting of Paul's Letter.* Minneapolis, MN: Fortress, 2003.

Esler, Philip F. *God's Court and Courtiers in the Book of Watchers: Re-interpreting Heaven in 1 Enoch 1–36.* Eugene, OR: Cascade, 2017.

Esler, Philip F. "The Social World of Early Judaism." Pages 45–68 in *Early Judaism and its Modern Interpreters.* Edited by Matthias Henze and Rodney A. Werline. Atlanta, GA: Society of Biblical Literature, 2020.

238 Bibliography

Estrada, Rodolfo Galvan III. *A Pneumatology of Race in the Gospel of John: An Ethnocritical Study.* Eugene, OR: Pickwick, 2019.

Fitzmeyer, Joseph. *The Gospel According to Luke.* Anchor Yale Bible Series; 2 volumes. New York: Doubleday, 1981–1985.

Fox, Nickolas. *The Hermeneutics of Social Identity in Luke–Acts.* Eugene, OR: Pickwick, 2021.

Fredriksen, Paula. "Mandatory Retirement: Ideas in the Study of Christian Origins Whose Time Has Come to Go." *Studies in Religion* 30 (2006): 230–246.

Fredriksen, Paula. *Paul: The Pagans' Apostle.* New Haven, CT: Yale University Press, 2017.

Fredriksen, Paula. "What 'Parting of the Ways'? Jews, Gentiles, and the Ancient Mediterranean City." Pages 35–64 in *The Ways That Never Parted: Jews and Christians in Late Antiquity and the Early Middle Ages.* Edited by Adam H. Becker and Annette Yoshiko Reed. Tubingen: Mohr Siebeck, 2003.

Fuller, Michael. *The Restoration of Israel: Israel's Re-Gathering and the Fate of the Nations in Early Jewish Literature and Luke–Acts.* Berlin: De Gruyter, 2012.

Gärtner, Bertil E. *The Areopagus Speech and Natural Revelation.* Uppsala: C. W. K. Gleerup, 1955.

Gill, David. "Achaia," Pages 433–453 in *The Book of Acts in its First-Century Setting,* vol. 2. Edited by David Gill and Corad Gempf. Grand Rapids, MI: Eerdmans, 1994.

Goodman, Martin. "The Persecution of Paul by Diaspora Jews." Pages 379–385 in *The Beginnings of Christianity.* Edited by Jack Pastor and Menachem Mor. Jerusalem: Yad Ben-Zvi Press, 2005.

Gowers, Emily. "Trees and Family Trees in the Aeneid." *Classical Antiquity* 30.1 (2011): 87–118.

Gray, Patrick. "Athenian Curiosity (Acts 17:21)." *NovT* 47 (2005): 109–16.

Grebe, Sabine. "Augustus' Divine Authority and Vergil's Aeneid." *Vergilius* 50 (2004): 35–62.

Green, Joel. *Conversion in Luke–Acts: Divine Action, Human Cognition, and the People of God.* Grand Rapids, MI: Baker Academic, 2015.

Green, Joel. *The Gospel of Luke,* New International Commentary on the New Testament. Grand Rapids, MI: Eerdman's, 1997.

Gruen, Erich S. "Christians as a Third Race." Pages 235–249 in *Christianity in the Second Century: Themes and Developments.* Edited by James Carleton Paget and Judith Lieu. Cambridge: Cambridge University Press, 2017.

Gruen, Erich S. *The Construct of Identity in Hellenistic Judaism.* Boston, MA: De Gruyter, 2016.

Gruen, Erich S. *Heritage and Hellenism: The Reinvention of Jewish Tradition.* Berkeley, CA: University of California Press, 1998.

Gruen, Erich S. "Philo and Jewish Ethnicity." Pages 179–196 in *Strength to Strength: Essays in Honor of Shaye J. D. Cohen.* Edited by Michael L. Satlow. Brown Judaic Studies. Atlanta, GA: SBL, Brown Judaic, 2018; later published as chapter 8 of Gruen, *Ethnicity in the Ancient World: Did it Matter?* DeGruyter, 2020.

Gruen, Erich S. *Rethinking the Other in Antiquity:* Princeton, NJ: Princeton University Press, 2011.

Bibliography

Gundry, Robert H. *Matthew: A Commentary on his Literary and Theological Art.* Grand Rapids, MI: Eerdmans, 1982.

Haenchen. *Acts of the Apostles: A Commentary.* Translated by Bernard Noble and Gerald Shinn. Philadelphia, PA: Westminster, 1971.

Hagner, Donald A. *Matthew 1–13.* Dallas, TX: Word Books, 1993.

Hakola, Raimo. *Identity Matters: John, the Jews, and Jewishness.* Leiden: Brill, 2005.

Haley, Shelly P. "Be Not Afraid of the Dark: Critical Race Theory and Classical Studies." Pages 27–49 in *Prejudice and Christian Beginnings: Investigating Race, Gender, and Ethnicity in Early Christian Studies.* Edited by Laura Nasrallah and Elisabeth Schüssler Fiorenza. Minneapolis, MN: Fortress Press.

Hall, Jonathan. *Ethnic Identity in Greek Antiquity.* Cambridge: Cambridge University Press, 1997.

Hall, Jonathan. *Hellenicity: Between Ethnicity and Culture.* Chicago, IL: University of Chicago Press, 2002.

Hamm, Dennis. "Luke 19:8 Once Again: Does Zacchaeus Defend or Resolve?" *JBL* 107.3 (1988): 431–437.

Harrington, Daniel J. *Matthew* (Sacra Pagina). Collegville, PA: Liturgical Press, 1991.

Harrisville, Roy. *The Figure of Abraham in the Epistles of St. Paul.* Lewiston: Edwin Mellis, 1992.

Hartman, Dorota. "The 'Children of Abraham' in Luke–Acts." *Henoch* 39.2 (2017): 351–365.

Hays, J. Daniel. *From Every People and Nation: A Biblical Theology of Race.* Downer's Grove, IL: Intervarsity Press, 2003.

Hodge, Caroline Johnson. *If Sons Then Heirs: A Study of Kinship and Ethnicity in the Letters of Paul.* New York: Oxford University Press, 2007.

Hodge, Caroline Johnson. "Olive Trees and Ethnicities: Judueans and Christians in Rom. 11.17–24." Pages 77–89 in *Christians as a Religious Minority in a Multicultural City: Modes of Interacting and Identify Formation in Early Imperial Rome.* Edited by Jürgen Zangenberg and Michael Labahn. New York: T&T Clark, 2004.

Hopkins, Keith. "Seven Missing Papers." Pages 623–630 in *Parenté et Stratégies Familiales dans l'Antiquité Romaine. Actes de la table ronde des 2 – 4 octobre 1986* (Paris, Maison des sciences de l'homme). Edited by Jean Andreau and Hinnerk Bruhns. Collection de l'École Française de Rome 129. Palais Farnèse: l'École Française de Rome, 1990.

Horrell, David G. *Ethnicity and Inclusion: Religion, Race, and Whiteness in the Construction of Jewish and Christian Identities.* Grand Rapids, MI: Eerdmans, 2020.

Horrell, David G. "Religion, Ethnicity, and Way of Life: Exploring Categories of Identity." *CBQ* 82.1 (2021): 38–55.

Horst, William. "From One Person?" *Perspectives on Science and Christian Faith* 74.2 (2022): 77–91.

Hubbard, Jeffrey M. "Paul the Middle Platonist? Exegetical Traditions on *Timaeus* 28c and the Characterization of Paul in Acts 17:16–31." *Harvard Theological Review* 115.4 (2022): 477–495.

Isaac, Benjamin. *The Invention of Racism in Classical Antiquity.* Princeton, NJ: Princeton University Press, 2004.

Jervell, Jacob. *Luke and the People of God.* Minneapolis, MN: Augsburg, 1972.

Jervell, Jacob. "Sons of the Prophets." Pages 96–121 in *The Unknown Paul: Essays on Luke–Acts and Early Christian History.* Collected essays, Jacob Jervell. Minneapolis, MN: Fortress, 1984.

Jipp, Joshua W. "Abraham in the Synoptic Gospels and the Acts of the Apostles." Pages 109–126 in *Abraham in Jewish and Early Christian Literature.* Edited by Sean Adams and Zanne Domony-Lyttle. New York: T&T Clark, 2019.

Jipp, Joshua W. "The Paul of Acts: Proclaimer of the Hope of Israel or Teacher of Apostasy from Moses?" *Novum Testamentum* 62.1 (2020): 60–78.

Jipp, Joshua W. "Paul's Areopagus Speech of Acts 17:16–34 as both Critique and Propaganda." *JBL* 131.3 (2012): 567–588.

Jokiranta, Jutta and Cecelia Wassen, "A Brotherhood at Qumran? Metaphorical Familial Language in the Dead Sea Scrolls." Pages 173–204 in *Northern Lights on the Dead Sea Scrolls: Proceedings of the Nordic Qumran Network 2003–2006.* Edited by Anders Klostergaard Petersen, et al. Boston, MA: Brill, 2009.

Josephus. Translated by H. St. J. Thackeray et al. 10 vols. Loeb Classical Library. Cambridge, MA: Harvard University Press, 1926–1965.

Kamudzandu, Israel. *Abraham Our Father: Paul and the Ancestors in Postcolonial Africa.* Minneapolis, MN: Fortress, 2013.

Kartveit, Magnar. "Josephus on the Samaritans – His *Tendenz* and purpose." Pages 109–120 in *Samaria, Samarians, and Samaritans: Studies on Bible, History, and Linguistics.* Edited by József Zsengellér. Boston, MA: De Gruyter, 2011.

Kartveit, Magnar. *The Origin of the Samaritans.* Boston, MA: Brill, 2009.

Keener, Craig S. "'Brood of Vipers' (Matthew 3.7; 12.34; 23.33)." *JSNT* 28.1 (2005): 3–11.

Keener, Craig S. "Human Stones in a Greek Setting: Luke 3.8; Matthew 3.9; Luke 19.40." *JGRChJ* 6 (2009) 28–36.

Keener, Craig S. *The IVP Bible Background Commentary: New Testament.* Downers Grove, IL: Intervarsity, 1993.

Kennedy, Rebecca F., C. Sydnor Roy, and Max L. Goldman. *Race and Ethnicity in the Classical World: An Anthology of Primary Sources in Translation.* Indianapolis, IN: Hackett, 2013.

Kinzer, Mark. *Jerusalem Crucified, Jerusalem Risen: The Resurrected Messiah, the Jewish People, and the Land of Promise.* Eugene, OR: Wipf and Stock, 2018.

Knowles, Michael P. "Serpents, Scribes, and Pharisees." *Journal of Biblical Literature* 133.1 (2014): 165–178.

Konstan, David. "Acts of Love: A Narrative Pattern in the Apocryphal Acts." *Journal of Early Christian Studies* 6 (1998): 15–36.

Konstan, David. "Defining Ancient Greek Ethnicity." *Diaspora* 6.1 (1997): 97–110.

Kuecker, Aaron. *The Spirit and the 'Other': Social Identity, Ethnicity and Intergroup Reconciliation in Luke–Acts.* New York: Bloomsbury, 2011.

Kuschel, Karl-Josef. *Abraham: A Symbol of Hope for Jews, Christians, and Muslims.* London: SCM Press, 1995.

Lee, Jae Won. "Paul and Ethnic Difference in Romans." Pages 141–156 in *They Were All Together in One Place? Toward Minority Biblical Criticism.* Edited by Randall C. Bailey, Tat-siong Benny Liew, and Fernando F. Segovia. Atlanta, GA: Society of Biblical Literature, 2009.

Levenson, Jon Douglas. *Inheriting Abraham: The Legacy of the Patriarch in Judaism, Christianity, and Islam.* Princeton, NJ: Princeton University Press, 2012.

Levin, Yigal. "Jesus 'Son of God' and 'Son of David': The 'Adoption' of Jesus into the Davidic Line." *JSNT* 28.4 (2006): 415–442.

Lieu, Judith. "The Race of the God-Fearers." *Journal of Theological Studies* 46.2 (1995): 483–501.

Long, A. A. and D. N. Sedley. *The Hellenistic Philosophers, Volume 1.* New York: Cambridge University Press, 1987.

Lopez, Davina. *Apostle to the Conquered: Reimagining Paul's Mission.* Minneapolis, MN: Fortress, 2008

Loubser, J. A. "Invoking the Ancestors: Some Socio-Rhetorical Aspects of the Genealogies in the Gospels of Matthew and Luke." *Neotestamentica* 39.1 (2005): 127–140.

Ludlow, Jared W. "Abraham in the Old Testament Pseudepigrapha: Friend of God and Father of Fathers." Pages 41–58 in *Abraham in Jewish and Early Christian Literature.* Edited by Sean A Adams and Zanne Domoney-Lyttle. London: T&T Clark, 2019.

Malina, Bruce J. and John J. Pilch. *Social-Science Commentary on the Book of Acts.* Minneapolis, MN: Fortress, 2008.

Malina, Bruce J., and Richard L. Rohrbaugh. *Social-Scientific Commentary on the Synoptic Gospels.* Minneapolis, MN: Fortress, 1992.

Malkin, Irad. "Introduction." Pages 1–28 in *Ancient Perceptions of Greek Ethnicity.* Edited by Irad Malkin. Cambridge, MA: Harvard University Press, 1990.

Manson, T. W. *The Sayings of Jesus.* Grand Rapids, MI: Eerdmans, 1979 (reprint of London: SCM Press, 1957).

Marciak, Michal. "Idumea and Idumeans in Josephus' Story of Hellenistic-Early Roman Palestine." *Aevum* 91.1 (2017): pages.

Marcovich, M., editor. *Origenes Contra Celsum libri VIII.* Leiden: Brill, 2001.

Mărculet, Ştefan. "Elements of Inculturation in Saint Paul's Speech from Areopagus." *Theological Review* 23.3 (2013): 28–40.

Mason, Steve. "Jews, Judaeans, Judaizing, Judaism," *Journal for the Study of Judaism* 38 (2007): 457–512.

Mason, Steve. *Josephus and the New Testament.* Peabody, MA: Hendrickson, 1992.

Matera, Frank J. *Romans.* Paideia Series. Grand Rapids, MI: Baker, 2010.

Matthews, Shelly. *Perfect Martyr: The Stoning of Stephen and the Construction of Christian Identity.* Oxford: Oxford University Press, 2010.

Matthews, Shelly. *Taming the Tongues of Fire: Acts of the Apostles: An Introduction and Study Guide.* London: Bloomsbury T&T Clark, 2017.

McCoskey, Denise Eileen. *Race: Antiquity and Its Legacy.* Oxford: Oxford University Press, 2012.

McEntire, Mark and Wongi Park. "Ethnic Fission and Fusion in Biblical Genealogies." *JBL* 140.1 (2021): 31–47.

McInerny, Jeremy, editor. *A Companion to Ethnicity in the Ancient Mediterranean.* Oxford: Wiley-Blackwell, 2014.

McWhirter, Jocelyn. *Rejected Prophets: Jesus and His Witnesses in Luke–Acts.* Minneapolis, MN: Fortress, 2013.

Meier, John. *A Marginal Jew: Rethinking the Historical Jesus,* Volume 2. New York: Doubleday, 1994.

Milgrom, Jacob. "The Penalty of *Karet.*" Pages 405–408 in *The JPS Torah Commentary: Numbers.* Philadephia, PA: JPS, 1989.

Miller, David M. "Reading Law as Prophesy: Torah Ethics in Acts." Pages 75–91 in *Torah Ethics and Early Christian Identity.* Edited by Susan Wendel and David Miller. Grand Rapids, MI: Eerdmans, 2016.

Mitchell, Alan. "Zacchaeus Revisited: Luke 19,8 as a Defense." *Biblica* 71.1 (1990): 153–176.

Moraff, Jason. "Children of the Prophets and the Covenant: A Post-Supersessionist Reading of Luke–Acts." *Religion* 14.120 (2023): 1–17.

Moraff, Jason. "Recent Trends in the Study of Jews and Judaism in Luke–Acts." *CBR* 19.1 (2020): 64–87.

Morgan, Teresa. "Society, Identity, and Ethnicity in the Hellenic World." Pages 23–45 in *Ethnicity, Race, Religion: Identities and Ideologies in Early Jewish and Christian Texts, and in Modern Biblical Interpretation.* Edited by Katherine M. Hockey and David G. Horrell. New York: T&T Clark, 2018.

Muddathir, Abdel Rahim, Georges Balandier, et al. "UNESCO Statement on Race and Racial Prejudice." *Current Anthropology* 9.4 (1968): 270–272.

Nasrallah, Laura. "The Acts of the Apostles, Greek Cities, and Hadrian's Penhellenion." *JBL* 127.3 (2008): 533–566.

Neusner, Jacob. "Was Rabbinic Judaism Really 'Ethnic'?" *CBQ* 57.2 (1995): 281–305.

Neyrey, Jerome. *The Gospel of John.* New York: Cambridge University Press, 2007.

Neyrey, Jerome. *Honor and Shame in the Gospel of Matthew.* Louisville, KY: Westminster John Knox. 1998.

Nickelsburg, George W. E. *1 Enoch.* Hermeneia, 2 volumes. Minneapolis, MN: Fortress, 2001–2012.

Nickelsburg, George W. E. "Abraham the Convert: A Jewish Tradition and its Use by the Apostle Paul." Pages 151–175 in *Biblical Figures Outside the Bible.* Edited by Michael E. Stone and Theodore A. Bergren. Harrisburg, PA: Trinity Press International, 1998.

Oliver, Isaac. *Torah Praxis after 70 CE: Reading Matthew and Luke–Acts as Jewish Texts.* Tübingen: Mohr Siebeck, 2013.

Olson, Daniel. *A New Reading of the Animal Apocalpyse of 1 Enoch: "All Nations Shall Be Blessed."* Boston, MA: Brill, 2013.

Palmer, Carmen Jane Heather. "Converts at Qumran: The *Gēr* in the Dead Sea Scrolls as an Indicator of Mutable Ethnicity." PhD Dissertation, St. Michael's College of the Toronto School of Theology, Toronto, 2016.

Palmer, Carmen Jane Heather. *Converts in the Dead Sea Scrolls: The* Gēr *and Mutable Ethnicity.* Boston, MA: Brill, 2018.

Penwell, Stewart. *Jesus the Samaritan: Ethnic Labeling in the Gospel of John*. Boston, MA: Brill, 2020.

Pervo, Richard I. *Acts: A Commentary*. Minneapolis, MN: Fortress, 2009.

Pomeroy, Sarah. "Some Greek Families: Production and Reproduction." Pages 155–164 in *The Jewish Family and Antiquity:* Brown Judaic Studies. Edited by Shaye J. D. Cohen. Atlanta, GA: Scholar's Press, 1993.

Popović, Mladen. "Abraham and the Nations in the Dead Sea Scrolls." Pages 77–104 in *Abraham, the Nations, and the Hagarites: Jewish, Christian, and Islamic Perspectives in Kinship with Abraham*. Edited by Martin Goodman, George H. van Kooten, and J.T.A.G.M. van Ruiten. Boston, MA: Brill, 2010.

Popović, Mladen. "God the Father in Flavius Josephus." Pages 181–200 in *The Divine Father: Religious and Philosophical Concepts of Divine Parenthood in Antiquity*. Edited by Felix Albrecht and Reinhard Feldmeier. Boston, MA: Brill, 2014.

Preisigke, Friedrich. *Sammelbuch Grieschischer Urkunden aus Ägypten*. Strasbourg: K. J. Trübner, 1915.

Pummer, Reinhard. *The Samaritans: A Profile*. Grand Rapids, MI: Cambridge University Press, 2016.

Punt, Jeremy. "The Politics of Genealogies in the New Testament." *Neotestimentica* 47.2 (2013): 373–398.

Ravens, David. *Luke and the Restoration of Israel*. Sheffield: Sheffield Academic, 1995.

Rhamie, Gifford. "Whiteness, Conviviality and Agency: The Ethiopian Eunuch (Acts 8:26–40) and Conceptuality in the Imperial Imagination of Biblical Studies." PhD Dissertation, Canterbury Christ Church University, Canterbury, 2019.

Richardson, P. *Building Jewish in the Roman East*. Waco, TX: Baylor University Press, 2004.

Richardson, P. *Herod: King of the Jews*. Columbia, SC: University of South Carolina Press, 1996.

Rosen-Zvi, Ishay. "Pauline Traditions and the Rabbis: Three Case Studies." *HTR* 110:2 (2017): 169–194.

Rowe, Christopher Kavin. *World Upside Down: Reading Acts in the Graeco-Roman Age*. Oxford: Oxford University Press, 2010.

Roy, James. "Autocthony in Ancient Greece." Pages 241–255 in *A Companion to Ethnicity in the Ancient Mediterranean*. Edited by Jeremy McInerney. Oxford: Wiley-Blackwell, 2014.

Saldarini, Anthony J. *Matthew's Christian-Jewish Community*. Chicago, IL: University of Chicago, 1994.

Schnabel, E. J. "Contextualising Paul in Athens: The Proclamation of the Gospel before Pagan Audiences in the Graeco-Roman World." *Religion and Theology* 12.2 (2005): 172–190.

Schodde, George H., translator. *The Book of Enoch: Translated from the Ethiopic with Introduction and Notes*. Andover, MA: Warren F. Draper, 1882.

Sechrest, Love. "Enemies, Romans, Pigs, and Dogs: Loving the Other in the Gospel of Matthew." *Ex Auditu* 31 (2015): 71–105.

Sechrest, Love. *A Former Jew: Paul and the Dialectics of Race*. New York: T&T Clark, 2009.

Sechrest, Love. *Race & Rhyme: Rereading the New Testament*. Grand Rapids, MI: Eerdmans, 2022.

Sedley, David. "Philosophical Allegiance in the Greco-Roman World." Pages 97–119 in *Philosophia Togata*. Edited by Miriam Griffin and Jonathan Barnes. Oxford: Clarendon, 1989.

Seim, Turid Karlsen. "Abraham, Ancestor or Archetype? A Comparison of Abraham-Language in 4 Maccabees and Luke–Acts." Pages 27–42 in *Antiquity and Humanity: Essays on Ancient Religion and Philosophy*. Edited by Adela Yarbro Collins and Margaret M. Mitchell. Tübingen: Mohr Siebeck, 2001.

Siker, Jeffrey. "Abraham in Graeco-Roman Paganism." *JSJiPHRP* 18.2 (1987): 168–193.

Siker, Jeffrey. *Disinheriting the Jews: Abraham in Early Christian Controversy*. Louisville, KY: Westminster John Knox, 1991.

Skarsaune, Oskar. "Ethnic Discourse in Early Christianity." Pages 250–264 in *Christianity in the Second Century: Themes and Developments*, edited by James Carleton Paget and Judith Lieu. Cambridge: Cambridge University Press, 2017.

Smith, David. *Luke and the Jewish Other: Politics of Identity in the Third Gospel*. Abingdon: Routledge, 2024.

Smith, David. "Luke, the Jews, and the Politics of Early Christian Identity." PhD Dissertation, Duke University, Durham, NC, 2018.

Smith, Mitzi. *The Literary Construction of the Other in the Acts of the Apostles*. Eugene, OR: Pickwick, 2011.

Smith, R. R. R. "The Ethne from the Sebasteion at Aphrodisias." *The Journal of Roman Studies* 78 (1998): 50–77.

Solevåg, Anna Rebecca. "Zacchaeus in the Gospel of Luke: Comic Figure, Sinner, and Included 'Other.'" *Journal of Literary and Cultural Disability Studies* 14.2 (2020): 225–240.

Somov, Alexey, and Vitaly Voinov. "'Abraham's Bosom' (Luke 16:22–23) as a Key Metaphor in the Overall composition of the Parable of the Rich Man and Lazarus." *CBQ* 79 (2017): 615–633.

Spilsbury, Paul. *The Image of the Jew in Flavius Josephus' Paraphrase of the Bible*. Tübingen: Mohr Siebeck, 1998.

Staples, Jason A. *The Idea of Israel in Second Temple Judaism: A New Theory of People, Exile, and Israelite Identity*. New York: Cambridge University Press, 2021.

Stern, Sacha. *Jewish Identity and Rabbinic Writings*. Leiden: Brill, 1994.

Stoler, Ann L. "Racial Histories and Their Regimes of Truth." *Political Power and Social Theory* 11 (1997): 183–206.

Stroup, Christopher. *The Christians Who Became Jews: Acts of the Apostles and Ethnicity in the Roman City*. New Haven, CT: Yale University Press, 2020.

Swain, Simon. "Polemon's *Physiognomy*." Pages 125–202 in *Seeing the Face, Seeing the Soul: Polemon's* Physiognomy *from Classical Antiquity to Medieval Islam*. Edited by Simon Swain. Oxford: Oxford University Press, 2007.

Taylor, Nicholas. "The Social Nature of Conversion in the Early Christian World." Pages 128–136 in *Modelling Early Christianity: Social-Scientific Studies of the New Testament and its Context*. Edited by Philip Esler. New York: Routledge, 1995.

Thiessen, Matthew. *Contesting Conversion: Genealogy, Circumcision, & Identity in Ancient Judaism & Christianity*. Oxford: Oxford University Press, 2018 [2011].

Thiessen, Matthew. "Luke 2:22, Leviticus 12, and Parturient Impurity." *Novum Testamentum* 54.1 (2012): 16–29.

Thiessen, Matthew. "Paul, the Animal Apocalypse, and Abraham's Gentile Seed." Pages 65–78 in *The Ways that Often Parted: Essays in Honor of Joel Marcus*. Edited by Lori Baron, Jill Hicks-Keeton, and Matthew Thiessen. Atlanta, GA: SBL, 2018.

Tiller, Patrick. *A Commentary on the Animal Apocalypse of 1 Enoch*. Atlanta, GA: SBL, 1997.

Toney, Carl. *Paul's Inclusive Ethic: Resolving Community Conflicts and Promoting Mission in Romans 14–15*. Tübingen: Mohr Siebeck. 2008.

UNESCO. "The Scientific Basis for Human Unity." *UNESCO Courier* 3 (1950): 6–8.

VanderKam, James C. *Jubilees: A Commentary in Two Volumes*. Edited by Crawford Sidnie White. Minneapolis, MN: Fortress, 2018.

Van der Lans, Birgit. "Belonging to Abraham's Kin." Pages 307–318 in *Abraham, the Nations, and the Hagarites: Jewish, Christian, and Islamic Perspectives in Kinship with Abraham*. Edited by Martin Goodman, George H. van Kooten, and J.T.A.G.M. van Ruiten. Boston, MA: Brill, 2010.

Van Zile, Matthew P. "The Sons of Noah and the Sons of Abraham: Origins of the Noahide Law." *Journal of the Study of Judaism in the Persian, Hellenistic, and Roman Period* 48.3 (2017): 386–417.

Wall, Robert W. *"Acts."* Pages 1–368 in *New Interpreter's Bible*, vol. X. Edited by Leander Keck, Marion Soards, William Lane, and Gail O' Day, New Testament editors. Nashville, TN: Abingdon, 2002.

Wan, Sze-Kar. "To the Jew First and also to the Greek." Pages 129–157 in *Prejudice and Christian Beginnings*. Edited by Laura Nasrallah and Elisabeth Schüssler Fiorenza. Minneapolis, MN: Fortress, 2009.

Williams, Margaret. "Abraham in Contemporary Greek and Latin Authors." Pages 165–182 in *Abraham in Jewish an Early Christian Literature*. Edited by Sean A. Adams and Zanne Domoney-Lyttle. London: T&T Clark, 2019.

Wilson, Stephen D. *Leaving the Fold: Apostates and Defectors in Antiquity*. Minneapolis, MN: Fortress, 2004.

Wise, Michael, Martin Abegg Jr., and Edward Cook. *The Dead Sea Scrolls: A New Translation*. New York: HarperSanFrancisco, 2005.

Wiseman, T. P. "Legendary Genealogies in Late Republican Rome." *Greece & Rome* 21.2 (1974): 153–164.

246 *Bibliography*

Xeravits, Géza G. "Abraham in the Old Testament Apocrypha." Pages 29–40 in *Abraham in Jewish and Early Christian Literature*. Edited by Sean A. Adams and Zanne Domoney-Lyttle. London: T&T Clark, 2019.

Yoder, John Howard. "In the Bosom of Abraham: The Name and Role of Poor Lazarus in Luke 16:19–31." *Novum Testamentum* 62 (2020): 2–3, 8–9.

Zetterholm, Magnus. *The Formation of Christianity in Antioch: A Sociological Approach to the Separation between Judaism and Christianity.* New York: Routledge, 2003.

Ziesler, John. *Paul's Letter to the Romans.* Philadelphia, PA: Trinity Press International, 1989.

Index Subjects

Abraham: as ancestor of Christians, even gentile ones, x–xi, 13, 16, 83–84, 95n121, 125–26, 129, 143, 156nn41–46, 163n148, 168–69, 189–90, 200, 210–12, 227–32; as ancestor of Judeans, vii, x, xxin38, 9, 16, 59–72, 85, 87n11, 90n39, 90n45, 101–4, 109, 118, 122, 128, 134–39, 143–45, 161n115, 167, 170, 200, 202; as ancestor of "many nations," 60, 62, 64, 73, 75, 87n9, 88n16, 95n121; as ancestor of proselytes, 65, 67, 80–85, 96n128, 203; as ancestor of specific gentile nations, x, 12, 16, 20, 61–64, 66–68, 73–78, 84–85, 91n58, 231; as astrologer/scientist, 79, 81, 94n101; as benefactor/intercessor, 68–69, 71–72, 84, 117, 131, 146, 150, 152; bosom of, 71, 145–49, 164n160; blessing to the nations, 68, 73, 78, 87nn10–11, 90n49, 94n92, 97–98, 104, 117–18, 151, 184, 209, 215n47; children from stones, vii, x–xi, xvii, xxin43, 122–26, 153, 180, 196, 202, 232; connections to gentiles, x, xxiin49, 12, 60–61, 75–80, 84–85, 94n101, 104–5, 118, 175; disinheriting some/disinheritance, xi, 68–72, 85, 87n17, 96n130, 110, 117–18, 122, 124–26, 128, 131–32, 135, 146–49, 151–53, 154n26–27, 163n147, 164n166, 167, 196, 225n210; as exemplar to be imitated, 16, 60–61, 69–72, 80–85, 86n6, 91n50, 92n66, 108, 110, 132–33, 137–40, 152–53, 163n144, 196–97, 221n149; as first to keep Torah, 70–73, 84, 92n63; God's promises to, xxn31, 59–60, 65, 67–70, 72, 87n11, 90n42–43, 92n76, 101–4, 106, 110–11, 112n21, 113n29, 118, 134, 167, 170, 181, 185; Jesus' family resembles, 97–100, 107, 110, 111n8, 112n12, 116n63, 118, 134, 225n186; as model convert/rejector of idolatry, x–xi, xxn27, 73, 80–82, 84, 189–90, 203, 219n110; name, 60, 72, 73, 86n4; seed/children of, x, 9, 59–60, 62–65, 68, 70, 72, 86n1, 87n11, 90n42, 101; tomb of, 20, 74, 93n82. *See also* hospitality

Abraham, Isaac, and Jacob, 69, 70, 88n27, 146, 149, 164n160, 196–97

Adam, xxin43, 6–7, 9, 65, 66, 72, 91n57, 92n75, 97, 109, 169–73, 177–80, 183–84, 213nn15–16, 214nn28–29

248 *Index Subjects*

Adiabene, Judean converts in the royal family of, 19–20, 26–27, 37, 50nn150–53

adoption, 10, 30–31, 61–62, 70, 75, 90n45, 91n56, 96n130, 110, 128, 132, 151–52, 213n13, 227

Aeneas, vii, 13, 45n76, 214n24

alienation. *See* estrangement

allogenos/allophulos/allotrios. *See* foreigner

Ammonites, 12, 49n138, 62, 73–75, 78, 95n121, 157n53

ancestral traditions, x, xx nn27–28, xxin37, 7–9, 19, 22, 24–30, 35, 50nn152–53, 52nn166–67, 69–71, 81–82, 137, 186–87, 205–6, 208–10, 228. *See also* way of life

ancestry/descent: as significant criterion of ethnicity, x, xviin1, 5–10, 36–37, 42n42; fluidity in attribution of, 11–16; seeming fixity of, x, 9–11, 16, 21–22, 36–37, 66, 89n33, 213n17. *See also* Abraham; ascriptive descent; subscriptive descent; resemblance

Anna, xi, xvi, xxin41, 1, 9, 107–8, 110, 219n113, 225n186

Antiochus IV, 28–29, 52nn167–68, 71

Anti-semitism, xvi, 19, 143, 228–32, 233n6

Aphrodisias, vii–ix, xv–xvii, 13, 228

Aphrodite/Venus, vii, 13

apostasy, x, 24, 26–31, 52nn166–68, 52n172, 53n175, 187, 198–99, 203–10. *See also* conversion; estrangement

appearance. *See* phenotype

Arabs, 2, 6, 12, 45n83, 62, 75, 78, 88n16, 95, 193

ascriptive descent, 13, 16, 55n199, 62, 71–80, 134, 137, 142, 168. *See also* subscriptive descent

"atheism," xvi, 24, 27–28, 51n157

Athens, 12, 173–80, 208, 216n58, 217n64

barbarians, xxin37, 44, 22, 25, 49n142, 76, 93n87, 95n121, 169

"brother,"; address applied to proselytes to Judaism, 32, 198, 223n162; address for members of one's race, 149, 184, 186, 200, 203–4, 223n166; address used among Christians, 33–35, 54n197, 162n135, 168, 199–202, 223n167, 227; address within voluntary associations, 31–34, 54n192; related races as "brothers," xxiin52, 73–77, 200–201, 231–32. *See also* kinship

Caria/Carians, vii–ix, xv, xxiin45, 12–13, 75, 95n121

centurions, xxiin48, 19, 51, 112n23, 152, 188, 191–92, 207. *See also* soldiers

"Christians," as convenient shorthand for early Jesus–followers, viii, x, xiv, xviin8

circumcision, 9, 26–29, 49n138, 56n221, 60, 64, 67, 99, 110, 112n23, 125, 129, 149, 156n42, 185–86, 188, 191, 204, 209–10, 230, 233n8

colonies/–izing, xii, 12, 25, 46n97, 75, 78, 88n16, 172, 180, 214n27, 229

constructed kinship. *See* kinship

conversion, 7–8, 19–20, 23–33, 35, 48n124, 48n135, 49n138, 50nn152–53, 83, 108, 168, 188, 197–210. *See also* apostasy

criteria of race/ethnicity, 5–11, 42n33, 42n42. *See also* ancestry; homeland; way of life

"cut off," biblical punishment, 128, 132, 135, 148–49, 164n163, 185, 210, 225n210

daughter of Abraham, an unnamed, 130, 136–39, 149, 158n75, 160n105

David, xi, xxnn30–31, 2, 9, 44n51, 98, 102, 105, 109, 114n34, 170–71, 213n14, 214n23, 225n186

Index Subjects 249

degeneration, racial, 17–18, 37, 46n97, 123, 187

descent. *See* ancestry/descent

deviance, ethnic, xxn28, 187–88, 197–212, 231–32. *See also* prototypicality

Edom/Edomites. *See* Idumeans

Elizabeth, x, 2, 44n51, 97–102, 110, 219n113, 225n186

endogamy, xiii, xxn27, 70, 91n62, 233n20

environmental theory of heredity, 9, 17–18, 35, 37, 46n93

Esau, 48n120, 62, 66–70, 73–74, 78, 85, 87n9, 89n31, 91n62, 95n121, 96n130, 100, 135, 148, 152, 157n53, 164n166, 200, 231, 233n14

estrangement: with members of one's family, 30–31, 197–200, 203, 206–7, 212; with members of one's (former) people, 24, 26–31, 197–212

Ethiopia, 128, 193, 195, 220n132, 220nn135–36

Ethiopian pilgrim, the, xixn17, 19, 57n224, 188, 193–95, 220n136

ethnē; personified, vii–viii, xv, xxin44; in the sense of "gentiles," 1, 39n4, 189, 214n27

ethnicity: ancient terms for, 1, 3–4; ethnic fluidity, xii, 7–38, 167; ethnic genealogies, xii, 11–13, 64–68, 73–80, 84, 157n53; polythetic nature of, 7–8, 10–11, 35–38, 42n42, 47n108, 56n210. *See also* criteria of race/ethnicity; race

ethno-cultural umbrella, 20–23, 35. *See also* Hellenism; Judaism

ethnos-conscious approach, ix, 3

family. *See* kinship, estrangement

fictive kinship. *See* constructed kinship

fig. *See* tree

foreigner, 14, 18, 23, 25–27, 29, 37, 41n31, 45n80, 46n97, 49n139,

50n153, 64, 70–71, 95n118, 132, 148, 169, 172, 175–77, 181, 190–95, 208, 214n27, 220n136, 224n179

genealogy: fluidity and, 11, 13–15, 47n113, 70, 74, 185; of Jesus, xxin43, 8–9, 39n14, 109–10, 169–73, 213nn14–16. *See also* ancestry; ethnic genealogies; intellectual genealogy

gentile, term, 1, 39n4, 189, 214n27. *See also ethnē*

God, children of, 170–75, 177–80, 214n23, 218n84

God-fearers, 3, 102, 112n23, 124, 155n34, 162n135, 172, 188–97, 200, 209–11, 220n119, 221n136, 223n162, 227

Greek, language, 3–4, 38nn1–2

Hagar, 63, 70, 73, 82–83, 88n20, 93n87

Hasmoneans, 15, 22–23, 49n138, 76–77, 200

Hebrew, language, 3, 38n2, 88n27, 115n43

Hebrew, term for ethno-linguistic group, 60, 72, 82–83, 98, 113

Hellen (ancestor), 11–12

Hellenes/Greeks, 3, 5, 11–13, 15, 17, 20–23, 25, 28–29, 36, 41n31, 47n108, 49n142, 57n223, 76, 89n35, 94n101, 173–80, 189, 204, 208, 223n171

Hellenism/Hellenizing, 51n164, 52n167

Herod Agrippa I, 205

Herod Antipas, 2, 134, 159n87, 119, 133

Herod the Great, xii, 2, 13, 15, 20–22, 37, 39n8, 44n51, 45nn83–87, 74, 80, 97, 119, 134

Hippocratic Oath, 33–34, 202

homeland: birthplace *vs.* racial homeland, 18–19; loyalty to another race's, 19–20, 26, 28, 37; potential for fluidity, 17–20, 35; as significant

250   *Index Subjects*

criterion of race in antiquity, 5–10.
See environmental theory of heredity
hospitality, 92n64, 132–33, 139–44,
150

Idumeans, ii, 2, 48n120, 66–67, 85,
135; as "brothers" of Israel, 16, 20,
57nn223–24, 73–75, 93n83, 200,
231; descendants of Abraham, 15,
20, 37, 62, 73–75, 85, 87n9, 135,
157n53, 160n102; reckoned as
Judeans, 11, 13, 22–23, 48n124,
49n138, 200, 222n159
imperial mimicry. *See* colonies/
colonizing
Infancy Narrative, 97–108, 110–11,
114n34, 119, 135, 152, 170
intellectual genealogy, xxn29, 33–35,
46n91, 55n207, 179–80
Ioudaioi. *See* Judeans
Isaac, 62–64, 66, 68–70, 74–75, 78, 83–
85, 86n1, 87nn10–11, 88n23, 91n62,
97, 99–100, 103–4, 111n8, 113n29,
128, 164n166
Ishmael/Ishmaelites, 12, 62–63, 66, 68,
73, 75, 85, 87n9, 95n121, 104, 135,
148, 164n166
Israel: restoration of, xi, xiii, xxn31,
1, 59–60, 67–69, 101–2, 104–8,
111, 114nn36 and 40, 115n47,
123, 143, 149, 190, 223n165;
term encompassing Judeans and
(Northern) Israelites, 14, 37,
45nn79–80, 68, 86n3, 90n39, 102,
108, 160n102, 167, 201–2, 209, 220–
21n136, 222n160, 223n165, 231. *See
also* Jacob; Judeans; Samaritans
Izates. *See* Adiabene

Jacob, 6–7, 9, 14, 45nn79–80, 49n120,
63–66, 68–70, 73–74, 78, 85, 87n11–
12, 89n33, 90n45, 91nn57–58, 97,
102, 106, 111n8, 112n21, 113n29,
114n36, 128, 164–65n166, 200,
225–26n210, 231, 233n14

Jews. *See* Judeans
John the Baptist, x, xiii, 2, 9, 44n52,
97–100, 170, 192, 196, 202, 212nn4–
5, 219n112, 225n186
Jonah, 192, 195–97, 222n150
Joseph, Mary's husband, 1, 8–9, 44n51,
98, 170, 213n13
Joseph, patriarch, 14, 75, 97, 100, 107,
109, 171, 185–86, 225n186, 223n13
Judaism: as Judeans' whole way of
life, 41n26, 49n149, 61, 153n8, 229;
distinct from Samaritan Yahwism,
108; Judaizing, 49n138, 84, 188–89,
193–95, 198, 210–11, 220n136,
229; prototypical, xiii, 2–3, 39n6,
70, 112n12, 97–100, 110, 118–19,
157n48, 170, 187–88, 205, 208, 210,
219n111, 233n8. *See also* apostasy;
conversion; proselytes
Judeans: others characterizations of,
xvi, 27–28, 51nn156–157, 93n87,
202–3, 211, 227–29; as translation of
Ioudaioi, xxn32, 4–5

karet. *See* "cut off"
Keturah, 12, 62–63, 73–75, 78, 87n9,
88n16
kinship: constructed/fictive, xiv, xxn29,
16, 30–35, 46n91, 83–85, 124,
142–43, 168, 180, 201–2, 211; and
ethnicity, ix, xxin37, 5–10, 42n42,
43n49, 73–77, 197–202. *See also*
brother; intellectual genealogy

Lazarus, parable of, 117, 142, 145–50,
159n87, 163nn150–53
leprosy, xxiin52, 190–92
light to the nations, 1, 60, 86n2, 105–7,
114nn36–39, 115n42, 123
lineage. *See* genealogy
Lot, 62, 73–75, 78, 93n84, 110, 119,
132, 140, 151–52

Mary, 1, 44n51, 91n52, 98–102, 107–8,
114n34, 115n41, 199–200, 219n113;

Song of, 100–102, 104, 110,
113nn23–25, 116n63, 136–37
migration/mobility, 17–18, 35, 37,
50n150, 79–81, 46n97, 163n146,
190–97
Moabites, 12, 49n138, 62, 73–75, 78,
157n53
Moses, xi, xxiin49, 19, 30–31, 49,
53n175, 66, 75, 88n27, 91n53,
93n87, 113, 117, 121, 164n163,
184–88, 203–5, 218n92, 219nn104–
112, 225n210, 230; Law of, 9, 25,
53n175, 71, 103, 204–5, 209–10,
233n8. *See also* Torah

Naaman, 51n155, 190–92, 195
Noah, xi, 6, 65–66, 70, 88n27, 91n57,
128, 151, 157n59, 170, 172, 213n16,
215n46

Paul: character in Acts, 53n175, 86n2,
106, 116n48, 175–80, 188, 200–202,
204–9, 217n64, 222n160, 223n162,
225n187, 227; the historical, ix,
xixn17, 13, 19, 31, 33, 53n177,
54n197, 83, 98, 125, 129, 132, 142–
43, 157n48, 158nn71–72, 202–3,
213n14, 224nn180–81
Persians, 5, 11, 21–22, 181
phenotype and race, 6, 8, 14, 16, 42n42,
37, 65–67, 193
prophets: like Moses, 164n163, 184–86,
219n112, 226n210. *See* Zechariah
proselyte: sons of the, 70, 117, 154n14,
181–88, 219nn112–13; sons of those
who killed the, xii–xiv, 168–69,
181–88, 203–4, 218n87, 218n91,
230; regarded as kin, 25–35, 50n152,
81–84, 128, 201–4, 211; in the
Qumran movement, 20, 32–33. *See
also* conversion
prototypicality, xiii, 2–3, 39n6, 83, 97–
100, 110, 118–19, 187–88, 205, 208,
210, 219n111. *See also* Abraham;
deviance

purity: food, and sharing meals, 23, 69,
192; gentiles and, 66–67, 89, 192;
impurity ascribed to some Israelites,
120–22, 154n27, 185; leprosy and,
xxiin52, 190–92

Qumran movement, 14, 20, 32–33, 70,
185, 200, 215n32, 222n160

race. *See* ethnicity; as term appropriate
for discussions of antiquity, xxn32,
3–5, 40n21; as used synonymously
with ethnicity, xxn32, 4–5, 41n25
"religion"; as anachronistic for
discussions of antiquity, 10–11,
41n26, 48n125; implicated in
construction of ethnicity, 5–8, 10–11,
20–24, 47n108, 48n135, 167, 212n2.
See also conversion; apostasy
resemblance confirming/disproving
descent, 16, 110, 140–45, 163n144,
172, 185–86, 188, 214n30
Roman empire, various races' place
within the, vii–ix, xv–xvii, xxiin45,
2–3, 13, 17–18, 22, 25, 39n13,
52n166, 119, 133, 205, 208,
215n46, 224n179, 227–30. *See also*
colonies/–izing

Samaritans, xiv, xvi, xxiinn51–52m,
3, 11, 14, 37, 45nn79–80, 86n3,
90n39, 102, 104, 108, 133, 159n87,
160n102, 167, 169, 201–2, 221n136,
222n151, 222n160, 223n165, 229,
231, 234nn20–21
Sarah, x, xiii, 39n6, 59, 63–64, 68, 74,
82–84, 88n17, 90n42, 98–100, 110,
111n8, 123, 140, 156n44, 158n59
sebasteion, vii–ix, xv–xvii, 2, 13
Simeon, xi, 1–2, 8, 38n2, 107–8, 110,
114–15n40, 161n115, 219n113
Sodom, 69–72, 119, 131, 140, 151–52,
165n179, 197
soldiers, 17, 21, 80, 119, 126, 132–33,
160n92, 191–92

252 *Index Subjects*

Spartans, 5, 12, 21–22, 41n31, 46n97, 76–78, 93n90, 200, 223n164
subscriptive descent, xi, xiii–xiv, 16, 20, 31–35, 55n199, 61–62, 69–72, 80–85, 110, 124–25, 135, 137–39, 142–45, 161n111, 168–69, 229
sungeneia. See kinship

tax collectors, 119, 132–33, 139–45, 161n118, 162n119, 162n130
temple: on Gerizim, 108; Jerusalem Temple, 1–2, 9, 18–20, 39n6, 50n150, 87n12, 107–8, 111, 115nn40–41, 119, 129, 131, 158n66, 158n66, 158n75, 183, 193–95, 199, 204–5, 221n138, 222n160, 231, 233n17; pagan temples, 2, 24–25, 28, 81, 51n155, 191, 208, 222n138; warning inscription, 193–94, 204. *See also* sebasteion (temple of the emperors)
Torah, xv, xxiin52, 9, 39n8, 53n175, 70–72, 84, 92n63, 133, 145, 148, 159n87, 177, 184, 188; redefining loyalty to the, xv–xvi, 125, 188, 204–5
tree: Abraham as root/trunk, 13, 62, 64, 75, 111n1, 127–31, 134–35, 157n59, 158n61, 158n69, 212n1; family tree symbolism, 12–13, 62, 75, 127–28, 132, 167, 189–90, 194–95; Israel as, 13, 62, 126–32, 158n66, 210, 212n1, 230. *See also* vineyard

tribes: must bear fruit, 92n75, 126, 128–32, 134, 158n75, 159nn77–78, 167; tribal identity, xvi, xxin41, 6, 9, 12, 14, 19, 40n15, 42nn33–35, 50n152, 68, 70, 76, 78, 86n3, 90n39, 106, 108, 231, 233n13, 223n16; twelve tribes, 12, 14, 62–63, 73, 75, 87n9

vineyard, Israel as, 127, 129–32, 158n76, 210, 218n91. *See also* tree
vipers, brood of, x, 9, 120–22, 125–27, 134, 136, 210
"The Way," viii, x, xviiin8, 168, 179, 187–88, 190, 201–2, 204–6, 208, 210–11, 219n111, 222n160, 223nn165–66, 225n194, 227–29, 231–32. *See also* "Christians"

way of life, xi, xxiin37, 44n54; potential for fluidity, xi, 15, 18, 20–35, 39n8, 46n97, 48n135, 224n179; as significant criterion of ancient ethnicity, xii, 5–10, 38, 43nn48–49. *See also* ancestral traditions

Zacchaeus, 136, 138–45, 152, 162n119, 163n144
Zarephath, widow of, xxn31, 190–91, 219n112, 220n127
Zechariah, father of John, 2, 9, 39n6, 44n51, 97–100, 102–6, 108, 110, 113n25, 114n40, 115n47, 116n63, 219n113
Zechariah, prophet, 183–84

About the Author

Andrew Benko is the academic dean of the Iona School for Ministry and serves as a priest in the Diocese of Texas (Episcopal). He has taught as an adjunct professor at Texas Christian University and Southwest University. His first book, *Race in John's Gospel* (2019), examined the racializing rhetoric of the Fourth Gospel.

www.ingramcontent.com/pod-product-compliance
Lightning Source LLC
Chambersburg PA
CBHW030813160425
25197CB00002B/20